THEORIES OF ADOLESCENCE

FOURTH EDITION

THEORIES OF ADOLESCENCE

FOURTH EDITION

Rolf E. Muuss

Goucher College

RANDOM HOUSE, NEW YORK

Fourth Edition

9 8 7 6 5 4 3 2 1

Copyright © 1962, 1968, 1975, 1982 by Random House, Inc.

Library of Congress Cataloging in Publication Data

Muuss, Rolf Eduard Helmut, 1924–
    Theories of adolescence.

    Bibliography: p.
    Includes index.
    1. Adolescent psychology.   I. Title.
BF724.M8   1982   155.5   82-3813
ISBN 0-394-32424-2   AACR2

Manufactured in the United States of America

Grateful acknowledgment is made for permission to quote from The
Growth of Logical Thinking from Childhood to Adolescence *by Bärbel
Inhelder and Jean Piaget. Translated by Anne Parsons and Stanley
Milgram. Copyright © 1958 by Basic Books, Inc. By permission of Basic
Books, Inc., Publishers, New York.*

ACKNOWLEDGMENTS

THE early origins of *Theories of Adolescence* go back to the author's doctoral dissertation, "Theories of Adolescence: An Analysis of Selected American and European Positions," University of Illinois, 1957. However, the fourth edition bears little resemblance to this earlier work because many new theories have emerged since then, and new research has contributed to our understanding of old theories. However, the author remains grateful to his Doctoral Committee, Norman Gronlund, Leon Helmer, Stewart Jones, and Hobart Mowrer. He is especially indebted to his advisor, Glenn Blair, who was instrumental in stimulating, guiding, and supporting the earlier part of this endeavor.

A book of this nature is never the accomplishment of just one person; its creation is nurtured, challenged, and encouraged by many people. The author is especially grateful for valuable suggestions and critical comments on earlier drafts of one or several of the new chapters from Drs. Barbara Long, Kent Robinson (M.D.), Linda Schuerholz, Clarence Schulz (M.D.), Eli Velder, and Gerald Whitmarsh. Sincere appreciation is expressed to my secretary, Kay Cornell, for her efficient, reliable, and competent assistance in all aspects of bringing this work to completion. In addition, there are many students who, at one time or another, have worked on parts of the manuscript; they are too numerous to mention, but many thanks to all of them.

In addition, I am indebted to the students in my courses, "Adolescent Development" and "Adolescents and the Secondary Schools," who have questioned, challenged, and continuously stimulated my thinking.

Most of all, I would like to express my deeply felt gratitude to the Elizabeth C. Todd Distinguished Professorship Foundation, through which my work gained recognition, released time, and financial support, all of which contributed in large measure to the speedy completion of this edition.

Finally, the author is grateful to his wife, Gertrude, for her support and patience, and to his son, Michale, who encouraged, taught, and supported me in using the computer as a word processor in writing the new chapters.

ROLF E. MUUSS
January 1982

CONTENTS

1 INTRODUCTION *1*
The Purpose of Studying Theories of Adolescence *1*
Adolescence and Pubescence: Their Definitions and Relationship *2*

2 THE PHILOSOPHICAL AND HISTORICAL ROOTS OF THEORIES OF ADOLESCENCE *8*
Early Greek Concern with Human Nature *9*
Medieval Christian View of Human Development *14*
John Amos Comenius' Development-Centered Theory of Education *17*
John Locke's Empiricism *19*
Jean Jacques Rousseau's Romantic Naturalism *22*
Charles Darwin's Theory of Biological Evolution *25*
G. Stanley Hall's Biogenetic Psychology of Adolescence *27*

3 THE PSYCHOANALYTIC THEORY OF ADOLESCENT DEVELOPMENT *30*
Introduction to Psychoanalytic Theory *30*
Conscious—Preconscious—Unconscious *33*
Id—Ego—Superego *35*
Development of the Ego *36*
Development of the Superego *38*
Freud's Stages of Psychosexual Development *39*
The Oral Stage *41*
The Anal Stage *41*
The Phallic Stage *42*
The Phallic Stage as "Little Puberty" *44*
Sexual Latency *44*
Puberty, or the Genital Stage *45*
Mechanisms of Defense *49*
Educational Implications *56*

4 ERIK ERIKSON'S THEORY OF IDENTITY DEVELOPMENT *60*

Erikson's Eight Stages of Development *60*
The Relationship of Erikson's "Stages of Man" to the
    Adolescent Identity Crisis *64*
    Trust versus Mistrust *64*
    Autonomy versus Shame, Doubt *65*
    Initiative versus Guilt *66*
    Industry versus Inferiority *67*
    Identity versus Identity Confusion *68*
    Intimacy versus Isolation *72*
    Generativity versus Stagnation *73*
    Integrity versus Despair *74*
James Marcia's Expansion of Erikson's Concept "Identity versus
    Role Diffusion" *74*
    Identity Diffusion *76*
    Foreclosure *79*
    Moratorium *81*
    Identity Achievement *83*
Research Findings on Identity Statuses *84*
    Intelligence *84*
    Academic Variables *85*
    Performance on Cognitive Tests *85*
    Personality Variables *86*
    Family Antecedents *88*
    Moral Reasoning *89*
    Autonomy *90*
    Drug Use *90*
    Sex Differences in Identity Statuses *90*
Educational Implications *92*

5 PETER BLOS' MODERN PSYCHOANALYTIC INTERPRETATION OF ADOLESCENCE *96*

Blos' Theory: An Introduction *96*
Blos' Second Individuation Process *99*
The Oedipus Complex in Blos' Theory *103*
The Six Phases of Adolescent Development *107*
    Latency *109*
    Preadolescence *110*
    Early Adolescence *113*
    Adolescence Proper *115*
    Late Adolscence *117*
    Postadolescence *119*
Educational Implications *120*

6 CULTURAL ANTHROPOLOGY AND ADOLESCENCE *125*

Benedict's Theory of Cultural Conditioning *126*
The Adolescent Girl in Samoa *130*
Cultural Anthropology and Some Theoretical Issues *131*
Educational Implications *135*

7 FIELD THEORY AND ADOLESCENCE *140*

Developmental Concepts of Field Theory *140*
Kurt Lewin's Theory of Adolescent Development *146*
Roger Barker's Somatopsychological Theory of Adolescence *152*
Educational Implications *157*

8 SOCIAL PSYCHOLOGY AND ADOLESCENCE *160*

Allison Davis' Concept of Socialized Anxiety *160*
Robert Havighurst's Developmental Tasks of Adolescence *162*

9 ARNOLD GESELL'S MATURATIONAL THEORY OF ADOLESCENT DEVELOPMENT *165*

Gesell's Theory of Development *166*
Gesell's Description of the Pubescent and Adolescent Period *169*
Educational Implications *173*

10 JEAN PIAGET'S COGNITIVE THEORY OF ADOLESCENCE *176*

The Major Developmental Concepts of Piaget's Theory *178*
Piaget's Stages of Cognitive Development *181*
    The Sensorimotor Stage *182*
    The Preoperational Stage *183*
    The Concrete Operational Stage *184*
    The Formal Operations Stage *187*
    Combinatorial System of Operations *191*
    INRC Group of Operations *195*
Evaluation of Piaget's Formal Thinking Stage *201*
    Is There an Adult Stage of Cognitive Development? *203*
Educational Implications *203*

11 LAWRENCE KOHLBERG'S COGNITIVE-DEVELOPMENTAL APPROACH TO ADOLESCENT MORALITY *209*

Levels of Moral Development *211*
Stages of Moral Development *213*
The Invariant Developmental Sequence in Moral Thinking *216*
Cross-Cultural, Socioeconomic, and Political Differences in
  Moral Thinking *217*

Relationship of Kohlberg's Stages of Moral Judgment to
  Other Stage Theories   *220*
Educational Implications   *223*

12 SOCIAL COGNITION, PART 1: ROBERT SELMAN'S THEORY OF ROLE TAKING   *227*

Social Cognition   *227*
Definition of Social or Interpersonal Cognition   *232*
Selman's Stage Theory of Social Cognition   *234*
  Stage 0. *Egocentric Undifferentiated Stage of Social
    Perspective Taking* (age three to six)   *239*
  Stage 1. *The Differential or Subjective Perspective-Taking
    Stage or the Social Information Role-Taking Stage* (age five
    to nine)   *240*
  Stage 2. *Self-Reflective Thinking or Reciprocal Perspective
    Taking* (age seven to twelve)   *243*
  Stage 3. *The Third Person or Mutual Perspective-Taking Stage*
    (age ten to fifteen)   *245*
  Stage 4. *In-Depth and Societal Perspective Taking*
    (adolescence to adulthood)   *248*
Educational Implications   *251*

13 SOCIAL COGNITION, PART 2: DAVID ELKIND'S THEORY OF ADOLESCENT EGOCENTRISM   *254*

The Concept of Egocentrism   *254*
Stages of Egocentrism   *256*
  Sensorimotor Egocentrism (birth to age two)   *256*
  Preoperational Egocentrism (age two to six)   *257*
  Concrete Operational Egocentrism (age seven to eleven)   *257*
  Adolescent Egocentrism (age eleven to adulthood)   *258*
Research Support for an Adolescent Egocentrism Theory   *263*
Educational Implications   *267*

14 THE IMPLICATIONS OF SOCIAL LEARNING THEORY FOR AN UNDERSTANDING OF ADOLESCENT DEVELOPMENT   *270*

Social Learning Theory   *270*
Modeling, Imitation, and Identification   *273*
Social Learning Theory Contrasted with Stage and
  Trait Theories   *276*
Social Learning Theory Contrasted with Behavioristic
  Learning Theory   *279*
The Antecedents of Adolescent Aggression   *283*
Educational Implications   *287*

REFERENCES   *293*

THEORIES OF ADOLESCENCE

FOURTH EDITION

1 : INTRODUCTION

THE PURPOSE OF STUDYING THEORIES OF ADOLESCENCE

The process of human growth and development has long been the subject of much theorizing. However, since the turn of the century, special attention has been directed toward the period of development commonly referred to as "adolescence." The prodigious amount of recent literature dealing with adolescence shows the deep and sustained interest manifested by psychologists, educators, physicians, lawyers, psychiatrists, sociologists, and parents.

Numerous theories have been advanced to explain the phenomenon of adolescence. These theories have resulted in many conflicting viewpoints. In previous centuries, the opposing camps in developmental psychology built their arguments mainly on personal experiences and philosophical considerations. In recent years, they have relied more and more on systematic studies, controlled observation, and experimental research. These scientific methods of investigation have eliminated some of the earlier misconceptions of adolescent development, but they have not settled many of the basic controversial issues.

Problems have arisen owing to ambiguous terminology and to disagreement on basic assumptions as to what actually constitutes adolescence. In many instances, theoretical differences concerning adolescence stem from more basic disagreements on the methods and aims of psychological inquiry and the nature of psychological knowledge. Since an advocate of a particular position tends to cite research that supports his theory, there is a need for analyzing and, to some extent, integrating the different theoretical positions on adolescent development. It is not the aim of this book to derive a new theory or to combine several existing theories into an eclectic one. The main purpose is to give a systematic and comprehensive picture of different theoretical positions and to show whenever appropriate the relationship among them.

ADOLESCENCE AND PUBESCENCE:
THEIR DEFINITIONS AND RELATIONSHIP

The word "adolescence" is derived from the Latin verb *adolescere* meaning "to grow up" or "to grow into maturity." For the purpose of this study, the following general definitions appear to be most suitable: Sociologically, adolescence is the transition period from dependent childhood to self-sufficient adulthood. Psychologically, it is a "marginal situation" in which new adjustments have to be made, namely those that distinguish child behavior from adult behavior in a given society. Chronologically, it is the time span from approximately twelve or thirteen to the early twenties, with wide individual and cultural variations. It tends to occur earlier in girls than in boys and to end earlier in more primitive societies. The terms "adolescence," "adolescent age," and "adolescent period" will be used interchangeably in this book. Laymen frequently use "teen-agers," but this term literally used includes only the ages thirteen to nineteen. Furthermore, "teen-ager" connotes a somewhat condescending attitude, as does the term "juvenile," which some people invariably associate with delinquency. A more appropriate word for the period between childhood and adulthood is "youth," but this term has different meanings for different writers. Whereas Gesell, Ilg, and Ames (1956) use it as the title of their study of the years from ten to sixteen, others have used it to describe the late adolescent period. Keniston (1970) goes even one step further and defines "youth" as a distinct new stage between adolescence and adulthood that has emerged only recently from the changing conditions in postindustrial society.

The words "puberty" and "pubescence" are derived from and related to the Latin words *pubertas*, "the age of manhood," and *pubescere*, "to grow hairy," "to reach puberty." Ausubel (1954) uses the term "pubescence" as the more restricted concept that refers only to the biological and physiological changes associated with sexual maturation. Adolescence is the broader, more inclusive concept that refers also to changes in behavior and social status.

Pubescence is the time span of physiological development during which the reproductive functions mature; it is phylogenetic and includes the appearance of the secondary sex characteristics as well as the maturation of the primary sex organs. Pubescence, then, corresponds to the period of early adolescence and ends with the appearance of all secondary sex characteristics and reproductive maturity. These changes take place in a time span of approximately two years. At perhaps no other period in human life, except birth, does a transition of such importance take place. And though physiological change takes place at all age levels, the *rate* of change during this period is immeasurably greater than in the years that precede and follow it (Ausubel, 1954).

The relationship between pubescence and adolescence becomes more complicated if material from cultural anthropology concerning initiation rituals is considered. In some instances, the transition from childhood to adulthood is smooth and without social recognition; in other instances, *puberty rites* bring about a transition not from childhood to adolescence, but from childhood to adulthood. Pubescence seems to be the only aspect of the process of maturation that some primitive societies recognize; after puberty the young man and woman obtain adult status and have adult privileges. The prolonged period of adolescence in more technologically advanced societies is not a physiological but a social invention.

It has been claimed that these initiation rituals may occur after, during, or even before the period of biological pubescence. While the duration of pubescence is determined by biological factors, the length of social adolescence is influenced by social institutions and social groups. A causal relationship between the physiological changes during pubescence and the behavioral and social phenomena has been questioned by cultural anthropologists and social learning theorists. However, Beach (1974) demonstrated a close relationship between levels of testosterone and the beginning of heterosexual interest and sexual behavior in boys during puberty (kissing, petting, dating, masturbation, nocturnal emissions). Ausubel emphasizes that social initiation into adulthood either corresponds to or follows physiological maturation, but that the attainment of biological sexual maturity "always precedes and never follows" the social inauguration of adolescence. Sherif and Cantril, after reviewing anthropological studies on the subject, conclude that the problems that adolescents face "vary from culture to culture, rendering the transition to adulthood more or less complicated, more or less conflicting, more or less prolonged" (Sherif and Cantril, 1947: 220). However, they assert that the "basic psychological principles which operate in all of these social settings should be the same" (1947: 220).

For a long time a specific causal relationship between pubertal change and the psychological adjustment of adolescence have been assumed to exist. This assumption is unwarranted, since the effects of physiological changes do seem to be greatly modified by social expectations. Psychological correlates of puberty, particularly noticeable in the area of sexual adjustment (see Figure 1), find behavioral expression and tie pubescence and adolescence together. Needless to say, the author does not imply that the kind of prolonged transition period found in Western societies is universal. Youth in Samoa has frequently been cited as a smooth, harmonious, and pleasurable transition period.

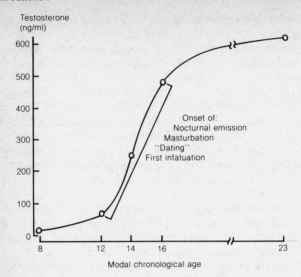

FIGURE 1.   Level of plasma testosterone in human males at different ages.

From F. A. Beach, *Levels of Plasma Testosterone in Human Males at Different Ages*. In W. Montaga and W. A. Sadler, eds., *Reproductive Behavior*. © 1974 Plenum, New York. Reproduced with permission.

However, even in Samoa there is evidence of change in status and conflict in sexual adjustment. The girl may be invited to a love affair by a *soa*, a messenger who may betray his friend in his own favor. The *moetotolo*, or "sleep crawler," hoping that the girl is expecting a lover may attempt a modified form of rape, since he has been unsuccessful in previous love affairs. Also, the prestige is enhanced for the families of both bride and bridegroom if the girl proves to be a virgin (Mead, 1950).

In Western culture, pubescence as a developmental period corresponds to early adolescence. The onset of pubescence can be ascertained by specific body changes (Greulich, 1944). The sequence of these changes, according to Ausubel (1954), remains fairly constant, even with retarded or precocious individuals.

Girls	*Boys*
Skeletal growth	Skeletal growth
Breast development	Enlargement of testes
Straight pigmented pubic hair	Straight pigmented pubic hair
Maximum annual growth increment	Early voice changes
	Ejaculation

Kinky pigmented pubic hair	Kinky pigmented pubic hair
Menstruation	Maximum annual growth increment
Appearance of axillary hair	Appearance of downy facial hair
	Appearance of axillary hair
	Late voice change
	Coarse pigmented facial hair
	Chest hair

Any of these criteria could be selected, and a variety of them have been used to determine the onset of pubescence. It is obvious that pubescence is not a single event but a constellation of events, none of them occurring instantaneously. Consequently, there is a great deal of overlapping in the developmental sequence. The main idea in the definition of puberty is attainment of reproductive maturity. Therefore, the most widely used single criterion for determining puberty in girls is the first menstruation (Shock, 1944). However, since it is generally believed that there is a period of one or more years of sterility between the first menstruation and the ability to conceive and reproduce, even menstruation is not a valid criterion for the determination of reproductive maturity. Furthermore, there is no corresponding event in boys. Ejaculation has been considered (Ausubel, 1954), but since it is less dramatic than first menstruation and is frequently not remembered, it is less accessible for research investigation. Furthermore, there is no evidence that menstruation and ejaculation are corresponding biological events.

The change in the excretion of gonadotropic hormones, determined through urinalysis, gives valid information concerning the endocrinological changes that accompany pubescence. Gonadotropic hormones are considered partly responsible for the development of primary and secondary sex characteristics and wholly responsible for the production of mature ova and spermatozoa. Studies have shown that few, if any, gonadotropic hormones are found in the urine of nonpubescent boys (Greulich, 1944; Shock, 1944). The adequate production of gonadotropic hormones appears to be of great importance in determining the onset, normality, or deviations of pubescent development.

The upper limit of adolescence is less clearly marked than the onset of pubescence, since there are no objective physiological phenomena that can be used to define the termination. Observable social phenomena such as financial independence, successful employment, and marriage are useful. But, in the first place, they do not necessarily indicate psychological independence. Second, no agreement has been reached as to their relative importance. Finally, the psychological and even the sociological meaning of such phenomena differ according to the socio-cultural environment; how to determine when adulthood, maturity, self-determination, and independence have been reached depends on the definition that these terms have in a given social setting.

In primitive society, the period of adolescence may be very brief and may be terminated by initiation rituals after which the individual obtains adult status. In contrast, the psychologist G. Stanley Hall wrote in 1904 that adolescence in the United States lasts until the twenty-fourth or twenty-fifth year. To speak of the termination of adolescence in terms of age is only possible if the sociocultural environment is taken into consideration.

In most cultures two different criteria have been applied to determine the end of adolescence. They are: (1) *functional definitions*— such as ability to support oneself—and (2) *status definitions*— such as having reached the age necessary to vote or having been given status through initiation rituals (Committee on Adolescence, 1968). Status definitions are easily determined and more obvious, but often less meaningful, since they depend on arbitrary convention and often neglect individual differences in development. Functional definitions are more related to the responsibilities that are required of adults to function effectively in a given society and relate to self, mate, off-spring, and society.

In the United States the legal recognition of the end of adolescence is changing in line with the accelerating growth patterns and earlier maturation of adolescents today as compared to a century ago. Considerable evidence has accumulated (Muuss, 1970a; Tanner, 1968) indicating that adolescents reach puberty earlier, experience the adolescent growth spurt earlier, and reach adult height earlier. The Twenty-sixth Amendment gives the eighteen-year-old the right to vote, and most states are also reexamining the definition of the end of adolescence and the beginning of adulthood. The legal age for buying liquor, to sue and be sued, and to enter into contracts is being lowered from twenty-one to eighteen in many states. Other legal rights not available to children—such as acquiring a license to drive a car, the option to drop out of school, permission to marry and enter full-time employment—may be granted at an earlier age with considerable variation from state to state. In a legal sense, the age of eighteen is increasingly recognized as the termination of adolescence, since at this age the law increasingly removes the last legal protective aspect of "immaturity" and gives a person his or her full legal rights and responsibilities.

Adolescence is widely recognized as a period of social, personal, sexual, religious, political, and vocational adjustments as well as a period of striving for increasing emotional and financial independence from parents. Therefore, from a psychological standpoint, the status definition for termination of adolescence is not related to a specific chronological age; it is instead the degree to which these adjustments have been made. A person who marries after graduation from high school and becomes successfully employed and financially self-sufficient is more likely to be regarded as having attained maturity than a friend who goes to college and is supported by parents. Furthermore, a person can be old in a chronological sense and still show the behavioral characteristics of the adolescent. However, if appropriate age norms must be given, they are suggested by the school organization: preadolescence, nine to eleven, covers elementary schoolchildren; early adolescence, twelve to fourteen, coincides with middle school and frequently with pubescence; middle adolescence, fifteen to eighteen, covers the senior high school years; and late adolescence, nineteen to twenty-one, applies primarily to the college-bound segment of youth.

2: THE PHILOSOPHICAL AND HISTORICAL ROOTS OF THEORIES OF ADOLESCENCE*

LONG before psychology became a science, there were philosophical, theological, educational, and psychological theories that contributed to an understanding of human nature and human development. G. Stanley Hall, as a result of his famous two-volume work *Adolescence* (1916), is considered the father of a scientific "psychology of adolescence." Prior to Hall it was frequently the philosopher-educator who was especially concerned with a theory of human development with its implications for teaching. This was the case with Plato, Aristotle, Comenius, Rousseau, Herbart, Froebel, and Pestalozzi.

One difficulty in identifying prescientific theories of adolescent development is that prior to Hall adolescence was not considered a separate part or stage of human development and received no special emphasis. The word "adolescence" first appeared in the fifteenth century, indicating that historically adolescence was subordinated to theoretical considerations about the general nature of human development. Contemporary theories of adolescence frequently have their historical roots in general theories of development. Some important ideas about human development come from philosophers who are primarily concerned with the question: What is the nature of man? For example, what Locke and Darwin had to say about the nature of man is so profound that it is utilized and reflected in the writings of Rousseau and Hall respectively and thus constitutes a philosophical basis for a theory of development.

In classifying theories of development, Ausubel (1958) distinguishes between preformationistic and predeterministic approaches to human development on the one side and tabula rasa approaches on the other

---

*Chapter 2 is a revision and extension of an article by the author, "Theories of Adolescent Development, Their Philosophical and Historical Roots," *Adolescence*, 1966, Vol. I, pp. 22–44.

side. The preformationistic theory is reflected in the theological proposition of man's instantaneous creation, in the homunculus theory, and in the doctrine of man's basic sinfulness as well as in the more recent theories emphasizing instincts and innate drives. Predeterministic theories postulate universally fixed stages of development, but allow for environmental influences, as is obvious in Rousseau's romanticism, Hall's theory of recapitulation, Freud's stages of psychosexual development, and Gesell's emphasis on maturation. In contrast to this are the tabula rasa approaches that minimize the biological and genetic factors and place heavier emphasis on environmental determinants of human development. As the name implies, this includes Locke's tabula rasa theory, the humanistic approaches, and the modern theories of behaviorism, social learning theory, and cultural determinism.

EARLY GREEK CONCERN WITH HUMAN NATURE

A historical approach to a theory of adolescence must begin with the early Greek ideas about human development. Their influence remained prevalent through the Middle Ages and is still noticeable today. The philosophical idea of dualism, for instance, is essentially Greek. Plato (427–347 B.C.) made a clear distinction between two aspects of human nature: soul and body. He expounded that body and soul are different substances and that although there is some interaction between them, the soul is an entity in itself, capable of leaving the body without losing its identity. It can perceive more clearly and reach higher realities when freed from the body; *soma sema* ("the body is the grave of the soul"), he declared. The body and sensuality are the fetters that hinder the soul in reaching those higher realities. Body is matter and has all the defects of matter. The idea of dualism between mind and body reappeared later in Christian theology and became of primary importance in the philosophical thinking of the seventeenth century, especially under Descartes, Leibnitz, and Spinoza.

Of greater interest from a development point of view is the idea of the layer structure of the soul which Plato developed in the dialogue *Phaedo*. According to Plato, the soul has three distinguishable parts, layers, or levels. Thus, probably for the first time in the history of psychology, a threefold division of soul, or mind, is advanced. The lowest layer of the soul is described as man's desires and appetites. Today we might describe this level in terms of drives, instincts, and needs, and its resemblance to Freud's concept of "id" can hardly be denied. According to Plato, this part of the soul is located in the lower part of the body and is primarily concerned with the satisfaction of the physical needs. ". . . it fills us full of love, and lusts, and fears, and fancies of all kinds, and endless foolery, and . . . takes away the power of thinking at all" (Plato, 1921: 450). The second layer of the soul, the spirit, includes courage, conviction, temperance, endurance, and hardihood; aggressiveness and fierceness also originate here. Man has both the first and the second layer in common with the animal world. These two layers belong to the body and die with it. The third layer is divine, supernatural, and immortal; it constitutes the essence of the universe. This is the real soul, which Plato described as reason and which has its temporary seat in the body. Plato's theory concerning the layer structure of the soul is reflected in several central European personality theories, which are developed on the assumption of a layerlike stratification of personality. They perceive development as a process by which the lower layers mature earlier and are superseded by higher layers as the child grows older. Plato had already postulated such a developmental theory. Reason is latent during the first stage when perception is most important. Among contemporary theorists, Piaget maintains that percepts develop into concepts. The second stage of development is characterized by conviction and understanding and brings the second layer of the soul, spirit, into the foreground of psychological development. The third stage, which we might identify with adolescence, but which, according to Plato, is not reached by all people, relates to the development of the third part of the soul, reason and intelligence.

Interspersed in most of Plato's dialogues—but particularly in *Laws* and *The Republic*—are descriptive accounts of children and youth as well as advice concerning the control of their behavior. While this material does not constitute a theory of development as we understand it today, it does give insight into Plato's conception of the nature of development.

During the first three years of life the infant should be free from fear and pain and sorrow. This point of view would be endorsed by many psychologists today. Interestingly enough, in the dialogue *Laws* Cleinias suggests that in addition to freeing the infant from pain we ought to provide pleasure. This is in agreement with Plato's basic goal, which is the possession of happiness. However, the Athenian Stranger objects that this would spoil the child, since during the early years "more than at any other time the character is engrained by habit" (Plato, 1953: 359). Character is formed at such an early age because the experiences and impressions leave a lasting influence. However, Plato did admit that "the characters of young men are subject to many changes in the course of their lives." The argument about the consistency of personality versus its modifiability has continued, and proponents for both of Plato's statements can be found today.

From three to six the child needs sports and social contact with age-mates in order to get rid of his self-will. Plato would punish but not disgrace the child. Social development is taken into consideration at this age, and children ought to come together in a kind of kindergarten arrangement under the supervision of a nurse. However, children should find for themselves the "natural modes of amusement" appropriate to their age.

Plato suggested a division of the sexes at six. "Let boys live with boys and girls . . . with girls." The boy now has to learn horsemanship, the use of bow and arrows, the spear, and the sling. Boys will not be allowed to drink wine until they are eighteen because of their easy excitability, "fire must not be poured upon fire." A related adolescent desire is argument for amusement's sake. In their enthusiasm they will leave no stone unturned, and in their delight over the first taste of wisdom they will annoy everyone with their arguments. Plato believed that the character is formed through habit at a very early age.

Plato developed his educational philosophy in *The Republic*. He perceived education as the development of the soul under the influence of the environment, "and this has two divisions, gymnastic for the body, and music for the soul." Reasoning in the young child is undeveloped, but since the young child is impressionable, Plato suggested establishing "a censorship of the writers of fiction," since "anything that he receives into his mind is likely to become indelible and unalterable: and therefore . . . the talks which the young first hear should be models of virtuous thoughts" (Plato, 1921: 642). Rational and critical thought develop mainly during adolescence. The training that began with music and gymnastics during childhood was continued through adolescence with mathematical and scientific studies. The latter brought out critical thought and dissatisfaction with direct sense knowledge; during this training students would develop methods of finding the truth and of distinguishing truth from opinion. In *Laws* Plato spoke of education as "that training which is given by suitable habits to the first instincts of virtue in children;—when pleasure, and friendship, and pain, and hatred are rightly implanted in souls not yet capable of understanding the nature of them, and who find them, after they have attained reason, to be in harmony with her" (Plato, 1953: 218). The meaning of education in this view is to provide experiences for children prior to the development of reason that are nevertheless in agreement with reason when it does develop during adolescence. Plato already recognized the importance of individual differences; children are born with different abilities and should be guided into those kinds of activities that are in line with their aptitudes.

Plato postulated that the attainment of knowledge might be explained by his doctrine of innate ideas. Though undeveloped, vague, and nebulous, innate ideas are nevertheless present at birth. Learning is a process of remembering these ideas, which once—probably before the soul entered the body—were clear. Sensations help in reawakening these partially lost ideas. The mind-body dualism is of relevance here, since the body contributes sensation while the mind contains the ideas. In this way, Plato's theory of innate ideas opens the discussion about the influence of heredity and environment.

Aristotle (384–322 B.C.), in contrast to Plato, denied the separation of body and soul and returned to the older Greek idea of the unity of the physical and mental worlds. Body and soul, according to him, are related in structure and function. The relationship between body and soul is the same as that between matter and form; body is matter and soul is form. Soul-life, for which Aristotle used the word "entelechy," is the principle by which the body lives. Aristotle accepted Plato's idea concerning the levels of the soul-life; however, he viewed soul structure from a biological, almost evolutionary, point of view. The lowest soul-life form is that of the plant, the life functions of which are supply of nourishment and reproduction. The next higher form of soul-life is also found in animals, its additional functions being sensation, perception, and locomotion. The third soul-life function is distinctly human and sets men apart from the animal world. It includes the ability to think and reason. Consequently, there are three layers of soul-life—the food-supplying, or plant, soul; the perceiving, or animal, soul; and the thinking, or human, soul. Aristotle further divided the thinking, or human, soul into two different parts: the practical soul by which we "deliberate about those things which depend upon us and our purpose to do or not to do" (Aristotle, 1925: 1196) and the theoretical soul, which deals with higher and abstract knowledge such as distinguishing between what is true and what is false.

Aristotle advanced a theory of development concerning the layer structure of the soul that appears to have some resemblance to Darwin's more scientific biological theory of evolution, even though it does not include the idea of evolution of one species from another. Furthermore, Aristotle made an impassable division between the different levels of soul-life. Plato, in describing the stages of development, held that the first (plant) soul level developed before the second (animal) soul level and this, in turn, was a prerequisite for the rational soul level. Aristotle followed this idea of the level structure of the soul and applied it to the development of the child, as becomes obvious from the following quotation:

> As the body is prior in order of generation to the soul, so the irrational is prior to the rational. The proof is that anger and wishing and desire are implanted in children from their very birth, but reason and understanding are developed as they grow older. Wherefore, the care of the body ought to precede that of the soul, and the training of the appetitive part should

follow; none the less our care of it must be for the sake of the reason, and our care of the body for the sake of the soul [Aristotle, 1941c: 1300–1301].

Aristotle divided the developmental period of the human being into three distinguishable stages of seven years each. The first seven years he named infancy; the period from seven to the beginning of puberty, boyhood; and from puberty to twenty-one, young manhood. This division of the period of development into three stages was generally accepted during the Middle Ages and recurs in some modern psychological theories of development.

Infants and animals are alike in that both are under the control of their appetites and emotions. "Children and brutes pursue pleasures" (Aristotle, 1941a: 1053). Aristotle emphasized that moral character is the result of choice, "for by choosing what is good or bad we are men of a certain character. . . ." Even though young children are able to act voluntarily, they do not have choice, "for both children and the lower animals share in voluntary action, but not in choice, and acts done on the spur of the moment we describe as voluntary, but not as chosen" (Aristotle, 1941a: 967–968). This seems to imply that children first go through an animallike stage of development; what distinguishes them from animals is that children have the potential for higher development than animals, "though psychologically speaking a child hardly differs for the time being from an animal" (Aristotle, 1941b: 635). It is the characteristic of adolescence to develop the ability to choose. Only if the youth voluntarily and deliberately chooses will he develop the right kind of habits and thus in the long run build the right kind of character. By making choices adolescents actively participate in their own character formation. Voluntary and deliberate choice thus becomes an important aspect in Aristotle's theory of development, since it is necessary for the attainment of maturity. This idea is expressed by several modern writers. For example, both Margaret Mead and Edgar Friedenberg have stated that today, with prolonged education and prolonged dependency, we have reduced choices for adolescents to the extent that we interfere with their attainment of maturity.

Although Aristotle did not offer us a systematically stated theory of adolescence, in *Rhetorica* he provided us with a detailed description of the "youthful type of character," part of which resembles descriptive statements that could have been writen by G. Stanley Hall or Arnold Gesell. "Young men have strong passions, and tend to gratify them indiscriminately. Of the bodily desires, it is the sexual by which they are most swayed and in which they show absence of self-control" (Aristotle, 1941d: 1403). Sexuality in adolescence is of concern in any contemporary text, whether theoretically, empirically, or clinically oriented. Aristotle in his description of adolescents commented on their instability: "They are changeable and fickle in their desires, which are violent while they last, but quickly over: their impulses are keen but not deep-rooted" (Aristotle, 1941d: 1403). Lewin and Barker among the contemporary writers deal with the instability of the psychological field of the adolescent since he stands in a psychological no man's land. This makes many sociopsychological situations unclear, indefinite, and ambiguous, and the resulting behavior is "changeable and fickle." "For owing to their love and honour they cannot bear being slighted, and are indignant if they imagine themselves being unfairly treated" (Aristotle, 1941d: 1403–1404). Adolescent complaints about being "unfairly treated" in home, school, and society in general are so common today that they need no further elaboration. The list of quotes from *Rhetorica* in which Aristotle described the characteristics of adolescence could be continued at length, and other analogies to contemporary theory, observation, and empirical data would not be too difficult to find. Aristotle discussed, among other issues, adolescents' desire for success, their optimism, trust, concern with the future rather than the past, their courage, conformity, idealism, friendship, aggressiveness, and gullibility.

The education of the adolescent in the fourth century B.C. was based on the study of mathematics and included astronomy, geometry, and the theory of music; these subjects taught abstraction but did not require the life experiences and the wisdom that were considered necessary in order to become a philosopher or a physicist.

Under the early impact of Christian theology, Aristotelian thought seemed to get lost; however, it was later combined with Christian ideas by Saint Thomas Aquinas. The Aristotelian Thomistic philosophy became dominant in the twelfth and thirteenth centuries, and its influence was felt during the Middle Ages—particularly in the form of Scholasticism. Aristotle is also considered as influential in laying the foundation for a more scientific approach to science and psychology.

MEDIEVAL CHRISTIAN VIEW OF HUMAN DEVELOPMENT

The theological view of human nature and development cannot as readily be identified in terms of one man, a specific historical period, or even a particular church. We find the idea of Original Sin expressed by Tertullian in the second century when he speaks of the depravity of human nature. It was emphasized by John Calvin in the sixteenth century and is prevalent in Catholic Scholasticism, Protestant Calvinism, and American Puritanism.

The theological view of human nature and development as found in the medieval early Reformation period encompassed several ideas relevant to our topic:

1. Mankind's unique position in the universe, being created in the image of God.
2. Mankind's evil due to Adam's original sin.
3. Mankind's dualistic nature, a spiritual, immortal soul and a material, mortal body. Salvation and life after death places the immortal soul on a higher level of importance.
4. Knowledge as revealed to mankind from without. It comes from God and is revealed to us through the Bible.
5. The homunculus idea of instantaneous creation. The last point is not so much biblical as medieval.

Most of these ideas can be found in biblical sources, but they were also influenced by Greek philosophy, especially Plato's dualism. We will see later that theories that followed in the seventeenth, eighteenth, and nineteenth centuries, especially those advanced by Locke, Rousseau, and Darwin, can partly be understood as antitheses to these earlier theological ideas.

The idea that God created mankind in his own image and thus gave it a unique position in the universe is expressed in Genesis 1:27–28: "And God created man to his own image: to the image of God he created him: male and female he created them." Furthermore, he gives them the power to rule over all living creatures. Prior to Darwin man was seen as being divinely created and basically different from the animal world.

The second important idea concerning the nature of humanity is the theological doctrine of human depravity. The human being is seen as having innate tendencies toward ungodliness and sinfulness, as fundamentally bad, with the badness becoming stronger during the developmental years if it is not counteracted by stern discipline. The idea of Original Sin as based on Genesis 3:6–7 relates the sinfulness of each individual to Adam's first sin. And "as sin came into the world through one man and death through sin, and so death spread to all men because all men sinned. . . . Yet death reigned from Adam to Moses, even over those whose sins were not like the transgression of Adam . . ." (Romans 5:12–14).

This pessimistic view of human nature, prevalent in Catholic theology before the Reformation, received a new impetus with Calvin's theology and thus set the intellectual climate for Puritanism. The educational objective in this theory was to bring forth the innate ideas that are God-given—knowledge of his laws and commands. Such a stern disciplinary approach to education was prevalent under the influence of Catholic Scholasticism and Calvinism in Europe and Puritanism in New England. There was little room for individual differences, since the quality of the mind was the same for all individuals and the child who failed to learn was seen as willfully resisting the efforts of the teacher. The role of the teacher was defined by the teacher's authority and a belief that learning could be facilitated by physical punishment. The role of the child was defined by obedience. Calvin in particular expressed a strong faith in the value of education.

The theological point of view that mankind is the result of instantaneous creation results in preformationist thinking (Ausubel, 1958). During the Dark Ages, it was believed that the child came into the world as a miniature adult. The difference between a child and an adult was considered to be only a quantitative one, not a qualitative one. If one were to accept this point of view, then it follows that there should be no difference in the physiological functions of the child and the adult. Therefore, girls wore long dresses and corsets of adult style, only smaller in size, as is obvious from many medieval paintings. The qualitative difference in body build, body function, and mental abilities was disregarded. Growth was understood to be only a quantitative increase of all physical and mental aspects of human nature, not a qualitative one. This is a regression of thought when contrasted with the logical theories of Plato and Aristotle. The theory of preformationism held that children had the same interests as adults and therefore should be treated correspondingly, which meant that adult requirements were put upon them and were enforced by stern discipline. According to this view, the child did not "develop" but was preformed. Figure 2 illustrates the homunculus concept; it represents a view of the preformed "little man" in the sperm as conceived by seventeenth-century scientists. This idea of "homunculism" was utilized in prescientific theory of embryology.

> It was seriously believed that a miniature but fully-formed litle man (i.e., an homunculus) was embodied in the sperm, and when implanted in the uterus simply grew in bulk, without any differentiation of tissues or organs, until full-term fetal size was attained at the end of nine months [Ausubel, 1958: 23–24].

This idea of homunculism was soon to be challenged by the beginning of modern science and advancements in the field of medicine. It was learned that young children have qualitative and quantitative characteristics of their own and are not miniature adults. One might speculate that the reason for the limited concern of pre-Hallian writers with the basic physiological changes that take place during pubescence—many of these changes are obvious to the keen observer, and

FIGURE 2. Drawing of a small man (that is, a homunculus) in a human spermatozoon. Adapted from Hartsoeker, 1694.

their detection does not require medical knowledge or technology—is due to the theoretical position that the child is a miniature adult. In the philosophical realm it was Rousseau who stated that "nature would have children be children before being man. If we wish to prevent this order, we shall produce precocious fruits which will have neither maturity nor flavor, and will speedily deteriorate; we shall have young doctors and old children" (Rousseau, 1911: 54). Thus a new conception of human nature contributed to a more scientific concept of growth and development.

JOHN AMOS COMENIUS' DEVELOPMENT-CENTERED THEORY OF EDUCATION

The Renaissance may be seen as a revolt against authoritarianism in church, school, and society. The Aristotelian logic, the presupposition of universal ideas, and Scholasticism in general were challenged by Erasmus and Vives. Vives felt that one had "to begin with the individual facts of experience and out of them to come to ideas by the natural logic of the mind" (Boyd, 1965: 179). Learning was no longer seen as a deductive process, but as an inductive process beginning with experiences, and he suggested that an understanding of the learning process came from psychology. Learning, it was believed, was determined by the mind of the learner, and, therefore, education became concerned with individuality in pupils.

Comenius (1592–1670) accepted these new ideas of the Renaissance, combined them with Aristotle's classification of development, and advanced a theory of education that was based on psychological assumptions. In his *Great Didactic*, first published in 1657, Comenius suggested a school organization based on a theory of development. Rather than dividing the developmental period into three stages of seven years, as Aristotle did, Comenius proposed four developmental stages of six years each and a different kind of school for each of these four stages.

The suggested school organization was based on assumptions concerning the nature of human development and a specific theory of learning, that of faculty psychology. Interestingly enough, present-day school organization in parts of the United States closely resembles this pattern. Comenius argued that the temporal sequence of the curriculum content should be borrowed from nature; in other words, it should be suitable to the psychological development of the child. "Let our maxim be to follow the lead of nature in all things, to observe how the faculties develop one after the other, and to base our methods on this principle of succession" (Comenius, 1923: 257).

In the first six years of life children learn at home in the mother-school at their mother's knees. They should exercise the external senses and learn to discriminate among the various objects around them. The nature of the development of the faculty of sense perception is such that it precedes all other faculties, and, consequently, sensory experiences and sensory knowledge should be provided first. The significance of early sensorimotor experiences is emphasized in Piaget's contemporary theory of development.

The child from six to twelve attends the vernacular-school and receives a general well-rounded elementary education, which is provided for all children, rich or poor, boy or girl. Included in the curriculum are the correct use of the vernacular language, social habits, and religious training. The program at this level would emphasize training of the "internal senses, the imagination and memory in combination with their cognate organs." Comenius accepted the faculty psychology point of view in respect to memory. "The memory should be exercised in early youth, since practice developes it, and we should therefore take care to practice it as much as possible. Now, in youth, labour is not felt, and thus the memory developes without any trouble and becomes very retentive" (Comenius, 1923: 152).

For the next six years, from twelve to eighteen, which include the adolescent period as we understand it today, education was to be provided in the Latin school. The psychological purpose of the school at this age was to train the faculty of reasoning. The student learned to "understand and pass judgment on the information collected by the senses." Included were judgments about relationships of the things perceived, imagined, and remembered. Understanding here implies utilization of the principle of causality. The curriculum of the school was divided into six years, which results in the following six classes: Grammar, Natural Philosophy, Mathematics, Ethics, Dialectics, and Rhetoric.

The following six years, from eighteen to twenty-four, consist of university education and travel, and during this period the faculty of the will is trained. Considering our present conception of will this appears to be a strange notion and becomes more meaningful only if we consider that the concept of will, as used by Comenius, includes the self-direction of one's life. Corresponding ideas can be found in the contemporary theories of Erikson and Piaget.

Comenius strongly advocated that the instructional procedure should fit the level of comprehension of the child in contrast to the Scholastic education, which he attacked. For Comenius, development is not uniform, continuous, and gradual—as the homunculus theory of development implies—but each stage of development has its own characteristics, "teachable moments" as Havighurst would say today. Development was seen as a process in which the intellectual functions gain progressively more control over the other aspects of the soul.

> To attempt to cultivate the will before the intellect (or the intellect before the imagination, or the imagination before the faculty of sense perception) is mere waste of time. But this is what those do who teach boys logic, poetry, rhetoric, and ethics before they are thoroughly acquainted with the objects that surround them. It would be equally sensible to teach boys of two years old to dance, though they can scarcely walk [Comenius, 1923: 257].

The right time for the education of each of the faculties must be chosen correctly, and the sequence must be "borrowed from nature." In Comenius' continuous focus on what children can do, know, and are interested in at each stage of development, we seem to find the historical roots of a child-centered theory of education.

JOHN LOCKE'S EMPIRICISM

The idea of homunculism with its emphasis on preformationism and Plato's theory of innate ideas—a basic scholastic principle—was most seriously challenged and opposed by John Locke (1632–1704). Locke was influenced by Thomas Hobbes' (1588–1679) idea that the human being, both body and mind, is part of the natural order; he further expanded Hobbes' theoretical position, known today as empiricism, that all of our knowledge is derived from sensation. Hobbes stated in *Leviathan* that "there is no conception in man's mind, which has not at first, totally, or by parts, been begotten upon the organs of sense" (Hobbes,1651: 7). Locke further developed the theory that there are no innate ideas; ideas that we hold in our consciousness are either obtained through our senses directly or are derived from those ideas that have been obtained through sensations previously. The child's mind at the time of birth is, according to an analogy used by Locke, a tabula rasa, a blank tablet. He made the following famous statement concerning the nature of the human mind:

> Let us then suppose the mind to be, as we say, white paper, void of all characters, without any ideas:—How comes it to be furnished? . . . To this I answer, in one word, from EXPERIENCE. In that all our knowledge is founded; and from that it ultimately derives itself. Our observation employed either, about external sensible objects, or about the internal operations of our minds perceived and reflected on by ourselves, is that which supplies our understandings with all the materials of thinking. These two are the fountains of knowledge, from whence all the ideas we have, or can naturally have, do spring [Locke, 1753: 76].

This assumption has had far-reaching influence on social theory and has with amplification become the cornerstone of democracy. Since the mind of each person at birth is a tabula rasa, all ideas and knowledge come from experience; since present differences and inequalities that can be found in people are due to environment and experiences, all are completely equal at birth. Thus the principle of democracy is in part derived from a philosophical-psychological theory concerning the child's mind at birth. Locke discussed his views concerning democracy in *Treatise of Civil Government* (1768). He blamed environmental conditions, such as poor education and poor social environment, for the human misery in the world and gave hope to those who lived under unfavorable conditions. Thus emerged a theory that is an expression of faith in the perfectibility of the human race.

Locke found rather enthusiastic followers in Helvetius and Condillac in France. They carried his empiricism to its extreme, since for them even the powers of faculties of the mind were the result of sensation. Furthermore, since poor living conditions existed for the French lower and middle classes prior to the Revolution, many people in France were especially susceptible to such ideas. Thus the words *liberté, egalité, fraternité* became the powerful symbols of a new concept of human nature. A new hope emerged; that by changing the environment, human nature could be changed. Mankind could determine its own destiny.

Locke's proposition that there are no innate ideas and that the human mind is a tabula rasa contrasts sharply with several theories of human development already discussed. The more outstanding examples are:

1. The doctrine of human depravity and Original Sin appeared to be in contradiction to Locke's new concept of the human mind. If our mind is formed by experience only, then it follows that whether a child becomes "good" or "bad" is due to environmental experiences. Locke's psychology stresses nurture rather than nature.

2. The medieval class system of Europe was based on what we would consider today as hereditary assumptions. The nobility was noble by birth, regardless of personal merits and qualities. This notion was challenged by the empiricist assumption that "all men are born equal." If everyone is alike and begins life at the same point, then everyone should have the same rights and opportunities to obtain better social positions. King and subject, rich and poor, begin life at the same zero point. Therefore, support for social mobility is found in this theory. Locke's early form of environmentalism, even though it is not directly related to behaviorism, social learning theory, and cultural relativism, may be viewed as a historical forerunner to these schools of thought.

3. The doctrine of innate ideas was interpreted during the medieval period to imply that the child is a miniature adult and grows only quantitatively. Locke's tabula rasa concept implied that the child at birth is fundamentally different from the adult both qualitatively and quantitatively. If ideas are not innate, then the newborn child is radically different from the adult in respect to intellectual properties. Locke pointed out that the child's personality is basically different from that of the adult and thus laid the foundation for a new theory of child development; he also urged the scientific study of human nature. Development, he believed, occurred in a gradual process from mental passivity in the early years of childhood to increased mental activity in adolescence. The rational faculty emerges toward the end of this developmental process and therefore was seen as characteristic of the period of adolescence.

Locke himself, even though he advanced many important ideas about human nature, foreshadowed rather than developed a specific theory of human development. It was Rousseau who, influenced by Locke, proposed a new theory of human development.

JEAN JACQUES ROUSSEAU'S ROMANTIC NATURALISM

Rousseau (1712–1778) was greatly influenced by Locke's ideas, but he developed his own theoretical positions concerning human nature. While for Locke reason was the most important aspect of human nature, Rousseau considered human nature as primarily feeling. While Locke was concerned with constitutional government, Rousseau made a great plea for individualism and individual freedom and directed his criticism and attack against society and social institutions. Although he, too, was concerned with the social well-being of all, he distinguished between the "will of all" (majority will, determined by vote) and the "general will" (that which is really best for every member of society). Rousseau was not truly democratic, for he was afraid that a majority vote could be as bad as any monarchy. Ideally the majority will and the general will would coincide. This, however, was only possible if men were educated and wise.

Rousseau brought about a revolutionary change in thought concerning the nature of human development with its corresponding educational implications, the main ideas of which he expressed in *Émile*, originally published in 1780. The traditional approach toward childhood education had been to see the child from the adult point of view, adult interests, and adult social life. Rousseau claimed that such an approach is not only false, it may even be harmful. He started with the needs and interests of the child and saw development as a natural preplanned process. If one were to free the child from the restrictions, unnatural limitations, and rigid discipline of the adult world, nature would assure a harmonious and healthy development. The child was innately good, but the restrictions of adult society and poor education had corrupted the child. To correct this, he advocated a natural development in a sound and healthy environment, which for him was one that posed few restrictions on the child, especially in the first twelve years. Rousseau was one of the strongest proponents of individualism in education, basing his proposition on a deep faith in the natural good of man.

Rousseau advocated a revision of the treatment children received at home and in school as well as changes in the methods of instruction; if development were left to the laws of nature, the outcome would be most desirable. Each of Rousseau's four stages of development had specific psychological characteristics. Consideration of these characteristics resulted in definite educational objectives, the attainment of which helped children grow toward maturity. The educational methods, the content to be taught, and the educational objectives at each age level were to be determined by the characteristics of the child at that developmental level. Learning was most effective if the child had freedom and could learn and grow according to his own impulses.

Rousseau (1780) most strongly opposed the homunculus idea and asserted that it was the plan of nature that children play, live, and behave like children before they become adults. "Childhood has its own way of seeing, thinking, and feeling, and nothing is more foolish than to try to substitute ours for them" (Rousseau, 1911: 54). Rousseau advised teachers and parents, "You ought to be wholly absorbed in the child—observing him, watching him without respite, and without seeming to do so, having a presentiment of his feelings in advance" (Rousseau, 1911: 169). Even though Rousseau himself had only limited and not always successful educational experiences—his five children lived in a foundling asylum—his theory had a tremendous impact on educational practice in the latter part of the eighteenth and most of the nineteenth centuries. Rousseau's ideas are obvious in the works of Pestalozzi, Froebel, Basedow, Spencer, Horace Mann, and Dewey and are reflected in a child-centered approach to education.

Rousseau, like Aristotle, saw the development of the child occurring in certain stages; however, he identified four stages rather than three and believed that teaching and training should be in harmony with the developmental nature of each of these stages. According to Rousseau, these various stages are breaks in the developmental process, and each can be distinguished by its special characteristics and functions. He spoke of a metamorphosis that takes place when the child changes from one stage to another. Thus, Rousseau introduced a saltatory theory of human development according to which the nature of development is seen as change that is more sudden at certain age levels than at others. He, like G. Stanley Hall, spoke of puberty as a new birth. New functions may emerge rather suddenly and become dominant in the psychological organization. We might better understand this saltatory aspect of development in Rousseau's theory in the light of his own temperamental saltatory experiences.

The first stage, that of infancy, includes the first four to five years of life. The child is dominated by the feeling of pleasure and pain. This period is called the animal stage, because the child is like an animal in regard to its physical needs and undifferentiated feelings. This notion we encountered earlier in the writings of Aristotle. Education, such as training motor coordination, sense perception, and feeling, is primarily physical. He advocated to mothers that the method of nature be followed in everything and proposed the following rule: "Observe nature, and follow the route which she traces for you. She is ever exciting children to activity; she hardens the constitution by trials of every sort; she teaches them at an early hour what suffering and pain are."

The second stage, which Rousseau characterized as the savage stage, includes the years from five to twelve. Dominant during this stage is the faculty of sense. Sensory experiences are provided by play, sport, and games, and the curriculum is centered on the training of the senses. During this stage self-consciousness and memory develop, and human life in the proper sense begins here. The child still lacks reasoning ability and is not yet sufficiently aware of moral considerations. Education during this stage should be free from external, social, and moral control. Formal training in reading and writing are seen as harmful and therefore postponed until the beginning of the third developmental stage. In the first twelve years education

> . . . ought to be purely negative. It consists not at all in teaching virtues or truth, but in shielding the heart from vice, and the mind from error. If you could do nothing and allow nothing to be done, if you could bring your pupil sound and robust to the age of twelve years without his being able to distinguish his right hand from his left, from your very first lesson the eyes of his understanding would be open to reason [Rousseau, 1911: 59].

Rousseau's method of "negative education," based on the assumption that there is an innate developmental plan in the organization that cannot be improved upon by environmental factors, finds its corresponding modern psychological concept in "maturation." The defenders of the maturational concept of development frequently advocate, as did Rousseau, a permissive and unrestricted atmosphere for childrearing.

The third stage, the years from twelve to fifteen, is characterized by an awakening of the rational functions, including reason and self-consciousness. Youth at this age possess an enormous amount of physical energy and strength. The excess of energy leads to curiosity, which the school curriculum should utilize by encouraging exploratory behavior and the desire to discover what is true about the world. The only book that should be read during this stage is *Robinson Crusoe*. Rousseau saw in Crusoe the great model and ideal for the preadolescent, since his style of life was characterized by exploration of the world and a primitive curiosity, which corresponds to the needs and interests of this developmental stage. The curriculum should be geared to the study of nature, astronomy, science, art, and crafts. Rousseau in agreement with contemporary educational theory emphasizes the learning process rather than the product. "He is not to learn science, he is to find out for himself." This is the age of reason; curiosity and personal utility are the main motives for behavior; social conscience and emotionality are still undeveloped. It is interesting to observe that, in opposition to other developmental theories, the rational aspect of personality develops prior to the emotional. Rousseau's theory was a reaction to the historically earlier philosophy of rationalism with which he had obvious differences.

The fourth period, adolescence proper, from the age of fifteen to twenty, finally culminates in the maturation of the emotional functions and brings about a change from selfishness to self-esteem and social consideration. The adolescent is no longer self-sufficient but develops a strong interest in other people and a need for genuine affection. This stage is characterized—late by comparison to knowledge about youth today—by the emergence of the sex drive, which Rousseau considered a second birth. "We have two births, so to speak—one for existing and the other for living; one for the species and the other for the sex" (Rousseau, 1911: 193). Now conscience is acquired, and morals and virtues become possible. This is the period of preparation for marriage, which ideally coincides with the attainment of maturity.

Maturity could be considered as a fifth stage in the process, but it appears to be less clearly defined. The faculty that becomes dominant during this period is will. Comenius also placed the development of the will at the time of late adolescence. The will is the faculty of the soul by which we choose between two alternatives.

These stages of development, according to Rousseau, correspond to certain stages in the development of the human race. Thus it was assumed by this recapitulation theory that the human race had gone through the stages of animallike living, the stage of savagery, the stage of reason, and, finally, through a stage of social and emotional maturity. He used the historical development of the race in order to explain the development of the individual child. This hypothesis was further developed by educators, such as Froebel and Ziller, as well as by G. Stanley Hall and the Child Study Movement of America.

Critics have pointed out that Rousseau overemphasized the individual nature of human growth and development and underemphasized the importance that education, society, and culture have in the developmental process and especially in the formation of the human personality. He saw the influence of society and culture as negative forces in personality development; he wanted to remove them to make possible the free natural development of what is good in the child.

CHARLES DARWIN'S THEORY OF BIOLOGICAL EVOLUTION

A new trend of thought concerning the nature of development emerged with the publication of Darwin's *Origin of Species* (1859). Darwin's (1809–1882) idea of evolution—growth and development from the simpler to the more complex forms of organic life—has been one of the most revolutionary and influential ideas in man's thinking about himself and the nature of his development. Every living organism from the simplest organic structure to the most complex, man himself, is brought together under the order of natural explanation. The psychological implications resulting from this biological concept of development were accepted, elaborated, and applied to adolescent development by G. Stanley Hall, thus leading to a science of adolescent development.

Since Darwin's theory is well known, only its basic principles will be stated. Darwin collected substantial, though not complete, evidence for a theory that claimed that the evolution of biological life is continuous, from a single cell organism, through numerous higher developmental stages, to the complexity of human mind and body. This evolutionary theory assumed variability and adjustability in all organisms as well as the overproduction in the number of offspring of each species. Darwin showed that the overproduction of offspring threatened a species' capacity to survive. The result is a "struggle for existence." In this struggle of the selection of some and elimination of others, a "natural selection process" takes place by which the increase in population is checked. The stronger, healthier, faster, more immune, more intelligent, and physically better developed and adjusted organisms survive and reproduce, while the weak, sick, and less adaptable species perish. In time this leads to the "survival of the fittest." The qualities that account for the survival of the fittest are inherited by the offspring. Since the conditions for survival frequently differ in various kinds of environments, basic changes in the organism occur. Thus in the selection process, variations, new kinds, new races, and eventually new organisms come into existence. This process began with the simple one-cell organism, and from the lower forms of organic life more and more complex forms have developed. The last link in this biological evolution is the human being. Since climatic, geological, and general life conditions change, the evolutionary process is a perpetual one.

This theory of evolution is in complete contrast to the theological doctrine of the divine creation of humankind. Through Darwin's theory mankind was placed in the order of nature. Most theological and many philosophical positions previous to Darwin's—for example, that of Aristotle—had postulated an essential dichotomy between man and nature. This absolute distinction between human nature and the nature of the organic world was seriously challenged by Darwin. Humans were now seen as part of the organic world, albeit a more advanced and more intelligent species.

G. STANLEY HALL'S BIOGENETIC PSYCHOLOGY OF ADOLESCENCE

G. Stanley Hall (1844–1924) was the first psychologist to advance a psychology of adolescence in its own right and to use scientific methods in his study of adolescence. It can be said that he bridged the philosophical, speculative approach of the past and the scientific, empirical approach of the present.

Hall expanded Darwin's concept of biological "evolution" into a psychological theory of recapitulation. In this theory he stated that the experiential history of the human species had become part of the genetic structure of each individual. The law of recapitulation asserted that the individual organism, during its development, passes through stages that correspond to those that occurred during the history of mankind. That is, the individual relives the development of the human race from early animallike primitivism, through a period of savagery, to the more recent civilized ways of life that characterize maturity.

Hall assumed that development is brought about by physiological factors. He further assumed that these physiological factors are genetically determined, that internal maturational forces predominantly control and direct development, growth, and behavior; there was little room in this theory for the influence of environmental forces. It follows that development and its behavioral concomitants occur in an inevitable and unchangeable pattern that is universal, regardless of the sociocultural environment. Cultural anthropologists and sociologists were able to challenge this point and to show that Hall's position was extreme and untenable in the light of accumulated evidence. They further refuted the claim that the behavioral predispositions of physiological drives, as expressed in the recapitulation theory, are highly specific. Hall held that socially unacceptable types of behavior—those characteristic of earlier historical phases—must be tolerated by parents and educators, since they are necessary stages in social development. He advocated childrearing practices of leniency and permissiveness. However, he reassured parents and educators that unacceptable behavior would disappear in the following developmental stage without any corrective educational or disciplinary efforts. Remnants of this assumption can be found in Gesell's conception of maturation.

A corollary of Hall's theory of recapitulation is his concept of stages of human development; the characteristics of a certain age in the development of the individual correspond to some primitive historical stage in the development of the human race. Hall did not divide human development into three stages as advocated by Aristotle and many present-day "stage" psychologists. He followed a four-division pattern similar to that proposed by Comenius and Rousseau. Hall's developmental stages are infancy, childhood, youth, and adolescence.

The period of infancy includes the first four years of life. While children are still crawling, they are reenacting the animal stage of the human race when the species was still using four legs. During this period, sensory development is dominant; the child acquires those sensorimotor skills that are necessary for self-preservation.

The period of childhood—the years from four to eight—corresponds to the cultural epoch when hunting and fishing were the main activities of man. This is the time when the child plays hide-and-seek, cowboys and Indians, uses toy weapons, and so on. The building of caves, shacks, and other hiding places parallels the cave-dwelling culture of early history.

Youth—from eight to twelve—includes the period that today is commonly referred to as "preadolescence." During this stage the child recapitulates the "humdrum life of savagery" of several thousand years ago. This is the period of life when the child has a favorable predisposition to practice and discipline, when routine training and drill are most appropriate.

> Never again will there be such susceptibility to drill and discipline, such plasticity to habituation, or such ready adjustment to new conditions. It is the age of external and mechanical training. Reading, writing, drawing, manual training, musical technic, foreign tongues and their pronunciation, the manipulation of numbers and of geometrical elements, and many kinds of skill have now their golden hour, and if it passes, unimproved, all these can never be acquired later without a heavy handicap or disadvantage or loss [Hall, 1916: xii].

Adolescence is the period from puberty (about twelve or thirteen) until full adult status has been attained. According to Hall, it ends comparatively late, between the twenty-second and twenty-fifth years. Hall described adolescence as a period of *Sturm und Drang*, "storm and stress." In German literature, the period of *Sturm und Drang* includes, among others, the works of Schiller and the early writings of Goethe. It is a literary movement full of idealism, commitment to a goal, revolution against the old, expression of personal feelings, passion, and suffering. Hall saw an analogy between the objectives of this group of young writers at the turn of the eighteenth century and the psychological characteristics of adolescence. In terms of recapitulation theory adolescence corresponds to a time when the human race was in a turbulent, transitional stage. Hall described adolescence as a new birth, "for the higher and more completely human traits are now born" (Hall, 1916: xiii).

The characteristics of adolescent *Sturm und Drang* are pictured in detail by Hall in the chapter "Feelings and Psychic Evolution" (Hall, 1916). He perceived the emotional life of the adolescent as an oscillation between contradictory tendencies. Energy, exaltation, and supernatural activity are followed by indifference, lethargy, and loathing. Exuberant gaiety, laughter, and euphoria make place for dysphoria, depressive gloom, and melancholy. Egoism, vanity, and conceit are just as characteristic of this period of life as are abasement, humiliation, and bashfulness. One can observe both the remnants of an uninhibited childish selfishness and an increasing idealistic altruism. Goodness and virtue are never so pure, but never again does temptation so forcefully preoccupy thought. Adolescents want solitude and seclusion, while finding themselves entangled in crushes and friendships. Never again does the peer group have such a strong influence. At one time the adolescent may exhibit exquisite sensitivity and tenderness; at another time, callousness and cruelty. Apathy and inertia vacillate with an enthusiastic curiosity, an urge to discover and explore. There is a yearning for idols and authority that does not exclude a revolutionary radicalism directed against any kind of authority. Hall (1916) implies these antithetical impulses of Promethean enthusiasm and deep sentimental *Weltschmerz* in his use of the concept of *Sturm und Drang*, which for him is so characteristic of the adolescent.

In late adolescence the individual recapitulates the stage of the beginning of modern civilization. This stage corresponds to the end of the developmental process: the adolescent reaches maturity. Hall's genetic psychology did not see the human being as the final and finished product of the developmental process; it allowed for indefinite further development.

3: THE PSYCHOANALYTIC THEORY OF ADOLESCENT DEVELOPMENT

INTRODUCTION TO PSYCHOANALYTIC THEORY

Sigmund Freud (1856–1939) developed a comprehensive theory of psychopathology, of personality, and of human development and in the process founded the psychoanalytic school of thought. His theory was revolutionary since it fundamentally changed the conceptual foundation of psychology and psychiatry of his time; it has remained influential to this day (see Chapters 4 and 5). Psychoanalysis was based on concepts and on insights into the workings of the human mind that had obtained little systematic attention in pre-Freudian psychology. The new ideas of physics and biology that emphasize energy and dynamics, and were prevalent toward the end of the nineteenth century, as well as Darwin's notion of evolution, influenced Freud's thinking and became part of his psychodynamic theory of psychology. He believed that all psychological events are tied to energy, drive, and instincts based on biological characteristics of the body.

Freud's theoretical assumption concerning the nature of man has dramatically changed man's conception of himself. Freud is often identified as one of the most important thinkers of the twentieth century, comparable in influence to Copernicus and Darwin. Copernicus changed our geocentric view of the world. Darwin's theory removed the human race from its special position in relationship to God and placed it within the continuum of natural evolution as part of the animal world; humans were seen as no more than just another animal with specific survival mechanisms. Freud, in turn, made explicit that humans were not the rational, logical, and intelligent beings they had been believed to be but were to a large extent irrational, influenced by hidden, dark, unconscious motives of which they themselves were often not aware. Freud implied that the crucial psychological reality is desire rather than reason.

The significance of Freud's work is not limited to psychology, psychiatry, and psychoanalysis proper, but his ideas have become influential in literature, art, advertisement, philosophy, sociology, medicine, and education. His contributions to our understanding of the mind have penetrated many areas of modern Western culture and thought to such an extent that his ideas have become part of each individual's "implicit psychology" to a much larger extent than is commonly acknowledged. Freud's contribution to our understanding of the nature of the mind contains several identifiable elements and ideas:

1. All behavior is motivated, and the motivating forces are often unconscious.
2. Freud's theory of dreams emphasized the meaningfulness of dreams as manifestations of the unconscious mind.
3. Similarly, Freud ascribes meaning to errors, forgetting, slips of the tongue, and other unintended behavior, believing that they reveal unconscious forces.
4. A major motivating force in human behavior is sexuality, including the idea of infantile sexuality. Freud emphasized the conflictual relationship between sexuality and civilization.
5. Early childrearing experiences, especially in weaning, toilet training, and the role of the family in the handling of sexuality and aggression, are seen as significant factors in personality development.
6. Freud gave new hope to the treatment of psychopathology and changed social attitudes toward the neurotic and psychotic.

After completion of his medical training, Freud began his medical career in Vienna as a research scientist in neurology, hoping to become a professor rather than a practicing physician. However, because of his limited opportunities for advancement in the university setting and since he needed to earn money and support his family, he was forced to practice medicine. As a medical specialist in neurology, he began to see patients with neuropsychological problems (psychoneuroses). The treatment of nervous disorders was a branch of medicine that was, at that time, primitive, and few treatment modalities existed that could successfully be used in dealing with patients with mental aberrations.

Freud's scientific inclination led him to the discovery and development of new treatment methods. He systematically collected observational and case study data, supplementing it with his own famous self-analysis, to which he devoted the last half hour of each day from 1897 until his death in 1939. Freud's theory evolved only slowly and was a multifaceted theory of various models and explanatory systems of human psychopathology, the nature of dreams, human motivation, and the inner workings of the mind. Like the theories of Copernicus, Darwin, and other revolutionary thinkers before him, Freud's new theoretical formulations were initially met with bitter resistance and objections from the scientific community.

A rather careful review of the empirical research literature attempting to test Freud's theoretical assumptions concludes:

> Large masses of experimental information are available for testing psychoanalytic propositions. We have been amused by the fact that while there is the stereotyped conviction widely current that Freud's thinking is not amenable to scientific appraisal, the quantity of research data pertinent to it that has accumulated in the literature grossly exceeds that available for most other personality or developmental theories. We have actually not been able to find a single systematic theory that has been as frequently evaluated as Freud's [Fisher and Greenberg, 1977: 396].

While not all of Freud's concepts receive unequivocal empirical support, many do, and many others receive at least partial support. Apparently, Freud's concepts of the oral and the anal personality, the etiology of homosexuality, several aspects of the Oedipus complex theory, and his theory of the origin of paranoid delusions seem to find substantial support from empirical investigations. Other aspects of Freud's theory, such as the nature of dreaming, the effectiveness of psychoanalytic therapy, Freud's psychology of women, and sex differences are not borne out by empirical studies. In general, there is much more support for Freud's overall theoretical propositions concerning human nature and personality development than for his practical suggestions about doing psychotherapy (Fisher and Greenberg, 1977).

Space does not allow a full discussion of the entire system of psychoanalytic theory. Therefore, in the context of theories of development and especially theories of adolescence, only those theoretical models especially relevant to an understanding of personality development and to the neopsychoanalytic theories that follow in Chapters 4 and 5 will be presented:

1. The topographical model of the mind consisting of three layers: the conscious, the preconscious, and the unconscious. This conceptualization of the tripartite organization of the mind grew out of Freud's book, *The Interpretation of Dreams* (1900/1953), which was his first major psychoanalytic work.
2. Another tripartite model of the mind, which Freud later developed in *The Ego and the Id* (1923a/1949), based on the structural hypothesis and consisting of the id, the ego, and the superego.

These two systems are not only compatible, but they overlap and have been integrated into a more dynamic view of the inner workings of the mind and thus contribute to our understanding of personality development as well as to the dynamics of psychopathology.

3. The psychosexual stages of human development are: the oral, anal, phallic, latency, and genital stages. These are of particular significance for our concern with theories of adolescence since they constitute the cornerstone of Freud's developmental theory.

4. The mechanisms of defense: repression, displacement, identification, rationalization, reaction formation, introjection, projection, undoing, and denial. These are mechanisms by which the ego, by one means or another, defends against the unacceptable and painful or anxiety-arousing wishes of the id. Anna Freud considered asceticism and intellectualization especially characteristic of pubescence. Otto Rank also viewed asceticism as typical for adolescents, but contrasts it with its opposite, promiscuity.

Freud's theory of psychosexual development has stimulated considerable research interest and further theoretical development in personality development in general and adolescent development in particular by such psychoanalysts as Hartmann, Horney, Sullivan, Winnicott, Fromm, Reich, Rank, A. Freud, Erikson, and Blos. Freud himself, partly because of his discovery of the role of infantile sexuality in normal and abnormal development and partly because of his emphasis of the importance on the first five years of life in human development, climaxing in the Oedipus complex, placed relatively little emphasis on pubescence and adolescence. Many neo-Freudians seem to agree with this neglect of the period of adolescence in Freud's original theory. Among the neo-Freudians, E. Erikson and P. Blos in particular have attempted to rectify this theoretical neglect of adolescence. However, a familiarity with Freud's basic concepts appears to be an essential prerequisite for understanding psychoanalytic and neopsychoanalytic theory.

CONSCIOUS—PRECONSCIOUS—UNCONSCIOUS

The first tripartite model of the mind emerged from Freud's efforts to explain the psychology of the dream processes. The mind, according to Freud (1900/1953, 1915/1957), consisted of three layers: the conscious, the preconscious, and the unconscious. This early comprehensive theory of personality and development is referred to as the topographical model.

The *conscious* is that layer of the mental apparatus of which the individual is aware. Conscious provides contact with both the external world—through perceptions, motor activity, and feelings—and with the internal personal world of dreams, images, and thoughts. Consciousness itself contains only a very small and limited part of the mental life. The metaphor often used is the iceberg, of which only a very small part floats over the surface while most of it is under the water. Freud emphasized that only a very limited part of our mental activity takes place in the conscious at any one time. However, the conscious also has the function of censorship, admitting or excluding material from awareness.

The much greater part of our mental activity remains more or less inaccessible in the lower regions of the mental structures. One of the major tasks of psychoanalytic treatment is, according to Freud, the uncovering of this hidden material to make unconscious content, motives, and dynamics conscious. Only the patient's conscious understanding of these hidden dynamics makes a realistic and thoughtful adjustment possible, hence therapy is primarily concerned with making unconscious material conscious.

The *preconscious*, in a certain sense, is part of the unconscious, since the individual is not aware of its content. Yet much of it, particularly in the upper regions of the preconscious, is easily accessible to the conscious, since the content can voluntarily be retrieved by directing one's attention to it. This can be achieved by asking relevant questions or by providing appropriate stimuli. The preconscious constitutes much of the mental warehouse of information and experiences, accessible through memory and, therefore, basically accessible to the conscious on specific request. Most of the ideas that are not at present in our awareness but that can, through the process of memory, retrieval, and thinking, be brought back into our conscious mind are, according to Freud, in our preconscious.

The preconscious, however, is not a passive storehouse of information but is actively involved in many mental activities. According to Kubie (1958), sudden insights into complex problems or creative thoughts and discoveries do emerge from preconscious processes. Often the solution to a problem does not emerge while one is consciously working on it but seems to pop into one's mind from the preconscious without any conscious thinking effort when one is relaxed or about to go to sleep, and sometimes solutions emerge even when one is not consciously aware of the problem.

The *unconscious* contains experiences and information that cannot readily be brought into awareness by volition, that require special efforts, treatment, hypnosis, or interpretation to be brought back into the conscious. However, for Freud, the unconscious was the dominant force in the mental apparatus, especially in psychopathology. The pathway between the unconscious and the conscious is normally blocked, but the pathway between the preconscious and the conscious is at least partially open. The content of the unconscious (traumatic experiences, unacceptable impulses, and such) are kept in the unconscious by repression; however, they are not dormant but remain dynamic and active. Although the constant process of repression itself is not conscious, it consumes psychological energy. However, repression is unable to suppress the unconscious impulses permanently, hence the unconscious impulses and experiences manifest themselves in distorted, nonrecognizable form in dream content, errors, accidents, and neurotic symptoms. Thus, an accident may be understood as an unconscious desire to hurt oneself or to punish oneself for forbidden thoughts or deeds. The craving for sweets is viewed as an unconscious symbolic repressed desire for human love. Dreaming is a process by which the repressed unconscious wish (the latent dream content) finds a distorted conscious manifestation in the dream experiences (the manifest dream content).

Considerable scientific evidence supports Freud's basic assumption that motives, wishes, feelings, and fantasies exist in an individual without the individual being consciously aware of these hidden dynamic forces; furthermore, these hidden forces are known to influence behavior (Fisher and Greenberg, 1977).

ID—EGO—SUPEREGO

Later Freud developed in *The Ego and the Id* (1923a/1949) another tripartite model of the mind that is closely related to the topographical model of conscious, preconscious, and unconscious; each component of this id–ego–superego model emerges during different stages of psychosexual development (the developmental model will be discussed later). In the structural model Freud conceptualizes the structure of the mind as consisting of three major systems: the id (biological), the ego (psychological), and the superego (social). In the healthy adult person these three systems, id, ego, and superego, form an integrated personality pattern, which aids the individual in conducting daily interactions with the environment and allows satisfaction of basic needs and desires within socially prescribed limits. In the neurotic person these systems are in conflict, necessitating the use of defense mechanisms or maladaptive manifestations and thus reducing the efficiency of that person's everyday functioning.

A number of psychoanalysts assert that some of the reemergence of infantile or childish behaviors that may occur in early adolescence is due to regression. Faced on the one hand by the problem of coping with a sudden upsurge in sexual and aggressive drives and the anxiety that they create, and on the other hand by greatly increased social demands, the adolescent may temporarily abandon anxiety-producing and not always successful efforts at more mature responding, and retreat to more 'primitive' responses that were successful and rewarding in an earlier, simpler period [Conger, 1977: 84].

The id is present at birth and governed by the pleasure principle. The id provides the mind with its psychological energy, impulses, and motivation to act. It represents the biological component of the mental apparatus, including untamed passion. It contains irrational instinctual appetites and impulses, and its purpose is to gratify basic instinctual and bodily needs and reduce the tensions produced by these biological needs. The contents and the processes of the id are primarily but not exclusively unconscious. Tension reduction, which comes about when basic biological needs are gratified, is pleasurable. Hence, the object that reduces bodily tensions becomes attached (or cathected) to the id. Freuians speak extensively of libidinal object finding, and the object can be a thing, the self or part of the self, or another person: oral object choice, anal object choice, parent object choice, Oedipal object choice, homosexual object choice, and heterosexual object choice. In the young infant the drive of the id is not yet restrained by moral or practical considerations but is directly oriented toward drive gratification. The operations of the id are, therefore, referred to as primary processes.

Even later in life, an id-dominated personality asserts little or no control over a person's instinctual wishes and sexual desires. Such a person's behavior is mainly influenced by the immediate gratification of the pleasure-seeking motive and would show little concern either for the demands of reality or for social or ethical values. The acting-out juvenile delinquent as well as the promiscuous sexual behavior of the adolescent seems to be id-dominated.

DEVELOPMENT OF THE EGO

According to Freud the ego develops in part out of the id during the end of the first through the second year of life and is defined by its reality-testing functions. The most important function of the ego is the adaptation of the individual to reality (S. Freud, 1933/1963).

Toilet training contributes greatly to ego development, since it contributes to the delineation of body boundaries or, in a more general sense, to a distinction between the self and the outside world. The ego represents the psychological component of the personality, but the id still remains the dominant element in the partnership between id, ego, and superego. This development of the ego out of the id takes place when the demands of the id are not met and transactions between the organism and the outside world become necessary to discharge tensions. When needs are not immediately satisfied two consequences can occur:

1. The infant remains in a state of tension.
2. The id, having to cope with unresolved tension, is transformed into a new structure, the "I" or the ego, which takes into account the external reality that does not allow the gratification of impulses, and in the process the maturing child learns to cope with the tensions stemming from the needs of the id that are in conflict with the demands of reality.

The ego serves several functions in the mental apparatus. First and foremost, the function of the ego is to compromise between the inner world of subjective experiences, the id, and the demands of the external (objective) world. It obeys the reality principle. The ego has a reality-testing function; that is, it delays, inhibits, restrains, and controls the demands of the id—not permanently, however, but only in order to maximize its gratification at the appropriate time and place, when short-range as well as long-range consequences are being considered, and when the gratification of a desire is actually in the individual's best interest. The ego also considers whether the object is appropriate for the gratification of the needs of the id. The ego takes on several other functions. It prevents the drive discharge when such behavior would not be in the individual's best interest; that is, it helps the individual develop frustration tolerance. It also controls the ideas that enter consciousness. Furthermore, through various defense mechanisms at the disposal of the ego, ideas that are dangerous or arouse anxiety may be prevented from entering the conscious or may be distorted. The ego thus guides the behavior of an individual toward acceptable goals. In that sense all cognition is a function of the ego. Finally, the ego encompasses logical thinking.

The ego represents the external world to the id. It consists of reason, common sense, and reality-testing functions, but serves the purpose of the id from whom it borrows its energies. The metaphor used by Freud was that of the horse (id), constituting instinctual drive and energy, and the rider (ego) who controls where and how fast the horse can go.

The ego's relation to the id might be compared with that of a rider to his horse. The horse supplies the locomotive energy, while the rider has the privilege of deciding on the goal and of guiding the powerful animal's movement. But only too often there arises between the ego and the id the not precisely ideal situation of the rider being obliged to guide the horse along the path by which it itself wants to go [Freud, 1933/1964: 77].

On the other hand, there often is no real difference between the goals of the id and the ego, only differences in the way these goals can be attained. The ego tries to avoid the negative consequences that could result from an uninhibited gratification of the id impulses.

DEVELOPMENT OF THE SUPEREGO

Later in human development, during the latency period, the superego develops, primarily as a function of the resolution of the Oedipus complex. Freud (1923b/1949) views the superego as the "heir of the Oedipus complex."

Research findings suggest that the development of the superego is less a direct outgrowth of oedipal tensions and conflicts with the father than Freud suggested. Instead, the mother's and other people's standards play a larger role and are more positively assimilated and gradually integrated in the self-structures than Freud had theorized. The oedipal struggle itself is resolved most effectively, not out of fear of the father (castration anxiety) but out of a nurturant, friendly attitude on the father's part (Fisher and Greenberg, 1977: 405).

The superego represents the social-moral component in the personality. It represents the ideal rather than the real and strives for perfection. The individual's internalized moral code develops out of a process of identification with one's parents and their standards as to what is good or bad, virtuous or sinful. Later, the superego becomes the internal representation not only of parental mores but, in a more generalized sense, of societal rules and cultural restrictions on the expression of instinctual drives. The development of the superego approaches its completion at the beginning of puberty, which means that self-control begins to replace the control through reward and punishment by parents, and anxiety and guilt become the self-administered punishment of the superego. The superego has two components. The *conscience*, which reacts when we transgress moral values and makes us feel guilty, and the *ego-ideal*, which makes us feel proud when we behave according to our ideals. At this point of development, when the tentative balance between id, ego, and superego is just beginning to emerge, the newly awakening sexual tensions of puberty demand id gratification and thus produce serious conflicts in the personality structure.

The superego serves three functions:

1. To inhibit, especially the aggressive and sexual impulses of the id that are not approved by society
2. To persuade the ego to substitute moralistic goals for realistic goals
3. To strive for perfection (Hall, 1954: 47)

Considering the relationship between the topographical model of the conscious, preconscious, and unconscious to the structural model of the mind as id, ego, and superego provides a more dynamic understanding of the mental apparatus as viewed by psychoanalysts. The id corresponds most closely to the unconscious in the topographical model. The ego is not sharply distinguished from the id, but its lower portions flow into the id and the unconscious. Repressed ideas merge into the id but are sharply segregated from the ego by the resistance of repression (S. Freud, 1923a/1961: 24). The ego cuts across all three layers of the typographical model; it is obviously present in the perceptual system of conscious. "It may be that much of the ego is itself unconscious, only part of it, probably is covered by the term preconscious" (S. Freud, 1896/1962: 18).

The superego is also located in all three layers of the topographical model, and while it is part of the ego, it also decides what part of the id may be allowed into the region of the ego.

It must be emphasized that the model set forth in Figure 3 is obviously only a human construct, developed to explain the inner workings of the mind. It is not material or physiological, and the dividing lines are not as neat and clear-cut as the illustration suggests. What are depicted are functions of awareness, not locations in the brain.

FREUD'S STAGES OF PSYCHOSEXUAL DEVELOPMENT

Psychosexual development, according to Freud, begins in early infancy and passes through a series of predetermined, highly differentiated stages, named according to the body zones or erogenous zones that provide libido satisfaction during a particular developmental period. Freud assumed that these stages are universal, in that each individual, regardless of society and culture, must move through this invariable sequence of psychosexual experiences to reach maturity, almost as if it was part of human nature. Development progresses because the child obtains pleasure from different parts of the body at different times, and therefore, each developmental stage is identified by the psycho-

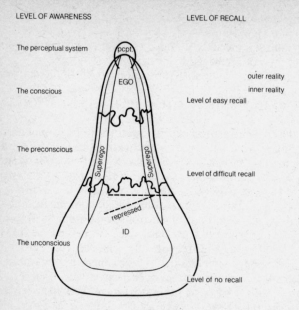

LEVEL OF AWARENESS   LEVEL OF RECALL

The perceptual system — pcpt

EGO   outer reality

The conscious   inner reality

Level of easy recall

The preconscious — Superego / Superego

Level of difficult recall

repressed

ID

The unconscious

Level of no recall

FIGURE 3.   A schematic presentation of Freud's theory of the mind in which the structural model and the topographical model are combined.

Adapted from S. Freud (1933) and Kaplan and Baron (1952).

sexual mode or the body area that dominates in its urge toward pleasure and satisfaction: oral, anal, phallic, and genital; during the latency period the libidinal drive is repressed. An adult personality structure can be classified into the oral, anal, phallic, or genital type.

This sequential order of normal development can be disrupted by *fixation* or *regression*. Fixation can occur at any point in development, with the individual remaining at least partially at an immature level of libido gratification and not moving on to more mature levels. Illustrations of oral fixation are alcoholism, excessive smoking, or compulsive eating. Regression takes place when the individual encounters serious frustration in psychosexual development and therefore returns to less mature and safer stages in order to attain libido satisfaction. The typical example is the child's return to thumb-sucking when a younger sibling is born.

The sexually rejected adolescent may regress to masturbation; the girl unsuccessful in dating may regress to playing with dolls. Fixation and regression occur when progress toward more mature levels of sexual development encounters serious frustration from the environment.

Fixation can also result from overgratification at a particular stage; thus, spoiling the child may impede progress toward heterosexual maturity.

THE ORAL STAGE

During the first year of life the oral region is the primary source of pleasure. The child gets pleasurable autoerotic stimulation not only from sucking, drinking, and eating but also through oral activity not motivated by hunger, such as thumb-sucking and sucking a pacifier or various other objects placed in the mouth. At this stage the mouth is the dominant erogenous zone. Displeasure is expressed by spitting out. Libidinal energies are directed toward an oral object choice. The love object at this early stage of development is the self. Self-love often precedes object love, since the young infant has no perception of objects in the outside world as separate from the self. Self-love is narcissistic, a concept Freud adopted from Greek mythology. During this stage the ego remains undeveloped, and the energies of the id seek satisfaction with little concern for reality or awareness of possible dangers.

Abraham (1921/1948) subdivided this stage further into the passive-dependent phase, when the infant expects to be fed and taken care of, and the oral-sadistic phase, when the infant exhibits oral-aggressive tendencies while teething. Oral characteristics manifest themselves later in life through overeating or by finding primary satisfaction through drinking, smoking, kissing, or talking. Even the aggressive component of this stage can express itself in making "biting" remarks or in oral sarcasm.

THE ANAL STAGE

During the second year of life, partly as a result of the social demand for toilet training, the primary erogenous zone shifts from the oral to the anal region of the body; libido is now invested in an anal object choice. During this stage the infant must learn to regulate natural impulses and to postpone immediate gratification to meet the demands of the external reality; hence, the ego develops. From anal activity the infant may derive not only pleasure but also a feeling of power over the mother from both "holding back" (prolonging evacuation in order to obtain stronger sensations) and "letting go" (experiencing relief and pleasure from evacuation). The oral and the anal stages are basically autoerotic phases of development.

Depending on how toilet training is administered, anal attributes may shape the development of personality characteristics. Fixation at the anal stage or regression to this stage may produce anal-erotic conflicts, which manifest themselves in one of the two modalities of the anal stage: retention or expulsion. The retentive component is most obvious in the stingy person who holds on to all kinds of things, especially money. This person is most likely stubborn, overcontrolled, fussy, and excessively concerned with neatness, cleanliness, and orderliness. The expulsive type, in contrast, lets go, both emotionally and physically (emotional outbursts, temper tantrums, and rage). This person cannot save, is a spendthrift, is rebellious, unclean, messy, sloppy, and disorderly.

Factor analytic studies have demonstrated that clusters of traits corresponding to the basic qualities of the oral or anal personality, such as parsimony, neatness, and obstinacy, do occur together in children and adults as would be predicted on the basis of Freud's theory (Fisher and Greenberg, 1977: 393, 397). There is a paucity of data, rather than negative evidence, to clearly show that the oral and anal personality traits originate in these crucial early developmental stages. Scattered bits of evidence suggest that such a relationship between early childhood experiences and adult personality patterns does indeeed occur, quite consistent with Freud's theory.

THE PHALLIC STAGE

Although the oral and the anal stages were basically pregenital stages, children in the phallic stage, from about age three to six, become interested in their own sex organs and feelings; fantasies and preoccupations with sexuality begin to predominate. Touching and manipulating one's sex organs is experienced as pleasurable, and masturbation can be expected at this stage, even though it does not necessarily lead to orgasm. The oral, anal, and phallic stages are narcissistic stages, since all libido satisfaction is derived from stimulation of one's own erogenous zones. However, during the phallic stage the object of the libido begins to change. The self as the love object is replaced by a parent object choice, and the parent object is the opposite-sex parent, leading to the *oedipal situation*. In Greek mythology Oedipus kills his father and marries his mother. Since the reproductive organs of the sexes are different and since the roles each parent plays in the life of the child are different, the events that occur during the phallic stage are also different for the two sexes. However, Freud is much more explicit in explaining the events in the boy, and his account of the male's oedipal situation receives stronger support from empirical investigations than the female's.

During the phallic stage the male child begins to take pride in his penis; he values and idealizes it. With increased sexual desire, his love for his mother becomes erotic, and he begins to view his father as a rival. Wanting exclusive possession of his mother leads to the oedipal conflict. His feelings toward his father are ambivalent. On the one hand he identifies with his father and loves him; on the other hand he sees his father as an obstacle to his incestuous wishes and has aggressive feelings toward him. Since he knows his father is more powerful than he is, he fears that the father may cut off the offending sex organ, something that apparently must have happened to girls, who lack the protruding penis. This insight leads to a fear that Freud identified as *castration anxiety.*

As an outgrowth of castration anxiety the incestuous wishes for the mother are repressed. Three additional factors contribute to the resolution of the Oedipus complex: (1) the realization that social taboos forbid him to possess the mother sexually, (2) disappointment from the mother, and (3) maturation. The child resolves the conflict by identifying with his father, hoping to become like his father, so that he too can eventually possess a wife. Through the resolution of the Oedipus complex the child begins to incorporate parental and later social moral values into his personality structure, thus contributing to the development of the superego during the latency period, which follows.

Fisher and Greenberg report, based on their extensive review of the research literature concerned with the oedipal concept, that there exists fairly convincing evidence "that men do have differential attitudes about their parents that mirror a history of sexually tinged rivalry with father for mother as a love object. The male does, as Freud proposed, experience castration anxiety, and this anxiety is intensified by exposure to erotic stimuli" (1977: 400).

The oedipal processes in the female are reversed, less complicated, less dramatic, begin later, and last longer than in the boy; and Freud is less specific in identifying the underlying dynamics. He has also received less empirical support for these conceptualizations. The girl, like the pre-oedipal boy, loves her mother. With the increasing awareness of her sex organs she discovers that she lacks something the boy has, feels castrated, and blames her mother for her missing organ. As her relationship with her mother weakens, she turns her love to her father and develops an attitude of both jealousy and sexual attraction, referred to as *penis envy.* Again, confrontation with the impossibility of attaining the desired penis, aided by maturational processes, leads the girl to the resolution of the Electra complex; however, the resolution of the Electra complex proceeds more slowly and continues throughout the latency period into adolescence. Empirical evidence suggests that the female is more likely to resolve her oedipal conflict out of fear of loss of love than the male and is less motivated by castration anxiety. In general, fewer empirical investigations have tested the oedipal theory as it applies to females; some of Freud's assumptions have been challenged, and others remain unsupported.

THE PHALLIC STAGE AS "LITTLE PUBERTY"

The phallic stage is sometimes referred to as "little puberty." Apparently, Freud felt at one point that in terms of evolutionary theory the human race had evolved from a species that reached its reproductive maturity at the age of about five or six. Thus, the "little puberty" is a hypothesized remnant of sexual development in evolutionary terms. Even the body zone identified by the names given to these two stages—"phallic" for "little puberty" and "genital" for "actual puberty"—refer basically to the same body zone. The masculine term "phallic" in the earlier stage reflects the strong male orientation of much of Freud's theory. However, the implications of this evolutionary aspect of Freud's theory allows for interesting comparison. "The phallic stage is then the vestige of the prehuman adolescence. The period between these two adolescences has some stability, while the period before and after latency are full of rapid change, conflict, and psychological problems stemming from urgent libidinal demands" (Baldwin, 1967: 368).

SEXUAL LATENCY

With the successful resolution of the Oedipus complex, the child enters the relatively calm period of sexual latency; the libido drive is less urgent, and more importantly, no new object choice emerges. It is during latency, as a by-product of the resolution of the Oedipus complex, that the identification with the parents becomes strong, and hence the superego develops. The period itself covers approximately the elementary school years, although there are wide individual variations. During this period the aggressive impulses, the sexual instincts, and the libidinal forces go under cover. The traumatic experience of having been deprived of fulfilling the sexual desires during the oedipal situation restrains the child for several years from seeking an overt affectionate relationship.

Several writers disagree with Freud's assumption of a period of sexual inactivity and sexual latency during this stage of development. For example, White states:

> His assumption about the quiescence of sexual energies seems to be simply wrong. Anthropological evidence and better observation in our society have combined to cast grave doubt on the hypothesis of a biologically determined sexual latency. For once we can almost say that Freud underestimated the importance of sex [1960: 127].

The latency period, during which the child identifies with parents, is viewed by psychoanalysts as a period when important social, cultural, and moral values are acquired. Schooling greatly facilitates the learning of general social values and the acquiring of fundamental social skills. New roles are tried in games and in play, and the development of motor ability is encouraged. Psychoanalysts are quick to point out that this is the period in the human life cycle when all known societies provide some formal training in essential skills for their young, even though not necessarily the academic schooling of most Western societies.

Toward the end of the latency period, orientation of interests, games, and play activities enter a homosexual phase in which friendship ties to one's own sex grow strong and often involve an exclusion of the opposite sex. During the transition from latency to puberty and with the increase in sexual tension, sexual awareness, and sexual interests, even these same-sex friendship patterns may become erotic in nature. Hence, homosexual activity in the form of genital exhibitionism, genital exploration, and masturbation are not uncommon during this prepubertal or early pubertal phase. Kinsey reports that 50 percent of all male teen-agers participated at one time or another in such forms of homosexual play. Other studies put this figure as high as 70 percent. Freud does see as one of the problems of this period "not missing the opposite sex" (S. Freud, 1925: 87), implying that friendship ties could become too strong, binding boys and girls to their own sex, with the possibility of an inversion of the sex object.

PUBERTY, OR THE GENITAL STAGE

Adolescence proper, brought about by the biological maturation of the reproductive system, is characterized by a rapid increase in sexual tensions demanding gratification. The sexual needs and fantasies become more explicitly concerned with tension release and later with the sexual union of male and female. However, these inclinations are restrained by the social demands for adaptation to the moral values of society and the norms of the community. The seriousness of this situation becomes obvious if one considers that pubescence requires—for the first time since birth—that a basic biological drive, which acquires full strength only as a result of the pubescent growth changes, must be integrated into the personality structure of the young, still developing adolescent. This fact is complicated further by the traditional social-moral-religious standards, which demand that the heterosexual gratification of this drive be postponed until marriage, often as long as ten to

A. Libidinal Localization (erotogenic zones)	B. Aim, or Mode of Pleasure-Finding	C. Libidinal Object-Finding		
INFANCY PERIOD				
Pregenital Period	*Infantile Sexuality*	Auto-eroticism	Narcissism	Allo-eroticism
1. Oral Stage				
a. early oral	Sucking, swallowing (incorporating)	at first objectless		Oral object-choice
b. late oral	Biting, devouring (destroying, annihilating)		Primary Narcissism	Oral-sadistic object-choice
2. Anal Stage				
a. early anal	Expelling (rejecting) (destroying) { looking exhibiting handling inflicting			Anal and anal-sadistic object-choice
b. late anal	Retaining (controlling) (possessing) { pain submitting to pain			
Early Genital Period (phallic stage)	Touching, rubbing, exhibiting and looking at genitalia, investigating, comparing, questioning, fantasizing (tender affection)			Parent object-choice Oedipus-phantasies
LATENCY PERIOD				
No new zone	Repression Reaction-formation Sublimation Affectional trends	Further decline of auto-eroticism	Diminished Narcissism	Development of social feelings
ADOLESCENT OR PUBERTAL PERIOD				
Late Genital Period Revival of zone sensitivity of infancy period	Reactivation of modes or aims of infancy period	Revival of auto-eroticism	Fresh wave of Narcissism	Revival of Oedipus object-choice
Later, functioning of vaginal zone	Emergence of adult mode of pleasure-finding			Homosexual object-choice
				Heterosexual object-choice

FIGURE 4. The theoretically normal development of children according to Freud's hypotheses of psychosexual development.

Reprinted from *The Structure and Meaning of Psychoanalysis*, by Healy, Bronner, and Bower, by permission of Alfred A. Knopf, Inc. © 1930 by Alfred A. Knopf, Inc.

fifteen years after the drive acquires its full biological strength. In terms of psychoanalytic conceptualizations, this means that the "id impulses" seek gratification with new urgency but clash with the recently developed and still formative "superego," producing guilt feelings because the superego finds the demands of the id unacceptable. The ego, unable to satisfy both, feels crushed between the two powerful contenders. Thus, the new balance between id, ego, and superego, recently established during the latency period, is suddenly thrown out of balance during puberty, producing conflict, turmoil, and a psychological disequilibrium. These conflicts can be internal, a psychological struggle between temptation and conscience, or they can be external, between parents and self. The ego attempts to cope with these conflicts, on the one hand, by denying the demands of the id through such mechanisms as repression or denial or, on the other hand, by quieting the superego through intellectualization, rationalization, asceticism, and regression.

Sexual attraction, once more as in the phallic stage, turns to the opposite-sex parent, and Freud does speak of a revival of the oedipal situation during puberty, accompanied by a reawakening of castration anxiety (Freud, 1925/1953). However, during latency the development of the superego has proceeded to the point at which an internalized "incest barrier" will no longer allow these taboo feelings into consciousness, and hence the ego uses defense mechanisms, especially displacement, to divert the incestuous demands of the libido toward somewhat more acceptable love objects. Freud (1925) commented that during early adolescence, a boy's first serious love object is most likely a mature woman—not unlike his mother—a very common theme in French literature and movies. In much the same way the pubescent girl often falls in love with older men (as seen in her crushes and infatuations for teachers, movie stars, and entertainment heroes) before she shows much interest in boys of her own age group. Thus, the first opposite-sex love object of the adolescent is often, symbolically speaking, a mother or father figure, allowing the oedipal wish an acceptable nonincestuous substitute. And even later in adolescence, when the sexual object choice begins to turn to an opposite-sex partner of the same age, the choice is often unconsciously motivated by patterns and traits prevalent in one's own parents. This phenomenon finds expression in the song that says "I want a girl just like the girl that married dear old dad." Thus, unconscious motives determine the adolescent's attraction to a particular individual when falling in love, allowing the fulfillment of the oedipal wish.

Related to this second oedipal situation is the adolescent task of freeing oneself from emotional dependency on one's parents. The boy's libidinal attachment to his mother must be released, and he must also free himself from the dominance of his father. This process of detachment from the incestuous love object brings the "problem of the generation" into the foreground and gives it its psychoanalytic explanation. This process of emotional detachment results, at least for a time, in rejection, resentment, and hostility toward parents and other authority figures. The conflict between the generations has been described frequently in the literature on adolescence and is a fairly common, everyday experience in many families. A fundamental task of the adolescent, as seen by psychoanalytic theory, is the "attainment of genital primacy and the definitive completion of the process of non-incestuous object finding" (Spiegel, 1951: 380). In other words, only through the emotional detachment from parents is the libidinal attachment to an opposite-sex partner possible.

According to psychoanalytic theory, the origin of a primary homosexual orientation is also related to an unresolved oedipal conflict rather than to the above-described homosexual interest of the late latency/preadolescent period, which may merely be an expression of the constitutional bisexuality of both male and female and generally is a normal developmental phase. However, a primarily homosexual orientation may be created if, during the height of the Oedipus complex, the male forms an intense "erotic attachment" to his mother and is received favorably by his mother, who responds with too much erotically tinted love while the father remains distant, cold, detached, and aloof. Such a family constellation of the seductive mother and the rejecting father enhances the castration anxiety to such an extent that the boy becomes concerned with the loss of his penis. Hence, he cannot tolerate the sight of female genitals because that is a dreadful reminder of what could happen to him. Any heterosexual contact would therefore re-create the guilt and anxieties related to the oedipal feelings toward his mother. In an extensive and comprehensive review of the empirical evidence pertaining to the family pattern of the homosexual, Fisher and Greenberg find partial support for Freud's proposition. "The father of a homosexual is likely to be an unfriendly, threatening person who would presumably be an unusually intense Oedipal competitor" (1977: 247). Similarly, Fisher and Greenberg report, "There is also moderate support for the view that the mother of the homosexual is particularly close, intimate, and restrictive in her relationship with her son. She fits well the stereotype of the seductive mother" (1977: 248). Finally, they also report that "the male homosexual has an elevated concern . . . about getting hurt" (1977: 248), which psychoanalysts would interpret as an indication of "castration anxiety."

MECHANISMS OF DEFENSE

One of Freud's major contributions to an understanding of the dynamics of the mind—widely recognized, even by people who tend to disagree with some of the general assumptions of psychoanalysis—is the identification and description of defense mechanisms. They help the ego cope with anxiety, frustration, and unacceptable impulses and help relieve tension and inner conflicts. Since anxiety is likely to increase during periods of rapid developmental changes and since adolescence is generally considered such a period—old ways of responding no longer seem to work and new patterns of adjusting have not yet been tried—the need for defense mechanisms is heightened during adolescence (Conger, 1977). Individuals develop such mechanisms of defense, especially if they cannot deal with anxiety in a rational fashion, to defend themselves against the demands of the id or against conflicts with reality. Some mechanisms of defense, such as denial, conversion, reaction formation, and projection, are considered more primitive since they reflect more of a loss of touch with reality; others, such as sublimation, undoing, rationalization, displacement, identification, and intellectualization, represent higher (closer to normal) levels of functioning. Everybody seems to utilize some defense mechanisms at one time or another to cope with conflictual situations and to protect the personality from the stresses, anxieties, and frustrations of everyday living. It is only when a particular defense is used exclusively to deal with the tension between inner psychological reality and the demands of the external world that use of defense mechanisms becomes symptomatic of neurotic tendencies, and even psychopathology.

> Of course, no individual makes use of all the possible mechanisms of defense; each person merely selects certain of them, but these become fixated in his ego, establishing themselves as regular modes of reaction for that particular character, which are repeated thoughout life whenever a situation occurs similar to that which originally evoked them [S. Freud, 1937/1953: 340].

The most common defense mechanism, widely used even by normal people, is *rationalization*, a process in which one advances more or less plausible reasons to justify an act or an opinion, concealing to others and even to one's self the true reason or motive. Sometimes this mechanism is referred to as the "sour-grapes reaction," based on the famous fable in which the fox who cannot reach the luscious grapes claims that he doesn't want them because they are sour.

The adolescent unable to attain a date with a highly desirable girl will tend to rationalize that he is better off without her because she talks too much or is too spoiled or is too popular or is likely to lose her pretty figure at an early age. The high school girl ignored by the student council president may rationalize that the latter does not recognize her because he wears glasses and is probably nearsighted, when the school leader actually does not even know she exists (Lambert, 1978).

Rationalization can help us to cope with disappointment in two ways: (1) it provides an acceptable justification for what we did, or what we believe, or what we really wanted but could not attain and (2) it helps soften the anxiety and the disappointment connected with unattainable goals. We often rationalize personal failure by blaming circumstances rather than ourselves; we thus avoid the feeling of anxiety and guilt that would result if we acknowledged our failures and inadequacies. Rationalization aids the ego by providing an excuse for something unattainable, unpleasant, or unacceptable. And we do use methods of rationalization, especially if criticized or called upon to explain unacceptable or undesirable behavior. Children use it *vis-a-vis* parents, and students *vis-a-vis* their teachers. However, frequent use of rationalization makes it impossible to learn from error and avoid mistakes, since such an approach prevents our recognizing the error or mistake or the personal shortcoming as such. By rationalizing, one is denying a personal responsibility for one's shortcomings. The student who fails the exam but blames the test or the teacher rather than himself frees himself from anxiety but also absolves himself from studying harder next time; the student believes that it was not his fault that he failed.

Repression to some extent is the purpose of all mechanisms of defense, and repressive components do accompany most of them. Repression deals with impulses from within, while denial relates to events that happen in the outside world. Repression should also be distinguished from suppression. Suppression is a conscious effort not to let ideas or impulses surface to awareness. Repression, in contrast, is an unconscious process of refusing to let into awareness the traumatic event, the stressful incident, or the unacceptable impulse. It was one of Freud's earliest constructs. Repression is less reality-oriented than rationalization since the impulse is cut off from awareness but remains dynamically operative in the unconscious. Most people are unaware of their earlier sexual feelings toward the opposite-sex parent. Socially taboo and highly traumatic early sexual experiences such as incest or rape may be repressed but dynamically operative in the adolescent's attitude toward sexuality. "Thus, for example, a girl who is sexually attracted to her father will simply remove this intolerable incestuous thought from her consciousness. It may come up again in her dreams, but upon awakening, these, too, will be repressed" (Calhoun, 1977:35). Repression is the metaphorical rug under which we sweep the garbage of our life to hide it, and although the garbage is no longer visible, it is still there.

Displacement is a very important psychoanalytic defense mechanism used to explain how the affect or libidinal energy toward one object is transferred to a substitute object, which, while logically inappropriate, is quite appropriate for unconscious thinking. The original emotions remain the same, but the object to which the emotions are directed changes. An adolescent girl who experiences an intense fear of snakes may be displacing her underlying fear of a male's sexual advances. Displacement seems to be common when the original impulse or object is accompanied by a high degree of guilt or anxiety or when libidinal energy is blocked. For example, the libidinal drive toward masturbation during adolescence may be transferred to a compulsive need to wash one's hands. The connection between the two behaviors appears inappropriate. However, the hand is the body part that executes the masturbatory behavior, and since masturbation is viewed as a "dirty habit," hand washing is an unconscious undoing of masturbation; it cleans what is dirty, it relieves anxiety, some of the libidinal energy seeking release in masturbation may actually find discharge in the substitute behavior, and even the motions of the hands around the soap may contain some similarity to masturbatory behavior. In a more general sense, the unavailable or unattainable gratification of sexual needs may find displaced expression in oral activities, such as smoking, kissing, applying lipstick, drinking, whistling, singing, talking, chewing gum, and spitting. The adolescent's first serious infatuation with a somewhat older, motherly teacher may be viewed as a displacement of the unacceptable love impulse toward his mother. However, since even the teacher is unavailable and socially unacceptable as a love object, a further displacement directs the love need to a more readily available girl of a similar age; however, she, too, may possess some characteristics of his mother. Thus, in the search for a mother substitute, one displacement may be put on top of an earlier displacement.

Identification is a process by which characteristics and qualities of an external object, frequently another person, are absorbed into one's own personality. Freud prefers the term "identification" over the term "imitation" since identification implies the involvement of deeper, more significant layers of the personality as well as a more permanent change. Imitation, which is part of identification, is superficial copying of behavior. The person with whom a child identifies changes as the child moves through the developmental stages. The successful resolution of the oedipal conflict requires an identification with the same-sex parent, a process that greatly enhances superego formation. However, with the beginning of adolescence, parental identifications dramatically decline and identification with movie heroes, entertainment personalities, and famous athletes as well as coaches and teachers is common, a process that aids in achieving independence and establishing a personal identity. A primitive form of identification finds expression in eating something in order to become more like the object eaten. Thus, the hunter may eat the lion's heart in an attempt to become as brave as the lion. In the Christian sacrament the body and blood of Christ is eaten in order to become more Christlike.

Conversion is one of the earliest defense mechanisms identified by Freud; however, conversion as a phenomenon has become less common in contemporary Western society. If a strong conflict exists between a sexual impulse and its opposing superego forces, the resulting psychological conflict may be transformed into a somatic illness, as happens in conversion hysteria. Thus, the manifest symptoms are paralysis, blindness, deafness, and loss of memory with no physiological cause. The symptom is indirectly connected to the unacceptable impulse. For example, paralysis of the arm could be a conversion of a strong but unacceptable impulse to touch girls' breasts.

In *isolation* or *intellectualization* the actual impulses reach the conscious, but they are isolated from the strong affect that usually accompanies such impulses. Feelings and intellect are separated so that a threatening situation loses its emotional impact. The feelings are repressed and the problem is viewed in abstract intellectual terms. The psychoanalyst refers to the process as decathexis, since the object has lost its cathexis. Cathexis is the concentration of mental energy on a specific idea or object. In other words, affect has become separated from content, as in a person who is insulted but does not feel anger. Isolation of affect means mental activities that usually occur together are separated, a phenomenon not at all uncommon in adolescent sexual development when, for example, sexual-sensual needs are gratified with one person (for example, a prostitute), while the erotic affectional feelings are reserved for the beloved sweetheart. In a religious, scientific sense, isolation would find expression in a dual incompatible belief system by the same person who, for example, as a religious person believes in the biblical story of creation and as a biological scientist believes in the Darwinian theory of evolution. Patients in therapy may develop an elaborate and abstract self-analysis of their problem but have no real feeling about it; instead, they try to convince the therapist of how much insight they already have.

Among the many defense mechanisms that the ego can use, Anna Freud (1948) considers two especially characteristic of the adolescent coping with the onslaught of sexual tensions: *intellectualization* and *asceticism*. Both may be used before pubescence, but they become especially important during this period of sexual disequilibrium. Asceticism is characterized by rigor, self-denial, and mortification of the flesh. It is typically seen as a phase in puberty, where it indicates a fear of sexuality and a simultaneous defense against sexuality. Asceticism in an adolescent results from a generalized mistrust of all instinctual wishes. This mistrust goes far beyond sexuality and includes eating, sleeping, and dressing habits. The increase in intellectual interest and the change from concrete to abstract interests (thinking) are accounted for in terms of these defense mechanisms against the anxiety produced by the libido.

Otto Rank (1945) contrasts promiscuity with asceticism as the two adolescent defense mechanisms that aid in maintaining independence. Having just freed themselves from the emotional dependence on parents, adolescents avoid any kind of strong emotional attachment, including an intimate personal love relationship, since it implies a new kind of mutual dependency. Being promiscuous satisfies sexual urges without the loss of the newly acquired independence, since such sexual gratification takes place without genuine love, personal commitment, and ego involvement. Separating the physical side of sexuality from its emotional component, as the idea of promiscuity implies, is of course a form of intellectualization as defined by Anna Freud. By being ascetic, adolescents retain their independence because they willfully reject any kind of involvement. Periods of asceticism may alternate with periods of instinctual gratification. In both instances the adolescent avoids the real love relationship in which self-restraint, self-subordination, and dependency are necessary to maintain permanent intimacy.

In *reaction formation*—also referred to as "reversal into the opposite"—the unacceptable impulse is repressed from consciousness but readmitted as its very opposite. Thus, the hostility an unmarried, teenage mother may feel toward her newborn baby is unacceptable and is replaced by kindness, resulting in overprotection. Over-compensation often accompanies reaction formation, so that, in this illustration, too much kindness is provided. The expression "killed with kindness" aptly illustrates the distinctive tendencies that underlie this kind of defensive kindness. The function of kindness is not really to help other people but to release the anxiety and guilt associated with the true feeling of hostility.

Similarly, hate may be transformed into love. The question arises, how can the new defensive emotion of kindness or love be distinguished from true kindness or love? Several characteristics suggest that an emotion may be the product of reaction formation: extreme forms of the defense emotion; some inconsistency, since the negative emotions may break through when one is off-guard; extravagant showiness; and compulsivity. The extreme and intolerant crusades against various vices are often a reaction formation against unconscious impulses toward that very same vice. The individual inclined toward criminal behavior may, through a reaction formation, become a highly effective police detective. Unacceptable homosexual tendencies may manifest themselves as extreme disgust and crusading against homosexuals. The puritanical censor of pornographic films and books may gain secret satisfaction from viewing the suspect material.

Introjection (internalization) has certain similarities to identification, such as the internalizing of outside events or characteristics of other people into the protagonist's personality structure for defensive purposes. However, introjection is more limited in scope. The whole personality is not restructured, only a specific part, as when an individual internalizes society's values as a guide to personal behavior. An extreme form of introjection is the "identification with the aggressor," seen even in German concentration camps among older, surviving inmates who assumed the behavior and the values of the hated Gestapo. Apparently, an attitude of "if you can't defeat your enemies, join them" prevailed.

Projection is the opposite of introjection, in that one attributes or projects to somebody else impulses unacceptable within oneself. In other words, we ascribe to others those feelings that we ourselves have but find unacceptable. Projection is, in certain respects, similar to rationalization. The adolescent boy, for example, claims that none of his peers like him, when actually he likes neither himself nor others. This mechanism of defense serves a dual purpose: (1) we free ourselves of the unacceptable and frustrating feeling (relieve anxiety) and (2) we get rid of some of our tension and frustration by complaining about the nastiness of the individual to whom we have assigned our own unacceptable impulse, and we can pretend that we are the innocent party. A highly irritated adolescent girl, for example, angrily accuses her parents of being inconsiderate and ill-tempered. If asked what the parents did, she might respond, "They irritate me." Or to take another example, if we dislike someone, projection allows us to interpret everything that individual does as an expression of personal dislike for us. Projection of sexuality apparently plays an important part in antiblack prejudice. The black man is accused of uninhibited sexuality and sexual prowess by the white man, who cannot accept, let alone express, his sexuality because of the more rigid social and moral restraints put on him since early childhood.

Although almost all mechanisms of defense distort reality in one way or another, *denial* is the most primitive defense because it not only distorts the cognition of reality but denies the existence of some emotionally significant part of reality. We refuse to acknowledge that the source of our distress actually exists. In contrast to repression, denial focuses on external reality; however, it does seem to serve a function quite similar to repression. This defense is not common in very young children, since they have not learned to distinguish between fantasy and reality. It begins to appear in the anal stage and is very common in neurotics and psychotics. In its extreme form, denial means that an existing sector of reality is blotted out. An example is the rejected bride in one of Dickens's novels who kept the wedding table set and her wedding gown on for years after the groom left her waiting at the altar. Another is the boy who plans and talks of graduate school and of becoming a lawyer even though he barely receives passing grades in his academic high school subjects. Still another is the girl who has no boyfriends but sits anxiously near the telephone every Friday evening in the hope that "someone may want to invite me out tonight."

Because the process of denial is unconscious, the person is not actually lying. The most common form of denial is blocking a past event out of memory; we say "I don't remember," and we actually do not, but everybody else remembers quite well. Less serious use of denial seems to occur when we attempt to avoid unpleasant events in our real environment; we look away from an unpleasant or disgusting sight. We postpone the unpleasant job, day after day, for a tomorrow that never comes.

There is some debate as to whether *sublimation* ought to be considered a defense mechanism, since it is basically a constructive and adjustive process. On the other hand, sublimation is really a specific kind of displacement. In sublimation the libidinal instincts, rather than being displaced in neurotic behavior, are rechanneled into constructive and socially acceptable behavior. According to Freud, the libidinal impulse, even though it is transformed, is actually discharged. In the sense that the unacceptable impulse is discharged, sublimation differs from all other defense mechanisms where the energy is repressed or distorted. The common illustration is the creative artist who sublimates his anal impulse to smear feces all over by painting a beautiful picture on canvas. More to the point, Freud maintained that the gorgeous male and female nudes created by Renaissance painters were really the result of sublimated erotic impulses. Lincoln chopped wood to sublimate his anger. For Freud, the development of civilization was the result of sublimation of instinctual energies. Sublimation takes place if a socially acceptable and closely associated substitute object can be found for the libido force, so that partial satisfaction can take place. This process of seeking and finding a substitute activity is still an unconscious one (except when the football coach demands sexual abstinence from his players two weeks before the big game). Psychoanalytic treatment is intended to direct the patient toward sublimation. The final goal of psychoanalytic treatment is to have the patient accept his desires and wishes, sublimate them in a socially acceptable way, and find a normal way for sexual satisfaction.

Undoing takes the form of atonement, penance, repentance, apology, restitution, and being punished or punishing oneself. When an unacceptable impulse has broken through and manifested itself in actual behavior, through the process of undoing we attempt to counteract the undesirable acts or desires or thoughts and to reduce our anxieties.

Children are taught at an early age that when they engage in socially disapproved behavior they are punished, or they have to make up for it, since it is only through punishment or atonement that the misdeed can be negated and the individual can start over with a clean slate. If this cleansing process does not take place, the anxiety, guilt, and self-debasement will threaten the ego. Hence, the individual, in combination with projection and introjection, tends to "undo" what has been done, just as one erases a misspelled word to start over.

Freud offered the following illustration of undoing. "His patient, while walking down a country road, kicks a stone onto the middle of the road. He then reflects that when his beloved's carriage comes down the road it will hit this stone, overturn, and kill her. To undo this potential murder, he now kicks the stone off the road. On reflecting further, he decides this is all very silly, and so he kicks the stone back to the center of the road. He repeats this sequence endlessly" (Corsini, 1977: 31).

The outcome of the use of defense mechanisms is a reduction in drive and anxiety. Defense mechanisms satisfy immediate needs and do reduce frustration, but often their benefit is short-lived. The damaging effects are evident in their long-range consequences and their negative impact on other people. Frequent use of defense mechanisms impedes learning, personal growth, and satisfactory interpersonal relationships in the individual using them, since most defense mechanisms tend to increase the social distance between the individual and others.

EDUCATIONAL IMPLICATIONS

Freud assumed that "frustration of normal sexual satisfaction may lead to the development of neurosis" (S. Freud, 1900/1953: 319). Even at the risk of overgeneralizing, the psychoanalytic argument may be stated as follows: therefore, if parents do not want their child to be neurotic, they must not discipline the child. This statement implies that educators should avoid frustrating adolescents unnecessarily and question the prudish Victorian attitude toward sexuality prevalent at Freud's time. But since "sexuality" for Freud is defined rather broadly—that is, to include everything that relates to and grows out of a person's love life—one might go one step further and assume that parents and educators should keep frustrations to a minimum, especially those frustrations that block the satisfaction of basic human needs. What is needed instead is an atmosphere of leniency, love, affection, approval, and attention in which the child can grow up feeling secure, wanted, and loved.

A similar idea was expressed in Rousseau's natural Romanticism and especially in his emphasis on "negative education." More recently psychoanalytic ideas have been influential in the creation of a variety of educational experiments, the best known of which is A. S. Neill's school, Summerhill, in Leiston, England. Summerhill attempts to remove all restrictions and frustrations from the educational process, including many of the common restrictions on children's sexual curiosity and exploratory sex behavior. The school is designed to fit the child rather than to make the child fit the school, and Neill hopes that the result is to make Summerhill the happiest school in the world.

But even for the regular classroom teacher in a more conventional setting some of Freud's ideas can be applied for the benefit of the pupil and the educational process. By applying psychoanalytic thought to classroom management, discipline becomes less authoritarian and therefore less frustrating. Even when the kind of freedom provided in Summerhill may be inappropriate, there can be a genuine concern with the underlying causes and dynamics of disturbing, disruptive, antisocial, acting-out behavior. Even for a teacher with only rudimentary understanding of psychoanalytic principles, misbehavior can no longer be viewed as arbitrary, as simple meanness or a personal affront, but rather it must be seen as a symptom of underlying conflicts and causes (Muuss, 1962). What an individual does or says is not meaningless but has a cause. Just as errors in conceptual development reflect lack of understanding, use of a false method, or incorrect reasoning, so errors in self-control or rudeness serve a psychological purpose. A basic assumption of psychoanalytic theory is that all behavior is meaningful. Dreams, neurotic behavior, even a slip of the tongue, and forgetting and losing things are motivated; if there is no conscious motive, there must be an unconscious one.

Education has been slow in providing a place for the "affective domain" in its structure and curriculum. However, much of the recent efforts to legitimize emotions in the educational process have their roots in the writings of Freud and are made explicit in the writings of some of his followers—Anna Freud (1948), Lawrence Kubie (1960), and Richard Jones (1960).

The child's fifth freedom is the right to know what he feels; but this does not carry with it any right to act out his feelings blindly. This will require a new mores for our schools, one which will enable young people from early years to understand and feel and put into words all the hidden things which go on inside of them . . . [Jones, 1960: vii–viii].

Psychoanalytic theory assumes that talking about and acting out dreams, fears, aggressive feelings, and feelings of hostility not only brings them out into the open but cleanses them and reduces their magnitude. In addition, openly sharing emotional problems in a classroom of peers leads to the realization that others have similar, if not the same, fears and feelings. "The freedom of one individual to express what another individual inhibits often results in freeing the latter" (Jones, 1960: 16). Adolescents in their concern about normality in regard to physical development, sexual needs, social sensitivities, and personal problems can benefit from the realization that their concern and most personal thoughts are not really too different from those of their peers.

The inhibition or frustration of sexual energies that most Western societies demand of their youths is the basis of Freud's concept of sublimation. Damming up libidinal energies "must swell the force of the perverse impulses, so that they become more powerful than they would have been had no hindrance to normal sexual satisfaction been present" (S. Freud, 1953: 319). It follows that early infantile sexual activities should not be repressed or pushed into the unconscious, unless normal sexual development be perverted. If libidinal energies are forced to regress to earlier stages of sexual development and denied any normal satisfaction, substitute satisfactions in the form of fetishism, homosexuality, sadism, masochism, narcissism, or other neurotic symptoms may manifest themselves. Yet psychoanalytic theory does not advocate uninhibited gratification of sexual impulses. Freud suggested redirecting sexual energy by means of sublimation. In Western culture most societies oppose unrestricted sexual gratification and assume that uninhibited sexuality would create new conflicts. Furthermore, since society's values are already represented in the adolescent's personality structure by means of the superego—which develops during the latency period—the sociosexual conflict is a psychological, internal one, a conflict of the conscience. Freud does not make a specific statement about adolescent sexual gratification. But since during this time the sexual drive and internal and external forces controlling the expression of sexuality are strong, sublimation can be a means of guiding these energies into productive educational activities, thus contributing constructively to the learning process.

In practicing sublimation an individual finds substitute forms of satisfaction and tension release for unsatisfied libidinal energies. It is assumed that nonsexual aims and socially useful activities absorb some of the sexual energy. Hence many educationally desirable activities may be stimulated by denying sexual gratification. For a long time football players and athletes have been advised prior to major sports events to abstain from sexual activity. Through sublimation "sources of sexuality are discharged and utilized in other spheres, so that a considerable increase of psychic capacity results" (S. Freud, 1925: 95). The connection between sexual energy and productivity in the fields that appeal more to emotion, such as music, art, poetry, and literature, is one of the assumptions of psychoanalytic theory. Freud himself went much further. He developed a theory of culture and civilization in which all human creations—from the learning of language to the composition of symphonies and scientific inventions—are due to sublimation. "Sexual impulses have contributed invaluably to the highest cultural, artistic, and social achievements of the human mind" (S. Freud, 1953: 27). Since sexual urges appear to be strongest in the late adolescent period—if Kinsey's "outlets" are taken as an indication of the strength of sexual drive—and since internal and external restrictions are also strongest during this period, at least for middle-class American youth, sublimation appears to be one important educational objective in this period. If society can use sublimation to provide a harmonious balance between realistic denial of gratification and fulfillment of basic needs without repression and utilization of sexual energies and thus avoid the two extremes of maladjustment—neurosis and delinquent behavior—the productivity and creativity of the individual could be vastly increased. Sublimation remains a theoretical model, and Freud stated quite frankly that very little is actually known about the physiological and neurological processes of sublimation.

Freud believed that applying psychoanalysis to education was most important. But he admitted quite openly that he had no "special understanding of it" (S. Freud, 1933/1964). He did credit his daughter, Anna, with making this aspect of psychoanalysis her life work and thus expanding his theories. Anna Freud's interest in child psychoanalysis and education is expressed in many of her publications, but it is especially clear in a lecture, "The Relation Between Psychoanalysis and Pedagogy" (A. Freud, 1931).

4: THE IMPLICATIONS OF ERIK ERIKSON'S THEORY OF IDENTITY DEVELOPMENT

ERIKSON'S EIGHT STAGES OF DEVELOPMENT

Erik H. Erikson's (1902–   ) theory reflects in part his psychoanalytic training, but it embraces social aspects of development to a much larger extent than Freud's original theory did. With little more than a German high school (Gymnasium) education, Erikson attended art schools and travelled in Italy, apparently in search of his own identity. (Erikson's later writings popularized the concept of "identity," a concept especially applicable to the period of adolescence.) As a young artist Erikson was offered a teaching position in a private school in Vienna that served the children of Sigmund and Anna Freud's patients. Peter Blos worked as a teacher in the same school, and the friendship of these two men stems from this time. During his tenure as a teacher Erik Erikson was invited to undergo psychoanalysis with Anna Freud, and in the process his interest changed from art and teaching to the theoretical study of psychoanalysis. He graduated from the Vienna Psychoanalytic Institute in 1933 as a lay analyst since he held no medical or academic degrees. Later that year he moved to the United States and became associated with the Harvard Psychological Clinic. He also held positions in several well known psychiatric institutions, including Yale, the University of California, Western Psychiatric Institute, and Austin Riggs Center. He returned to Harvard in 1960.

Erikson has published extensively, his best known and most widely read book being *Childhood and Society*, published in 1950 and revised in 1963. Of particular interest to our understanding of adolescence is his *Identity: Youth and Crisis* (1968). However, the idea of identity formation appears in other book titles, such as *Identity and the Life Cycle* (1959), and is the underlying theme of much of Erikson's writing. Even when he examines historical figures, as in *Young Man*

Luther (1958), *Gandhi's Truth* (1969), and more recently Thomas Jefferson, he is concerned with the identity crisis of each of these men as well as with the respective national identity crises at the time of their most notable contributions. Revealing his basic philosophy, he says one cannot separate "the identity crisis in individual life and contemporary crisis in historical development because the two help to define each other and are truly relative to each other" (Erikson, 1968: 23). Erikson has written about his own identity crisis as well as the philosophical and psychoanalytic foundation of the concept in "Autobiographic Notes on the Identity Crisis" (1970).

In his chapter "Eight Stages of Man" Erikson (1950) greatly modifies and expands the Freudian theory of psychosexual development. The modifications come from anthropological findings and a concern with social forces and thus shift from an emphasis on the sexual nature of development to a new theory of psychosocial development. The core concept in this theory is the acquisition of an ego-identity, and the identity crisis becomes the most outstanding characteristic of adolescence. Although the specific quality of a person's identity differs from culture to culture, the accomplishment of this developmental task has a common element in all cultures. In order to acquire a strong and healthy ego identity, the child must receive consistent and meaningful recognition of his achievements and accomplishments.

Human development proceeds according to the *epigenetic principle of development*, which is borrowed from embryology and states "that anything that grows has a ground plan, and that out of this ground plan the parts arise, each part having its time of special ascendancy, until all parts have arisen to form a functional whole" (Erikson, 1968: 92).

In the epigenetic model (see Figure 5) the basic ground plan of increasing psychosocial differentiation is depicted. The diagonal axis, beginning with "Trust vs. Mistrust," shows the developmental sequence of the well-known eight stages of man. Movement upward along the diagonal axis represents development and shows the successive differentiation of the originally undifferentiated structure, and thus represents increasingly more mature levels of functioning. This diagram demonstrates:

1. That each item of the vital personality is systematically related to all others, and that they all depend on the proper development in the proper sequence of each item; and
2. That each item exists in some form before "its" decisive and critical time normally arrives [Erikson, 1968: 93, 95].

	1	2	3	4	5	6	7	8
VIII								INTEGRITY vs. DESPAIR
VII							GENERATIVITY vs. STAGNATION	
VI						INTIMACY vs. ISOLATION		
V	Temporal Perspective vs. Time Confusion	Self-Certainty vs. Self-Consciousness	Role Experimentation vs. Role Fixation	Apprenticeship vs. Work Paralysis	IDENTITY vs. IDENTITY CONFUSION	Sexual Polarization vs. Bisexual Confusion	Leader- and Followership vs. Authority Confusion	Ideological Commitment vs. Confusion of Values
IV				INDUSTRY vs. INFERIORITY	Task Identification vs. Sense of Futility			
III			INITIATIVE vs. GUILT		Anticipation of Roles vs. Role Inhibition			
II		AUTONOMY vs. SHAME, DOUBT			Will to Be Oneself vs. Self-Doubt			
I	TRUST vs. MISTRUST				Mutual Recognition vs. Autistic Isolation			

FIGURE 5. Erikson's Epigenetic Diagram

From Identity: Youth and Crisis, by Erik Erikson, © 1968 by W. W. Norton, New York. Reproduced by permission.

Each of the eight developmental stages is characterized by a conflict that has two opposing possible outcomes. This dual aspect of the social crisis gives each stage it name, rather than the body zones that give pleasure as in the original Freudian theory. If the conflict is worked out in a constructive, satisfactory manner, the positive quality becomes part of the ego and further healthy development is enhanced. However, if the conflict persists or is resolved unsatisfactorily, the negative quality is incorporated into the personality structure. In that case the negative quality will interfere with further development and may manifest itself in psychopathology.

Each crisis or conflict is never completely solved but appears to be most pronounced at the age level at which it is placed. However, as in psychoanalytic theory, these stages occur in a sequential order. Ego "identity is never 'established' as an 'achievement,'" as something static or unchangeable, but is a "forever to-be-revised sense of reality of the Self within social reality" (Erikson, 1968: 24, 211). Although the identity crisis is most pronounced during adolescence, a redefinition of one's ego-identity is not at all uncommon when the college freshman leaves home and has to learn to fend for himself. Any time a major role change takes place, such as one's first job, marriage, parenthood, divorce, unemployment, serious illness, widowhood, or retirement, identity issues may reemerge. The ability to cope with identity issues that result from changes in one's role in life may well depend on the degree of success with which the adolescent identity crisis was mastered.

The vertical sequence in Figure 5, beginning with "Mutual Recognition vs. Autistic Isolation" and ascending until it coincides with "Identity vs. Identity Confusion" in the diagonal sequence, demonstrates how each of the four stages preceding adolescence contributes significantly to the development of an ego-identity or identity diffusion during adolescence. Thus "Mutual Recognition," "The Will to Be Oneself," "Anticipation of Roles," and "Task Identification" are secondary outcomes of the earlier stages in psychosocial development that are essential contributing factors to the achievement of a positive identity in adolescence. On the other hand, failure in the earlier stages resulting in "Autistic Isolation," "Self-Doubt," "Role Inhibition," and a "Sense of Futility" may contribute to a personal estrangement or identity confusion in adolescence.

The horizontal sequence in Figure 5 beginning with "Temporal Perspective vs. Time Confusion" depicts the derivatives of earlier relative achievements that now become part and parcel of the struggle for identity. "It is necessary to emphasize [that] the early relative achievements [diagonal] must be . . . renamed in terms of that later stage. Basic Trust, for example, is a good and a most fundamental thing to have, but its psychosocial quality becomes more differentiated as the ego comes into the possession of a more extensive apparatus, even as society challenges and guides such extension" (Erikson, 1959: 140–141).

The symptoms of confusion that make up the negative alternative on the horizontal sequence represent the earlier failures to progress normally and to resolve conflicts; they become therefore part of the identity confusion issue. The common experience of time confusion during adolescence, for example, arises out of the undifferentiated mistrust that may have occurred much earlier. Time confusion may develop into an attitude of not trusting time, of interpreting an unnecessary delay, lateness, or forgetfulness related to a meeting-time as deceit.

THE RELATIONSHIP OF ERIKSON'S "STAGES OF MAN" TO THE ADOLESCENT IDENTITY CRISIS

TRUST versus MISTRUST

During infancy—Erikson's first stage in the human life cycle—the major developmental crisis is between becoming a trusting or a mistrusting person. The development of trust includes becoming trustful of others and gaining a feeling of one's own trustworthiness. The necessary healthy experience for the development of trust is maternal love and care. Initially, the infant "lives through, and loves with, his mouth" (Erikson, 1968: 97). Being fed regularly does contribute to trust. However, the infant is receptive to maternal love in many ways besides orality. Children learn to trust because mother does come and take care of them regularly. They thus experience living in a predictable, secure world in which basic needs are being satisfied. Later, as motor skills develop and they are given freedom to explore their environment, they also learn to trust themselves and their own body, especially as they begin to control body movements such as grasping, holding, and reaching, and later crawling, standing, walking, and running.

The mistrust of time and the *time confusion* that Erikson sees as "more or less typical for all adolescents at one stage or another" (Erikson, 1968: 182) grow out of unhealthy experiences at this early stage and are related to the regularity of the cycle in which the infant's basic needs are satisfied. Repeated delay or irregularity in essential body satisfactions results in mistrust of time.

The conviction that emerges from this receptive state is "I am what I am given," and it is an incorporative stage. The healthy, positive outcome is the ability to trust others and to trust oneself. Later in the life cycle the capacity to experience faith is a result of the positive experiences at this early stage. The trusting infant has developed the first requisite for later developing confidence, optimism, and finally a feeling of security. The trusting infant recognizes people and smiles at them. *Mutual recognition* and mutual trustworthiness are the earliest and most undifferentiated experiences of what is later to become a sense of identity.

The negative outcome of this stage is mistrust of others and mistrust of oneself. Lack of trust in infancy may contribute to the identity confusion in adolescence. Absence of experiences leading to the development of trust in early childhood may impair the "capacity to feel identical" with others during adolescence (Erikson, 1968: 105). *Autistic isolation* in infancy is the earliest contribution to identity diffusion in adolescence.

AUTONOMY versus SHAME, DOUBT

The issue at the second stage of life is between becoming an *autonomous,* creative individual and a dependent, inhibited, and *shameful individual* filled with *self-doubt*. The stage falls approximately between the ages of eighteen months and three and one-half years. During this stage children—although still dependent on others in many ways—begin to experience the autonomy of free choice. They now develop the motor ability and the intellectual capacity to experience themselves as entities in their own right. They realize that they are different from father and mother. This newly gained sense of autonomy is often used in an exaggerated fashion, which leads to conflicts. The battle for autonomy may show in stubborn refusal, temper tantrums, and the "yes–no" syndrome. An important task is the beginning mastery of self-control; particularly important in this process is the control of body waste products. Toilet training means "holding on and letting go" when the child wishes, representing highly autonomous activities over which nobody has direct control. The child can—and at times does—retain body wastes even though his mother may want him to let go. On the other hand, he can release them even though his mother wishes him to hold back. However, with proper training the child can develop a feeling of mastery for a job well done and a sense of autonomy of choice in a general sense as well as in regard to toilet training.

The conviction that emerges during this stage is "I am what I will be," reflecting the child's new sense of autonomy. The positive attributes that can be gained during this stage are pride, control, self-assurance, autonomy, *self-certainty*, and the *will to be oneself*. The development of a rudimentary form of the *will to be oneself* during the autonomy stage is an essential prerequisite for the development of a mature ego-identity during adolescence. "There are clinical reasons to believe that the adolescent turning away from the whole childhood milieu in many ways repeats this first emancipation" (Erikson, 1968: 114). The autonomy attributes gained during this period contribute to the formation of an identity in adolescence, leading to the conviction: "I am an independent person who can choose freely and who can guide my own development and my own future."

The negative outcome is *shame, self-doubt,* dependency, *self-consciousness*, and meek compliance resulting from too many restrictions, unfair punishment, and the parents' inability to cope with the budding *autonomy* of their young child in a realistic fashion. The identity crisis of adolescence revives and grows out of an unresolved autonomy crisis. Since autonomy is one of the essential ingredients for the development of identity during adolescence, the battle for autonomy becomes once more an important issue in the adolescent's struggle for independence from the family and in early attempts at self-determination. This involves two problems. Adolescents may become so self-conscious and lacking in autonomy that they are afraid of being seen in an exposed and vulnerable situation. They may question their self-worth and the reliability of the whole experience of their childhood and therefore be unable to achieve an identity. On the other hand, entering adolescence with too much autonomy may contribute to brash and shameless defiance of parents, teachers, and other authorities.

INITIATIVE versus GUILT

The psychosocial conflict in the third stage of life is the development of a *sense of initiative versus a sense of guilt*. A conflict exists between an aggressive intrusion into the world by way of activity, curiosity, and exploration or an immobilization by fear and guilt. The child from about three and one-half to six years of age normally shows a great deal of exuberance, a feeling of power, curiosity, a high level of activity, and surplus energy. In play activities the child moves around much more freely and more aggressively and develops an increasingly larger radius of operations. This is also the stage when language develops rapidly. The child expresses his emerging intellectual initiative by endless questions. Beginning early in this stage he starts with an endless number of "what" questions that later lead to long sequences of "why" questions. These questions are basically learning tools, since new words, concepts, and ideas are acquired in this fashion. In addition, one can observe aggressive manipulation of toys. The child takes things apart to see what is inside, not because of destructive tendencies but out of curiosity. However, if this curiosity is interpreted as destructiveness, the child is made to feel guilty, and as a result initiative may wane. Children will also explore and manipulate their own bodies as well as those of friends, and this exploration does involve curiosity about the sex organs. Social criticism and punishment may foster the development of guilt feelings in regard to sex. The aggressive behavior, including exploration of the bodies of other people, is accompanied by a rudimentary form of cooperation with others in play activities.

The conviction that emerges from this intrusive mode is: "I am what I can imagine I will be." The intrusive mode is characterized by a variety of thoughts, wishes, fantasies, and behaviors: "(1) the intrusion into space by vigorous locomotion, (2) the intrusion into the unknown by consuming curiosity, (3) the intrusion into other people's ears and minds by the aggressive voice, (4) the intrusion upon or into other bodies by physical attacks, and (5) often most frighteningly, the thought of the phallus intruding the female body" (Erikson, 1968: 116).

If the crisis of this stage is mastered successfully, a sense of initiative emerges that will later in adolescence become the basis for curiosity, ambition, and *experimentation with different roles* just as the child's play activities often reflect an *anticipation of different roles*. The sexual self-image and the differentiation between masculine (making) and feminine (catching) initiative become important prerequisites for the sexual identity crisis during adolescence. The ability to take the initiative contributes to the development of an identity in adolescence since it fosters the anticipation of what one might become and of one's future role in life by "freeing the child's initiative and sense of purpose for adult tasks which promise a fulfillment of one's range of capacities" (Erikson, 1968: 122).

A negative outcome is likely if parents restrain, resist, and punish the newly developing initiative too much, for example, by making the child feel guilty for taking toys apart or exploring his own body. If the child's exploration and initiative encounters severe reprimand and punishment, the result may be a more permanent immobilization by guilt, inhibition by fear, *role inhibition, role fixation*, and too much dependence on adults. Since these attributes interfere with identity formation during adolescence, a negative outcome at this stage would contribute to the development of identity diffusion in adolescence.

INDUSTRY versus INFERIORITY

The task at the fourth stage is the development of a *sense of industry versus the emergence of feelings of inferiority*. Freud's idea of the Oedipus complex followed by a period of sexual latency is adopted by Erikson. Unable to marry his mother, the boy must learn to become a potential provider, so that he eventually will become a husband who has his own sexual partner. Therefore, this period between school entry and puberty becomes a period of learning and mastering the more basic skills needed in society. Children do acquire much fundamental knowledge during this period, and even more important, they learn to take pride in their work and acquire an attitude to do well in their work. This period is therefore described as *the apprenticeship* of life. In all known cultural groups children receive during this stage some kind of formal training, although not necessarily the kind of schooling provided in Western societies. The child must learn to win approval, recognition, and a feeling of success by producing things and doing his job well. An important aspect of industry is the "positive identification with those who know things and know how to do things" (Erikson, 1968: 125). The free play of the earlier period now becomes subordinated to rules and regulations and more structured activities. The child must learn to follow and respect rules and become committed to the ideas of cooperation in team effort and fair play. Through team activities, games, and cooperative play the child learns to anticipate the behavior, roles and feelings of others. This idea receives greater emphasis in the social cognition theory of Selman (see Chapter 12).

The conviction that emerges during this apprenticeship is: "I am what I will learn" or even more production oriented: "I am what I can learn to make work." If the *sense of industry* is established successfully, the child will need and want accomplishments and strive for completion of tasks and for recognition for work well done. He will develop a sense of duty, a feeling for workmanship and work participation, and an attitude of wanting to do well that is based on industriousness and a desire for success. The contribution that this stage makes to identity formation is "the capacity to *learn* how to be, with skill, what one is in the process of becoming" (Erikson, 1968: 180)—that is, an *identification of the task* ahead and a willingness to learn and master it.

If the child fails in the task to acquire a feeling of success and a desire for recognition for work well done, there will be a lack of industriousness and a feeling of uselessness. Such children may not develop the feeling of enjoyment and pride for good work. On the contrary, they may be plagued by feelings of inadequacy and inferiority and may become convinced that they will never amount to much. As a result there is *work paralysis* and a *sense of futility* that is most likely to contribute to ego diffusion in the next stage.

IDENTITY versus IDENTITY CONFUSION

Adolescence has been characterized by Erikson (1950) as the period in the human life cycle during which the individual must establish a *sense of personal identity* and avoid the dangers of *role diffusion* and *identity confusion*. Identity achievement implies that the individual assesses his strengths and weaknesses and determines how he wants to deal with them. He must answer for himself where he came from, who he is, and what he wants to become. Identity, or a sense of sameness and continuity, must be searched for. Identity is not readily given to the individual by society, nor does it appear as a maturational phenomenon when the time has come, as do the secondary sex characteristics. Identity must be acquired through sustained individual effort. Unwillingness to work actively on one's identity formation carries with it the danger of role diffusion, which may result in alienation and a lasting sense of isolation and confusion.

The search for an identity involves the establishment of a meaningful self-concept in which past, present, and future are brought together to form a unified whole. Consequently, the task is more difficult in a historical period in which the anchorage of family and community tradition has been lost. Hence, the present is characterized by social change, and the future has become much less predictable. In a period of rapid social change the older generation is no longer able to provide adequate role models for the younger generation. Keniston (1965) has even suggested that in a rapidly changing society the search for an identity is replacing the socialization process, since the latter implies that there actually exist stable, socially defined roles into which the adolescent can be guided.

Since the older generation no longer provides effective role models to the adolescent who is in the process of searching for a personal identity—or if they do provide them, the adolescent may reject them as personally inappropriate—the importance of the peer group in helping the individual answer the identity question "Who am I?" cannot be emphasized enough. The answer that will be found for this question depends on social feedback from others giving their perception and evaluation of the individual. Therefore, adolescents "are sometimes morbidly, often curiously, preoccupied with what they appear to be in the eyes of others as compared with what they feel they are and with the question of how to connect to earlier cultivated roles and skills with the ideal prototypes of the day" (Erikson, 1959: 89).

Since an identity can best be found in interaction with significant other people, the adolescent may go through a period of almost compulsive peer group involvement. Conforming to the expectations of peers helps adolescents find out how certain roles fit them. The peer group, the clique, and the gang, even the lover, aid the individual in the search for a personal identity, since they provide both a role model and quite specific social feedback. The bull session and the seemingly endless telephone conversations, for example, serve a genuine psychological purpose by providing this kind of feedback. As long as the adolescent depends on role models and feedback, the in-group feeling that the peer group provides will remain quite strong. The ensuing clannishness and intolerance of "differences"—including petty aspects of language, gesture, hair style, and dress—are explained by Erikson as the "necessary defenses" against the dangers of self-diffusion that remain prevalent as long as an identity has not yet been achieved. Particularly during the time when the body image changes so rapidly, when genital maturation stimulates sexual fantasies, and when intimacy with the opposite sex appears as a possibility with simultaneously positive and negative valences, the adolescent relies on peers for comfort and companionship and as a sounding board. Eventually adolescents must free themselves from this new dependency on peers—which has just replaced their dependency on parents—in order to become themselves—that is, to attain a mature identity. Such an identity, once it has been found, gives the young adult "a sense of 'knowing where one is going,' and an inner assuredness of anticipated recognition from those who count" (Erikson, 1959: 118).

Pubescence, according to Erikson, is characterized by the rapidity of body growth, genital maturity, and sexual awareness. Because these changes are qualitatively quite different from those experienced during childhood, an element of discontinuity from previous development may be experienced during early adolescence. Youth is not only confronted with an internal "physiological revolution" that interferes with the establishment of a reliable body image but also with a "psychological crisis" that revolves around the issue of identity formation. Erikson maintains that the study of identity has become more important than was the study of sexuality in Freud's time. Particularly for the adolescent, identity—the establishment and reestablishment of sameness with one's previous experiences and a conscious attempt to make the future a part of one's personal life plan—seems to become subordinated to sexuality. Adolescents must establish ego-identity and learn to accept physiological body changes and the new libidinal feelings as being part of themselves. The identity crisis depends at least in part on these psychophysiological factors. If ego identity is not satisfactorily established during adolescence, there is the danger that role diffusion will endanger further ego development. "Where this is based on a strong doubt as to one's sexual identity, delinquent and outright psychotic incidents are not uncommon" (Erikson, 1950: 228).

Falling in love, a common occurrence at this age, is seen by Erikson not so much as a means of satisfying sexual needs, as it will be at a later age, but as an attempt to project and test one's own diffused and still undifferentiated ego through the eyes of the beloved person. The various love affairs through which adolescents pass contribute to the development of an identity; the feedback received in the love relationship aids the individuals in defining and revising their own self-definition and encourages them to clarify and to reflect on their own self-concept and their own definition of their ego. Thus, the numerous crushes and infatuations, not at all uncommon at the high school and even the college level, serve a genuine developmental purpose. "This is why many a youth would rather converse and settle matters of mutual identification, than embrace" (Erikson, 1950: 228).

Of great concern for many adolescents is the issue of developing a vocational identity, and during the initial attempts some role diffusion is not uncommon. The problem—widely identified through empirical investigations—is that adolescents at this stage hold highly glamorized, idealized, and sometimes unrealistic conceptions of the vocational roles they dream about. Furthermore, goal aspirations are often much higher than the individual's perseverance and ability warrants. Frequently, the adolescent chooses vocational goals that are attainable by only a very few—models, actors, actresses, rock musicians, athletic champions, car racers, astronauts, and other glamorized "heroes." In the process the adolescents overidentify with and idolize their models and heroes to the extent that they yield their own identity and imitate the heroes. At this point youths rarely identify with their parents; on the contrary, they often rebel against parental dominance, value systems, and intrusions into their private life. This is a necessary part of growing up, since they must separate their own identity from that of the family and develop autonomy in order to attain maturity.

The adolescent's search for a personal identity also includes the formation of a personal ideology or a philosophy of life that will give the individual a frame of reference for evaluating events. Such a perspective aids in making choices and guides behavior, and in this sense a personal identity based on a philosophy of life may greatly influence the individual. In a society such as ours, where many different ideologies compete for followers and new ideologies emerge constantly, the formation of a personal ideology that has both consistency and conviction is made increasingly difficult. While it is easy to adopt a ready-made existing ideology, such a philosophy is often less flexible and less effective than a personally developed one. The adopted ideology rarely becomes truly integrated into the personality and can, therefore, lead to foreclosure in identity development.

A positive outcome of the identity crisis depends on the young person's willingness to accept his own past and establish continuity with previous experiences. To complete the search for an identity the adolescent must find an answer to the question "Who am I?" He must also establish some orientation toward the future and come to terms with the questions "Where am I going?" and "Who am I to become?" The adolescent must develop a commitment to a system of values—religious beliefs, vocational goals, a philosophy of life—and accept his sexuality. Only through the development of these aspects of ego-identity can intimacy of sexual and affectionate love, deep friendship, and personal self-abandon without fear of loss of ego-identity take place and thus make possible the developmental advance to the next stage in the human life cycle: *intimacy vs. isolation*. The intimacy stage has been investigated in greater detail by Orlofsky (1978) and Orlofsky, Marcia, and Lesser (1973).

The adolescent who fails the search for an identity will experience self-doubt, role diffusion, and role confusion; such an individual may indulge in self-destructive one-sided preoccupation or activity. He will continue to be morbidly preoccupied with the opinion of others or may turn to the other extreme of no longer caring what others think and withdraw or turn to drugs or alcohol in order to relieve the anxiety that role diffusion creates. Ego diffusion and personality confusion, when they become permanent, can be observed in the chronic delinquent and in psychotic personality disorganization. In its more severe form the clinical picture of identity diffusion may lead to suicide or suicide attempts. "Many a late adolescent, if faced with continuing diffusion, would rather be nobody or somebody bad, or indeed, dead . . . than be not-quite-somebody" (Erikson, 1959: 132). The increase of suicide attempts among adolescents in the last decade is well documented.

INTIMACY versus ISOLATION

Once a personal identity has been achieved, the need for personal intimacy moves into the foreground of the psychosocial development of the young adult. The conflict at the next higher level of development is between finding *intimacy or isolation* in interpersonal relationships. At this stage peer group conformity has lost much of its earlier importance. The peer group may aid in finding an identity and may even be helpful in making contacts with the opposite sex; however, it does not directly provide for intimacy. Intimacy involves establishing emotional closeness to other people as a basis for enduring relationships. Physical closeness and sexual and affectional intimacy are only part of the issue. A basic theoretical insight emerges from the sequential order of Erikson's stages: the prerequisite for genuine and lasting intimacy is the achievement of an ego-identity, since intimacy implies the fusion of the identities of two people. It follows that ego-identity must be established before the possibility of marriage can be realistically considered. One must first find an answer to the question "Who am I?" before one can find a partner to match to this "I." As long as the "I" remains undefined or is still forming, the selection of a partner appears futile. "The giving of oneself to another, which is the mark of true intimacy, cannot occur until one has a self to give" (Constantinople, 1969: 359). If marriage is begun before one or both partners have established an identity, the chances for a happy, lasting marriage are quite low. This may partly explain why the divorce rate of teen-age marriages is so very high and is much higher than for the population in general.

The conviction that emerges during the intimacy stage is: "We are what we love." The plural pronoun "we" rather than the singular "I" is a significant reflection of the mutuality and the intimacy of the relationship. The positive outcome of this stage in the human life cycle is intimacy, including sexual intimacy, genuine friendship, stable love, and lasting marriage. The negative outcome is isolation and loneliness, and if intimacy is not based on a permanent identity, divorce and separation may result. The young adult who still has basic uncertainties in his identity will shy away from interpersonal relationships or may seek promiscuity without intimacy, sex without love, or relationships without emotional stability. As a counterpoint to intimacy, detachment and distancing in interpersonal relationships may emerge—that is, "the readiness to repudiate, isolate, and, if necessary, destroy those forces and people whose essence seems dangerous to one's own" (Erikson, 1968: 136).

GENERATIVITY versus STAGNATION

The developmental issue of adulthood is the achievement of *generativity*; the negative possibility is *stagnation*. This stage encompasses the productive years of the human life cycle, and generativity is the driving force in human behavior. Erikson discusses in some detail why he prefers the term "generativity" to its more widely used synonyms "productivity" and "creativity." Generativity is a productive creativity in terms of vocational and professional contributions to society. Marriage, giving birth to children, and guiding the growth of children are creative, productive activities. The successful resolution of the conflict implies that the mature person wants to be useful and productive, wants to be needed. The conviction that emerges is "I am what I create," or "I am what I can produce." The giving of oneself to another person, an ideal, or to one's work leads to an expansion of ego interests. If failure should occur at this stage, there would be no further development, and stagnation would be the outcome. Stagnation implies a routine repetition in vocational activities and social stagnation. The individual becomes egotistical, self-absorbed, and self-indulgent and in turn expects to be indulged. Stagnation means that "individuals begin to indulge themselves as if they were their own one and only child" (Erikson, 1968: 138).

INTEGRITY versus DESPAIR

The last stage of the human life cycle encompasses old age and retirement from the productive years of life. The developmental task of this stage is between the achievement of *ego integrity versus disgust and despair*. The conflict here is between combining, integrating, and appreciating one's life experiences or becoming bitter, resentful, and negative. The successful resolution of the seven preceding stages culminates in *integrity*. The conviction that emerges is: "I am what survives of me." The positive outcome at this last stage in life is an acceptance of one's self and one's life without bitterness and regret and coming to terms with the approaching finality of life. Ideally, there is independence, autonomy, and maturity, rather than a regression to childlike dependency. Ego-integrity is based on self-discipline and the wisdom that can give old age its positive quality.

The negative outcome, on the other hand, is a feeling that one's life was wasted—a basic discontentment with one's life, one's self, and others. There is fear of death and a regression to childhood dependency that characterizes the disintegration of old age, resulting in disgust and despair.

JAMES MARCIA'S EXPANSION OF ERIKSON'S CONCEPT "IDENTITY VERSUS ROLE DIFFUSION"

James Marcia wrote his dissertation, "Determination and Construct Validity of Ego Identity Status," at Ohio State University in 1964. Subsequently, he has continued his research interest in Erikson's theoretical construct *Identity vs. Identity Confusion*.

What emerges from these research efforts (Marcia, 1966; 1967; 1968; 1976a; 1976b; 1980; Marcia and Friedman, 1970) constitutes an interesting expansion and elaboration of Erikson's theory. Marcia identifies various patterns and common issues operating in youths who are coping with the adolescent identity issues. In addition, Marcia's conceptualizations have stimulated others to pursue identity status research relying heavily on Marcia's interview assessment technique. Especially noteworthy in this respect is the work by Cross and Allen (1970; 1971), Donovan (1975), Orlofsky (1973; 1978), Schenkel (1975), Schenkel and Marcia (1972) and the studies from A. S. Waterman and Goldman (1976), A. S. Waterman and C. K. Waterman (1970; 1972;

1974), C. K. Waterman and Beubel (1970), and C. K. Waterman and Nevid (1977).

According to Marcia, the criteria for attainment of a mature identity are based on two essential variables that had already been identified by Erikson: crisis and commitment. "Crisis refers to times during adolescence when the individual seems to be actively involved in choosing among alternative occupations and beliefs. Commitment refers to the degree of personal investment the individual expresses in an occupation or belief" (Marcia, 1967: 119).

In applying Marcia's criteria of the absence or the presence of crisis and also commitment to Erikson's developmental stage *identity versus role diffusion*, four identity statuses emerge. They provide the conceptual structure for Marcia's taxonomy of adolescence.

1. The *identity-diffused* or *identity-confused subject* has not yet experienced an identity crisis nor made any commitment to a vocation or a set of beliefs.
2. The *foreclosure subject* has not yet experienced an identity crisis but has made commitments. However, these commitments are not the result of personal searching and exploring; rather, they are handed, ready-made, to the individual by others, frequently parents. These superimposed commitments are accepted without the individual's raising fundamental and personal questions about them.
3. The *moratorium subject* is in an acute state of crisis; he is exploring and actively searching for values to eventually call his own. In other words, this individual is actively struggling to find his identity but has not yet made a commitment or has only developed very temporary kinds of commitments.
4. The *identity-achieved subject* has experienced personal crises but has resolved them on his own terms. As a result of the resolution of these crises the individual has made a personal commitment to an occupation, a religious belief, a personal value system and has resolved his attitude toward sexuality.

These four identity statuses may be perceived as a developmental sequence, but no one is necessarily and inevitably the prerequisite for the others, as is the case in Erikson's "Eight Stages of Man." Only the moratorium appears to be an essential and inevitable prerequisite for the achievement of an identity, since a true identity cannot be achieved without the kind of searching and exploring that is the defining characteristic of the moratorium. Any one of these identity statuses could become terminal, but the foreclosure subject is of course in greater danger of this than the moratorium subject. If the identity-diffused status becomes terminal, the probability of psychopathology or delinquency is especially great.

An individual in the process of moving to a higher status may well exhibit some of the characteristics of two or even three statuses at the same time. For example, a young man may already have developed a clear commitment to a vocation based on personal choices while still actively searching for a personal value system and remaining committed to a puritanical attitude toward sex indoctrinated by his parents. Marcia found that as students moved through the four years of undergraduate college experiences, the proportion of identity-diffused subjects declined significantly while the proportion of identity-achieved subjects increased steadily. This movement toward more mature identity statuses was not a function of college selectivity but of increased psychosocial maturity. Constantinople reports a "consistent increase in successful resolution of identity, both from the freshman year to senior year across subjects and from one year to the next within subjects" (Constantinople, 1969: 367). In a more recent study, Meilman (1979) investigated the age changes in identity status and found, in accordance with Erikson's and Marcia's theoretical assumptions, that twelve-year-olds were identity-diffused (68 percent) or foreclosed (32 percent). Several studies have clearly demonstrated that with increasing age adolescents steadily but slowly shifted toward a more mature identity status. Marcia (1980) believes that late adolescence (eighteen to twenty-one years) is the crucial period for identity formation. According to Meilman, by the age of twenty-four the majority (56 percent) had achieved an identity, but the other statuses were still represented: moratorium, 12 percent; foreclosure, 8 percent; and identity-diffused, a surprisingly high 24 percent (Meilman, 1979).

In Marcia's research (1966; 1967; 1970; 1976a; 1976b) the individual's identity status is determined by means of an individual semi-structured interview designed to assess the subjects' commitment to a vocation, a personal value system, and religious beliefs, the extent to which the subjects actually experienced a personal crisis in regard to any of these, and their attitude toward sexuality.

The remainder of this chapter will examine more closely the four identity statuses and the research literature that has defined the psychosocial characteristics of each.

IDENTITY DIFFUSION

The identity-diffused individual has no apparent personal commitment to occupation, religion, or politics and has not yet developed a consistent set of personal standards for sexual behavior. He has not experienced an identity crisis in respect to these issues nor gone through an active struggle in terms of reevaluating, searching, and considering alternatives. Erikson (1968) maintains that identity diffusion is not a diagnosis of a psychological problem but a description of a normal developmental process—which, if it persists and only if it persists into late adolescence and adulthood, could become a diagnostic classification. Consequently, identity diffusion can encompass a variety of different behavior or personality patterns. This appears to be one reason why some of the research findings concerned with identity-diffused subjects are not always entirely consistent.

First, identity diffusion may exist due to a precrisis lack of commitment—not at all uncommon when entering early adolescence. Apparently, it is a kind of psychological chaos typically experienced by early adolescents, as the data by Meilman (1979), cited above, clearly demonstrate. Thus, some degree of identity diffusion should be considered a normal characteristic of early adolescent development. Second, there is also the narcissistic type of identity diffusion. These youths live and let live and in their selfish approach "use" others for their own pleasure and try to get for themselves whatever they can get away with. Apparently suffering from an unresolved ego crisis of Erikson's first stage, *trust versus mistrust*, and not being able to trust people, they use them. Third, identity-diffused subjects avoid anxiety, crisis, and confrontation by means of drugs or alcohol or by otherwise denying that crises exist. Finally, as mentioned before, prolonged stagnation in the identity diffusion stage without further development may lead to personality disintegration, thus becoming a diagnosis of psychopathology that may lead to schizophrenia or suicide.

Identity-diffused subjects are in a state of psychological fluidity, still uncommitted to a personal value structure; consequently, they are open to all kinds of influences, and when opportunities arise they may take advantage of them, often without design or purpose. Such individuals may take a smorgasbord approach to ideological systems and be most influenced by and overly receptive toward whatever politician or minister was last heard. The diffused college student can become quite vehement in his demands on the college professor to tell him which of the various theories is best, which is right, or which one he is to believe in. Erikson (1965) maintains in *The Challenge of Youth* that the high rate of recidivism among young offenders can be explained by the fact that during the years of identity formation, especially identity diffusion, these youth were forced by society into intimate contact with other criminals.

On Kuhn's (1954) Twenty Statement Test (TST) the identity-diffused subject may reveal confusion in answers to the question, "Who am I?" Some such answers might be "I am a nobody," "I don't know who I am," "I wish I weren't me," "I wish I knew who I am,"

"I am confused," "I am mixed up," "I am not me," "I am unsure of what I am," "I am dead," "I wish I were dead," "I am intelligent"/ "I am stupid," "I am a child of God"/"I am a child of the devil." Identity in these responses is defined negatively by the lack of something, the reversal of an identity, the denial of an identity, death, and contradictory statements revealing confusion.

The classical example of identity diffusion in literature is Shakespeare's Hamlet. He is confused about his sex role: "Man delights me not, no, nor woman either." He is also estranged from love and procreation, as when he says: "I say we will have no more marriage." And finally he appears alienated from the ways of his country ". . . though I am native here, and to the manner born . . ." (Erikson, 1965: 6). In Arthur Miller's *Death of a Salesman*, Biff admits his identity diffusion quite succinctly: "I just can't take hold, Mom, I can't take hold of some kind of life."

In Marcia's studies (1966; 1967; 1968; 1976a; 1976b) subjects were independently classified as to their identity status. In addition, personality tests were administered to all subjects. Identity-diffused male subjects showed little resistance to self-esteem manipulation—that is, they quite readily changed their own opinions about themselves. They were vulnerable to evaluative feedback about themselves, since they did not have a firmly established identity. Gruen (1960), too, found that ego-diffused subjects were more willing to accept incorrect personality sketches about themselves than subjects who had achieved an identity. Marcia's subjects scored low on a stressful concept attainment task. They had lower self-esteem and experienced more difficulty than the other identity statuses in interpersonal relationships. Marcia and Friedman's (1970) identity-diffused female subjects were enrolled in the easiest college majors as compared to the other three identity statuses, even though they were no less intelligent. Females, too, obtained low self-esteem scores but high anxiety and authoritarianism scores. Block (1961) found a direct relationship between role variability and the individual's identity status. That is, subjects lacking a clear personal identity behaved quite differently in interaction with people having different roles, such as parent, lover, friend, coworker, boss, or acquaintance. Identity-achieved subjects, in contrast, revealed more internal consistency in their interpersonal behavior. Bronson (1959), contrasting those who have achieved an identity with those who have not, characterized identity-diffused subjects as:

1. Less certain about the relationship between the past and the present as it pertains to themselves and their self-concept. Their self-concept is not yet firmly rooted in earlier identifications.
2. Showing a high degree of internal tensions and anxieties.

3. Less certain about their own personality traits, and they experienced considerable variability over a short period of time as to their own feelings about themselves. They have no clear definition of who they are and cannot estimate their own personality traits effectively.

FORECLOSURE

Foreclosure subjects are committed to goals and values, an occupation, and a personal ideology. Consequently, in everyday life they superficially may appear very much like identity-achieved subjects, with whom they actually have some characteristics in common. However, foreclosure subjects differ from identity-achieved subjects in that they have not experienced a psychological crisis or seriously considered other goals, other values, and other alternatives as being applicable to themselves. The goals they aim for and the values they hold were determined by others—parents, religion, or peers. The foreclosure subjects frequently tend to become their parents' alter egos. When a young man is asked what he wants to become, he may answer, "I want to be a dentist," and when asked why he may respond, "Because my father is a dentist." And even further probing would not change the essence of the first response. No personal reason is given; no personal searching seems to have taken place. When talking to foreclosure subjects, it becomes difficult to distinguish between their own goals and those that parents have planned and emphasized for them. Foreclosure subjects were "socialized" by their parents in the sense that parents determined what they were to become. College serves mainly to reconfirm the childhood value system and provide an opportunity to attain the parent's goals rather than as a process by which to explore vocational options. The danger is that foreclosed subjects may become so solidified in their position and so authoritarian in their attitudes that the foreclosure status becomes terminal, and the subjects do not reach the status of identity achievement. There appears to be a certain rigidity in personality structure. If these subjects are not sufficiently challenged or guided to question their preprogrammed assumptions and values, foreclosure may become a permanent part of their personality structure and they may remain dependent on others, even later in life.

On Kuhn's Twenty Statement Test (TST) foreclosure subjects seem to define their own identity in terms of relationships to other people or to see themselves as extensions of other people. The following responses of three college students from the author's files suggest foreclosure: "I am a daughter, a sister, an aunt, a sister-in-law, a niece"; "I am a girl, a daughter, my father's little girl"; "I am my mother's daughter, my father's daughter, my sister's sister, my brother's sister, my boyfriend's girl friend, my girl friend's friend, my next door neighbor's neighbor, my aunt's niece, my cousin's cousin."

Responses from Marcia's (1968) interview protocol may serve to illustrate the commitment of foreclosure subjects to parental values. One adolescent comments on his political affiliation with a Republican ideology quite similar to that of his parents: "You still pull that way, Republican, if your parents are that way. You feel like it is where you should be." Another foreclosed subject who holds the same religious beliefs as his parents states: "Maybe it's just a habit with me, I don't know. I have thought a lot and you meet all kinds of people here, but I really haven't changed any of my beliefs. . . . I plan to bring up my children in the church, just the way dad did with me" (Marcia, 1968: 329). Keniston seems to be referring to the foreclosure phenomenon when he writes that "total lack of conflict during adolescence is an ominous sign that the individual's psychological maturity may not be progressing" (Keniston, 1971: 364). Kubie and other psychiatrists have observed that an unusually smooth and conflict-free adolescence is often followed by mental breakdown or serious emotional problems in middle adulthood.

The foreclosure status is most frequently viewed as being shaped through the dominant influence of the subjects' parents. However, the dynamics do not necessarily involve the parents; they could be applied to other influential forces—such as the individual's peer group. For a certain developmental period young adolescents may lose themselves and may lose their budding identity to the peer group. In this situation, foreclosure occurs because the individuals' identity submerges too readily into the role given to them by others. As a result they define themselves primarily by their group membership, and they act, dress, select food and entertainment, and use language and slang predominantly in the light of peer-group standards, expectations, and pressures. At the same time intolerance and even cruelty toward those who behave differently is not uncommon, especially in the junior high school years.

The youth group movement of totalitarian systems, such as the Hitler Youth in Nazi Germany, provides such group identity with uniforms, flags, rituals, beliefs, and even heroes as models. A similar vicarious identity is provided by belonging to a gang, a hippie subculture, and other less formal subcultural youth groups. Many junior high school students conform rather unquestioningly to the dress and behavior standards of their peer group in order to be accepted, to benefit from the feeling of group solidarity, and to boost their sense of identity through identification with the peer group. In the process, they often overidentify with the peer group, with its heroes and idols, to the extent that they may lose for some time their own personal value system and even the capacity to make independent decisions. According to Keniston, if the "conformity to peer group norms merely replaces conformity to parental norms . . . adolescent development is foreclosed before real self-regulation and independence are achieved" (Keniston, 1971: 377).

The youth group of the totalitarian system may serve as an illustration of political foreclosure, since the youth movement provides the adolescent with a ready-made system of beliefs and even a personal identity that the democratic society does not provide. The totalitarian system's appeal to many adolescents might be based on these considerations, since the totalitarian system supplies convincing and suitable identities—or symbols of identity—for this age group. Democratic identity has less extrinsic appeal and it is much harder to attain because it involves freedom of choice. Democratic values, rather than supplying a ready-made identity, insist on a self-made identity. Adolescent imagery, which frequently tends to classify into black and white, has an affinity to the totalitarian system, which supplies this kind of dichotomy. The democratic system, in contrast, allows for many different shades of ideological beliefs and therefore provides more ambiguity. It even is tolerant of totalitarian belief systems, such as the Moonies, which cater to the need of some adolescents for a ready-made totalitarian value structure. The democratic value structure requires that individuals develop their own ego-identity in order to withstand ambiguity and the persuasive arguments of totalitarian ideologies; the problem is that it provides little help to the individual in establishing an identity.

MORATORIUM

The word "moratorium," in a general sense, means a period of delay granted to somebody who is not yet ready to meet an obligation or make a commitment (Erikson, 1968: 157) The moratorium of the adolescent is defined as a developmental period during which commitments either have not yet been made or are rather exploratory and tentative. However, the concept implies that there are many crises and unresolved questions. The individual is in an active struggle to find an answer, explore, search, experiment, try out a different role, and play the field. It is in this sense that the moratorium is considered the adolescent issue *par excellence.* According to Marcia, about 30 percent of today's college students are in the moratorium stage.

Erikson and Margaret Mead (1961) both postulated that the adolescent period is a psychological moratorium, or an "as-if period" when individuals can experiment with different roles "as-if" they were committed to these roles. However, since it is only an "as-if period," they are not really committed and not held fully accountable for errors that might be made in trying out new roles. They can still change their values and commitments, and they frequently do so in the process of gaining experience and becoming more mature. Therefore, the as-if period is the delay society grants to its youth to try on different roles—like trying on clothes—to see which fits best. It is in this sense that the moratorium adolescent may try out radical political philosophies, try out new religious belief systems such as Oriental mysticism, or even try different vocational activities such as social work or the Peace Corps. Finally, the moratorium adolescent may try new and different sexual relationships, such as coed apartment living, bisexuality, or homosexuality.

If adolescents, while experimenting with moratorium issues, have sufficient opportunity to search, experiment, play the field, and try on different roles, there is a very good chance that they will find themselves, develop an identity, and emerge with commitments to politics, religion, a vocational career orientation, and a more clearly defined sex role and sexual preference. These final commitments are frequently much less radical than some of the tentative and exploratory commitments during the moratorium. According to Marcia, moratorium is truly an essential and necessary prerequisite for identity achievement. However, while the adolescent is in the process of searching and exploring, the world does not look very stable or predictable and does not appear to be a very desirable place; rather, the youth views the world, society, and social institutions as badly in need of improvement. Moratorium subjects are inclined to express their disenchantment by challenging what they see. Their desire is to change government, politics, education—in short, "the system." While frequently very good diagnosticians and effective critics in pointing to the limitations, problems, and imperfections of the "system," they are not equally effective in producing viable, realistic alternatives because to do so requires identity, willingness to compromise, and a more permanent commitment.

In responding to Kuhn's (1954) test question "Who am I?" moratorium subjects typically reveal their lack of commitment, their uncertainty, and their search for an identity with such responses as: "I am searching, I am confused, I am thinking, I am wondering, I am calculating"; "I am a curious person, I am unsure of what I am, I am many people at different times, I seek new experiences to find out what I really am, I am looking for something, I am looking for myself."

Mead and Friedenberg both have expressed concern that in society's emphasis on success, progress, and production as symbolized by scout badges, good grades, promotion, honors, recognition, awards, and diplomas, we exert too much pressure on our youth and in the process deprive them of the opportunity to experience a moratorium, an "as-if period," without the pressure for accountability. It has been found that the need for a moratorium is reflected in the motives for volunteering in the Peace Corps, and it seems to have been one of the reasons for the existence and the popularity of the hippie counterculture.

IDENTITY ACHIEVEMENT

After an individual has experienced a psychological moratorium and has resolved the adolescent identity crisis and as a result has begun to develop lasting personal commitments, an identity has been achieved. Identity achievement contributes to an increment in ego strength. It means that adolescent development has been successfully completed and maturity has been attained. Successful adolescent development has been defined by Keniston (1971: 363) as ". . . integration of impulses into life . . . the humanization of conscience . . . the stability of a sense of self. . . ."

An identity has been achieved after the individual has seriously and carefully evaluated various alternatives and has considered different choices, and has come to conclusions and decisions on his own terms. Actually, it is not at all uncommon for such individuals to take a position that is fairly close to their parents' values; however, unlike the moratorium subjects, they have considered various other options, tried more liberal or even more radical approaches, and finally accepted or rejected them on their own terms. This process contrasts with that of the foreclosure subject, who remains very close to parental values and expectations, without ever making a genuine personal choice in the matter and without having seriously questioned parental values. The achievement of an identity gives the individual an awareness of and an acceptance of personal continuity with the past and a more stable orientation toward the future. Identity means that a new synthesis has been found which "will link the past, the present, and the future" (Keniston, 1965: 212). The function of this sense of identity is to create a new outlook toward the self which provides inner self-sameness and continuity and stabilizes values and purposes (Keniston, 1965). Once an identity has been achieved there is an increase in self-acceptance, a stable self-definition, a willingness to make commitments to a vocation, a religion, a political ideology and also to intimacy, engagement, and marriage. Orlofsky, Marcia, and Lesser (1973) were able to show that the identity-achieved subjects had by far the greatest capacity for engaging in interpersonal intimacy; lower levels of identity had a much greater probability of being stereotyped, pseudointimate, or even isolate in their interpersonal relationships. To achieve a mature ego-identity the individual must overcome "his irrational rebelliousness as well as his irrational urge to conform" (Keniston, 1971: 364).

Individuals who have attained an identity, according to Erikson (1968), feel in harmony with themselves, accept their capacities, limitations, and opportunities. Such an individual realizes "where he fits (or knowingly prefers not to fit)" into social situations in terms of his own personal development. Four college students' responses to the "Who am I?" test from the author's file may serve again to illustrate this sense of identity achievement: "the future Mrs. Jones, a future English teacher; a future resident of Colorado, a happy-go-lucky person"; "a woman, a potential wife, a potential mother, a student, a teacher"; "I am me, outgoing, well-liked, intelligent"; "A contained person, a free-willed individual, a leader, a self-sufficient young adult." These responses convey the feeling that adolescence has been or is about to be terminated. There is a sense of direction and a positive orientation toward the future, which is one of the characteristics of the identity-achieved individual.

RESEARCH FINDINGS ON IDENTITY STATUSES

A summary of the ego-psychoanalytically oriented identity research, based in part on review articles by Bourne (1978) and Marcia (1980), may show the extent to which Erikson's theory has stimulated contemporary research. Such a presentation may demonstrate the extent to which the concept of "identity statuses" has recently become a major research construct leading to the investigation of personality development in adolescents, including college students and young adults. Furthermore, this summary will demonstrate the broad range of issues and variables to which identity is related. Much of the identity research has been conducted with male subjects, hence the data presented are for males unless indicated otherwise. This section of the presentation will be organized by the major cognitive, educational, adjustment, and personality correlates of identity rather than by the identity statuses. Not all research specifically identifies Marcia's four identity statuses or uses Marcia's identity assessment technique; some studies contrast only the attributes of high and low identity subjects (LaVoie, 1976).

INTELLIGENCE

A frequently reported finding is that the four identity statuses are not systematically related to level of intellectual functioning or scholastic ability (Bob, 1968; Cross and Allen, 1970; Marcia, 1966; Marcia and Friedman, 1970; Schenkel, 1975). However, since many of these studies use college students as subjects, this finding may be influenced by the narrower range of mental ability characteristic of the college student population.

ACADEMIC VARIABLES

Grade Point Average. Cross and Allen (1970) found that identity achievers received higher grade point averages than the other three identity statuses, even if scholastic ability is controlled; Waterman and Waterman (1972) found that identity achievers have better study habits. Donovan (1971), in contrast, found that the foreclosures obtained the highest grades.

College Major. Among female college students, the achievers and the foreclosures tend to choose more difficult fields of study than the other two identity statuses (Marcia and Friedman, 1970).

Achievement Motivation. Among a combined group of men and women, identity achievers and moratorium subjects showed a higher level of achievement motivation than the remaining two statuses (Orlofsky, 1978).

Fear of Success. Findings on Horner's "Fear of Success Variable" revealed a surprising reversal in the performance of the sexes. Among college women, the identity-achieved subjects and the moratorium subjects admitted greater fear of success; among college men, the foreclosure and the identity-diffused subjects showed more fear of success than the remaining two statuses (Howard, 1975; Orlofsky, 1978).

PERFORMANCE ON COGNITIVE TESTS

Concept Attainment. Marcia (1966) found that the identity achievers do better on a concept attainment task than the other three statuses. However, attempts to replicate this finding (Bob, 1968) have not been entirely successful—hence, the generalization is only tentative.

Performance under Stress. Identity achievers performed better on the concept attainment task when under stress than in nonstress conditions. When under stress the moratorium and the diffused subjects did more poorly than in the nonstress situation. The performance of the foreclosures did not change as a function of stress (Bob, 1968). This finding is reminiscent of the observation that the foreclosures' level of aspiration did not change, even when confronted with failure experiences (Marcia, 1966).

Field Independence and Conformity. On a Witkin type field-independence task, college women who were identity achievers and foreclosures showed more field independence than those of the other two statuses (Schenkel, 1975); that is, they were better able to analyze and structure their experiences. This constitutes an implicit agreement with an earlier study by Toder and Marcia (1973) that demonstrated that identity-diffused and moratorium women displayed the greatest degree of conformity in an Asch-type experiment. Apparently a lack of identity increases the need to conform in the identity-diffused subjects; however, in general it is assumed that foreclosures have a propensity toward accepting and conforming to traditional values.

Formal Operations. Studies investigating the relationship between Piaget's stages of formal operations and Marcia's identity statuses have been less conclusive than studies on many of the other variables, a finding consistent with the earlier reported findings of no differences between the identity statuses and intelligence. Cauble (1976) concluded that the four identity statuses did not show a significant distribution over several of Piaget's formal thinking stages. Wagner (1976) reported only scant evidence for a relationship between identity statuses and formal operational reasoning. Even the conclusions by Rowe and Marcia (1980), since based on a very small sample, can only be considered as tentative findings. They did report that subjects who were in an advanced stage of formal operations (IIIa or beyond) were also identity achievers. And a similar but less pronounced relationship existed for moratoriums.

Problem-Solving Strategy. Identity achievers and moratoriums scored higher on a reflective problem-solving task; foreclosure and diffusion subjects were more impulsive (Waterman and Waterman, 1974).

PERSONALITY VARIABLES

In general, students who score high on measures of identity are as a group better adjusted, have a more integrated personality, and are more self-accepting than individuals who score low. This was demonstrated by LaVoie (1975) on measures of defensiveness, general maladjustment, personality disorder, neurosis, and personality disintegration. Donovan's (1975) identity-achieved and moratorium subjects displayed highly developed ego functioning and independence.

Authoritarianism. A frequently replicated finding, well based in theory and equally obvious in males and females, is that foreclosures score as significantly more authoritarian and more conventional than all other identity statuses. They endorse authoritarian values, tend to be obedient, respect authority, and are loyal to conventional values (Breuer, 1973; Marcia, 1966; 1967; Marcia and Friedman, 1970; Matteson, 1974; Schenkel and Marcia, 1972). Foreclosures also showed a surprising willingness to administer a high level of electric shock to a victim in a Milgram-type obedience task (Podd, 1972). In contrast, the moratorium subjects scored significantly lower than all other identity statuses on authoritarianism; they seem to challenge traditional authority and question existing values.

Anxiety. Among the college males, the moratorium subjects are the most anxious of all the identity statuses (Mahler, 1969; Marcia, 1967; Oshman and Manosevitz, 1974; Podd, Marcia, and Rubin, 1970). One theoretical explanation is that they actually are in a developmental period of insecurity, vulnerability, and crisis, and hence anxiety would be quite natural. However, it could also be that they are more open with themselves and more willing to admit experiencing anxiety. Foreclosure males, in contrast, are rigid and defensive, and hence their self-reported anxiety scores are the lowest. The diffused males apparently have too much apathy or lack of commitment to experience a high level of anxiety. Among females, more in line with common-sense expectations, the diffused subjects display more anxiety than all other statuses (Marcia and Friedman, 1970); female foreclosures, like males, display the least amount of anxiety.

Affect. Identity-achieved and foreclosure women showed significantly less negative affect than the remaining two statuses (Toder and Marcia, 1973).

Self-Esteem. Quite surprisingly, since identity and self-esteem are related constructs, Marcia (1966) reported only a very low correlation ($r = .26$) between self-esteem and an overall identity score and no significant differences between the four identity statuses. However, Breuer (1973) did report that identity-achieved and moratorium subjects obtained higher self-esteem scores than foreclosure and identity-diffused subjects. Furthermore, LaVoie (1976), who compared high- and low-scoring mid-adolescents, was able to demonstrate that the former had significantly higher self-concept scores than the latter and showed that self-concept improves with age. Donovan (1975) also reports that his identity-diffused subjects "seemed to have the lowest sense of self-esteem."

In a study conducted by Marcia and Friedman (1970), women displayed a different pattern from that reported by Breuer for males. Foreclosure women obtained the highest self-esteem scores; identity-achieved women, surprisingly, scored lower on self-esteem than all other statuses. However, Dye, Marquiss, and LaVoie (1975) support only the earlier findings pertaining to foreclosure, challenging those related to identity achievement. They reported that identity-achieved and foreclosure women obtained significantly higher self-concept scores than either moratorium or diffused women. In this context it is important to recall that identity-achieved women also had the greatest fear of success. Apparently the identity statuses have a different meaning for males and females, as will be discussed in more detail later.

Self-Esteem Manipulation through Feedback. The identity achievers and the moratorium subjects appear to be little influenced by external feedback about their personality. They are secure in knowing who they are and where they are going. They are least likely to accept false personality sketches about themselves; hence, they are not as easily manipulated as the foreclosure and diffused subjects (Gruen; 1960, Marcia, 1967).

Internal-External Locus of Control (Rotter). Male identity-achieved and moratorium subjects scored significantly higher on internal locus of control than did foreclosure and diffusion subjects, who were externally oriented (Waterman, Beubel, and Waterman, 1970). Apparently, subjects with an established or developing sense of identity believe that they themselves are in control of the events that shape their lives. For women, the identity-achieved and the foreclosure subjects obtained higher internal locus of control scores (Howard, 1975). Again, as in the case of self-esteem, foreclosure women emerged with different—and more positive—attributes than males.

Cooperation versus Competition. Podd, Marcia, and Rubin (1970), using a prisoners' dilemma game, found no significant overall differences in the competitive versus cooperative responses to the four identity statuses. However, one situation arose in which moratorium subjects were not very cooperative—when playing with an authority figure rather than with peers. Their unwillingness to cooperate is understandable in the light of the above-discussed finding that the moratorium subjects scored lowest on measures of authoritarianism since they are obviously in a stage of rebelling against authority.

FAMILY ANTECEDENTS

Several studies (Cross and Allen, 1970; Donovan, 1975; Jordan, 1970; 1971; LaVoie, 1976; Marcia, 1976a) have investigated the relationship between identity status and adolescents' perceptions of their parents. The findings of these various studies are not entirely consistent, except for the following generalizations.

1. The moratorium subjects saw their parents as ambivalent. Parents appeared to be inconsistent from the moratoriums' point of view; that is, parents were perceived as both accepting and rejecting. Among moratoriums the discrepancy between the parents and their son's point of view was great, as one might expect from the theoretical consideration that the moratoriums are actively questioning and challenging parental and established values. This discrepancy was greatest between sons and mothers.

2. The above statement also holds true for the identity achievers; however, for them the relationship had become more relaxed and more moderate. In a comparison of high and low identity mid-adolescents,

subjects with a high level of identity did perceive less distance between themselves and their fathers and mothers than did subjects with low identity scores (LaVoie, 1976).

3. Foreclosure subjects were—as one would expect, based on the theoretical definition of foreclosure—very close to and felt highly valued by their parents. Foreclosure males reported an intermediate—neither too harsh nor too limited—degree of control from their fathers (Cross and Allen, 1969). Foreclosures perceived their parents as accepting and supportive, but also as emphasizing strict superego functions. They saw their home as being loving and affectionate and had internalized their parents' goals for them (Donovan, 1975). The relationship between the foreclosure son and his father was especially strong. Apparently, the parents of foreclosure sons are quite effective in guiding them into the preconceived roles that they, the parents, have determined.

4. The parents of the identity-diffused subjects were perceived—again as suggested by theory—as detached, distant, uninvolved, and unconcerned. This observation was most noticeable in the father-son relationship. The diffused adolescents either didn't respect their parents or feared them and in general felt that there was a lack of understanding (Donovan, 1975). Identity-diffused students are more likely to come from broken homes than any of the other statuses (Jordan, 1970). Finally, it is interesting that college males who had grown up without a father attained lower overall identity scores than those who had come from intact families or whose mothers had remarried (Oshman and Manosevitz, 1974).

MORAL REASONING

The development of moral reasoning is closely related to the development of an ego identity. The identity achievers and the moratorium subjects scored significantly higher than the other statuses on moral reasoning and functioned at postconventional levels of moral judgment. Rowe and Marcia (1980) demonstrated a highly significant relationship between identity achievement and Kohlberg's postconventional level of moral judgment. The identity-diffused subjects still tended to function at the preconventional level of moral reasoning and attained the lowest moral judgment scores. However, because there are obvious individual differences, it was not possible to classify each of the four identity statuses in terms of specific corresponding stages of moral reasoning as defined by Kohlberg (Podd, 1972; Poppen, 1974). Hayes (1977) reported, in a more general sense, that adolescents who had a high level of identity were also more highly ethical, empathetic, and socialized than low-identity adolescents.

AUTONOMY

Both the identity achievers and the moratorium subjects, male as well as female, accepted more responsibility for their own behavior than did the identity-diffused subjects (Neuber and Genthner, 1977). The orientation of high-identity males is toward independence and active achievement; low-identity subjects tended to be passive and more affective (Andrews, 1973). Josselson (1973) reported that females who had achieved an identity displayed better psychological adjustment and more autonomy than those who had not yet mastered the identity crisis. Orlofsky, Marcia, and Lesser (1973) found foreclosure and identity-diffused subjects to be low on self-directedness. The foreclosure subjects scored lowest in personal autonomy and highest in their need for social approval.

DRUG USE

Foreclosure subjects, committed to traditional values, are the most adamant nondrug users (Dufresne and Cross, 1972). Moratorium and identity-diffused subjects are more likely to use drugs; however, each may use drugs for somewhat different reasons. The identity-diffused subject may use drugs and alcohol in an attempt to avoid crises, loneliness, and the feelings of confusion and diffusion; their use serves a defensive function. Based on clinical case studies, Flynn reports that he frequently sees this kind of defensive use of drugs by young adolescents who are confronted with identity issues of aggression, sexuality, dependency on parents, and dating problems. ". . . They were using drugs and associated themselves with the drug using crowd as a kind of spurious identity in order to drop out, for a time, from the struggle for psychosocial and psychosexual maturity" (1970: 149). For moratorium subjects, in contrast, drug use may be a manifestation of their openness to new experiences, their concern with trying different life styles, and their exploration of their own sense of awareness. Thus, under the rationalization, "I will try anything once," they may try out a great variety of different substances.

SEX DIFFERENCES IN IDENTITY STATUSES

Several major generalizations emerge from this brief review of the research literature:

1. It appears obvious that on most variables of mental health, cognitive performance, and life adjustment in general, the identity-achieved subjects score significantly higher than the identity-diffused

subjects. It has been found that this generalization applies to males as well as to females.

2. There exist sex differences in the personality correlates for these four identity statuses. However, the sexes also have much in common; in particular, the pattern for the identity-achieved and the identity-diffused is quite similar for both sexes. Sex differences become most obvious in the comparison of the foreclosure and the moratorium subjects. Apparently the route toward identity achievement follows a different course and may have different meanings for the two sexes—at least in the late 1960s and early 1970s when most of these studies were conducted.

3. Among men, identity achievers and moratorium subjects are often close together and perform better than the other two statuses on such variables as ego development, concept attainment, performance under stress, resistance to manipulation of self-esteem, internal reflectivity in decision making, and intimacy in interpersonal relationships.

4. Among females, identity-achieved and foreclosure subjects appear to be grouped together more often; they have higher self-esteem, show less conformity to peer group pressures, give evidence of a low level of self-reported anxiety, choose a more difficult college major, consider themselves straight rather than hip, and have attained higher levels of independence. One might further consider that there may be sex differences in the components that make up the identity of an individual. For example, Bell (1969) indicates that vocational identity plays a more central role in the identity of the male, and affiliation may play a greater role in the identity of the female (Douvan and Adelson, 1966). Erikson has emphasized that ". . . womanhood arrives when attractiveness and experiences have succeeded in selecting what is to be admitted to the welcome of the inner space" (1968: 283); for this reason, Marcia added a section about attitude toward premarital intercourse to the assessment of crisis and commitment in women as part of the identity interview. Schenkel and Marcia (1972) demonstrated that sexual ideology actually accounts for more variance in identity status than politics, occupation, and religion (which was second).

To interpret these reported sex differences is difficult since earlier identity studies were primarily concerned with validating the construct "identity," and usually used males as subjects. Even later studies limited their population to either males or females and often investigated different variables. Nevertheless, all of these variables do not explain away the rather noticeable sex differences found in much of the identity research. Marcia and Friedman (1970) have suggested, based on social, cultural, and historical factors, that achievement and foreclosure are "stable identity statuses for women, while achievement and moratorium are "stable" identities for males.

Most of our research with men suggested that *chronological proximity* to Identity Achievement was a crucial factor in the grouping of the statuses. That is, Moratoriums could be expected to behave most like Identity Achievements on measures involving general ego strength, while Foreclosures would perform most like Identity Diffusions. However, with women, the *stability* of the identity status was emerging as the important issue. Identity Achievement and Foreclosure are both fairly stable statuses; both groups have an identity, even though one is achieved and the other foreclosed. Moratorium and Identity Diffusion are unstable statuses; neither one has a firm set of identity, although Moratoriums are moving towards it [Marcia, 1976b: 103].

It will be interesting to observe whether these relationships between sex and identity status will begin to change as women become less traditional and more liberated in their pursuits of vocational careers, their striving for independence from their families, and their developing more liberated attitudes toward sexuality and sex roles. Schenkel (1975) suggests that such changes are taking place, and that women make increasingly more demands for autonomy. Erikson does perceive some rather fundamental differences in the achievement of a mature identity for males and females.

Understanding of female development in adolescence is a far more complicated task than the understanding of male development. Female development is quieter, subtler. And because the end-points of female development are ambiguous, it is harder to identify significant markers along the way. . . . Because the Erikson stages of identity and intimacy are probably merged for girls . . . identity development proceeds at a deeper and less tangible level [Josselson, Greenberger, and McConochie, 1977: 162, 164].

EDUCATIONAL IMPLICATIONS

One basic issue regarding education during adolescence that emerges from Erikson's theory is: To what extent and how do educational institutions enhance youths' efforts in self-finding? Contemporary critics of the school system—Dennison, Friedenberg, Goodman, Holt, Silverman, and others—have maintained that schools require adolescents to suppress their creativity, individuality, and identity to the demands of the skill- and knowledge-oriented curriculum in order to succeed. Thus, schools seem to be encourging foreclosure, since they demand conformity to the way things are and submission to authority, rather than aiding the adolescent in his search for a personal identity. Considering the Waterman and Waterman (1970) findings, it appears that foreclosure subjects were more comfortable in school and held more positive attitudes toward their educational experiences while the uncommitted, searching, and experimenting moratorium subjects evaluated their educational experience rather negatively. Apparently, the structure of the school, the curriculum, schedules, grades, hall passes, and so on, encourage foreclosure rather than efforts toward self-finding and self-definition, which implies questioning and challenging existing patterns, values, and authorities. One might speculate whether the all-pervasive indifference toward school and the frequent discontent of adolescents with education and with their teachers is in part a result of the lack of concern on the part of many educators with what Erikson and Marcia consider a fundamental developmental issue, namely, the resolution of the identity crisis. It has long been recognized that the problem of the high school dropout is not simply a matter of lack of ability, or even lack of achievement, but a desire for independence, a search without a goal, an expression of inner discontent and restlessness. Youth dissatisfaction with college, students questioning the value of their college education, the increasing pattern of "dropping in and dropping out" of college, as well as the increasing pattern of transferring from one college to another, do make sense in view of Erikson's "adolescent identity crisis" concept and Marcia's assumption that a moratorium requires this kind of Wanderlust and exploration and is an essential prerequisite for the achievement of a mature identity.

The cry for relevance in the curriculum and in the total educational experience might also be better understood in view of the moratorium issues: developing a sexual identity, finding religious values, selecting career goals, and developing a commitment to a political ideology. The adolescent often has difficulty in seeing the relationship among these burning personal issues and conjugating French verbs, studying ancient Rome, proving the Pythagorean theorem, and examining the finer points of Shakespeare's *Macbeth*; and teachers are often remiss in making these relationships obvious, even in those content areas where they are most readily apparent. The junior high school student's and even the senior high school student's choices of different courses are limited, and the adolescent has relatively little to say about the curriculum. The curriculum should become more closely related to the adolescent's search for self-understanding by including more identity relevant topics. This could include drug education and sex education, areas in which considerable misinformation exists even among sophisticated youth. Furthermore, such topics as human development, sociology, interpersonal relations, consumer economics, social organization, career opportunities in the future, ecology, sex roles and sex stereotypes, and a study of values could aid adolescents in developing a philosophy of life. All of these topics could be taught in a way that makes them academically respectable, as well as personally meaningful. In their English courses high school students could study the problems of adolescents as reflected in the literature dealing with adolescents. In addition, present teaching styles frequently include lecturing, rehearsing, reviewing, drills, quizzes, tests, and assignments—which means that even when these activities are meaningful, they are teacher directed and the learning activities are controlled by the authority of the teacher. Consequently, the high school student is often placed in a docile and submissive role, so that there is little opportunity to fulfill the needs of the moratorium subjects, and the foreclosure subjects are not encouraged to move out of their developmental stagnation but may be rewarded for foreclosure behavior.

In contrast to Freud's emphasis on the dangers of frustration and the possible contribution of frustration to neurosis, Erikson distinguishes between meaningful frustration and neurotic frustration. Meaningful frustration can serve useful ends as an educational experience and implies that even though the adolescent initially does not see a possible solution to the teacher's question, problem, or assignment—and consequently feels frustrated—he can, with work and perseverance, find the solution by himself. The teacher who has become an effective frustrator does not contribute to neuroses but instead helps his students to develop frustration tolerance. Therefore, parents and teachers might introduce more culturally meaningful but frustrating challenges that the adolescent can resolve with effort. As part of the process of growing up, children must learn to accept some of the inevitable limitations and restrictions that may be frustrating. Erikson objects to a frustration-free educational environment—like Summerhill—in which children's natural tendencies and interests determine the learning activities and the curriculum. An educational policy characterized by the child's questioning his freedom to learn— as implied in the often quoted "Teacher *must* we do today what we *want* to do?" (Erikson, 1968: 127)—can be as detrimental to the establishment of a healthy identity as the traditional emphasis on duty, obedience, self-restraint, and arbitrary rules. Learning occurs more effectively and the development of identity is enhanced in an educational climate that avoids the pitfalls of both these extremes. Youth do benefit from being "mildly but firmly coerced into the adventure of finding out that one can learn to accomplish things which one would never have thought of by oneself, things which owe their attractiveness to the very fact that they are not the product of play and fantasy, but the product of reality, practicality and logic" (Erikson, 1968: 127). Consequently, meaningful ways of frustrating adolescents by challenging them with new ideas, problems, and subjects may increase their efforts to learn and master and, ultimately, contribute to their process of maturing.

In the past, societies through puberty rites, initiation ceremonies, the apprenticeship-journeyman system, confirmation, bar mitzvah, and coming-out parties have provided some fairly clearly defined social roles that gave the individual a kind of identity by providing self-definition and social status. As these social role definitions have virtually disappeared—and as confirmations and bar mitzvahs have become primarily private, religious matters—the individual's search for his own unique identity and for his place in society has become more pronounced, and more of a burden is placed upon the individual. "Some of the adolescent difficulties in Western society may be better understood if one considers the adolescent as the marginal man who stands in a psychological no-man's-land without clear understanding of what is expected of him, struggling to attain adult status" (Muuss, 1970b: 113). The adolescent struggle to attain an identity and achieve adult status can be a frustrating experience, and society, educational institutions, and teachers may well ponder how they can make this experience more meaningful.

PETER BLOS' MODERN PSYCHOANALYTIC INTERPRETATION OF ADOLESCENCE*

5:

BLOS' THEORY: AN INTRODUCTION

Peter Blos (1904–) is a psychoanalyst in private practice in New York; he holds a Ph.D. rather than an M.D. and is a biologist by training. Blos has devoted a great deal of attention to the period of adolescence, both in his practical clinical work and in his theoretical formulations. More recently, he has "returned to his psychoanalytic beginnings," working with juvenile delinquents, as he did in the 1920s with A. Aichhorn in Vienna. His commitment to the period of adolescence is reflected in the titles of his numerous journal articles, as well as his four books: *The Adolescent Personality* (1941), *On Adolescence, A Psychoanalytic Interpretation* (1962), *The Young Adolescent: Clinical Studies* (1970), and more recently, *The Adolescent Passage* (1979).

Blos' theory of adolescent development has not been as widely accepted in the developmental literature as, for example, Erikson's theory, partly because it lacks popular concepts such as trust, autonomy, initiative, industry, and adolescent identity crisis; partly because emphasis falls on psychopathology; and partly because normal development is less systematically presented and emerges more as a by-product. Finally, the conceptual frame of reference is heavily laced with traditional psychoanalytic concepts such as the Oedipus complex, castration anxiety, penis envy, regression to the pre-oedipal, and archaic mother. Most of Blos' efforts are devoted to a description of deviancy in development, juvenile delinquency, psychoanalytic treatment, and cases of psychopathology. His theory has therefore been more popular among psychiatrists than among developmental psychologists, whereas Erikson's theory (1950), with its emphasis on the

---

*Chapter 5 is a revision and extension of an article by the author, "Peter Blos' modern psychoanalytic interpretation of adolescence," *Journal of Adolescence,* 1980, *3,* 229-252.

normality of the "Eight Stages of Man," has in contrast had a more profound influence on education and psychology, especially child and adolescent development.

Blos' theory is not incompatible with the theoretical concepts advanced by Erikson, who added a psychosocial dimension but did not give up the basic Freudian psychosexual concepts. Both men emphasize different dimensions of adolescent development. Blos seems to have remained closer to the original writings of Freud, trying to expand and elaborate rather than modify fundamental psychoanalytic constructs, especially those pertinent to adolescence. However, he frequently cites Erikson and uses some Eriksonian constructs in his own writings.

In addition, Blos draws on the various constructs emerging from ego-psychology—the second individuation process, regression to earlier experiences in the service of ego development, separation from parents, and turning to peers as a necessary developmental progression—rather than on Freud's notion that conflict defines all developmental tasks. Furthermore, Blos accepts many of the basic psychoanalytic assumptions concerning the nature of man and the psychodynamics of development and utilizes Freudian constructs throughout his writing. Freud emphasized the revival of the Oedipus complex and the reawakening of castration fear during the genital period (adolescence). Blos relies heavily on such ideas; however, he has developed a much more elaborate system that views adolescence as the psychological adjustment to sexual and biological maturation. "Puberty is an act of nature and adolescence is an act of man" (Blos, 1979: 405).

Another concept that Blos stresses is the separation experience from parental dependencies and familial love objects as a crucial task for normal adolescent development, an idea he refers to as the second individuation process (Blos, 1979: 141–170). This developmental process of adolescence requires a partial regression to earlier stages of development, which is necessary, not as a defense mechanism, but in the service of adolescent development (Blos, 1979: 161–168). The Oedipus complex receives elaborate treatment and is used as a fundamental dynamic principle to explain drive and ego orientation during adolescence, as well as sex differences in development. Throughout his writings, Blos emphasizes and describes how males and females differ in their development. More recently, Blos has written a paper, "Modification of the Traditional Psychoanalytic Theory of Female Development" (1980), in which he contrasts the classical Freudian theory of feminine development with more recent observations. Blos emphasizes that the orthodox psychoanalytic view of female adolescent development requires considerable realignment with more recent findings, and he suggests a need and a direction for further investigations. His purpose is to provide a new interpretation of the traditional psychoanalytical theory of the psychological development of females during adolescence. On the basis of Green's (1966) behavioral observation of children, Blos maintains that a biologically determined male-female dimorphism exists that permits us to speak of a primary femininity and masculinity. It has been observed that newborn babies already show sex differences in their behavior patterns (Hamburg and Lunde, 1966), such as the much greater behavioral continuity of fearfulness in males when exposed to visual novelty (Bronson, 1973).

Freud identified adolescence as the genital stage and viewed it as the final developmental stage before sexual maturity is reached. Blos, in contrast, as an indication of his highly differentiated conceptualization of the period of adolescence, suggests six different adolescent phases, that is, if one includes latency as the preparatory stage for adolescence and postadolescence as the transition phase between adolescence and adulthood. These six phases are:

1. Latency
2. Preadolescence or prepuberty
3. Early adolescence or early puberty. Phases 2 and 3 are sometimes treated as one stage and are then referred to as "Young Adolescence"
4. Adolescence proper—middle adolescence or advanced puberty
5. Late adolescence—a phase of consolidation
6. Postadolescence—the transition from adolescence to adulthood

In addition to these six developmental phases, five phase-specific issues emerge and undergo reorganization in normal development and provide the structure for the discussion of each of the above phases:

1. Drive organization
2. Ego organization or ego function
3. Somatic maturation
4. Conflict formation
5. Conflict resolution

The overall pattern of these five phase-specific issues and six developmental phases is not readily identifiable at any one point in Blos' books but emerges sporadically throughout his writing, providing an underlying systematic theoretical structure of normal adolescent development.

One of the major distinctions between Blos' formulation and Freud's original conception of psychosexual development is that Freud emphasized that personality formation took place very early in life, primarily during the oral, anal, and phallic stages, and that personality formation was conceived to be almost completed once the Oedipus complex had been resolved. Such statements as "the personality patterns attained by the end of the oedipal period are seen as set and relatively unresponsive to changing conditions" (Wachtel, 1977: 51) have become commonplace in the developmental literature. In contrast, Blos, Jones, and Erikson, among others, placed an increasing emphasis on the importance of adolescence in personality development. Blos' major theoretical contribution is an identification of the reorganization and restructuring of personality during adolescence, a process he referred to as the second individuation process. Only after the second individuation process has been completed is a certain degree of permanence and stability reached within the personality structure. Only when writing about postadolescence does Blos speak of "developmental achievement of personality organization" (Blos, 1962: 149), "harmonizing drive and ego organizations" (Blos, 1962: 150), and "the organization of a stable self" (Blos, 1962: 153).

> At the close of adolescence, as I have remarked earlier, conflicts are by no means resolved, but they are rendered specific; and certain conflicts become integrated into the realm of the ego as life tasks. It remains the task of postadolescence to create the specific avenues through which these tasks are implemented in the external world [Blos, 1962: 150].

Before we discuss Blos' six phases of adolescence we must consider the second individuation phase and the impact of the Oedipus complex in adolescence. At this time, there is relatively little empirical research especially designed to assess the specific psychoanalytic propositions of Blos' theory. However, the reader is reminded that Fisher and Greenberg (1977)—discussed in more detail in Chapter 3—have reviewed an enormous amount of psychoanalytically oriented research that does support some but not all of Freud's basic theoretical assumptions. Considerable support was cited in support of the male's Oedipus complex. The support for the female oedipal situation was less positive, and it is especially this part of the theory that Blos modifies and expands.

BLOS' SECOND INDIVIDUATION PROCESS

The first individuation process, a concept developed by Mahler (1963), is normally completed toward the end of the third year of life. Its completion is characterized by the attainment of "object constancy," and by the child's ability to distinguish between inside and outside reality— between "me" and "not me"—and the ability to differentiate between self and mother. "Mobility, language, and social experiences widen the child's life space and bring to his awareness the desirability of being like others, most importantly, like the parent or sibling" (Blos, 1962: 4). While the first individuation process aids in the differentiation between child and parent, it also contributes to the child's desire to model himself after the admired parent and contributes to the dependency of childhood. The first individuation process establishes independence from the concrete physical presence of the mother, and the mother becomes internalized. It is only in the second phase, at the dawn of puberty, that the "independence from internalized infantile objects" (Blos, 1979: 483) is attained.

By viewing adolescence as a recapitulation of psychoanalytically significant childhood experiences (e.g., a second Oedipus complex), Blos (1967) introduced as a major theoretical construct of adolescent development the "second individuation process"—a psychological weaning. It is initiated with the increase in the libidinal drive at puberty, continues until late adolescence, and reaches completion only when the adolescent can find external and extrafamilial love objects. As a result of the disengagement from parental control and from internalized, immature attachments of familial love and hate objects, the individuation process leads to a more realistic evaluation of parents and aids in the process of self-definition and ego maturity. Individuation involves "the shedding of family dependencies, [and] the loosening of infantile object ties in order to become a member of the adult world" (Blos, 1967: 163). The disengagement of childhood dependencies at the adolescent level takes place not only in relation to external concrete objects—as in the first individuation process—but also in relation to the internalized love objects of early childhood (Blos, 1979: 412). Only on completion of adolescence do these internalized self- and object-representations acquire firm boundaries and develop stability and resistance to change.

The adolescent individuation process helps to establish a personal, social, and sexual identity. It requires a turning away from parents and—because of still insufficient autonomy—a temporary turning toward the peer group culture. The peer group serves several functions—for example, helping the adolescent to resolve the oedipal conflict during this period and to sever parental dependencies. The peer group may actually serve some functions better than the family for several reasons:

1. The peer group helps adolescents to resolve internal conflicts within themselves and reduces anxiety, since peers can serve as a sounding board without arousing guilt or anxiety.
2. The peer group respects competencies—although these are often defined differently by adults and by various peer groups—as seen

in the different emphases placed on social and athletic skills.
3. The peer group provides practical and personal guidance in social situations, especially in heterosexual relationships and behavior.
4. The peer group provides honest and critical evaluative feedback about the individual's behavior and personality attributes.

Since adolescents cannot find sexual gratification within their family of origin, and in order to sever family dependencies, they turn toward the peer group for support, values, and security. Security is found in the shared code of what constitutes adequate behavior and in the dependency on mutual recognition of sameness (Blos, 1962: 188). However, in the attempt to free themselves from the control and restrictions of parents, adolescents may fall prey to the tyranny of peers who require conformity to their standards in return for the security they provide. Ample research evidence (Brittain, 1966; Brownstone and Willis, 1971; Costanzo, 1970; Costanzo and Shaw, 1966; Iscoe, Williams, and Harvey, 1963; Patel and Gordon, 1960; Schmuck, 1963) has identified this developmental trend toward greatly increased conformity in early adolescence and continuing into adolescence proper, followed by a decline in conformity with increased maturity. Blos views this trend as a defensive denial of the adolescents' dependency needs and describes it as "uniformism." The importance of the influence of the peer group is nowhere more pronounced than in sexual behavior. Recent trends indicate that sexual intercourse is now being endorsed by the peer group and is considered mature behavior: "The peer group with its characteristic fostering of conformity has come to equate adolescent heterosexual behavior with independence, individualism, and adulthood" (Blos, 1979: 249). The peer group provides the kind of support that the adolescent often loses in the separation process from his own family: "stimulation, belongingness, loyalty, devotion, empathy, and resonance" (Blos, 1967: 177). For the time being, the adolescent too readily accepts the norms of the peer group as guides to regulate feelings, impulses, and sexual behavior. The peer group can become an emotional alternative to the family, a substitute family. One danger is that the family dependencies will be replaced by permanent peer group dependencies, with emotional independence remaining unresolved. The opposite danger, for the adolescent who does not want to fit into the model of uniformism, is to be "avoided, ridiculed, ostracized, or condescendingly tolerated" (Blos, 1962: 118).

The second individuation process requires a fundamental restructuring of drive organization and ego functions. During adolescence the ego becomes weaker relative to the id due to (1) the new urgency of sex drive intensity during puberty and (2) the rejection of parental ego support, which was available during latency as a legitimate ego extension. Individuation is not without negative manifestations, such as internal turmoil, heightened vulnerability in personality organization, and emotional complications. A sense of "discouragement, helplessness, despair, incompetent rage, weakness, and worthlessness" represent the emotions of abandonment and regression (Blos, 1970: 235). However, the experiences of these negative by-products is a developmental necessity before the individuation process can be completed. Adolescent turmoil is viewed as the *sine qua non* of development, the assumption being "that only through conflict can maturity be attained" (Blos, 1979: 14). For a new reorganization to take place, the old psychological organization needs to be loosened, resulting in temporary fragmentation, disorganization, instability, insufficiency, estrangement, and self-consciousness. To consolidate a new organizational structure necessitates experimentation, "the testing of the self by going to excess," as well as oppositional attitudes, rebellious behavior, and resistive strivings (Blos, 1962: 12). The resulting structural change will eventually become permanent personality attributes.

The second individuation process is a process in which both "regressive and progressive movements alternate" (Blos, 1967: 164), providing the psychological basis for the inner turmoil, external rebellion, unpredictability, and chaos that make adolescence a period of crisis. According to Blos, it is only during adolescence that developmental regression must be viewed as a necessary, integral, and healthy part of development. He speaks repeatedly of the regressive movement that is activated by the sudden increase in the sexual and aggressive drives and that creates anxiety. That anxiety is increased externally by the greatly increased social demands and expectations. The idea that adolescence typically is a period of heightened anxiety is generally acknowledged (Conger, 1977: 64–70) and even depicted in the developmental literature (McCandless, 1970: 3). The idea received its empirical support through the work of Cattell, who maintains that "anxiety is very high in the adolescent, drops sharply as adulthood is reached, and continues to drop steadily throughout middle age until it rises very steeply again in old age" (1961: 262). Confronted with such demands and with internal conflicts related to sexual and aggressive drive, anxiety and conflict may be avoided by returning to more primitive responses, such as narcissism, oral greediness, and sadism, which were effective in earlier periods of life. Adolescent progress cannot take its normal path without this detour of regression; regression is seen as a precondition of progress, "without which emotional maturity cannot be attained" (Blos, 1979: 27). Individuation implies "a forward movement of the ego" and a "regression of the ego in the service of adolescent development." The meaning of these two apparently contradictory statements can best be illustrated by Nietzsche's famous aphorism, "They say he is going backward, indeed he is, because he attempts to jump." The backward movement manifests itself in an increase in narcissism, exhibited in arrogance, rebellion, defiance, and challenges to parents' authority (Blos, 1962: 91). Fantasies and acts of aggression are common during adolescence to an extent unusual among adults: "Rapaciousness, smuttiness, oblivion to unkemptness, dirtiness and body odors; motoric restlessness, and experimentation in every direction of action and sensation" (Blos, 1971: 964). However, the process of "disengagement from primary objects and the abandonment of infantile ego states" (Blos, 1967: 185), requires a regressive return to earlier periods of development.

> . . . the task of the psychic restructuring by regression represents the most formidable psychic work of adolescence. Just as Hamlet longs for the comforts of sleep but fears the dreams that sleep might bring, so the adolescent longs for the comforts of drive and ego gratification but fears the reinvolvements in infantile object relations. Paradoxically, only through drive and ego regression can the adolescent task be fulfilled [Blos, 1967: 171].

Failure to succeed in this emotional disengagement process interferes with the future task of finding extra familial ties of affection, impedes the movement toward autonomy and independence, and may contribute to deviant development and psychopathology. Difficulties in the successful completion of the second individuation process may manifest themselves in acting-out behavior, feelings of a lack of purpose, learning disorders, patterns of procrastination, moodiness, apathy, and negativism. In addition, some of the negative outcomes share with the individuation process the basic goal of adolescence, namely, a movement away from infantile dependencies without producing the necessary reorganization in psychic structure. Blos speaks of a "derailment of the individuation process" in which behavior and social roles are oppositional to parents' wishes and often constitute a more permanent break and unrealistic evaluation of these wishes.

THE OEDIPUS COMPLEX IN BLOS' THEORY

Although it has received less emphasis in Erikson's writing, the Oedipus complex remains a core concept for understanding Blos' theory of adolescent development. Blos distinguishes between the familiar Oedipus complex toward the end of the phallic stage and the reemerging of a second oedipal situation during puberty. The resolution of the pubertal Oedipus complex is an important part of the second individuation process. In a developmental sense the Oedipus conflict is biphasic. The phallic-oedipal conflict constitutes the first phase. According to the psychoanalytic recapitulation theory, the revival of the second phase occurs during puberty with the increase in drive intensity. Adolescence is the completion and final resolution, not just a repetition of the Oedipus complex. Since the oedipal situation is different for boys and girls, sex differences must be taken into consideration.

The issues become further complicated by the distinction between a negative passive oedipal position and a positive aggressive oedipal situation. The former is referred to as the early oedipal position, during which the child is primarily receptive; the latter is the more commonly acknowledged oedipal conflict during which the child's love turns toward the opposite-sex parent. The term "negative" refers to the child's love for the same-sex parent, while "positive" implies a love relationship directed toward the opposite-sex parent. Oedipal love always implies a sexual component; however, oedipal love must be distinguished from nonsexual affection, admiration, respect, and loyalty, which children experience in relation to both parents.

During the negative oedipal-phallic period, the boy identifies with his mother while his passive-receptive libido is attached to his father. For example, the passive-receptive oedipal boy may fantasize or wish for a baby from his father. The early passive oedipal period terminates when the boy realizes that the female has no penis and when the more active mode of the phallic stage begins to prevail. The active, or positive, oedipal position brings forth a more aggressive, masculine, libidinal drive, now directed toward possessing the mother. Thus emerges the well-known triangular relationship in which the father is seen as the son's rival and competitor; both hostile impulses and fantasies are aimed at the father. The consequence is castration fear. Three factors eventually lead to the abandonment of the oedipal position: (1) fear of the father, especially in the form of castration anxiety, which exists simultaneously with (2) love for the father and (3) the boy's own immaturity (Blos, 1962: 26). The mother who does not encourage the symbolic seductive attention of her son also enhances the normal progression toward latency.

Blos distinguishes between two possible outcomes of the Oedipus complex: (1) to identify with the father and to attempt to become like him in the future or (2) to give up the competitive striving and regressively and passively submit to the mother. The first solution enhances the development of the ego and the superego during latency and brings forth an orientation in accordance with the reality principle.

The second solution is a regressive return to the preoedipal mother; it enhances the id and the drive orientation directed towards the pleasure principle and leads to difficulties during puberty when biological maturation reintroduces the oedipal situation once more.

With the beginning of puberty the negative oedipal situation reemerges, resulting in a strong idealization and glamorization of the father. The father provides comfort and assurance, reviving "remnants of the boy's passive oedipal love for the father" (Blos, 1970: 221). The father is seen as the "protector against the pre-oedipal archaic mother," who represents the castrating threat during this phase (Blos, 1970: 154). This preadolescent castration fear generalizes and influences the boy's negative attitudes toward women. However, it also requires the adolescent boy to come "to terms with the homosexual component of pubertal sexuality" (Blos, 1979: 479). With the reorganization in libido drive from bisexual to heterosexual orientation on entering adolescence proper, the boy experiences the phase of the positive oedipal complex once more. Sexual attraction now turns to the mother while both fear and hostility are aimed at the father. In normal development, the social taboo against incestuous love has been internalized in the superego to the extent that the oedipal impulses are unacceptable, producing considerable guilt and anxiety. The resolution of the positive Oedipus complex constitutes a major developmental task during advanced puberty, and a successful resolution of this task becomes the necessary prerequisite for progression into late adolescence and adulthood.

The oedipal development of the girl contains elements that make the task and the resolution of the conflict quite similar to that of the boy, and the four phases of oedipal development are the same. However, there are important variations that influence the different patterns in heterosexual development. Blos does not assume that the resolution of the male and the female oedipal situation is parallel. The difference between the sexes lies in the necessity for the adolescent male to thoroughly resolve the positive as well as the negative aspects of the Oedipus complex in order to move more vigorously toward adulthood and maturity. "In contrast, the adolescent girl tolerates—within limits, to be sure—a far greater fluidity between the infantile attachment to both parents and her adult personality consolidation, without being necessarily encumbered in her advance toward emotional maturity" (Blos, 1980: 14).

In the prephallic stage the girl shares with the boy a passive receptive position *vis-à-vis* the active preoedipal mother. All children, regardless of their sex, see the mother as their first love object, and in this situation the archaic mother is always active, and in relation to her, the child during the oral and anal phases is always in a passive and receptive position. The sexes differ in that, for the male, the female always remains the ultimate love object, but the girl must abandon her first love object and turn toward the father and later toward other masculine love objects. Entry into the phallic stage brings about a change from the passive receptive mode to an active aggressive mode, the latter becoming more pronounced for the boy. This active phase emphasizes autonomy, initiative, and mastery of the world. "Femininity and passivity or masculinity and activity" are not synonymous, but are viewed as potential tendencies (Blos, 1979: 227). The girl's identification with the active mother during this early phallic stage ushers in the initial active, negative, oedipal situation for the girl. The stronger the attachment of the female to the mother during this period, the greater will be her dependence on the father later on. Curiosity, about the world in general and sexuality in particular, leads to the recognition of sex differences, an awareness that is burdened with meaning, encourages fantasy, and leads to body damage anxiety. It is when the shift from active to passive takes place—due to disappointment with the mother who has not provided the girl with a penis—that the aim of instinctual libido shifts from the mother to the father, leading to the passive, or positive, oedipal position. It is this shift from the active (phallic) stance to the passive position that threatens the female with a return to the original infantile dependency position. "Only when the girl succeeds in abandoning her passive tie to the mother and advances to a passive (positive) oedipal position, can she be spared the adolescent regression to the preoedipal mother" (Blos, 1979: 227). The oedipal situation remains part of the emotional life of the girl during the latency period. "Girls remain in it [the oedipal situation] for an undetermined length of time; they demolish it late, and even so, incompletely" (S. Freud, 1933/1964: 129).

During preadolescence, the girl resists the regressive pull toward infantile passivity, which arouses anxiety. In contrast to the boy at this stage, she turns toward activity as a defensive maneuver against this regressive pull toward passivity and takes on a sexually aggressive masculine role, in which she becomes the sexual instigator and initiator. Blos refers to this identification with the male role among girls, as "the oedipal defense of the pre-adolescent girl" (Blos, 1970: 42). The preadolescent girl approaches heterosexuality more speedily and more directly than the boy. During adolescence proper, the girl takes on the positive passive role *vis-à-vis* her father and rejects her mother. However, as in the case of the boy, abandoning this oedipal position is the necessary step toward nonincestuous object finding and toward progression in development.

THE SIX PHASES OF ADOLESCENT DEVELOPMENT

The second individuation process and the second oedipal complex provide the basic framework within which Blos traces the epigenetic pattern of adolescent development. Normal development proceeds in an orderly progression identified by six adolescent phases: latency, preadolescence, early adolescence, adolescence proper, late adolescence, and postadolescence. Each of these six phases represents phase-specific tasks and experiences, and the progression from one to the next is not just a matter of maturation but requires psychic restructuring. The transformations produce developmental characteristics that distinguish each phase from the one that follows or precedes it. Each phase, especially during the early stages, harbors the potential danger of "developmental derailment," leading to adolescent disturbances. However, the emphasis here, in contrast to Blos' original writing, will be on normal development rather than on the etiology and the dynamics of deviancy in development. The connecting and recurring issues around which the psychic restructuring of adolescent development takes place—and which Blos emphasizes, particularly in the description of the earlier phases—are: drive organization, ego development, somatic maturation, conflict formation, and conflict resolution. These phases will be dealt with in turn.

Drive Organization. Restructuring of drive organization refers to both the quantitative increase and the directional reorientation of libidinal and aggressive drive during puberty. According to Blos, drive intensification is equally strong for both libidinal and aggressive drives, a quantitative change that marks the progression from latency into preadolescence and early adolescence. The initial drive direction is diffuse, the bisexual orientation of childhood remains dominant into early adolescence and may include transitory homosexual experiences. A distinct restructuring of the direction of drive orientation characterizes the progression from early adolescence into adolescence proper with the advent of predominant heterosexual orientation. The movement from incestuous to nonincestuous object findings dominates drive organization in the late and postadolescent phase.

Ego Development. Ego development does not directly parallel modification in drive organization. The ego experiences an upsurge in maturity and strength during latency with a movement toward greater autonomy, increasing ego differentiation and, in general, ego expansion. But with the onset of puberty, there is a flooding of the ego with the newly emerging instinctual pressures, leaving the ego relatively weak *vis-à-vis* the ascendency of libidinal and aggressive drives. The ego insufficiency during the earlier phases of adolescent development is partly responsible for some of the chaos, turmoil, and crisis. It is only later, as a result of the resolution of the Oedipus complex, that the ego once more asserts its autonomy in relationship to the id, and the superego and the ego-ideal emerge out of the structure of the superego. The ego-ideal constitutes idealized goals and aspirations that lie in the future.

Somatic Maturation. The process of somatic maturation provides the physiological background for the progression in psychosexual development, and it is only against this biological aspect of development that changes in drive organization, ego development, the nature of conflict, and conflict resolution can be meaningfully understood. Somatic maturation is responsible for the profound changes in the primary and secondary sex characteristics, and hence, the preadolescent and the early adolescent frequently show much concern about these bodily changes. These concerns become obsessive and problematic when the adolescent discovers deviation in physical development—imagined or real. All of this contributes to an acute and heightened self-consciousness about the body. Pubertal maturation draws adolescents' attention particularly to the changing sex organs; they are curious about the functions of these organs and whether their own are normal and are anxious about their protection. "It is this preoccupation (unconscious and preconscious) with the sexual organs, their function, intactness, protection, and not the relationship theme of love and its fulfillment which stands out in the play construction of the preadolescent" (Blos, 1962: 58).

Blos is less specific in describing the maturational changes that take place in the body than, for example, Tanner (1962), who provides a detailed account of the process of somatic maturation. Blos sees it as his task to elaborate on the psychological consequences of these pubertal body changes, and he maintains that the "synchronicity between somatic and psychological changes," which is quite obvious during the early phases of adolescent development, disappears as the end of adolescence is approached.

Conflict Formation and Conflict Resolution. Each phase brings with it its own phase-specific set of conflicts requiring conflict resolution before normal progression to the next higher phase becomes possible. The more significant conflicts are the previously discussed negative oedipal conflict of preadolescence and early adolescence and the positive oedipal conflict of adolescence proper. Related to oedipal issues are the conflicts that emerge from the change from bisexuality during early adolescence to heterosexuality. The infantile dependency on parents produces conflict when heterosexual object choice becomes paramount. Conflicts are both essential and normative for developmental progress; only through conflict and resolution can maturity be attained. "The formation of a conflict between generations and its subsequent resolution is the normative task of adolescence" (Blos, 1979: 11). It is only through the resolution of conflicts that the normal movement through the adolescent phases is made possible, and this process is referred to by Blos as "the adolescent process."

In the remaining discussion of the six phases of adolescent development, an outline of this normal adolescent process will be presented and organized around the themes of drive organization, ego development, somatic maturation, conflict, and conflict resolution.

LATENCY

The latency period is viewed by Blos as an important preparatory phase for entry into adolescence, and much deviant development seems to emerge later from lack of success in ego consolidation—a major developmental task of latency. During latency, the libidinal drive—not entirely under cover—is less intense, more diffuse, and more easily diverted into constructive educational endeavors than during the oedipal periods that precede or those that follow it. The expansion of the ego renders the libidinal drive less dominant in the psychological structure. According to Blos, the latency period distinguishes itself from all other psychoanalytic stages of development in so far as no new instinctual aim or libidinal object emerges. The bisexual orientation of earlier developmental phases continues to be tolerated. The end of latency has arrived when the resurgence of libidinal drive is imminent. Indications that the transition between latency and prepuberty is taking place are the deterioration in manners, lack of concentration, decline in cooperativeness *vis-à-vis* authorities, and the increasing conformity to peer group pressures (Blos, 1970: 71).

Latency is a period of ego expansion, ego differentiation, and increased ego autonomy. The increased ego autonomy is accompanied by growth in several areas: cognition, judgment, logic, memory, empathy, anticipation, tension tolerance, self-awareness, the ability to distinguish between reality and fantasy, and a more precise differentiation between action and thoughts (Blos, 1970: 9). The confusion between internal and external, which is characteristic of early childhood—what Piaget calls the subjective and the objective—must be overcome before the end of the latency period. Healthy ego development during latency greatly facilitates the acquisition of basic knowledge and skills in school and contributes to the mastery of the environment, a major achievement of the latency period. The ego functions are also becoming increasingly resistant to regression and disorganization during latency (Blos, 1962: 57) and hence—if all goes well—provide the necessary strength to deal effectively with the increase in drive intensity that will occur during the period of puberty.

During latency the body continues to grow at a fairly even and stable rate, without any dramatic changes in body configuration or body sensations. The growth in physical stature makes possible greater physical mobility and independence and provides the somatic basis for increasing mastery of the environment. There is now a decline in the expressive use of the body, for increased verbal facility results in separation of verbal expression from motor activity (Blos, 1962: 55). In general, the unself-conscious body spontaneity and body expressiveness of the younger child declines during latency, a decline that leads to the high degree of self-consciousness, body awareness, physical awkwardness, and body preoccupation observed during adolescence.

The latency period is relatively free of intrapsychic conflicts, especially if the conflicts surrounding the Oedipus complex during the phallic stage have been successfully resolved. During latency the boy represses the remaining oedipal attachments more successfully than the girl, rendering entry into latency somewhat more conflictual. For girls, the transition is smoother since the oedipal issues linger on and become part of the emotional life of latency; the oedipal conflicts do not require repression or a definitive conclusion but may actually continue into adolescence (Blos, 1962: 55).

Intrapsychic development is characterized by increasing ego autonomy and ego maturity, reducing conflict between id, ego, and superego. Thus, a successful latency provides the strength for successful conflict resolution in adolescence and contributes to the development of tolerance in handling conflictual and painful experiences. Deficits in ego development during latency make the later resolution of adolescent conflicts difficult, if not impossible, and may impede the "adolescent process."

PREADOLESCENCE

With the beginning of preadolescence, also referred to as prepuberty, the most significant change is a pronounced increase in the energy level of pubertal drive, both libidinal and aggressive (Blos, 1941: 196–197). This drive is still quite diffuse and not yet focused on one specific love object or an instinctual aim but rather is experienced as general tensions that demand to be discharged. These instinctual tensions manifest themselves in restlessness, moodiness, and an increase in aggression. Preadolescence typically is the time when delinquent behavior begins. The aim of the drive is still diffuse—literally anything can become sexually stimulating: fear, shock, anger, or general excitement, even if void of erotic content (Blos, 1962: 57). Girls during this stage often appear "horse crazy," and boys are more preoccupied with "dirty jokes" than with sex. The push toward genital organization is counterbalanced by a strong regressive movement toward infantile modalities—oral (overeating, oral greediness); anal (preoccupation with buttocks and the process of elimination); phallic (sadism) (Blos, 1970: 22). Traits such as smuttiness, neglect of body care, gluttony, and motor excitability emerge at this stage. The effects of the increase in drive energy manifest themselves in a growing intensity of affect, making for unpredictability and uncontrollability of affective responses (Blos, 1979: 195).

> Temper tantrums, day dreams, bragging, swaggering, sulking and weeping, lying, cheating—these are the reactions of the small child faced by powers too strong for him, and these are the defenses to which he returns when the strains of adolescence are more than he can face. As temporary reactions they are usual and entirely to be expected at this time. Many types of behavior which would be considered dangerously neurotic during adulthood or middle childhood must be viewed as normal during the preadolescent period [Blos, 1941: 280].

The loss of responsiveness to parental control, already begun in late latency, continues. The preadolescent begins to withdraw from the family group, simultaneously entering the gang stage (Blos, 1941: 236–237). Parents often react with ambivalent feelings to this new attitude, revealing not only anger and resentment but also acceptance and support. Their inconsistency contributes further to the disturbance of adolescent-parent relationships. "Puberty constitutes a period of intensified stress and, as a consequence, it readily exposes certain inadequacies of psychic structure that were previously either nonexistent or seemingly irrelevant" (Blos, 1970: 9).

In preadolescence the demands for gratification of the increased instinctual tension meets the disapproval of the ego and the superego and thus introduces a disequilibrium in the psychic structure. Various mechanisms of defense are drawn on by the ego in order to deal with the tension between id and superego: repression, reaction formation, and displacement. (For definitions and illustrations of the various defense mechanisms, see Chapter 3.) In addition, there is "the revival of such primitive defenses as magical thinking, projection and denial, as well as all kinds of obsessive-compulsive traits, habits and thoughts" (Blos, 1970: 71). An illustration of reaction formation is the preadolescent boy who develops antagonism toward the opposite sex; he has no use for attention from his mother and avoids close contacts with females in general. The restructuring of the preadolescent ego is best characterized by the contradictory emotions: "the desire to go ahead," and "the fear of losing familiar ground" (Blos, 1970: xxi).

A qualitative maturational shift takes place with the beginning of pubescence and "pubertal maturation remains the biological initiator of adolescence" (Blos, 1971: 962). Some of the psychological restructuring of preadolescence actually precedes the physical changes of pubescence.

The conflict of preadolescence emerges out of the changes in somatic maturation. The sudden increase in sex drive upsets the balance between ego and id and manifests itself in castration anxiety for boys and renewed penis envy in girls (Blos, 1962). Anxiety and worry about the possibility of injury to the sex organs is not at all uncommon, emerging partly from castration anxiety, and partly from guilt feelings as an accompanying emotion of masturbatory behavior.

The direction of psychosexual development, as well as the developmental time schedules of the two sexes, begins to take different routes with the onset of puberty. The spurt of physical development in girls takes place earlier; girls during puberty are actually more mature than boys, perform better in school, are superior in social development, show more mature interest patterns, and are superior to boys in introspection.

With the onslaught of pubescence, there is a rejection of the opposite sex, who are treated with derision and contempt. Instead, there is a turning toward the same-sex peer group. Sex differences in physical development are most pronounced at a time when the individual experiences a "heightened group- and self-consciousness" (Blos, 1941: 231), which has a significant influence on the social adjustment and the intellectual and emotional development of the adolescent.

During preadolescence and early adolescence, the boy directs his aggressive impulses and his castration fears primarily toward his mother but also toward females in general; actual conflicts with the father reach a low point. As a defensive reaction against castration fear, the boy shows an exaggerated idealization and aggrandizement of his father. During this negative passive oedipal phase of early puberty, it is the castrating mother rather than the father who is feared and avoided.

Preadolescent boys fear and even dream of what Blos refers to as the "phallic castrating, preoedipal mother" and develop a defense against female sexuality. During this phase boys may actually be repulsed by advances from the opposite sex, including affection from their mothers. The same-sex peer group provides a masculine identification and moral support, but at the price of conforming to its standard and values. Same-sex friendships often involve shared secrets, intimacies, and erotically tinted homosexual attractions and experiences. Preadolescent boys avoid girls (Blos, 1962: 60), belittle them, and have no use for female sentimentality, "affection, endearment and amorousness"

(Blos, 1979: 121). Fondling, kissing, protecting, and punishing by the mother is frowned upon and avoided, especially when it might be seen by peer-group members.

Only later, during adolescence proper, with the reemergence of the positive aggressive Oedipus complex (about age fourteen to seventeen) does the hostile-aggressive impulse once more turn against the father and the sexual impulses toward the mother.

The female, as she enters the negative oedipal conflict of puberty, encounters a complex crisis, especially in relationship with her mother. Underlying this conflict is a fear of passivity, which stems from the girl's earlier relationship to her mother during the negative Oedipus complex in the phallic stage. As a defense against her fear of passivity and infantile dependency, she tends to overidentify with the male and aggressively turns toward the opposite sex. She "exaggerates her heterosexual desires and attaches herself to boys" (Blos, 1979: 110), and in the process she becomes either the "tomboy" or "the little woman." Attachments of this nature are defensive reactions against the pull toward passive, infantile dependencies and should be considered a necessary step in the movement toward mature femininity (Blos, 1980). Such heterosexual interest can lead to actual sexual involvement, which at this age lacks genuine personal-affectionate intimacy, in spite of the experience of passion. Blos, speaking of this thrust toward activity, refers to the preadolescent girl as being "boy crazy" and being an Amazon, pushing the boy into heterosexual social activities for which he is emotionally unprepared and in which he is not yet interested (Blos, 1962; 1979).

Girls are inclined to make demands on boys that boys cannot meet adequately and that merely force the boys into stronger defensiveness. As a result girls are likely to encounter defeat in their first heterosexual advances toward boys of their age group (Blos, 1941: 250–251).

If the girl should succumb to the regressive pull toward passivity during this stage, her drive orientation would more closely resemble that of the boy, since she too would experience homosexual yearnings and an antagonism toward the male.

EARLY ADOLESCENCE

Early adolescence, or early puberty, distinguishes itself from preadolescence by a higher degree of goal orientation of the libidinal drive and an increase in aggressive drive. The new goal consists of a beginning movement toward libidinous extrafamilial object finding, resulting in a more intense, richer, emotional life. With the onset of puberty, identification with parents declines rapidly and is replaced by an identification with others through friendship, admiration, hero-worship, idealization, crushes, and infatuations. This developmental pattern of a frequently strong identification with parents and parental figures during childhood (latency), followed by a stage of identification with glamorized and romanticized persons during adolescence, and culminating in the identification with an imaginary character who is a composite of many desirable qualities during late adolescence has been demonstrated empirically (Engelman, 1962; Havighurst and Mac-Donald, 1955). These early adolescent identifications frequently have an erotic undertone; however, the libidinal love objects of early adolescence are not necessarily heterosexual in nature, since a strong bisexual tendency still prevails. The newly emerging drive manifests itself in "crushes" on sports and entertainment heroes of both sexes, people often considerably older than the adolescent.

Friendships with members of the same sex similarly take on an idealized quality, show a high degree of intimacy, which thrives on secrecy and may become eroticized and sexualized.

> The phase of early adolescence is the time of friendship (still confined to the same sex) with unmistakably erotic overtones, either attenuated or more or less consciously experienced. Mutual masturbation, transient homosexual practices, mutually granted scotophilic gratification, shared transgression or crimes, idealization, feelings of bliss and elation in the presence of a friend—these are experiences in which the narcissistic object choice is manifested [Blos, 1965: 161].

The increase in the libidinal drive and the strong clash between the id and the superego during early adolescence leaves the ego weakened, inefficient, and fumbling, because, even though independent from parental authority and control, the ego has also lost its legitimate support from the parental ego. In order to cope with the increasing internal conflicts with parents, which grew out of the oedipal situation and the reorganization of the emotional life—creating a feeling of chaos—the ego draws on various mechanisms of defense and "the gap between the ego and the superego" widens (Blos, 1962: 76).

Blos maintains that the continuing maturation of the pubertal drive toward heterosexual genitality eventually pushes the individual out of the preadolescent phase. In the male particularly there is a noticeable increase in masturbatory behavior and, while it produces tension reduction and drive gratification, the dynamic meaning relates to counteracting castration anxiety and fear of homosexuality, which are still prevalent during this stage of strong bisexual tendencies. "The adolescent boy's defensive reaction toward passive homosexual strivings or fantasies far exceeds in intensity anything we witness in an adolescent girl who might sense or become aware of lesbian feelings" (Blos, 1980: 10).

The conflicts of early adolescence emerge from the bisexual nature that still prevails during that developmental phase. Early adolescence is a state of chaos and conflict, since the newly emerging goal in drive orientation requires abandoning homosexual and bisexual tendencies, resulting in a total reorganization of the libidinal drive and the emotional life. This qualitative change in drive orientation toward genitality requires the preoedipal and oedipal love objects be given up in favor of nonincestuous love objects. This process requires a detachment from parental dependencies and is often accompanied by outright conflict. "The conflict seems to focus on the mother and 'severance action' is required to resolve the passive dependency on the mother." At the same time the still-prevalent bisexual tendencies produce conflict in drive organization. In order to progress to the next higher stage, these tendencies will need to be replaced by a heterosexual orientation. The beginning of a sexual identity during early adolescence is the prerequisite to adolescence proper, which is based on a heterosexual orientation (Blos, 1970: 171). However, heterosexual orientation does not imply premarital sexual intercourse. Blos warns that too early a sexual initiation may interfere with ego development and the growth toward emotional maturity. Some empirical support for this assertion comes from the Jessor and Jessor (1975) study demonstrating that the transition from a virginal to a nonvirginal state, when it occurs already in early adolescence, is commonly associated with a variety of deviant behaviors.

ADOLESCENCE PROPER

Adolescence proper, or middle adolescence, is characterized by a decline in bisexuality and a further modification in drive organization, which involves an intensification of the sexual drive as well as the aggressive drive. Libido is now directed toward new love objects; that is, the goal of the drive is heterosexual object finding. The recognition of the heterosexual tendencies of this phase requires both a separation from the family of origin and a new and final resolution of the positive oedipal conflict (Blos, 1962). This is a period of psychological restructuring (Blos, 1979), of chaos, of mood swings, of turmoil and crisis, of experimentation, and it manifests itself in the unpredictable, vacillating, and rebellious behavior typical of adolescents. Hence Blos uses the expression "proverbial adolescence" to characterize this period.

At about fourteen or fifteen, sometimes sooner or later, the pattern seems to shift. The child is still an unstable, moody, and rather unpredictable person—battling with adult authority and with himself—overanxious, self-conscious, and overconfident by turns, apparently sophisticated but frequently only on the verbal level, desperately wanting help and guidance but often quite unable to ask for it or accept it from those he likes best. Yet in many ways he is much more grown up than he was and much easier to teach. By this time his interest in the opposite sex is ordinarily open and frankly expressed. He is as meticulous about appearance and manners as he was careless a few years before; he is clean and more orderly again and considerably more responsible [Blos, 1941: 272].

Adolescence proper is not only a period of heightened turmoil and crisis but also a period of heightened ego experiences. The ego rather than restraining and diverting the libido, as in the two preceding stages, now joins the libido in its movement toward heterosexual object finding. This process involves a disengagement from the earlier family object ties and immature dependencies, a resolution of the second, positive Oedipus complex, and a movement toward heterosexuality.

Oedipal wishes and their attending conflicts come to life again. The finality of this inner break with the past shakes the adolescent's emotional life to the center; by the same token, this break opens up to him unknown horizons, raises hopes, and generates fears [Blos, 1962: 88].

The developmental task of this period is the emotional disengagement from parents. "The definitive resolution of the [Oedipus] complex is the inherent task of adolescence" (Blos, 1979: 325). The resolution of the pubertal Oedipus complex implies a distinct turn toward the achievement of a sexual identity and independence.

Somatic maturation continues into adolescence proper, also referred to as advanced puberty. With the movement away from bisexuality and toward heterosexual object finding, sexuality now becomes sensitive to stimuli that are exclusively heterosexual—erotic in nature—in contrast to the more diffuse and global expression in the nature of the jokes that fascinate early adolescents. Jokes, anal in content in the preceding stages, now reveal a distinct sexual and erotic flavor. Concurrent with this change in sexual sensitivity is the newly emerging experience of tender love, affection, devotion, and deep-burning emotions, as well as the idealization of the heterosexual love object.

However, as a counterforce restraining the movement toward extrafamilial heterosexual love, there is a fear of a new dependency on the love object especially at this point when the dependence on parents is just beginning to decline (Blos, 1962: 101). The adolescent often expresses this conflict by stating that he is fearful of getting "too involved," or "going too far" with his heterosexual love object. He is fearful of love and new dependencies because he is just beginning to escape from the intense emotional involvement with his parents. Anna Freud and Otto Rank speak of the adolescent's defense mechanisms of asceticism, intellectualization, and promiscuity as being based on the fear of a new emotional dependency on a heterosexual partner when dependency conflicts with parents are still lingering on. Even the striving for independence from parents is not without some ambivalence, since it not only contains a strong desire for adult freedom and independence but also an unacknowledged wish for childlike dependence and parental protection coupled with fear of loss of security and adult guidance. "The wish for independence augments the feeling of loss and of security as derived from the infantile parent image. The price of independence is the tolerance of loneliness, as well as the acceptance of personal limitations and of the temporality of life" (Blos, 1970: 235).

The pubertal conflicts that began in preadolescence and early adolescence find their climax in the turmoil and the chaos of adolescence proper. The oedipal wishes reemerge once more, this time in their active positive form, which means that for the boy the active libidinal drive turns toward the mother and the aggressive, hostile impulses turn toward the father. Oedipal wishes emerging from the id collide with the superego when confronted with a relatively weak ego and increase internal conflicts. Guilt feelings and anxieties grow out of these oedipal desires. Oedipal thoughts, which are unacceptable to the superego, constitute the typical internal conflict of adolescence proper.

Somatic maturation, which reaches its peak during adolescence proper, not only intensifies the libidinal drive but also increases "the aggressive drive in equal measures." The aggressive drive manifests itself in quarrelsomeness and emerges in dreams and fantasies, including those of murder and suicide. "Aggression turns against the self, the object, or the nonhuman environment, indicating a fateful imbalance or defusion of the two basic drives" (Blos, 1979: 24). The reduction in bisexuality in drive orientation, which was characteristic of the earlier adolescent phases, contributes now to its very opposite—namely, a pronounced polarity of masculinity and femininity. Research evidence actually suggests that sex role conceptualizations, including sex role stereotyping, especially in terms of the opposite sex ideal, seem to reach their height in adolescence (Urberg, 1979).

LATE ADOLESCENCE

Drive organization during late adolescence continues to focus on heterosexual object finding and becomes more permanently entrenched in that position; however, some of the chaos, turmoil, reorganization, and restructuring that characterized adolescence proper has by now subsided. The ego emerges strengthened from the chaos of adolescence proper and begins to achieve a more stable and lasting organizational structure. A new character synthesis begins to take place; the sexual identity is more firmly entrenched and becomes irreversible. There is a consolidation of social roles and personal identifications, which gives this phase its descriptive title, "personality consolidation." Blos identifies the developmental task of late adolescence as the "elaboration of a unified ego" and the achievement of a "stable ego organization," terms highly reminiscent of Erikson's notion of the achievement of an ego identity. "During normal adolescence the growing child uses his advanced cognitive faculty and somatic maturity to gain emotional, moral, and physical independence. This is a time when he forms his own view of his past, present, and future" (Blos, 1979: 415). As the ego stabilizes there is decline in the experience of inner crisis, and many of the conflicts, the disorganizations, and the disunity that were so prevalent in the previous phase of development suddenly begin to decline (Blos, 1962).

The new ego organization is reflected in an integrated personality pattern in which id, ego, and superego are no longer in an adversary relationship. A more harmonious and cooperative personality structure is established in which both the id and superego serve the purpose of the ego. Now the individual is able to conduct various daily interactions with the social and physical environment and satisfy basic needs within socially prescribed boundaries.

One major change in the tripartite structure of the id, ego, and superego takes place during late adolescence. According to psychoanalytic theory, the superego develops primarily after the resolution of the phallic-oedipal situation during latency. The function of the superego is that of prohibition (moral conscience). It sets boundaries and punishes the ego for transgressions through guilt and anxiety. As a result of the resolution of the pubertal-oedipal situation, the superego differentiates itself further, and the ego-ideal emerges as a new structure within the superego. The ego-ideal attains a clear and definitive structure within the superego during late adolescence. "The ego ideal becomes the heir to the regulatory function of the superego" (Blos, 1962: 152). It contains not only an individual component but a social component as well (Blos, 1979). It becomes the agency of aspiration and wish fulfillment, and its function is to set goals, to punish by shame and by lowering self-esteem.

The model of stages of ego development advanced by Loevinger (1966; 1976) does not readily fit Blos' theory of adolescent development since Loevinger challenges both the clinical-psychoanalytic conceptualizations of ego development as well as the ego constructs emerging out of more narrowly defined research endeavors. However, her stage five, defined as the conscientious stage, implies that morality has been internalized and that long-term goals and personal ideals have begun to emerge. The imperatives emerging from internalized moral values now take precedence over conformity to values sanctioned by the peer group. Loevinger's conceptualizations—not without some empirical support—appear to be quite analogous to the psychoanalytic notion of the ego-ideal and the conscience emerging out of the structure of the superego in the late adolescent phase. The differentiation of the superego into conscience and ego-ideal in psychoanalytic theory also appears to be a necessary prerequisite for the attainment of stage five (social contract orientation) and stage Six (universal ethical principles orientation) in Kohlberg's theory of moral development (see Chapter 11).

The ego-ideal aims for perfection and sets goals that can never be fully attained; however, even the striving for perfection produces a sense of well-being. The ego must maintain a careful balance between the narcissistic internal self-idealization and the formation of realistic external ideals. The new ego-ideal of late adolescence is behind "the proclivity of youth for high ideals, for idealizations and ideologies" (Blos, 1979: 320), including not uncommon personal vocational goals that lie beyond resources and/or capabilities. A recent Project Talent (Flanagan, 1979) investigation indicates, for example, that of those twelfth-grade boys who planned a career in law, 41 percent had academic aptitude scores below the overall average; similarly, of those who planned a career in mathematics, 33 percent scored below average in academic aptitude.

Late adolescence sees the resolution of instinctual conflicting tendencies that contributed to the turmoil and the chaotic disorganization of adolescence proper. Somatic maturation comes to completion during late adolescence, sexual needs reach their peak, and according to Kinsey, even "sexual outlets" reach an all-time high for the male adolescent. Drive and ego now combine in the search for a heterosexual love object, reducing ambiguous and conflictual emotions in the search for identifications and intimacies outside the family of origin (Blos, 1979).

Late adolescence is the consolidation phase of adolescent development during which most conflicts are resolved. The sexual identity takes on a final form and is no longer easily reversible. There is a gain in purposeful actions, behavior becomes predictable, self-esteem acquires stability, and emotions gain constancy. Recreational, avocational, vocational, and devotional commitments and preferences emerge with greater stability (Blos, 1962).

POSTADOLESCENCE

Postadolescence marks the transitional phase between adolescence and adulthood and brings to completion the ultimate goal of the adolescent process, namely, the establishment of a stable drive organization that is in harmony with the ego organization and ushers in the final achievement of a stable self. Because self and object representation have developed firmer boundaries (Blos, 1979: 118), self-esteem becomes more constant and more stable. Self-esteem is less vulnerable to manipulation from outside sources and has come under control of the ego-ideal. Confronted with defeat, failure, or criticism, the ego, seeing itself now as separate from the ego-ideal, does not use rationalizations as defenses; it can nondefensively identify the boundaries between personal responsibility, situational circumstances, and unrealistic goals and can admit to errors and personal shortcomings. The completion of the adolescent crisis results in a more stable personality structure, and individuals can now reject false evaluations that do not correspond with their own self-evaluations (Gruen, 1960). Feelings become more consistent as a stable sense of self leads to a greater certainty about one's own personality characteristics, and there is a noticeable reduction in anxiety (Bronson, 1959).

The developmental task already begun during adolescence proper and late adolescence—that is, the attainment of identification, loyalties, and intimacies outside of the family of origin—becomes more urgent and more dominant at this point. With clearer boundaries established between self and object representation, the rebellious and conflictual elements that prevailed in these earlier phases subside and the adolescent's perception of the parents becomes more realistic, acknowledging, and accepting of positive as well as negative attributes. There are no more developmental road blocks to nonincestuous heterosexual object finding.

During postadolescence, the stabilizing tendencies of successful conflict resolution contribute to character formation. The ego has now become heir to the idealized parent of childhood. The adaptive and integrative functions of the ego continue to grow. What emerges during postadolescence is the moral personality, firmly anchored in society; there is a renewed experimentation with ego interests and with potential love objects. Postadolescence sees the emergence of a clearer conception of social roles, a sense of purpose, and a sense of direction (Blos, 1962).

EDUCATIONAL IMPLICATIONS

Blos recognizes the historical trend toward earlier physiological development and sexual maturation, described in more detail by Muuss (1970a), Tanner (1968), and others, but he remains dubious that the earlier sexual maturation of today's youth is accompanied by a corresponding acceleration in emotional, social, moral, and cognitive maturation. Hence, he warns that parents, schools, and other institutions should not simply allow and encourage this downward extension of adolescent heterosexual behavior under the rationalization of the typical American preoccupation with "the earlier and the faster, the bigger and the better." On the contrary, he feels that social institutions should retain their protective and containing functions rather than supporting or even rewarding this trend toward earlier and earlier heterosexual interest and involvement.

In addition, the physical and sexual maturation of boys and girls proceeds—as has been demonstrated by Tanner and others—according to very different time schedules. The earlier-maturing girls may make demands on boys, for which the less mature boys are totally unprepared. Because of these well-known sex differences in onset and speed of social-sexual development, the general acceleration of sexual development, the direction of sexual orientation, and the nature of conflict at the preadolescent and early adolescent phase (from the ages of about eleven to fourteen), Blos seriously suggests "that the separation of the sexes in school during these early years [not during the entire adolescent period] is, psychologically and biologically, well advised" (Blos, 1971: 970). During these years, when sex differences in intellectual, physical, social, and psychological development are most pronounced, boys and girls are poorly matched companions in work and play. Even Mead has expressed ideas quite similar to those of Blos: "The junior high school has become a forcing ground for inappropriate and socially maladjusted attitudes in boys and girls, laying the basis for hostility to females on the boys' part . . ." (Mead, 1961: 38). Blos, instead of identifying hostility as the crucial outcome, speaks of this situation as forcing boys into "stronger defensiveness." He continues his argument by pointing out that those boys who do develop a precocious preference for girls and bypass the strong identification with their own sex, experience more concern about the adequacy of their own masculinity later in life while preadolescent and early adolescent boys who keep the company of boys of their own age seem to establish a firmer and more lasting masculine identity. Similarly, Blos views early sexual intercourse as severely interfering with the normal developmental and preparatory functions characteristic of this stage.

We have ample evidence that an acceptance of the young adolescent as a self-directing, sexually active "young person" interferes severely with the preparatory functions of this stage. We can say that ego building at this time augurs more promisingly for the attainment of maturity than the early adolescent striving for a full sex life [Blos, 1971: 970].

Evidence for the assertion that frequent sexual intercourse during early adolescence interferes with ego development and is often associated with numerous other psychosocial problems emerges from such varied sources as Jessor and Jessor (1975), Loevinger (1976), and a summary review by Muuss (1982).

One rather novel, insightful, and quite significant educational implication emerges from Blos' writings in regard to parents' methods of discipline, their socialization efforts, and their teaching of values. Blos calls into question the contemporary preoccupation with, and the all-too-ready absorption of, so-called expert advice by parents and educators. Blos maintains that with the gradual but radical change in family structure and with the increasing significance of the mass media and commercialism, advertising and continuing education, the traditions of families in matters of childrearing, nutrition, learning expectations, values, manners, and moral stringencies have become replaced by a superabundance of so-called expert advice. Such expert advice flows freely and continuously into the home via newspapers, TV, magazines, books, lectures, films, PTA, and even church meetings. Thus, expert advice has or is in the process of replacing established family traditions.

However, the various forms of expert advice are not based on a systematic, well-integrated, and uniform system of values; nor do they maintain an underlying coherent philosophy. Quite to the contrary, they come from very different and frequently even contradictory theoretical, philosophical, political, scientific, or religious systems. Furthermore, they often enter the home only in bits and pieces or as simplified and predigested summaries of serious work, presented by newspaper journalists or popular magazine writers. They sometimes support, sometimes contradict, and sometimes replace family tradition. Furthermore, today's expert advice may support, contradict, or replace yesterday's expert advice. Parents faithfully try out what they have heard or read today only to abandon that approach without having reaped the benefits of their efforts, replacing it a few weeks or months later with a quite different approach encountered more recently—one that sounds better or happens to be "in." Parents who too eagerly, or even reluctantly, begin to apply this bewildering jumble of advice to their own offspring thereby "abdicate their personal responsibility in favor of choices made by the expert." In this process parents by necessity surrender their own values and convictions as well as family tradition. "This submission to the expert has drained ever larger sections of parental actions or attitudes of consistency, integration, and integrity" (Blos, 1971: 972).

Childrearing has become "synthetic" and often inconsistent; hence, it is no wonder that parents have become confused and children unresponsive. Blos feels rather strongly that this strange mixture of so-called scientific advice concerning all areas of childrearing has itself become a major problem, contributing to family disorganization, alienation, ineffective childrearing practices, and unresponsive and recalcitrant children. Children, in turn, as soon as they can read and understand what is being said, get plugged into the expert advice circuit themselves and, as adolescents, pick out ideas and advice contradictory to that put forth by their parents. Thus, at an age when it is natural for adolescents to question and challenge parental values, adolescents quote expert advice on marijuana, smoking, dating, fashion, and sex to bolster their arguments, exposing their parents as "old-fashioned," "narrow-minded," "past the time," "out of it," or simply authoritarian. All these charges are based on the adolescents' claim that "scientific evidence has shown that . . ."

Schools seem to neglect an important responsibility in not teaching the adolescent about the phenomena of pubescence. It is a well-known fact that during adolescence the variations in somatic maturation are so pronounced that the identification of children by their chrono-logical age is meaningless and sets up the incorrect notion that all twelve-and-a-half-year-old girls are in the same or even a similar stage of development. Actually, half of these girls are premenarcheal and half postmenarcheal; they espouse different values and different interests, prefer different types of activities, and have different degrees of feminine identification. The picture would be further complicated if one were to introduce twelve-and-a-half-year-old boys into the discussion. We know that the physical changes that accompany puberty pose a heavy emotional burden for the adolescent who is behind others in physical growth. Furthermore, adolescents are so preoccupied with physical normality that they are disturbed even by minor deviations. However, the adolescent usually does not know that most of these deviations that he observes on his own body and that disturb him are really quite normal. Thus, even minor or imagined deviations can become major psychological problems. The morbid preoccupation with normality, as well as curiosity about the function of sex organs and protection of primary and secondary sex characteristics, is most pronounced during pubescence. Since adolescents usually have little or no scientific basis by which to evaluate the actual adequacy of their own development, many uncertainties and anxieties arise, stemming primarily from furtive comparison with peers and peers' teasing comments, especially in the shower room. Any deviation from the "group average" can become a matter of concern and a source of worry. The emotional impact is magnified greatly when development does not progress in a sex-appropriate fashion—for example, when there are such sex-inappropriate characteristics as breast development or a feminine physique in boys, not at all uncommon during early adolescence. Boys especially are disturbed by such deviation from the normal course of development, even though most of these developmental "deviances" fall well within the normal range and are frequently only temporary. Such physical deviations negatively influence adolescents' social and emotional responsiveness and their general attitude toward themselves and toward life (Blos, 1941: 233). As a defense, during this phase an exaggerated preoccupation with maleness and masculinity emerges in boys. Some of the emotional significance of these well-known facts of very pronounced individual variations in the pubescent growth pattern and even the normality and the temporary quality of some sex-inappropriate secondary sex characteristics could be alleviated, or at least reduced, through a well-timed educational program devoted to the psychological significance of the physiological changes during early adolescence.

6: CULTURAL ANTHROPOLOGY AND ADOLESCENCE

DURING the late 1920s a number of systematic anthropological field studies of primitive societies opened a new area of thinking about personality development, the socialization process, and human instincts. Two books by Margaret Mead (1901–1978), *Coming of Age in Samoa* (1950) and *Growing Up in New Guinea* (1953), are relevant to a discussion of adolescence. We will be concerned primarily with the former book, since it is devoted entirely to the adolescent period.

The findings of cultural anthropology constitute a serious challenge to earlier theoretical propositions—especially those of G. Stanley Hall and Sigmund Freud—that held that certain important patterns in the development and behavior of human beings are universal and part of human nature. Since relatively little was known about the social structure of primitive societies prior to these anthropological investigations, earlier theories of adolescence had too readily assumed that the pattern of development found in the most widely studied Western cultures was universal. On the other hand, cultural anthropologists were stimulated in their theorizing and in their investigations by hypotheses derived from psychoanalysis. Consequently, the reciprocal influence of more recent psychoanalytic theory and cultural anthropology has been fruitful and stimulating. The theoretical ideas of these two schools of thought have actually converged to a rather remarkable extent during the past decade. Mutual recognition and research evidence have produced the emergence of theoretical ideas in which the extreme positions of environmental determinism and genetic universalism have yielded to a composite position in which biogenetic factors and environmental forces are weighed more carefully and recognized as mutually interacting. Comparing writings of Erikson (1950) and Mead (1961) we find a degree of accord that one could not have imagined when comparing early psychoanalytic theory with the writings of cultural anthropologists in the late 1920s and early 1930s. However, in order to facilitate an understanding of the controversial arguments in their historical perspective, we will first consider the early anthropological position.

BENEDICT'S THEORY OF CULTURAL CONDITIONING

Coming of Age in Samoa is a field study; it uses anthropological methodology, but does not contain an explicitly stated theory of adolescent development. However, Ruth Benedict (1887–1948), in "Continuities and Discontinuities in Cultural Conditioning" (1954/1980), does provide us with an explicit theory of development from a cultural anthropological point of view. This theory of cultural conditioning relates directly to Mead's study of adolescence in Samoa. By combining the theoretical writings of Benedict with the empirical study by Mead, we derive a systematic statement concerning the importance of cultural factors in the developmental process. "Cultural relativism"— a term more appropriate to the earlier than to the later writings of Mead— contributes new and important ideas to the understanding of the phenomenon of adolescence. It emphasizes the importance of social institutions and cultural factors in human development and describes the rituals of pubescence as well as adolescent experiences in primitive societies.

Human beings show far greater plasticity and modifiability than lower animals. This accounts for the progress the human species has made as well as for the wide intercultural differences. The biological constitution of man does not determine particular patterns of behavior; germ cells do not transmit culture. Few, if any, human traits are universal; even if there are universal traits, they may not be biogenetically determined. An early form of learned behavior— Benedict (1950) calls it a "cradle trait"—may have become a universal institution, for example, exogamous restriction on marriage.

Benedict (1980) offers a theoretical means of relating the way of life of a given culture to the growth and development of individual personality. She sees growth as a gradual, continuous process. Newborn infants depend on other people for survival. From this infantile dependence, they must grow into a state of relative independence; as adults they will have to provide for and protect offspring who then will be dependent on them. The pattern by which the child obtains independence varies from one culture to another. In some cultures, such as the American, the difference between a child and an adult is emphasized sharply by social and legal institutions. The change from one mode of interpersonal relationship to another creates discontinuity in the growth process. Lewin (to be discussed in Chapter 7) also accounted for adolescent difficulties in terms of the existing dichotomy between children and adults.

One example of this discontinuity in our society is the emphasis on the sexless nature of the child as contrasted with the sexual orientation of adults. The child never, or rarely, sees childbirth, sexual intercourse, and death; pregnancy is camouflaged, evacuation veiled with prudery, breastfeeding hidden, and some girls menstruate the first time without knowing what it is all about. The child gets very incomplete information about the life cycle of the sexes.

In contrast, the Samoan child follows a relatively continuous growth pattern. Youth has an opportunity to see birth and death near home, and many have seen a partly developed fetus, the opening of dead bodies, and occasional glimpses of sex activities. The child is not considered basically different from the adult. Sex life is not repressed or inhibited by society but is considered natural and pleasurable. Perversion, homosexuality, promiscuity, and other sexual activities, which because of their social and moral stigma divert emotional development toward neuroses in American society and may result in unsatisfactory marriage, are relatively harmless in Samoa; they are considered "simply play" and are without moral stigma. In Samoan society, most experiences follow a relatively gradual, continuous line of development without severe interruptions or restrictions. By contrast, in Western society many experiences that are approved for adults are restricted or forbidden to children. Attitudes, values, and skills that children have learned must be unlearned when they become adults.

Benedict discusses three specific aspects of discontinuity versus continuity in cultural conditioning. The major changes in Western society occur during adolescence. They are:

1. Responsible versus nonresponsible status role
2. Dominance versus submission
3. Contrasted sexual role (Benedict, 1980: 15).

The difference between continuous and discontinuous behavior in development from nonresponsible to responsible status can be demonstrated by the issue of work and play. In American society, especially in urban areas, work and play are considered separate and distinct. A child makes no important labor contributions to society; he is even forbidden by law to do so. But when young men and women reach maturity, they must compete on an equal basis with older adults. In some societies, development from a nonresponsible to a responsible status role is much more gradual. Play and work are not necessarily separated; they often involve the same activities. Among the Cheyenne Indians, a boy receives a bow and arrow at birth. As he grows, the bows are increased in size. His first contribution of a snow bird to the family meal is celebrated as a feast. The boy's contribution is valued even if his father brings home a buffalo. Nor does his status change when he finally brings home a buffalo himself.

In Samoa, the girls, sometimes only six or seven years old, are responsible for caring for and disciplining the younger siblings. Thus, each girl is socialized and develops responsibility by her early involvement in family duties. The boys at an early age learn the simple tasks of reef fishing and canoeing while the girls, after they are released from their duties as nursemaids for their younger brothers and sisters, work on plantations and help carry food to the village. No basic change takes place during the adolescent period; the degree of responsibility increases, and the amount and quality of work increases as the child grows stronger and matures. In our society—especially in urban and suburban communities—the shift from nonresponsible play to responsible work generally occurs during adolescence as a rather sudden shift. It creates a conflict in the adolescent since it requires a redefinition of essential roles.

The difference between submission and dominance is even more extreme in our culture. The child must drop his childhood submission and adopt its very opposite—dominance—in adulthood. Submission to parental authority is often enforced by emotional attachments that are hard to break later. Our emphasis on respect for parents and elders creates strong elements of discontinuity, since the submissive child must himself become a dominant parent.

During adolescence, a rather sudden shift takes place from submission to dominance. Frequently only a short time elapses between the adolescent's leaving home and founding his own family. At times this change is consciously experienced as a discontinuity by the adolescent who is ready to leave home, but who has received little training for independence. According to Erikson (1950), it is "Mom" who accentuates the difference between child and adult status to the extent that young men and women feel ill prepared for life. In contrast, some primitive societies have patterns of continuous conditioning in respect to submission-dominance. Benedict reports a case among the Crow Indians in which a father boasted "about his young son's intractability even when it was the father himself who was flouted; 'He will be a man,' his father said. He would have been baffled at the idea that his child should show behavior which would obviously make him appear a poor creature in the eyes of his fellows if he used it as an adult" (Benedict, 1980: 17). In Samoan society the seven-year-old girl dominates her younger siblings as their nursemaid, but she herself may still be under the dominance of older sisters. As the child becomes older, she dominates and must discipline younger children while she in turn is restricted and disciplined by older children. If a youth gets into conflict with his parents, he simply moves to his uncle's house or village without social, moral, or emotional stigma. Parents have only limited influence over their children; discipline is always the job of an older sibling. As a result, Samoan society does not know the intensely emotional conflict between dominance and submission that often erupts during adolescence in our society.

A most important discontinuity in the life cycle is the fact that the child must assume a sexual role leading to parenthood. Benedict does not deny that the contrasting sex role has an important biological source in the distinction between sterility before pubescence and fertility after maturation is reached. However, whether the contrasted sex roles of child and adult are experienced as continuous or discontinuous is not determined by physiological maturation but by social institutions, since they channel and alter the influence of the physiological factors. Our culture emphasizes the discontinuity of the sexual role. Childhood sexual experiences are frowned on and restricted, and sex is considered wicked. Until marriage, virginity and sexual abstinence are upheld as social ideals. But on the wedding night, sexual responsiveness is expected. Clinical evidence shows that the young bride frequently cannot make a good sexual adjustment after marriage because she has failed to unlearn the "danger" and "evil" of sex that she learned during adolescence. Benedict defines continuity in the sexual role as meaning "that the child is taught nothing it must unlearn later" (Benedict, 1980: 18). Mead, in describing the Samoan girl as she grows up, gives an example of a continuous pattern of sex expression; the Samoan girl does not have to unlearn anything about sex. She has the opportunity to experiment and to become familiar with sex with almost no limitations except a rigid taboo against incest. Parental indulgence toward masturbation is common. The postpubescent girl expends "all of her interest . . . on clandestine sex adventures" (Mead, 1950: 31). No sex repression is practiced, and she actually postpones marriage so she can enjoy the carefree adolescent period. Sexual maladjustment in marriage is unknown; psychic impotence does not occur. The adolescent does not experience moral conflicts, and what we call "storm and stress" behavior is hardly known in Samoa.

Benedict (1980) assumes that discontinuity in childrearing necessarily results in emotional strain, whereas cultural conditioning that is continuous in nature is marked by smooth and gradual growth. Societies that emphasize discontinuity of behavior are described as "age-grade societies." In these societies, stages in child development can be observed, since different behavior is demanded by the society at different age levels. Children in a certain age-grade are grouped in formal institutions such as school, Scouts, or informal peer groups. Their activities are organized around those forms of behavior considered appropriate for that age level. Individuals often "graduate" from one stage or age-grade with social recognition and public celebrations.

THE ADOLESCENT GIRL IN SAMOA

Mead is concerned primarily with the adolescent girl. A brief summary of her description of the transition from childhood to adulthood in Samoan society follows. The Samoan pattern of childrearing shows no signs of the extreme discontinuity between childhood and adulthood we see in America. The Samoan child is born into a permissive society, and permissiveness remains an outstanding characteristic. When the child becomes an adult, the demands do not increase very much; they remain continuous with past contributions. The adolescent does not experience any sharp break in activities and social expectations. The personality ideal of Samoa can be described as uncomplaining, cooperative, yielding, avoiding conflict and trouble, with little emphasis on personal prestige and material success. This attitude and the lack of pressure produce comparatively few maladjustments and neuroses.

Life in Samoa is unhurried, casual, and without deep feelings. No one fights for ideals or suffers for convictions. The gifted are held back and the slow coddled; family organization is a matter of expediency and involves no deep emotions and loyalties. The wife may go home to her family and the husband may select a new mate. The injury of adultery can be settled with the exchange of a few mats. Samoan society, in contrast to American society, is homogeneous and, at the time of Mead's study, showed little evidence of social change. Behavioral cues in interpersonal relationships are less ambiguous in Samoa than in more complex societies. In primitive societies, courtship patterns are frequently clearly established. Consequently, a girl in an encounter with boys knows rather clearly what effect her smile will have, how boys will react to her laughing, casting down her eyes, or softly walking past the group. In the United States, such behavior cues have greater ambiguity, and the boys' responses can be predicted with less precision. The girl smiling while passing a group of boys may bring forth a variety of reactions: embarrassment, a casual returning grin, a flirtatious remark, a wolf whistle, a direct advance, or even a follower along the streets—"not because each boy who answers feels differently about the girl, but because each understands differently the cue that she gives" (Mead, 1949: 257). Fewer choices have to be made in Samoa by both the child and the adult, and these choices have less severe consequences and can be reversed more easily. There is only one religion, not dozens as in the United States. There is only one moral standard, which includes very few restrictions. The American adolescent experiences several standards with a multitude of restrictions. One important characteristic is the lack of specialization of feeling in Samoan society. Casual sex relations occur without strong emotional ties and without moral disapproval, but they lack the romantic sentimentality that is so characteristic of adolescent love in Western culture. In Samoa "love and hate, jealousy and revenge, sorrow and bereavement, are all matters of weeks" (Mead, 1950: 132). Disciplining is a matter of convenience; it is not systematic. Punishment is administered by the child-nurse, not by the parent. There is a slow increase in responsibilities and a willingness to accept family duties as the child grows older. The young girl begins her work at six or seven by caring for a younger sibling; as she grows older, she learns to weave firm round balls, make pinwheels of palm leaves, open coconuts, tidy the house, bring water from the sea, spread out the copra, weave, and cook. The boy in a similar fashion learns to fish, plant taro, transplant coconuts, take the canoe over the reef safely, and husk coconuts and cut out their meat.

CULTURAL ANTHROPOLOGY AND SOME THEORETICAL ISSUES

Is adolescence a biological or a psychosocial phenomenon? Cultural anthropologists consistently emphasize the differences in human behavior, social institutions, habits, mores, rituals, and religious beliefs in various societies. Underlying most anthropological research and writing is the assumption that the social environment into which infants are born plays a tremendous role in their personality development. In other words, cultural anthropologists believe in cultural determinism. Since the economic, ideological, and institutional patterns of societies vary widely, we are justified in speaking of cultural relativism. One of Benedict's (1950) objectives was to help people understand relativity in the patterns of culture.

Though cultural anthropologists emphasize social and cultural environment—critics say they overemphasize it (Ausubel, 1954; Sherif and Cantril, 1947)—they do not deny the influence of biological factors. They just disregard them. This can be demonstrated by Mead's comparison of adolescents in primitive and complex societies. "If we lay aside the purely physical definition of maturation and consider adolescence as a period following childhood during which the individual becomes placed in his society, we are struck at once by the enormous difference in range" (Mead, 1952: 538–539). In the earlier writings of Benedict and Mead the physiological aspects of pubescence seem to have been laid aside.

Since cultural anthropologists assume the plasticity of human nature and the importance of social environment, it follows that they do not consider pubescence to be causally related to adolescence. The social nature of adolescence is indicated by statements such as: "At whatever point the society decides to stress a particular adjustment, it will be at this point that adjustment becomes acute to the individual" (Mead, 1952: 537). Comparison of adolescence in various primitive societies demonstrates that adolescent problems can be solved in different ways and at different age levels, or they may not exist at all. It does not seem reasonable to consider these problems inherent in adolescent development. A few examples from the writings of Mead (1952) and Benedict (1950) dealing with the attitudes of various societies toward menstruation will demonstrate this point:

1. Northern California Indian tribes held the attitude that the menstruating girl was dangerous to the village because she could dry up the well and scare the game.
2. The Yuki Indians in North Central California emphasized the goodness of the menstruating girl; their rituals were mainly concerned with the improvement of the crops. By lying quiet, the girl could increase the food supply. They emphasized the resources of society rather than the girl.
3. Among the Thompson Indians a menstruating girl's observance of symbolic rituals and taboos increased her chances for a career and a happy life. She lived in a hut away from other people and performed ritual acts of magic.
4. In the Gilbert Islands the menstruating girl was considered especially prone to enemy magic. By sitting still and facing west, she protected herself from evil.
5. In Samoa no taboos and rituals were connected with menstruation; the girls were not even forbidden to prepare food.
6. The Apache Indian girl's first menstruation was considered a potent supernatural blessing. The priest knelt before her to obtain the blessing of her touch.

These examples demonstrate that physiological maturity, if it is recognized at all, may be recognized in different ways. The social attributes of puberty are part of the traditional cultural pattern.

In the later writings of Mead we find that the earlier extreme position—frequently identified as cultural relativism—has undergone modification and moderation to include some universal aspects of development (Mead prefers to call them "basic regularities") without yielding any of the insight gained from her earlier writings. This new position might best be demonstrated by a few selected quotes from

Male and Female: "there are basic regularities that no known culture has been able to evade" (Mead, 1949: 143). "In all known societies, we find . . . some manifestation of what psychoanalysts call latency . . ." (Mead, 1949: 109). "The child is not only a *tabula rasa*, but a vigorous, maturing organism with modes of behavior appropriate to its age and strength. But it is not a maturing organism in a glass box . . ." (Mead, 1949: 145).

The controversial issue of stages versus continuity is resolved by the view that social environment, institutions, and the specific pattern of cultural conditioning determine whether development takes place in stages or is continuous. A similar position is taken by social learning theory (discussed in Chapter 14). According to Benedict the cycle from infantile dependence to adult independence is "a fact of nature and inescapable" (Benedict, 1980: 14); thus it contains an element of discontinuity. But this transition takes place in different ways in various cultures, so that no one way can be considered natural and universal. In Western cultures society reinforces stages of development by social institutions organized around those stages—grades of school, types of school, and the legal and moral concept of "underage." Graduation from one age level or school to the next brings about socially expected changes in behavior. These changes are frequently discontinuous in nature, especially during adolescence, giving support to a theory of developmental stages. For example, the fourteen-year-old is not allowed to drive a car, whereas the eighteen-year-old is often expected to. If a boy begins dating at ten or eleven, he is considered precocious, and parents become concerned; if he does not date when he is seventeen or eighteen, parents also become concerned, wondering whether his sexual development is normal. In Samoa, the unrestricted, unhurried, and noncompetitive pattern of development allows a continual and gradual development without any actual "graduation" and without any far-reaching disturbances or basic changes in behavior as a function of age.

Cultural anthropology challenges the universality and general validity of any stage theory. "Theories of developmental stages would also suffer serious revision if submitted to primitive tests. Not only the cruder theories of the inevitable stress and strain at physiological puberty, or of a 'collecting stage' go by the boards, but many smaller variations occur" (Mead, 1933: 918).

Mead, in her more recent writings, postulates that menstruation does constitute a dramatic experience and an unmistakable indication of the attainment of a new social status. "The girl's first menstruation marks a dividing-line between childhood and womanhood" (Mead, 1949: 176). For the boy no such specific experience exists, and his pubescence is characterized by a long series of slow developmental changes.

How are cultural and individual differences explained? Mead asserts that personality development is "jointly influenced by heredity, cultural, and individual life-history factors" (Mead, 1942: 55). Cultural anthropologists, even though they do not deny hereditary factors, neglect them in their earlier theoretical consideration and do not supply any systematic concepts by which to incorporate heredity into anthropological theory.

Culture is more homogeneous in primitive societies; one can expect greater similarities in the behavior of adolescents, since they have limited opportunities to make choices. Their behavior can be predicted more easily than that of youths in a modern Western city, whose individual differences would be greater because of (1) heterogeneity of culture, (2) rapidity of cultural change, and (3) diversified cultural and hereditary background. In primitive society, certain forms of behavior can be predicted through knowledge of the cultural pattern; in a modern city the behavior of a given individual is less directly conditioned by the total culture than by more specific subcultural and family patterns. It is better understood through a case-history approach.

Certain patterns of educational practices are related to patterns of personality development in primitive societies. Cultural anthropologists assume considerable homogeneity in the educational pattern of a given primitive society. But anthropological studies have shown that variations exist among different societies in methods of childrearing, forms of cultural conditioning, and the kind of restrictions and limitations enforced upon youth. The particular cultural pattern of childrearing accounts for intercultural differences. Mead (1942) rejects the early psychoanalytic notion that a few outstanding events in childrearing, such as weaning, toilet training, and thumb-sucking, determine character development. She asserts that the total cultural pattern and the nature of social interaction—especially the continuity or discontinuity of cultural conditioning—are the important factors in the development of personality. Specific aspects of childrearing in a culture selected for detailed study by anthropologists are not selected because a preconceived theory assumes that they are determinants of personality, but because they are outstanding and striking features of the given culture. These outstanding patterns of childrearing may be quite different in the socialization process of other societies.

Mead credits biogenetic inheritance with more importance as a determining factor in human development in her later writing than she did in *Coming of Age in Samoa*. Biological inheritance as a developmental factor may help account for considerable variation of intercultural and intracultural differences. Even in highly inbred and isolated groups with a great deal of uniformity in patterns of childrearing, she found remarkable "differences in physique and apparent temperament'' (Mead, 1949: 133). Furthermore, she hypothesizes that the same constitutional types that are found in our society are likely to be found—in different proportions—in most, if not all, societies.

Stimulated by Gesell's growth studies (discussed in Chapter 9). Mead and Macgregor (1951) compared and contrasted the growth pattern and sequence of Balinese infants with the pattern Gesell reported for children in New Haven, confirming some of his findings and challenging others. Mead raises a theoretical question as to the extent to which innate patterns of maturation are interfered with, altered, or supported by cultural factors. Mead's later position appears to deviate from her Samoan findings: ''. . . any alternative to following the developing child's manifestations of its mammalian ancestry and generic humanity, has been conceived as a distortion of the human being by cultural pressures'' (Mead, 1954: 175).

As the more recent psychoanalytic concepts have been expanded to include social determinants, cultural anthropological theory has moved from an early position of ''cultural relativism'' to a broader theoretical position that takes biogenetic factors into consideration. Though the two schools of thought place emphasis on different determinants, they have become highly compatible and complementary.

EDUCATIONAL IMPLICATIONS

Though the Samoan way of life contrasts sharply with life in America as well as with life in ''most primitive civilizations,'' Mead (1950) draws far-reaching conclusions, with important educational implications, from her study of Samoan culture.

In her later writings, Mead includes among the factors responsible for adolescent difficulties in American society ''the contradictions and unevenness of physical puberty'' (Mead, 1961: 37). However, her emphasis is on social factors. Since certain cultural conditions in the United States produce stress, strain, anxiety, and emotional instability in the adolescent, Mead suggests modification of these conditions through social planning.

In complex Western societies, which are characterized by a rapid rate of social and technological change, adolescents are confronted with many alternatives. Consequently, problem situations involving genuine choice arise more frequently than they do in primitive societies, and the possibility of an inappropriate choice increases. Adolescent difficulties in complex societies relate to ''the presence of conflicting standards and the belief that every individual should make his or her own choices, coupled with the feeling that choice is an important matter'' (Mead, 1950: 154). This conflict of choice is facilitated by the fact that physiological puberty occurs earlier now than in the past and that a number of other forms of behavior—dating, going steady, wearing lipstick, dance parties, and so on—have slowly moved down to earlier ages (Muuss, 1970a). At the same time, the expectations for prolonged formal education are increasing to the extent that an ever-increasing number of parents with children of school age expect their children to go to college. The earlier imitation of "adultlike" behavior, on the one hand, and the extended period of education, on the other hand, have increased the duration of social adolescence and created a "mass adolescent culture pattern" characterized by conformity to peer group standards and unresponsiveness to parental values and expectations. Mead feels that the junior high school in particular has contributed to adolescents' increased anxiety* about their growth patterns and appropriate sex behavior. The slow-maturing male is especially vulnerable to anxiety during this period. Owing to the differential growth rate of boys and girs, he is forced into association with members of the opposite sex at a time when he is not yet psychologically or physiologically ready for that kind of relationship. Instead of developing deep personal friendships and associations with members of his own sex, which would help him in developing his own masculine identity, he learns to distrust his male companions as competitors in the dating process. Consequently, boys and girls begin too soon to depend too much on each other "for social and intellectual companionship" (Mead, 1961: 44). Mead feels that this premature and early heterosexual interaction, which junior high schools invite and the peer group expects, contributes to the development of a negative attitude and hostility between the sexes. It lays "the basis for hostility to females on the boys' part and, on the girls' part, pressure toward marriage combined with contempt for males" (Mead, 1961: 38).

The emphasis in our society on installment-plan buying, conspicuous consumption, and early vocational success has brought about a basic shift in attitude from the saving of money, postponement of desires, and pursuit of long-range goals to an emphasis on immediate consumption and an enjoyment of the gratifications that the present provides. This shift to the immediate consumption of goods has been accompanied by a similar shift in attitude with respect to the consumption of sex. This places an increasing demand on the adolescent boy whose sexual desires are strong, but who has not yet learned to control them. His desire for sex brings him into conflict with the moral values of society. He can satisfy his desire through marriage, but early marriage may conflict with the continuation of his education. Mead hy-

---

*Cattell (1961) found that anxiety reaches its peak at about fifteen and only returns to such height again in old age.

pothesizes that premature domesticity may prevent the full development of the "higher mental capacities" in both sexes. Students need to explore the world, stimulate their curiosity, and find out who they are. The emotional commitment and the domesticity of early marriage may inhibit the desire to test, explore, discuss, mediate, and repudiate ideas and the intellectual maturity resulting from such processes. Self-finding, role exploration, and search for an identity must precede the dependency of intimacy and marriage, according to Erikson. The major motive of the married student often becomes "to get through," "to get established," "to make money," rather than to experiment, explore, and search for knowledge.

With Erikson (1950) and other contemporary writers, Mead maintains that the major task facing adolescents today is the search for a meaningful identity. This task is immeasurably more difficult in a modern democratic society than in a primitive society. The behavior and values of parents no longer constitute models, since they are outmoded as compared with the models provided by the mass media. Furthermore, adolescents in the process of freeing themselves from dependency on parents are not only unresponsive but frequently antagonistic to their parents' values. Since they have been taught to evaluate their behavior against that of their age-mates, they now discard the values of their parents and exchange them for the standards of their peers. Rapidity of social change, exposure to various secular and religious value systems, and modern technology make the world appear to the adolescent too complex, too relativistic, too unpredictable, and too ambiguous to provide a stable frame of reference. In the past there has been a period, which both Erikson and Mead call a "psychological moratorium," an "as if" period during which youth could tentatively experiment without being asked to show "success" and without final emotional, economic, or social consequences. The loss of such a period of uncommitted experimentation, during which youth can find itself, makes it difficult to establish ego-identity. As a substitute for psychological identity, youth utilizes peer-group symbols to establish a semi-identity by way of special clothes, special language, and special attitudes toward the world; in the past these were symbols of identity of deprived and/or semicriminal groups. Even education has become functional and "success" oriented. Consequently, the goals and values of adolescents are directed toward success, security, immediate gratification of desires, conformity, and social acceptance with little room for experimentation, idealism, utopianism, and personal martyrdom. "Failure to adopt our educational and social system . . . may be held responsible for some of the sense of self-alienation, search for negative identities, and so forth, characteristic of this present group of young people" (Mead, 1961: 49).

Mead discusses the possibility of a "return to nature" in the Rousseauian sense, but she rejects it because it presupposes a total change of our social structure and way of life. Although a communal living pattern and a Thoreauvian way of life among youth who are dissatisfied with the rigid structure of school, college, and society reflect this "return to nature" philosophy, Mead rejects a return to more primitive forms of life as a realistic solution for parents of an adolescent. While it is true that in Samoan society children witness, with no negative effect, reproduction, birth, illness, and death, the same experiences provided in an American family could do more harm than good, since society considers these experiences inappropriate and taboo for children.

However, Mead does advocate greater freedom and less emphasis on conformity to family, peer group, and community expectations so that adolescents can realize their creative potential. "We can attempt to alter our whole culture, and especially our childrearing patterns, so as to incorporate within them a greater freedom for and expectation of variations" (Mead and Macgregor, 1951: 185). This alteration can be achieved by a combination of freedom and training that is based on both an understanding of the students' "maturational psycho-dynamics" and insight into the patterns of culture.

Mead criticizes the American family for its too intimate organiza-tion and its crippling effect on the emotional life of the growing youth. She believes that too strong family ties handicap individuals in their ability to live their own lives and make their own choices. She suggests that "it would be desirable to mitigate, at least in some slight measure, the strong role which parents play in children's lives, and so eliminate one of the most powerful accidental factors in the choices of any indi-vidual life" (Mead, 1950: 141). However, even though she objects to the pattern of the American family that produces conformity and dependency on its children, she considers the family a tough institution and demonstrates that it is nearly universal. Mead knows of no better way to produce wholesome individuals than through a tolerant family system in which "father says 'yes' and mother says 'no' about the same thing" (Mead, 1947: 330), and in which adolescents can disagree with their parents without a resulting loss of love and self-respect or an increase of emotional tensions.

Mead demands more emphasis on mental and physical health in the classroom. Making choices is an important aspect of growing up in America and of maintaining mental health, especially at that period of development when sexual urges begin to play a more important role but when society does not condone sexual behavior. The adolescent will be increasingly confronted with conflicting choices, in sexual as well as other matters. This choice situation is complicated by a lack of a definite, generally accepted social canon in American society, and the advice received from parents, teachers, peers, and commercials are frequently in conflict. Consequently, many choice situations produce anxiety during adolescence. To help youth in overcoming this dilemma, a special educational effort ought to be made to train children and adolescents to consider alternatives and consequences when confronted with a choice situation. "Children must be taught how to think, not what to think" (Mead, 1950: 16).

Finally, returning to Benedict's theory of continuities and discontinuities in cultural conditioning, the educational implications become quite obvious: our educational practices at home as well as in school should emphasize continuity in the learning process so that the child becomes conditioned to the same set of values and behavior in childhood that will be expected from him in adulthood. The child should be taught nothing that he will have to unlearn in order to become a mature adult. The implementation of this idea is obviously difficult in our modern and complex society. Many social roles are defined by age and by social expectations. Changes in behavior, often constituting a discontinuity, are expected as the individual moves from elementary to high school, from college into the labor market, and from denial of sexuality before the wedding to sexual responsiveness following it.

7: FIELD THEORY AND ADOLESCENCE

KURT Lewin (1890–1947) was a pupil of the early Gestalt school of psychologists at the University of Berlin. He was also influenced by Freud's psychoanalytic theory, particularly in regard to motivation in human behavior. However, Lewin's theory of adolescence is conceptually quite different from any of the theories discussed so far. Lewin's field theory—especially as it relates to social psychology and learning theory—is widely known and frequently discussed in the psychological literature, but comparatively few references are made to his theory of adolescent development, which is explicitly stated in "Field Theory and Experiment in Social Psychology" (1939). His field theory explains and describes the dynamics of behavior of the individual adolescent without generalizing about adolescents as a group. His constructs help to describe and explain, and if the field forces are known, to predict the behavior of a given individual in a specific situation. In a sense, the field theory of adolescence is expressed explicitly and stated more formally than other theories of adolescent development. At the same time, however, Lewin's theory strongly opposes those conceptual schemes that require placing the phenomenal world in rigid and mutually exclusive categories.

Lewin assumed the "lawfulness" of all psychological events, even those that occur only once. He maintained that general psychological concepts and laws derived on the basis of frequency of occurrence created a dilemma, since these laws are abstracted from many individuals and are true in terms of probability only. Such laws may or may not apply to a specific individual. Therefore, there is no way back from these generalizations to a particular individual except by way of probability.

DEVELOPMENTAL CONCEPTS OF FIELD THEORY

One of Lewin's core concepts is the law "that behavior (B) is a function (f) of the person (P) and of his environment (E), B = f(PE), and that P and E in this formula are interdependent variables'' (1939: 34). How a child perceives his environment depends on the stage of his development, his personality, and his knowledge. An unstable psychological environment during adolescence brings about instability in the behavior of the individual. Therefore, to understand a child's behavior, one must consider the child and the environment as a constellation of interdependent factors. The sum total of all environmental and personal factors in interaction is called the "life space" (LSp), or the "psychological space." Behavior is a function of the life space and not only of the physical stimuli, $B = f(LSp)$. The life space includes physical-environmental, social, and psychological factors, such as needs, motives, and goals, all of which determine behavior. To demonstrate the dynamics of the life space, Lewin introduces two constructs that are to represent the situation of a particular individual at a particular time in a particular environment:

1. A map or geometrical representation of the life space, in which the person, available goals, and possible barriers between an individual and his goals are depicted (see Figure 6).
2. A representation of the forces that act on the individual and bring about locomotion toward or away from a goal.

Within the life space, objects or goals can have positive (attraction) or negative (repulsion) valence. If goals allow the fulfillment of needs and desires, they have a positive valence; barriers that interfere with the attainment of a goal have a negative valence. If the attracting and repulsing forces are in balance, a person experiences conflict. If the forces are not in balance, they produce locomotion and the individual moves, psychologically speaking, toward or away from the goal. When several forces act simultaneously, the locomotion is called a "resultant." A barrier between an individual and the goal may increase the individual's efforts to reach the goal, but it may also result in frustration.

In Figure 6 the person (P) is strongly attracted to the goal (G1), such as passing a course or getting a good grade in high school. However, to reach this goal various barriers having negative valences—for instance, quizzes, exams, papers, and reports, which require effort and time—must be overcome. If another attractive goal (G2), wanting to earn money, is operative at the same time and also requires overcoming barriers—namely, mowing the lawn, washing the car, and so on—the adolescent may experience conflict if the forces are in balance. Actual behavior would be determined by the strength of the forces, as one individual may be more attracted to earning money, or less repulsed by mowing the lawn, whereas another may be more interested in passing the course or may actually enjoy writing the required paper.

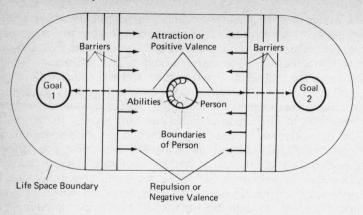

FIGURE 6. An individual's life space in a conflict situation.

The psychological field, or the life space, includes the individual with his biological and psychological dimensions as well as the environment with its social relations and physical objects. Since person and environment are seen as a constellation of interrelated factors, this theory achieves harmony among the many aspects of development by combining biological, sociological, environmental, and psychological factors in the concept life space. Field theory has successfully integrated the biological and sociological factors, which are frequently considered contradictory (for example, the nature-nurture issue). Lewin made explicit his position on this issue in several of his publications: "the social aspect of the psychological situation is at least as important as the physical" (Lewin, 1946: 793); "the psychological influence of environment on the behavior and development of the child is extremely important" (Lewin, 1931: 94); "psychology in general [is regarded] as a field of biology" (Lewin, 1935: 35). "Psychological ecology" is seen as the biological science that deals with the relationship between the organism and its environment or, as Lewin states the issue, "the relationship between psychological and non-psychological factors" (Lewin, 1951: 170). Thus he attempts to combine biological, social, and environmental forces into one system, and he accomplishes this with the construct of the life space, which can be readily illustrated as a map of the objects, goals, and valences that are operative.

In infancy, a child's life space is unstructured and undifferentiated; the child depends on outside help and external structuring of the environment by other people. An individual's space of free movement is limited by "(a) what is forbidden to a person, (b) what is beyond his ability" (Lewin, 1936: 219). As the child grows older and as the life space increases in structure and differentiation, the child learns to be more and more self-reliant. Fewer restrictions are placed on the child's freedom to move; hence ability to deal effectively with the increased life space grows. To acquire maximal differentiation of life space, the child must have the freedom to advance into new regions, to explore and include new experiences. Lack of freedom of movement will place restrictions on the child's attempt to expand his life space; psychological rigidity of personality will result. Conversely, if the life space, especially in early childhood, remains unstructured, the personality will lack integration and organization. Thus Lewin not only emphasizes the child's developmental need for independence, but he also adds the idea of a developmental need for a kind of dependency that provides the child with structure and guidance toward favorable personality development. The importance of the dependency need and the structure in the home contributing to the socialization of the child is a major concern of social learning theory discussed in Chapter 14. Research findings reported by Harris (1958) support this idea. Studies were made of the feelings, attitudes, and ideas of adults who, as children, attended the University of Minnesota Nursery School in the late 1920s. Those who had been reared in structured situations were decisive, confident, self-accepting, and achievement-oriented. Those raised in an unstructured home situation were indecisive, distrustful, pessimistic, and perceived success and failure in terms of good or bad luck.

The space of free movement—that region in the physical and psychological life space that is accessible to an individual—differs from person to person both in scope and nature, thus providing for a conceptualization of different experiences and thereby explaining individual differences. But even more important are the restrictions that limit free movement. Individual differences in forbidden and permitted regions are important in understanding the achievement of independence and personality development. As the adolescent's life space increases, many more regions become potentially accessible (see Figure 8). But often it is not at all clear to adolescents whether or not they are supposed to enter these regions. Sometimes they enter such a region when they are not supposed to and experience conflict; at other times they do not enter such a new region when they are supposed to and experience reprimand. The difficulty arises because these regions are no longer "beyond their ability"; because these regions may not be explicitly allowed or explicitly forbidden, they are part of the space of free movement but remain undefined and unclear. If they are forbidden, adolescents realize that these regions are not forbidden for some of their peers, and hope that their own restrictions will soon be lifted. Consequently, the definition and redefinition of the space of free

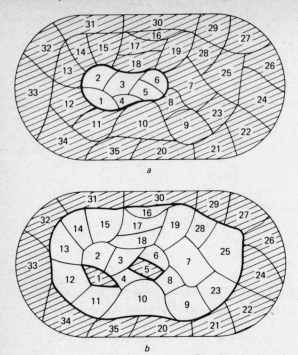

FIGURE 7. Comparison of the *space of free movement* of child and adult. The actual activity regions are represented. The accessible regions are blank; the inaccessible shaded. (*a*) The space of free movement of the *child* includes the regions *1–6* representing activities such as getting into the movies at children's rates, belonging to a boy's club, etc. The regions *7–35* are not accessible, representing activities such as driving a car, writing checks for purchases, political activities, performance of adult's occupations, etc. (*b*) The *adult* space of free movement is considerably wider, although it too is bounded by regions of activities inaccessible to the adult, such as shooting his enemy or entering activities beyond his social or intellectual capacity (represented by regions including *29–35*). Some of the regions accessible to the child are not accessible to the adult, for instance, getting into the movies at children's rates, or doing things socially taboo for an adult which are permitted to the child (represented by regions *1* and *5*).

From Kurt Lewin, The Field Theory Approach to Adolescence. *American Journal of Sociology*, 1939, *44*, 868–897. Reproduced by permission from The University of Chicago Press.

movement in the adolescents' life space may take innumerable hours of discussion and argumentation between them and their parents. This uncertainty of the undefined space of free movement illustrated in Figure 8 is the psychological construct by which field theory explains

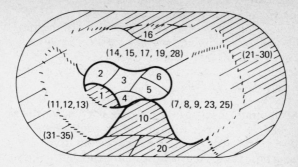

FIGURE 8. The *space of free movement* of the *adolescent* as it appears to him. The space of free movement is greatly increased, including many regions which previously have not been accessible to the child, for instance, freedom to smoke, returning home late, driving a car (regions *7–9*, *11–13*, . . .). Certain regions accessible to the adult are clearly not accessible to the adolescent, such as voting (represented by regions *10* and *16*). Certain regions accessible to the child have already become inaccessible, such as getting into the movies at children's rates, or behaving on too childish a level (region *1*). The boundaries of these newly acquired portions of the space of free movement are only vaguely determined and in themselves generally less clearly and sharply differentiated than for an adult. In such cases the life space of the adolescent seems to be full of possibilities and at the same time of uncertainties.

From Kurt Lewin, The Field Theory Approach to Adolescence. *American Journal of Sociology,* 1939, *44,* 868–897. Reproduced by permission from The University of Chicago Press.

some of the unpredictable aspects of adolescent behavior. Many of the undefined regions in Figure 8 are "new psychological situations" in the sense that Barker uses this term (as will be described in the second part of this chapter).

Lewin speaks of developmental stages, but his conceptualization of stages is quite different from the stages of Freud, Erikson, Gesell, and Piaget. Lewin's stages relate to differences in the scope of the life space and the degree of life space differentiation. In accordance with the all-inclusive definition of the life space, these developmental differences are concerned with the psychological environment as well as with the individual, his body, his goals, and his self-perception. According to Lewin, the differences between developmental stages manifest themselves in the following ways:

1. An increase in the scope of the life space in regard to
   a. what is part of the psychological present
   b. the time perspective in the direction of the psychological past and the psychological future

    c. the reality-irreality dimension
2. An increasing differentiation of every level of the life space into a multitude of social relations and areas of activities
3. An increasing organization
4. A change in the general fluidity or rigidity of the life space [Lewin, 1946: 797–798].

Figure 9 illustrates the change in life space as a function of age, comparing the child's (a) life space with that of an adolescent (b). Several important developmental differences become obvious from this comparison. (1) The main difference is the increased differentiation in the life space of the adolescent as compared to the undifferentiated and unstructured area of the child's life space. Both the child and his perception of the environment become differentiated and structured in the developmental process. This holds true in respect to many different aspects of development, such as language skills, social relations, and emotions, as well as the child's understanding of his world. Change in the differentiation of the life space occurs slowly at certain times and more rapidly at other times. Slow changes result in harmonious periods of development, whereas rapid changes are more likely to result in periods of crisis. Adolescence is characterized by a relatively rapid change in the structure of the life space, and the rapidity of the growth of the life space during adolescence may be responsible for the so-called adolescent crisis. (2) The comparison between (a) and (b) makes clear that the time perspective has expanded, since it now includes a more distant future and a more distant past. Such change in time perspective is a fundamental aspect of development; it has far-reaching consequences for education, the curriculum, and vocational planning. The adolescent develops the ability to understand the past, adopt a new outlook toward the future, and plan his own life more realistically. (3) Since the life space differentiates and the time perspective expands, the reality-irreality level also takes on new dimensions. The reality-irreality dimension is an important concept of Lewin's (1946) theory. "Irreality" refers to fantasies, dreams, wishes, fears, and certain forms of play. Young children are not able to distinguish clearly between wishes and facts, hopes and expectations. As they grow older, their reality enables them to distinguish with increasing accuracy between truth and falsehood, perception and imagination. One characteristic of adolescents is that they have learned to distinguish between reality and irreality.

Kurt Lewin's Theory of Adolescent Development

Fundamental to Lewin's theory of development is the view that adolescence is a period of transition during which adolescents must change their group membership. While both the child and the adult

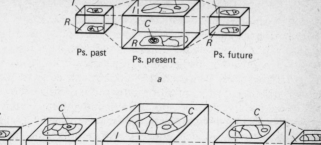

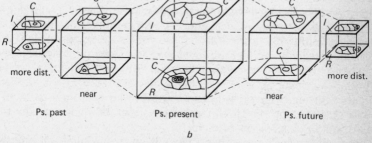

FIGURE 9. The life space at two developmental stages. Figure 9a represents the life space of a younger child. Figure 9b represents the higher degree of differentiation of the life space of the older child in regard to the present situation, the reality-irreality dimension, and the time perspective. C, child; R, level of reality; I, level of irreality; Ps Past, psychological past; Ps Present, psychological present; Ps Future, psychological future.

From Kurt Lewin, Behavior and Development as a Function of the Total Situation. In L. Carmichael (Ed.), *Manual of Child Development*. © 1946 by John Wiley & Sons, New York. Reproduced by permission.

have a fairly clear concept of how they fit into the group, the adolescent belongs partly to the child group, partly to the adult group, without belonging completely to either group. Parents, teachers, and society reflect this lack of clearly defined group status; and their ambiguous feelings become obvious when they treat the adolescent at one time like a child and at another time like an adult. Difficulties arise because certain childish forms of behavior are no longer acceptable. At the same time some of the adult forms of behavior are not yet permitted either, or if they are permitted, they are new and strange to the adolescent. The adolescent is in a state of "social locomotion," moving into an unstructured social and psychological field. Goals are no longer clear, and the paths to them are ambiguous and full of uncertainties—the adolescent may no longer be certain that they even lead to the desired goals. Such ambiguities and uncertainties are illustrated well by the boy asking or hesitating to ask for his first date. Since the adolescent does not yet have a clear understanding of his social status, expectations, and obligations, his behavior reflects this uncertainty.

A life space—as illustrated in Figure 6—has different regions that are separated by boundaries with varying degrees of permeability. For example, the adolescent is confronted with several attractive choices that at the same time have relatively impervious boundaries. Driving a car, smoking pot, dropping acid, having sexual relations are all possible goals with positive valence, and thus they become part of the adolescent's life space. However, they are also inaccessible because of parental restriction, legal limitations, or the individual's own internalized moral code. Since the adolescent is moving through a rapidly changing field, he does not know the directions to specific goals and is open to constructive guidance, but is also vulnerable to persuasion and pressure. Unfamiliar situations cause crises that can produce withdrawal, sensitivity, and inhibition as well as aggression, inappropriate emotional outbursts, rebellion, and radicalism. Consequently, because of a lack of cognitive structure, the adolescent frequently is not sure whether certain behavior will lead toward or away from a particular goal. This concept of "lack of cognitive structure" helps explain the uncertainty in adolescent behavior.

The self-image of individuals depends on their bodies. During the normal developmental process body changes are so slow that the self-image remains relatively stable. The body image has time to adjust to these developmental changes so that individuals know their own bodies. During adolescence changes in body structure, body experience, and new body sensations and urges are more drastic, so that even the well-known life space of the body image becomes less familiar, unreliable, and unpredictable. Adolescents are preoccupied with the normality of their bodies and how their bodies are perceived by others; they are concerned about and may actually be disturbed by their body image. They spend considerable time studying their image in the mirror and are concerned about the development of primary and secondary sex characteristics in relationship to age-mates. This is understandable; obviously, the body is especially close to and vital to one's feelings of attractiveness, stability, security, and one's sex role. Negative feelings about one's own body are related to a negative self-concept (Rosen and Ross, 1968) and may lead to emotional instability that can change one's orientation toward life. Due to these uncertainties, adolescent behavior is characterized by an increased plasticity of personality that can lead to personality changes and even religious conversions.

The change in a child's life space from being limited in scope but relatively structured to the increased but often unknown regions of the adolescent's life space includes not only more extensive social relationships, a new body image, and expanding geographic surroundings, but also an increased perception of the future and a better understanding of his own past.

Field theory defines adolescence as a period of transition from childhood to adulthood. This transition is characterized by deeper and far-reaching changes, a faster rate of growth, and differentiation of the life space as compared with the preceding stage of late childhood. The transition is also characterized by the fact that the individual enters a cognitively unstructured region that results in uncertainty of behavior. Transition from childhood to adulthood is obviously a universal phenomenon, since children become mature adults in all societies. However, the shift from childhood to adulthood can occur in different patterns. It can take the form of a sudden shift, such as has been observed in primitive societies in which the puberty rites end childhood and signify the beginning of adulthood. Mead reports, for example, that for the Manus girl, puberty "means the beginning of adult life and responsibility" (Mead, 1953: 107). There can also be a gradual shift, especially if the child group and the adult group are not as clearly separated and defined as they are in our society. Thus development would be continuous and the adolescent crisis would be mild. This appears to be the case in Samoan society discussed in Chapter 6. If the transition period is prolonged and if the children as a group are clearly distinguished from adults, as they are in Western societies, adolescents find themselves in a social situation in which their group membership is not clearly defined. The adolescent in such an in-between situation is referred to by Lewin as the "marginal man," and the adolescent's in-between standing is represented in Figure 10 by the overlapping area (Ad) of the child region (C) and the adult region (A). The assumption of the marginal-man concept is that the adolescent no longer belongs to the social group of children and does not want to be considered a child; yet he is not yet accepted into the social group of adults, and to the extent that this in-between situation is operative in his personal life space, his behavior will reflect this marginality. Being a marginal man implies that the adolescent may at times act more like a child, often when he wants to avoid adult responsibilities; at other times he may act more like an adult and request adult privileges. Parents and teachers, too, may interpret the marginal-man situation in their own way; however, they are more likely to remind the adolescent to be mature, grown-up, and adultlike when the issues involve responsibilities, chores, work, and study. They perceive their charges as "still so young" and "immature" when it comes to adult rights and privileges. Such a situation is most characteristic of youth in Western society, and it is partly responsible for some of Western society's "adolescent difficulties." The marginal man, topographically speaking, stands on the boundaries that separate two groups. "They are people who belong neither here nor there, standing 'between' the groups" (Lewin, 1948: 179). Marginality, even in other social situations, increases social tensions. Minority group members may find themselves in such a situation when they attempt to establish close personal relationships within the majority group—that is, by changing their group belonging. The psychological problems confronting the marginal man are both internal—instability, uncertainty, and self-hate—and external—a constant conflict over group belonging and a lack of role definition, with ostracism by either group possible.

From these basic assumptions about the nature of human development, Lewin (1939) derives a number of statements that describe, explain, and if the field forces are known, predict adolescent behavior:

1. The adolescent may show shyness and sensitivity, but at the same time aggressiveness may occur, mainly because of the unclearness of the situation and the disequilibrium in the adolescent's life space.

2. As a marginal man, the adolescent experiences a continuous conflict among different attitudes, values, ideologies, and life styles, since he is shifting his orientation from the childhood group to the adult group, but he really does not belong to either. Therefore, he experiences lack of social anchorage, except in relationship to his peer group.

3. These conflicts in values, attitudes, and ideologies result in increased emotional tension.

4. There is a predisposition in the adolescent to take radical positions and to change behavior drastically; consequently, one can find radical, rebellious attitudes and actions side by side with sensitivity and withdrawal tendencies.

5. "Adolescent behavior" can be observed only if and to the extent that the structure and the dynamics of the life space involve the following: (1) expansion and differentiation of the life space; (2) marginal-man standing in relationship to childhood and adult groups; and (3) biologically determined changes in the life space, as a result of body changes. The particular type of behavior that emerges and the degree of "adolescent behavior" depend greatly on the strength and nature of these conflicting forces. Above all in importance is the amount of difference between—and the factors that separate—adult society and child society in a particular culture.

The question of universality of the adolescent phenomenon is one of statistical frequency. Lewinian field theory (1935) considers this question irrelevant as well as the question of whether heredity or environment is the greater influence on development. They are irrelevant

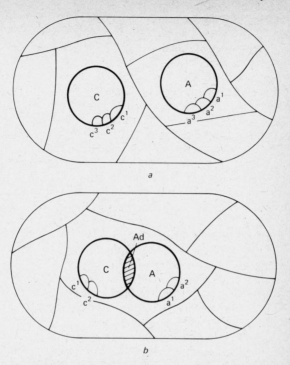

FIGURE 10.   The adolescent as a marginal man. (a) During childhood and adulthood the
"adults" (A) and "children" (C) are viewed as relatively separated groups, the individual
child (c^1, c^2) and the individual adult (a^1, a^2) being sure of their belonging to their respective groups. (b) The adolescent belonging to a group (Ad) which can be viewed as an
overlapping region of the children's (C) and the adults' (A) group belonging to both of
them, or as standing between them, not belonging to either one.

From Kurt Lewin, The Field Theory Approach to Adolescence. *American Journal of Sociology*, 1939,
44, 868–897. Reproduced by permission from The University of Chicago Press.

because knowing that a certain phenomenon, such as adolescence, occurs 100 percent, 80 percent, or 60 percent of the time does not give any
insight into the dynamics of the developing individual. Nor does it
show the relative influence of physical development, social, and emotional factors, or how they oppose and influence each other.

What is . . . important to the investigation of dynamics is not to abstract
from the situation, but to hunt out those situations in which determinative
factors of the total dynamic structure are most clearly, distinctly, and purely

to be discerned. Instead of a reference to the abstract average of as many historically given cases as possible, there is a reference to the full concreteness of the particular situations [Lewin, 1935: 31].

The dynamic aspect of adolescent behavior, not the statistical frequency of one event or another, is the concern of field theory.

According to Lewin, specific characteristics of individuals cannot be classified in categories of overt behavior. Field theory moves away from classification systems; it assumes that there are great individual differences and sees as its objective the systematic explanation of these differences. Sensitivity to environmental influences varies greatly among people. The speed with which the differentiation and structurization of the life space takes place also varies considerably in different people. Therefore, we must expect great individual variations in behavior. Furthermore, since sensitivity as well as rate of change in the life space increases during the adolescent period, we must expect that behavior changes also will differ widely and probably be more noticeable than at other times.

Moreover, field theory assumes not only individual differences, but cultural differences as well. Thus, while the life space varies from individual to individual within a given culture, the differences from culture to culture are even greater. Two aspects that will be relatively stable within a given culture but quite different from culture to culture are (1) the ideologies, attitudes, and values that are recognized and emphasized and (2) the way in which different activities are seen as related or unrelated; for example, religion and work are more closely related in Mennonite society than in American society as a whole (Lewin, 1942).

Another factor that may account for cultural differences in adolescent behavior is the varying length of the adolescent period from culture to culture and from social class to social class within a culture. Furthermore, the degree to which the child group and the adult group are differentiated in a given culture has far-reaching consequences for adolescent behavior. The more clearly the groups are separated, the more difficult the transition.

ROGER BARKER'S SOMATOPSYCHOLOGICAL THEORY OF ADOLESCENCE

Roger Barker and others (1953) expanded and elaborated Lewin's theory of adolescent development. Particularly significant is the chapter "Somatopsychological Significance of Physical Growth in Adolescence." Barker applies field theory to show the effects of physiological changes on behavior during adolescence. His goal is to develop hypotheses that provide insight into the dynamics by which changes in physiological structure influence behavior. Barker bases his hypothesis of a somatopsychological mechanism on these assumptions:

1. Adolescents are moving toward the social status, physical maturity, strength, and motor control of adults. But they are not yet adults; they are in an intermediate position between adults and children. They are in a marginal or transitory period, to use Lewin's terms.
2. Body dimensions, physique, and endocrinological changes occur at an accelerated speed, as compared to the preadolescent years.
3. The time and speed of changes in physique vary greatly among individuals, and these differences are more noticeable than during any other period of development. They are also more consequential, as the research on early and late maturation clearly demonstrates.
4. There are great differences within a given individual in the degree of maturity attained by different parts of the body. This phenomenon of asynchronous body growth is widely recognized by developmental psychologists such as Stolz and Stolz and Tanner and Zeller.

We can predict two psychological situations from these known facts about adolescent physical development: first, "new psychological situations" will arise during adolescence; and second, experiential psychological situations will take place in which "overlapping of the psychological field" occurs.

Lewin stated that great cultural differences in adolescent behavior can be explained in terms of whether the child group and the adult group are two clearly distinguishable social groups or one undifferentiated social group with easy locomotion from one segment to the other. Barker continues this argument by assuming that in the United States the child group is clearly separated from the adult group, for whom different forms of behavior are accepted. Children have a social position equivalent to that of a minority group; this increases the difficulty of moving from one group to the other. The possibility of moving from one social group to the other is determined informally by one's physique: looking like an adult makes it easier to get adult privileges. Formally, adult privileges and responsibilities are determined by law and come at a legally established age.

Barker applies the properties of the "new psychological situation" to adolescence in this way:

1. In a new psychological situation, the course of action to be

followed to reach a certain goal is unknown. This means that a given individual cannot accurately predict what behavior will bring the desired goal closer. Lewin (1942) describes this situation in detail, comparing it to moving into a strange town.

2. In an unknown situation, the valence is positive and negative at the same time, because the individual does not know whether a certain kind of behavior will bring the goal closer or move it further away.

3. In an unknown situation, "the perceptual structure is unstable" (Barker, 1953: 30), the psychological dynamics that result from an unknown situation are unclear, indefinite, and ambiguous. Small changes in the perceptual field of a given individual may change the total field.

From these considerations Barker derives behavioral characteristics that can be observed in an individual who operates, as the adolescent does, in a new psychological situation in which directions are unknown (Assumption #1).

a. The behavior will not be parsimonious as it was in the familiar situation in which the direction was known and the individual responded by habit, selecting the simplest route to a goal. In the new and unknown situation, he again must respond by exploration and trial and error to reach the goal. When the individual pursuing a course of action finds that it does not bring the goal closer, he will begin another course of action and repeat this trial-and-error process until the goal is reached. Awkwardness and timidity in dating behavior of early adolescence is an illustration of such a situation.

b. Since a person cannot foresee the consequences of a course of action, frequent errors will encourage caution. But, in addition to caution, this exploratory situation also produces a tendency toward radical and extreme moves. The discrepancy in adolescence between ideals and aspirations on the one hand and actual achievements on the other has been reported frequently both on theoretical and on empirical grounds (Flanagan, 1979, Wylie and Hutchins, 1967). Adolescents are quicker in providing verbal solutions to basic social problems than are more experienced adults. This is due partly to the increased time perspective and a desire to grow up, to achieve, and to succeed, which invites the making of long-range goals, and is also partly due to the inability to foresee obstacles and consequences of actions.

c. The unknown in the new situation, since it offers resistance to locomotion, is actually experienced as a barrier to the goal. Frustration builds up; aggressive, emotional, and disruptive behavior must be expected as a result.

Similarly, Barker derives behavioral characteristics from the assumption that the "valence is simultaneously positive and negative" (Barker, 1953: 36) (Assumption #2).

a. Positive valence will bring an advance toward the goal; negative valence will bring about a withdrawal. Since both are present simultaneously, the adolescent will be in conflict, trying to advance and withdraw at the same time. Consequently, emotionally disruptive behavior may occur, especially if the goal is important.

b. If the positive or negative valences shift, the individual will advance or retreat accordingly.

c. If in a given situation the valence is simultaneously positive and negative, the adolescent will be on the lookout for cues; he will move cautiously, trying to "feel" whether his behavior leads to success or failure.

From the third definition in which the new psychological situation is characterized as "perceptual structure is unstable" (Barker, 1953: 36), Barker derives the following behavioral characteristics (Assumption #3).

a. Behavior will depend on the perception of the situation. Since the adolescent's perceptual structure is unstable, his behavior will be unstable and vacillating. The first adolescent realization of the contradictions between the values taught by adults and the failure of adults to live and succeed by their own beliefs presents a new psychological situation that may change the child's outlook toward life, since a discrepancy between the ideal and the real is not easily reconciled.

b. The less stable the situation, the more the individual depends on small and sometimes unimportant cues. Behavior can be influenced easily; the adolescent has little resistance to suggestion. This is especially true for suggestions coming from the social group the adolescent wants to belong to. Peer group conformity is the psychological response to living in an unstable situation. The high degree of uniformity observed among adolescents can be explained as an attempt to structure the field, which is experienced as unstable by the individuals.

The alternative overlapping situation refers to the uneven rate of maturity of different organic or functional aspects of adolescence. For example, an adolescent may show signs of emotional immaturity, but he may look like an adult. Or an adolescent may have a child's physique but already have had a voice change. While Lewin emphasizes that the adolescent is the marginal man in regard to his social group belonging, Barker stresses the ambiguous situation that results from overlapping in body growth, emphasizing the somatopsychological significance of development. His hypothesis is this: because of the rapidity and ambiguity of their physical changes, adolescents are in a marginal situation; their behavior often is determined at the same time by childhood and adult values and expectations. This lack of consistency in value orientation accounts for the problems involved in so-called adolescent behavior.

Barker says there are three aspects in the overlapping situation:

1. *Congruence.* ". . . two or more overlapping psychological situations differ in the degree to which the behavior in each is congruent" (Barker, 1953: 39). The degree to which forms of behavior in a certain overlapping situation differ or agree makes a further breakdown necessary. In the first instance, the "overlapping consonant situation," the behavior required to reach two or more goals is practically identical. An example from the adolescent world would be the behavior needed to learn to box and develop muscular strength. Learning to box systematically makes muscles strong. The forces involved will "strengthen instead of weaken each other" (Lewin, 1938).

In the second overlapping situation, the actions taken to reach the one goal do not interfere with the behavior needed to reach the second goal; they are compatible. For example, an adolescent can get a high school education and make friends. But going to school does not automatically result in making friends, in the way that boxing increases strength. Barker (1953) calls this the "overlapping compatible situation."

In the third instance, we have a situation in which behavior necessary to reach one goal interferes with, but does not completely disrupt, behavior required to obtain another goal—say, getting an education and supporting a family. This is the "overlapping interfering situation.

Finally, there is the situation in which the behavior that is necessary to obtain one goal is incompatible with that required to reach another goal. An illustration would be the adolescent kissing his girl while driving in heavy traffic. This is referred to as the "overlapping antagonistic situation."

Adolescents frequently find themselves in one of the latter two situations when desires, ambitions, and aspirations reach into the adult world, where age, law, limited experience, and parents interfere.

2. *Potency.* The concept of potency represents the relative influence a particular factor or goal in a given psychological field has upon behavior, as a result of an overlapping situation. Thus, learning to box and wanting to develop physical strength are, probably, subordinate to other goals in the life space and have a relatively low potency. Conversely, it may be assumed that if an adolescent supports a family and continues to get an education, both factors consume a relatively large

segment of his life space and have a relatively high potency. "The relative potency is important for group membership in case of belonging to several overlapping groups" (Lewin, 1938: 202). It is not primarily the fact that the adolescent belongs to several groups that causes adjustment difficulties; it is the uncertainty concerning group loyalties. The adolescent may have to choose between old childhood friends or belonging to the "in-group." Also, the relative importance of the family over the peer group during the transition years is not always clear, and sometimes this uncertainty creates conflict.

3. *Valence.* Of further importance in an overlapping situation is the valence which each of the goals holds for the individual. From the examples given, either of the two possible forms of behavior could have a relatively large or small valence in comparison to the other. In Lewin's terminology, the valence a goal has can vary. For example, for one individual making friends can be far more important than getting an education; for another, making friends is secondary to getting an education. The behavior and attitudes of these two individuals would differ greatly. "Potency" refers to the relative influence of one goal as compared with all other goals, whereas "valence" refers to the actual attraction or repulsion of one given goal. In the case of the adolescent, generally speaking, adult privileges have a higher positive valence than those of childhood, which frequently have a negative valence.

EDUCATIONAL IMPLICATIONS

Adolescents and their problems are related to the change in group belonging. They no longer belong to the child group and are no longer considered children. Nor do they yet belong to the adult groups and receive their privileges, even though adult activities may have a positive valence for them. Thus, adolescents are in a stage of social locomotion; they are transferring from one group to another but do not belong to either one. Adolescents are "social outcasts," to use a somewhat extreme term. This condition necessarily makes them more dependent on their own age group for support, inspiration, fellowship, and idols than either children or adults are dependent on their age groups. These insights gained through field theory may be used as psychological arguments in favor of the junior high school, since this is the age group in which the accelerated change in body maturity and the shift in group belonging is most obvious. Counterarguments concerning the psychological effects of the junior high school are advanced by Mead and were presented in the previous chapter.

An important factor in adolescent development is the enlargement, differentiation, and conceptualization of the time perspective. The young child lives mainly in the present; the past and the future include only a few days or weeks and have relatively little effect on behavior. As a child grows older, and especially during the adolescent period, he develops a time concept that makes the past significant; historical occurrences can now be understood in their chronological sequence. Lewin's concept of the enlargement of the time perspective during adolescence coincides with the teaching of history at the onset of adolescence and has been supported by research studies. But the time concept expands not only into the past but also into the future, which now becomes meaningful for the child, who begins to form a life plan and set goals. The older child has to make choices in training and preparing for a vocation. This bespeaks the necessity for vocational guidance.

Adolescence is a period in which reality and irreality should be clearly distinguished, even though irreality will not necessarily disappear completely from the thought of the adolescent. It is important for the educator to emphasize the understanding of reality and to confront the adolescent with facts when responses become fabrications based on fantasy or irreality.

The adolescents' social awareness of group belonging undergoes great change, as do their bodies and body images. The child "knew" his body or showed little interest in it, but sexual maturity disturbs the adolescent, and the new bodily dimensions, qualities, and functions are sometimes threatening. Thus, a very close and vital part of life space, one's own body, becomes foreign and produces tension. Since body image is a fundamental region in the life space, this change leads to confusion, conflict, and uncertainty of behavior. Education probably will not be able to overcome all the difficulties related to body change, but it can at least prepare the adolescent boy and girl for these changes by helping them understand human growth and by giving them knowledge of the great normal variations in physical development.

The infant and the child must have their life space structured by their parents and other adults. But as they grow older, the restrictions and limitations should be removed slowly so that young adults are allowed to structure their own world. From an educational point of view, this means that the adolescent should be encouraged to develop independence and responsibility by setting his own goals and choosing his own methods to reach them.

Field theory presents the total situation, with all the aspects that make up the child's life space. If teaching is to be successful and produce the maximum amount of learning, the activities involved should have a positive valence for the student. Field theory holds that success in teaching depends on all of those conditions of learning that have been singled out by one or another educational theory—the social atmosphere, the amount of security, the interest and meaningfulness of the material, its psychological appropriateness for the developmental level of the learner, and the atmosphere in which the material is taught.

Lewin suggested, as do other phenomenologically oriented psychologists, that what is more important psychologically speaking is the subject's perception of an event rather than the objective reality. This implies that a teacher must make a genuine effort to understand the student's perception of the situation—that is, to try to empathize with the adolescent's point of view. An illustration is the not uncommon observation that two students perform about the same on an examination and both receive a B grade. However, their psychological experience of success or failure is not so much dependent on the objective reality of their performance, but on their expectation. The student who expected an A is disappointed and perhaps even angry. The student who feared a C or worse is encouraged and feels elated. Understanding behavior is only possible through a reconstruction and understanding of the perceptual field of the behavior. Facts acquired in this way may be quite different from those obtained by an objective approach. Psychoanalysis, clinical psychology, Gestalt psychology, and field theory have applied this method within its natural limitations. However, this phenomenological viewpoint raises the question of whether it is possible to fully see and understand the world in the same way as another person perceives it.

8: SOCIAL PSYCHOLOGY AND ADOLESCENCE

ALLISON DAVIS' CONCEPT OF SOCIALIZED ANXIETY

Allison Davis (1902–), in "Socialization and Adolescent Personality" (1944), defines "socialization" as the process by which individuals learn the ways, ideas, beliefs, values, and norms of their culture and make them part of their personality. He sees development as a continuous process of learning socially acceptable behavior by means of reinforcement and punishment. Acceptable and unacceptable behavior are defined by society, its socializing agents, social classes, or castes. Cultural behavior is acquired through social learning. Understanding the effects of social learning on adolescents is the crucial issue in Davis' theory.

Since punishment, threats, and withdrawal of love are used to foster the development of acceptable forms of behavior and inhibit the expression of undesirable forms, they are frequently anticipated in new learning situations. This anticipated fear of punishment as a result of repeated social reinforcement brings about what Davis calls "socialized anxiety," which becomes an important factor in facilitating the socialization process.* Socialized anxiety is adaptive in nature and culturally useful. The child learns to aspire to socially approved behavior and to avoid behavior that is punished. However, what is approved and what is punished are dependent on a person's age, sex, race, and social class. Socialized anxiety must be distinguished from neurotic anxiety, which is nonadaptive and irrational. Socialized anxiety serves as a motivating and reinforcing agent in the socialization process: it brings about, in Mowrer's (1939) words, "anticipation of discomfort" and becomes a behavior-controlling mechanism. During

---

*Davis sees the first source of anxiety in the cleanliness training of the child.

adolescence, it becomes internalized and increasingly independent of its reinforcing or socializing agents. It is Davis' (1944) hypothesis that the effective socialization of adolescent behavior is dependent on the amount of adaptive or socialized anxiety that has been implanted in an individual. If an individual's socialized anxiety becomes strong enough, it will serve as an impetus toward mature, responsible, normal behavior. The concept "socialized anxiety" could be compared to Freud's "superego." It is implied that if socialized anxiety is too weak or too strong, the attainment of mature behavior is less likely.

The goals of socialization differ not only from culture to culture, but also from social class to social class within a given culture, as demonstrated by social psychologists such as Davis and Havighurst. Consequently, social anxiety becomes attached to various forms of behavior depending upon the expectations, values, and definition of what is normal in a given social class. For example, the middle-class child acquires moral values, needs, and social goals different from those of either the lower- or the upper-class child. Furthermore, since the middle class is more concerned with normality, success, morality, and status, the amount of socially instilled anxiety is greater than in the other classes. It is characteristic of middle-class youth that their social anxiety increases with the onset of adolescence, since they face new developmental and behavioral tasks, such as preparation for work and heterosexual adjustment. Furthermore, as they become increasingly aware of their own social needs—having prestige, friends, being accepted by the peer group, relating to the opposite sex—they become more sensitive to social cues and social pressures. Since they depend greatly on social acceptance, prestige, and status, their social anxiety increases. This produces an increased striving for socially desirable goals. "Adolescents with a strongly developed social anxiety, therefore, usually strive for the approved social goals most eagerly and learn most successfully" (Davis, 1944: 208).

Lower-class adolescents behave differently from those in the middle class in such areas of socialization as sex expression, attitudes toward long-range goals, aggression, and schooling. Lower-class adolescents have been exposed to socializing agents whose attitudes toward these areas are quite different from those of the middle class. They do not develop the kind of socialized anxiety that motivates their middle-class counterparts to achieve and to postpone immediate pleasure for long-range goals. Furthermore, they have learned that they are not likely to receive the rewards available to middle-class adolescents even if they study their lessons, are "good little boys or girls," and avoid the sexual and recreational activities of their peers. "This means that the culture determines (1) what the goal-responses are for a given adolescent,

(2) the degree to which the goal-responses are available to him. With regard to a great many goals, what is rewarding to a middle-class adolescent is not at all so to a lower-class adolescent" (Davis, 1944: 209).

ROBERT HAVIGHURST'S DEVELOPMENTAL TASKS OF ADOLESCENCE

With Robert Havighurst's (1900–   ) book *Developmental Tasks and Education* (1951) the emphasis shifts from the social motivation that guides the behavior of the individual, namely social anxiety, to the criteria by which society defines the attainment of certain stages of development; however, these criteria are related to the needs of the organism. "A developmental task is midway between an individual need and a social demand" (Havighurst, 1951: 4). Developmental tasks are defined as skills, knowledge, functions, and attitudes that an individual has to acquire at a certain point in life; they are acquired through physical maturation, social expectations, and personal efforts. Successful mastery of these tasks will result in adjustment and will prepare the individual for the harder tasks ahead. Failure in a given developmental task will result in a lack of adjustment, increased anxiety, social disapproval, and the inability to handle the more difficult tasks to come. A rather important aspect of the concept of developmental tasks is its sequential nature; each task is the prerequisite for the next one. Furthermore, there is for at least some of these tasks a biological basis and, consequently, there is a definite time limit within which a specific task must be accomplished. Inability to master a task within its time limit may make later learning of that task much more difficult if not impossible. In other words, there is a "teachable moment" for many developmental tasks. Through its socializing agents and methods of reinforcement and punishment, society attempts to help the individual learn those developmental tasks at their proper age levels. Psychologically speaking, the teachable moment is the correct time for teaching and learning a given task. This time element is determined by maturation, social pressures and demands, and motivation. These three factors should be considered in curriculum planning if the student is to learn most effectively and with the least waste of energy by both the teacher and the student.

It is Havighurst's assumption that the specific nature of the developmental tasks differs from culture to culture, the degree of difference depending on the relative importance of biological, psychological, and cultural elements in a given task. If the cultural element in a task is dominant over the biological, then greater differences in the nature of that task are likely to be observed from culture to culture.

Havighurst (1951) describes the nature of the task; the biological, psychological, and cultural bases; the differences in the upper, middle, and lower classes in America; and educational implications. The developmental tasks for adolescence (from about twelve to eighteen) are:

1. Accepting one's physique and accepting a masculine or feminine role.
2. Developing new relations with age-mates of both sexes.
3. Gaining emotional independence of parents and other adults.
4. Achieving assurance of economic independence.
5. Selecting and preparing for an occupation.
6. Developing intellectual skills and concepts necessary for civic competence.
7. Desiring and achieving socially responsible behavior.
8. Preparing for marriage and family life.
9. Building conscious values in harmony with an adequate scientific world-picture (Havighurst, 1951: 30–55).

The achievement of these tasks might be taken as an indication that adulthood and maturity have been achieved. However, a new set of developmental tasks awaits the "Early Adulthood" period, just as a set of "Middle Childhood Tasks" preceded those listed.

A study by Schoeppe and Havighurst (1952) demonstrates that good achievement on one developmental task is positively related to good performance on another task at the same age. They also found that the performance in any one of these areas is positively related to future performance in that area. Furthermore, the early period of adolescence, between ten and thirteen, is crucial for socialization in that most changes in level of performance were found before thirteen, but relatively little change was observed between thirteen and sixteen.

Developmental tasks 1, 2, and 8 from the list above have an obvious biological basis and should therefore be found in every society, even though the specific behavior may vary somewhat because of social mores. The biological basis in 3, 5, and 6 is less obvious but nevertheless present. These adolescent tasks exist in every society, though the behavior involved may differ greatly from one society to another. Developmental tasks 4, 7, and 9 have no biological basis and therefore are characteristic of some societies but not of others. Havighurst included them because he is especially concerned with adolescence in the United States, where these tasks are required in order to meet the Early Adulthood Tasks.

Havighurst, in the formulation of his theory of developmental tasks, draws on several theories of adolescence that emphasize only certain aspects of adolescent development. He credits Williams (1930) with the original idea of specific tasks that are most important for the adjustment of boys and girls of this age group: "(1) to become emotionally independent of the family and (2) to achieve a good relationship with age-mates of the opposite sex" (Havighurst, 1951: 1). Also, Rank, in his theory of adolescence, puts great emphasis on the achievement of emotional independence (task 3). For Adler, the acceptance of the feminine or masculine role takes on great importance (task 1). For Freud, sexual adjustment, as expressed in developmental tasks 2 and 8, seems to be fundamental. Blos' theory of the adolescent's individuation concepts encompasses tasks 1, 2, 3, and 8. Erikson's concept of ego-identity is reflected in tasks 1, 3, and 7. Lewin's concept of increased organization and differentiation of the adolescent's life space encompasses tasks 2, 3, 5, and 7. Obviously, Havighurst's developmental tasks theory is an eclectic one combining previously developed concepts and constructs.

9: ARNOLD GESELL'S THEORY OF ADOLESCENT DEVELOPMENT

ARNOLD Gesell's (1880–1961) theory of adolescent development is a natural and integral part of his general developmental theory. His three best known works, *Infant and Child in the Culture of Today* (Gesell and Ilg, 1943), *The Child from Five to Ten* (Gesell and Ilg, 1946), and *Youth: The Years from Ten to Sixteen* (Gesell, Ilg, and Ames, 1956), constitute a trilogy describing human growth and development from birth to adolescence. A systematic statement of Gesell's general theory of development can be found in his "The Ontogenesis of Infant Behavior" (1946). Gesell's biologically oriented theory of predetermined maturation reflects the strong influence of Hall's theory of development. Gesell drew certain parallels between the evolution of the human race and the ontogenesis of the growing child, returning in a way to Hall's theory of recapitulation. He assumed, as did Freud, that development is biological in nature; however, he rejected the idea that unconscious motives direct and form actions, emotions, and personality structure. Gesell's emphasis on overt observable behavior and the more tangible aspects of personality is reflected in his definition of personality as "the total psychic individual as manifested in action and attitude" (Gesell, Ilg, and Ames, 1956: 32). Gesell was mainly interested in the behavioral manifestations of development and personality, rather than their structure.* His constructs of growth gradient as revealed in stages and cycles of development are similar to certain developmental theories advanced in central Europe.

---

*Gesell's comments on the three levels of reality that embrace the mental life are similar to Aristotle's three-layer concept of the human soul. Gesell's three levels of reality are: "1. the vegetative functions of respiration, alimentation, elimination; 2. the world of things, in time and space; 3. the world of persons, in home and community" (Gesell and Ilg, 1943: 20). However, whereas for Aristotle the lower layers of the soul had to develop before the higher could develop, Gesell saw the organism as an integrated unit, with all three levels growing simultaneously. The "mind does not grow on the installment plan" (Gesell and Ilg, 1943: 20).

In the introductory chapter of *Youth*, Gesell refers to his subjects as "adolescents" as well as "youths." However, in an earlier publication (Gesell and Ilg, 1946), he states, as did Hall, that adolescence is a period from about eleven to twenty-four; the term "youth" refers only to the earlier half of the adolescent period.

Gesell's study of growth and development is fundamentally normative. In his trilogy, he described the overall pattern of developmental trends and the "norms" of behavior in their chronological sequence. One can compare a given child with this schedule of development in order to assess the degree of precocity or immaturity. However, critics have pointed out that there are certain dangers in relying too much on normative descriptive data, especially when the concern is with a particular individual. Parents cannot really compare their own child's development to tables of averages without considering the great diversity and variability in human behavior and development. Lack of awareness of the difference between an average and an individual can result in much anxiety, since the average is too closely associated with "normality" and any deviation from the average, "abnormality." These not uncommon difficulties of a normative descriptive approach stem from the well-known and conclusively proved principle that there are great individual differences in onset, rate, and nature of almost all developmental phenomena. Children may deviate widely from the average without being "abnormal." Gesell was aware of this criticism; anticipating it, he devoted a whole section to "The Uses and Misuses of Age Norms" (Gesell and Ilg, 1943). Nevertheless, he proceeded normatively and described the twelve-year-old as if twelve-year-olds had highly specific generalizable characteristics and as if twelve-year-olds in general were substantially different from eleven- and thirteen-year-olds.

GESELL'S THEORY OF DEVELOPMENT

The concept of growth, both mental and physical, forms the core of Gesell's theory. He saw growth* as a process that brings about changes in form and function; it has its seasons and lawful sequences. To reveal these sequences, seasons, and principles of development was Gesell's objective. He emphasized that "mental growth is a patterning process; a progressive *morphogenesis* of patterns of behavior" (Gesell 1940: 7). Growth is a process of progressive differentiation and integration. It is the concept that unifies "the dualism of heredity and environment," since environmental influence stimulates, modifies, and supports growth (Gesell, 1946: 316). However, environmental factors do not

---

*Gesell used the terms "growth" and "development" interchangeably.

generate the sequence of growth. This is brought about by matura- tion—the appearance of functions, abilities, and skills without the influence of special training or practice. Maturation is considered the intrinsic component of the more comprehensive term "growth." The relationship between growth and maturation can best be described in Gesell's own words:

> Growth is a process so intricate and so sensitive that there must be powerful stabilizing factors, intrinsic rather than extrinsic, which preserve the balance of the total pattern and the direction of the growth trend. Maturation is, in a sense, a name for this regulatory mechanism [Gesell, 1933: 232].

Furthermore, "maturation is mediated by genes" (Gesell, Ilg, and Ames, 1956: 27). Biology determines the order of the appearance of be- havioral traits and developmental trends. For example, infants raise their heads first, then their trunks; they sit before they stand; they bab- ble before they talk. Gesell's theory assumes that there is an inborn biological force that determines the sequence of the occurrence of basic developmental phenomena, motor control, skills, abilities, and behav- ior patterns.

Even though Gesell theorizes about an "inherent maturational mechanism," the term "maturation" is not connected to or identified with specific physiological processes. Genetic factors guide and control the direction and sequence of the maturation mechanism. The concept of maturation implies that the individual masters certain forms of behavior with no known direct external influence. Gesell (Gesell and Thompson, 1929; Gesell, 1941) demonstrated the genetically deter- mined concept of maturation in studies of identical twins. The devel- opmental principle that results from these studies—that maturation is an essential prerequisite for learning—has been verified by others. Gesell summarized: "There is no conclusive evidence that practice and exercise even hasten the actual appearance of types of reactions like climbing and tower building. The time of appearance is fundamentally determined by the ripeness of neural structures" (Gesell and Thomp- son, 1929: 114). Although the appearance of maturationally acquired skills can be demonstrated more easily with infants and young chil- dren, Gesell (1933) applied this principle to development in general, in- cluding the period of adolescence.

Gesell rejected as early behavioristic the idea that infants are alike at birth and that differences are due to conditioning. He advanced the following idea to reconcile his normative descriptive approach with the principle of individual differences: The child is born a unique indi- vidual with an inherited pattern of growth, but also with great plas- ticity. Two factors account for individual differences:

1. The "genetic factors of individual constitution and innate maturation sequence" (Gesell, Ilg, and Ames, 1956: 22).
2. The "environmental factors ranging from home and school to the total cultural setting" (Gesell, Ilg, and Ames, 1956: 22). This latter process he called "acculturation."

Both processes interact to form a particular individual growth pattern, but since maturation is of primary importance, "acculturation can never transcend maturation" (Gesell and Ilg, 1943: 41).

Although development is basically a continuous process of patterning, there are fluctuations in the acquisition of specific functions. Growth takes place according to the principle of reciprocal interweaving in neuromotor development (Gesell, 1939). These developmental fluctuations and trends, corresponding to the ancient process of human evolution, are illustrated by the mechanical model of a spiral. Gesell (1933) spoke of a "process of continuous differentiation." Development takes place in sequential patterns or cycles. It oscillates along a spiral course of development toward maturity. Children progress as they acquire specific functions until they reach a certain degree of mastery. Then they revert to earlier forms of behavior before they are able to surpass previous performance. Plateaus may occur at either the high or low point of the developmental spiral. This theory helps explain why children return to earlier forms of development and why, for a time, they seem to be unable to accomplish those skills they were able to do well at an earlier age. Gesell perceived this downward gradient as nature's way of giving the child an opportunity to consolidate abilities and potentialities for further development. The developmental spiral of interchanging upward and downward gradients is a growth mechanism of self-adjustment. This concept of downward gradient is like Freud's concept of regression, with one basic difference: Psychoanalytic regression has a pathological aspect because it takes place when a person is unable to master a new situation. Downward gradient is an important, necessary, and natural part of the developmental process, since it provides the organism with rest and consolidation so it can move on to higher forms of achievement.

The concept of gradient of development may also be applied to adolescence. But the downward gradient cannot be demonstrated in adolescents as easily as it can with acquisition of the simple motor skills in early infancy. Growth gradients for the adolescent are well-defined stages of maturity by which the youth advances toward more complex and more mature functions. Gesell warned that growth gradients do not constitute a psychometric scale, but rather a theoretical construct that explains the growth process and helps identify and assess levels of maturity.

GESELL'S DESCRIPTION OF THE PUBESCENT AND ADOLESCENT PERIOD

Gesell, like Lewin, considered adolescence the crucial transition period from childhood to adulthood. The beginnings of adolescent behavior appear at approximately eleven and final maturity is reached in the early twenties. The central task of adolescence is to find oneself. The period is approximately two years shorter for girls because they develop faster. The more important changes occur in the first five years of adolescence. This is the time span Gesell, Ilg, and Ames (1956) called "youth" in their book on adolescence.

In the description of adolescent maturity profiles, maturity traits, and trends, Gesell drew his conclusions from a selected population segment in one geographic area of the United States. His subjects came from the high-average to superior ability range of the school population, and many of them planned to go to college. In the light of insight gained from cultural anthropology and social psychology, this is a serious limitation. But because of the postulated biological nature of development, Gesell considered many of the important and broad developmental principles, trends, and sequences to be universal. He described the innate maturational sequence and the pattern of growth as "more or less characteristic of the human species" (Gesell, Ilg, and Ames, 1956: 22–23).

Gesell did not systematically distinguish between pubescence and adolescence. He believed that biology controls not only changes in growth, glandular secretion, and the development of primary and secondary sex characteristics, but also abilities and attitudes; for example "the instinctive basis of reasoning ability is repeatedly shown in the adolescence of individuals . . ." (Gesell, Ilg, and Ames, 1956: 181). Again, when he discussed the characteristics of sixteen-year-old girls, he stated: "the girls instinctively stressed interpersonal relationship" in describing their future husbands (Gesell, Ilg, and Ames, 1956: 253).

Gesell did not see adolescence as necessarily turbulent, erratic, and troublesome, as Hall pictured it in his "storm and stress" concept. He considered it a ripening process, though not without irregularities. Furthermore, the age levels he used to define the different stages of development were considered as only approximates, with a slow process of change from one level to the next.

Gesell objected to a purely functional psychology and to a purely theoretical developmental system; he used maturity profiles to describe the characteristics of each age level. The concepts and ideas presented in the following synopsis are from *Youth: The Years from Ten to Sixteen* (Gesell, Ilg, and Ames, 1956), and all direct quotes refer to this book unless otherwise indicated.

The Ten-Year-Old. Gesell described the ten-year-old as being in a state of equilibrium. Ten may be considered a golden age of developmental balance; children are able to accept life and the world with ease. Ten-year-olds are fond of their homes, recognize authority, have confidence, and are obedient. They enjoy family activities such as picnics. They are also fond of friends and join groups and organizations. They are intrigued by secret societies and other forms of secretiveness. However, sociability is limited to their own sex. The ten-year-old boy might say, "We sort of hate girls," and the ten-year-old girl might retort, "We are not interested in boys *yet.*" Care of clothes is at a low point; so is body care. However, educationally, ten-year-olds are assimilative. They have a sense of fairness, and it is important to them that their teachers be fair. With the age of ten, childhood culminates its subcycle and adolescence is in the making.

The Eleven-Year-Old. The eleven-year-old arrives in the foothills of adolescence. Gesell, in analogy to Lewin's new situation and new field, said that the terrain is new; the organism is in a state of change; even physiological functions undergo far-reaching reconstruction. This shows up in impulsiveness and moods, anger and enthusiasm, negativism and argumentativeness, quarreling with siblings and rebellion against parents. In agreement with the basically biological orientation of his theory, Gesell saw some of these symptoms as almost instinctive manifestations of those biological changes that mark the dawn of adolescence.

The Twelve-Year-Old. By the age of twelve, much of the turbulent behavior of eleven has disappeared. Twelve becomes more reasonable, more companionable, and more sociable: "Twelve is predisposed to be positive and enthusiastic rather than negative and reticent" (p. 105). Twelves are trying to grow up and do not wish to be considered babies. They achieve some independence from their homes and parents and are now influenced more by peer groups. The twelfth year demonstrates integration of personality. Basic personality traits are reasonableness, tolerance, and humor. They are ready to take initiative and enter self-chosen tasks with enthusiasm. Twelves become aware of their appearance, especially under the influence of the crowd; they want to wear what the crowd wears. There is a change in boy-girl relationships. Ten's antagonism toward the opposite sex has faded away. "No twelve-year-old party can be guaranteed immune from some sort of kissing game—a most natural expression for Twelve" (p. 122).

The Thirteen-Year-Old. The chief characteristic of thirteen-year-olds is their thrust inward. They are reflective and enter a period of introversion. Thirteens become their own critics and seem to be overconscientious. They worry frequently and from time to time withdraw into themselves. They are sensitive to criticism, quite aware of the emotional state of others, and, generally speaking, fascinated by the term "psychology." At this age, they indulge in detailed criticism of their parents and also in searching self-appraisals. They have fewer friends than twelves, and they choose friends with whom they have many things in common. Great changes in body structure and body chemistry affect behavior in many ways: posture, motor coordination, voice change, facial expression, and related tensions and attitudes. These changes increase their awareness of the fact that they are growing up. Somatic events are related to fluctuations in mood from despair to self-acceptance.

The Fourteen-Year-Old. The general developmental trend now reverses itself from a thrust inward to a period of extroversion characterized by energy, exuberance, and expansiveness. A degree of integration affects both interpersonal relationships and self-concept. Thus, fourteen-year-olds achieve a degree of self-assurance that makes them feel content and relaxed. Their sociability is expressed by a great interest in people and an understanding of personality differences. Fourteens are fascinated by the word "personality" and like to compare and discuss personality traits. Friendships are built on identical interests and compatibility of personality traits. We may describe the fourteen-year-old's preoccupation with the intricacies of human personalities as "an instinctive amateur form of applied psychology" (p. 178). Interest in their own personality is also demonstrated by frequent identification with heroes and characters in movies and literature; they may exclaim, "That's me. That's me all over" (p. 180).

The Fifteen-Year-Old. Fifteen-year-olds cannot be "readily summed up in a simple formula" (p. 214). The description of the fifteen-year-old emphasizes individual differences, but some generalizations are proposed. The most important is a rising spirit of independence that manifests itself in increased tensions, with occasional blowups and hostility in parental and school relationships. Fifteen-year-olds are neither antischool nor antihome, but since they are now starting to think about founding their own home and family, they want to outgrow parental control. They wish to have free time and free choice and may show defiance of external control. Furthermore, they are increasingly self-aware and perceptive. This shows itself in perfectionistic tendencies, self-criticism, and a beginning of self-control. Fifteens are in a vulnerable maturity zone; they can be led into behavior problems and delinquency which, along with their spirit of independence, may bring about an urge to leave school and home.

The Sixteen-Year-Old. Sixteen, the last age described, is characterized as mid-adolescence and as the prototype of the preadult. Self-awareness, self-dependence, and personal social adjustment have now achieved a remarkable degree of balance and integration. Emotions are generally controlled. Sixteens are cheerful, friendly, outgoing, and well adjusted. The rebellious spirit, so characteristic of the fifteen-year-old, has given way to a sense of independence based on self-confidence; it has lost its rebellious component. Sixteen is oriented toward the future; the girls may already have matrimonial plans. There is much companionship between boys and girls, but, generally speaking, it is still on a nonromantic basis.

The developmental principle underlying these descriptions appears to be that growth occurs not in a straight, gradual, continuous pattern, but in fluctuations and oscillations. These descriptions also imply a stage theory that, rather oddly, is determined by time intervals that approach our calendar year rather than by physiological changes or psychological characteristics. However, we observe a progression from immature to more mature stages, culminations of development, and partial reversion to less mature stages.

In spite of Gesell's emphasis on the "continuity of the growth cycle," the descriptions of age levels show some lack of gradualness and steadiness that is theoretically not fully accounted for. Emphasis is placed on cycles, subcycles, and stages, and Gesell attempted purposely "to sharpen the contrast" between personality structure and behavior in one age level and the next. "The tight, withdrawn ways of Thirteen have loosened up at Fourteen. A profound change has occurred, not only within Fourteen but also in his impact upon the world around him" (p. 182). An example of behavioral change is the contrasting boy-girl relationships at eleven, twelve, and thirteen. For the twelve-year-old, Gesell reported strong interest in the opposite sex, with kissing games, regular dancing groups, and first dates. "Some boys who were not interested in girls at eleven and won't be at thirteen enjoy a short period of genuine interest in girls at twelve" (p. 127). Gesell used many such examples to highlight the difference between the preceding and the succeeding age-stage.

These differences in behavior, and even in personality structure, which in Gesell's descriptions so clearly distinguish one age group from another only twelve months older, appear to be unrealistic and mystical. Actual development appears to be more continuous than Gesell's theory admitted. Even more mystical is Gesell's description of the kinship and similarity found between children and youth in the same stage of development but in a different subcycle. Gesell impresses upon his reader again and again the similarities of children at various age levels in different subcycles of development. "The 8-year-old is indeed an elaborated and elaborating version of the 4-year-old" (Gesell and Ilg, 1946: 159). Also: "Then as Two becomes Two-and-a-half and as Five becomes Five-and-a-half or Six, a change occurs—a change in the same direction in each case. Behavior 'loosens up,' perhaps even 'goes to pieces'; life becomes charged with equally attractive, yet incompatible, dual alternatives; 'No' and 'Mine' become prominent items of vocabulary'' (p. 18). A more specific example of this kind of emphasis on the similarities between various subcycles is his observation that freckles are especially evident at both six and twelve; he does not mention them at five and eleven nor at seven and thirteen, almost as if six and twelve had greater similarities with each other than with the age level that preceded or followed each of them.

EDUCATIONAL IMPLICATIONS

Since, in Gesell's theory, maturation is an internal ripening process and since growth cannot be facilitated by external factors, it is frequently assumed that time alone will solve most of the minor problems in the majority of children. Difficulties and deviations will be outgrown. This permissive attitude turns up in Gesell's support of infants' self-regulation of sleep and self-demand for food. Gesell advises against the use of emotional methods of discipline and recommends that parents make the baby "with all its inborn wisdom a working partner" (Gesell and Ilg, 1943: 57). His philosophy of child care lies somewhere between the authoritarian and the laissez-faire approach and attempts to combine a belief in self-regulation with developmental guidance. He, like Rousseau, believed in the wisdom of nature and emphasized that educators must take their cues from the child.

Gesell identifies this idea of cultural guidance with democracy and relates the future of democracy to an understanding of the principles of child development. "Indeed the further evolution of democracy demands a much more refined understanding of . . . children than our civilization has yet attained" (Gesell and Ilg, 1943: 11). Since he attempts to bring about this understanding among parents, his writing appeals to the lay public rather than to the academic world. Understanding of children must be anchored in understanding the processes of growth, maturation, and acculturation. By applying the idea of innate growth potentialities, the realization of which he sees as an inalienable right, Gesell makes growth into a philosophical political concept. The child embodies a "spirit of liberty" based on the developmental principle that "growth tends toward an optimum realization" (Gesell, 1933: 230). Environmental factors alone prevent optimal development—an idea more radically expressed by Rousseau. A developmental philosophy of child care based on empirical research has far-reaching consequences for a democratic society. "The new biological doctrines of growth have vast social implications—implications for child guidance, for mental diagnosis, for health supervision, for the conduct of education, and for the very arrangements of our ways of living" (Gesell, 1948: 10). Gesell compares the influence his biological psychology will have to the impact of Darwin's theory of evolution.

Gesell maintains that the school curriculum should be founded on a psychology of development rather than on a psychology of learning. Furthermore, he hopes that with increased knowledge of development, the laws of learning will "be reformulated in terms of the biology and physiology of development" (Gesell and Ilg, 1946: 298). This belief follows from his emphasis on the interdependence of maturation and learning. Gesell demonstrated with identical twins that successful learning cannot take place until the maturational level appropriate for the particular kind of learning is reached. Consequently, a school curriculum should be based on psychological knowledge of the nature and sequence of maturation. The cultural pattern of teaching and learning must be adapted to the genetically determined growth pattern.

In considering the educational implications of specific age zones, we must emphasize the pupils' attitudes toward school and learning and their behavior in school. But this information may also indicate maturational trends and thus have bearing on curriculum development. The discussion will be limited to ages ten to sixteen.

Tens seem to be especially well suited for the educational processes; they are assimilative, love to memorize, and are more inclined to identify facts rather than correlate, conceptualize, or generalize. Their attention span is short, but their interests vary widely. They are sociable and need social organizations. If the community does not provide healthy outlets for this social need, youth will form its own gangs.

The restless, seething, and explosive form of behavior that characterizes eleven-year-olds will manifest itself in the classroom too. They will wriggle in their seats, but their exuberance will be followed by pronounced fatigue. A rather unorthodox suggestion for overcoming this fatigue is half-day school attendance. Eleven is highly competitive and especially enjoys group competition. Gesell suggests nonacademic activities such as music, art, shop, and dramatics for eleven's spontaneity and creativeness.

Twelves' sociability results in an increased interest in group work. The group may become so important that they lose their own identity and conform to group norms. Their greater independence from adults and longer attention span make them less in need of supervision. They show a remarkable increase in conceptual thinking and can define such abstractions as time, space, life, law, loyalty, crime, and justice. Their ability to classify and generalize also shows considerable improvement. They like to debate and can become involved and enthusiastic in defending or advancing the "right" idea.

Thirteens become more reflective and evaluative; they remain cooperative and are more careful in selecting the right words, phrases, and ideas. They criticize their own performance and may limit their arguments by adding "I think." They have a better sense of responsibility and they are more dependable in their work, but they are also absent-minded. Now, for the first time, they distinguish between liking the teacher and liking the subject. Since they are getting interested in hobbies, they need extracurricular activities. Their interests now include world affairs, political history, the solar system, nuclear science, and the weather. They show interest in the different branches of science; psychology seems especially fascinating.

Fourteens attempt to improve their command of language and enter the ideational realm. Their tendency toward sociability becomes of greater importance than their academic interest. They are curious about themselves and their personality traits; this makes guidance and counseling especially important. Gesell suggests a school unit just for fourteen-year-olds because fourteen is the pivotal year in the cycle of human development.

Fifteens show a craving for independence that may make them rebel against school, especially if they feel controlled and restricted. The need "to be on their own" may make them want to leave school and home. Participation in community experiences is suggested for this age. Fifteens are susceptible to peer group influences and may be quite a challenge to the teacher. But a teacher who meets their need for independence can produce integration of knowledge and high achievement.

Sixteens show the first signs of a mature mind, and the maturity traits are balanced and integrated. Attitudes toward school, teacher, learning, and themselves improve. They begin to "buckle down," work on their own, and accept responsibility. Gesell's description of the cycle breaks off at sixteen, even though this is not the end of the adolescent period.

10: JEAN PIAGET'S COGNITIVE THEORY OF ADOLESCENCE

JEAN Piaget's (1896–1980) contribution to our understanding of human development is reflected in the increasing attention that psychologists—especially those with a cognitive development orientation—have devoted to his theory. In his earlier work, Piaget emphasized the cognitive development in infancy and childhood; only in his later research did Piaget give systematic attention to the more advanced levels of cognitive reasoning characteristic of adolescents. The book most explicitly designed to describe cognitive development in adolescence is *The Growth of Logical Thinking from Childhood to Adolescence** (Inhelder and Piaget, 1958).

After completing his dissertation Piaget worked in Paris on the standardization of intelligence tests. Even though Piaget showed little interest in the psychometric and statistical procedures essential for test construction, he became fascinated with the underlying reasoning and the thought processes that children revealed while trying to solve test problems, and he found their explanations of incorrect responses particularly revealing. The Geneva group still feels that standardized test questions frequently lead to stereotyped responses that do not fully reveal the underlying thought structure. They instead gather data through a "clinical method" that assesses thought processes rather than knowledge and allows children to explain the reasons for their thinking. In the meantime Piaget-type cognitive assessment batteries have been developed by Pinard and Laurendeau (1964), Furth and Wachs (1975), Patterson and Milakofsky (1980), and others. In general, the emphasis in such procedures is not so much on the answers given and whether or not they are correct as on the reasons for the answers. Piaget's preoccupation with qualitative changes in children's

---

*References will be to Piaget and his theory, even though major contributions were made by Bärbel Inhelder, who is the senior author of this volume, which provides the major source material for this chapter.

thought processes is obvious in much of his work. However, the lack of statistical analysis, noticeable in most of his earlier work, has long been a source of criticism.

Among contemporary schools of psychological thought, Piaget takes a relatively unique and independent position. There are no immediate predecessors with whom Piaget studied or whose ideas he expanded. Nevertheless, Piaget was influenced by a number of thinkers. Philosophically, he was influenced by Kant's epistemology and Bergson's metaphysics. Piaget read Freud, but references to Freud appear only in his earlier work. Piaget did not share Freud's interest in the subconscious, in conflicts, in behavior dynamics, or in the affective aspects of human development. Instead he focused his theory on the conflict-free and rational side of human development and emphasized thought processes, the structure of intelligence, and the development of logical thinking. Nevertheless, Piaget's concept of "egocentrism" (see Chapter 13), which characterized the language, thought, and social judgment of developing children, is quite compatible with some psychoanalytic notions, such as the subject-object differentiation. Piaget also stimulated the present concern with moral judgment (see Chapter 11) and social cognition (see Chapter 12).

In certain respects, Piaget's theory (1947b) appears to be closer to the German school of Gestalt psychology, and Piaget once said that if he had studied with the Gestalt psychologists in Berlin he probably would have become a Gestalt psychologist himself. His kinship with Gestalt psychology is especially clear in his emphasis on the patterns of organization, the structural whole, and the total system. Piaget was concerned, as are the Gestalt psychologists, with the relationship between the parts and the whole. However, he disagreed with several of their basic assumptions. For example, Gestalt principles do not seem to be useful in explaining the "logical operations in thought" that Piaget attempted to discover. Furthermore, he emphasized structural changes as a function of development, whereas Gestalt psychology maintains that the "laws of organization" and "perceptual structure" are independent of age.

Piaget, who has been characterized as a "zoologist by training, an epistemologist by vocation, and a logician by method," is best known for his contributions to developmental psychology. He regarded himself as an interdisciplinary thinker and can best be identified as a "genetic epistemologist." Epistemology is the branch of science concerned with the methods, the limits, and the validity of knowledge. The term "genetic" implies that the acquisition of knowledge is influenced by genetic or biological factors; however, Piaget was not a maturationalist but is better characterized as an "interactionist." He emphasized that development is an interaction between biology and environment, or between nature and nurture. Coming from philosophy and biology, his methodology as well as his theoretical conceptualizations initially were unique and even suspect, but they have slowly and steadily been integrated into the mainstream of psychological thought and have become a dominating influence in cognitive and developmental research in the last twenty years. The popularity of "cognitive psychology" as a new field is, in part, a result of Piaget's contributions. The following presentation of Piaget's developmental theory can only highlight a few of the more salient features of a very complex theoretical construct.

THE MAJOR DEVELOPMENTAL CONCEPTS OF PIAGET'S THEORY

Piaget's theory of development contains two components which, even though closely interrelated, can be analyzed separately: the stage-dependent and the stage-independent theory (Flavell, 1963a). The elements of the stage-dependent theory are the four well-known developmental stages: sensorimotor, preoperational, concrete operational, and formal operational stages. Each will be discussed in more detail later. In addition, Piaget advanced a system of interrelated concepts, borrowed primarily from biology, that make up his stage-independent theory of development. The important constructs of the stage-independent theory are: schema, structure, operation, assimilation, accommodation, adaptation, equilibrium, and disequilibrium. These ideas cut across all levels of the stage-dependent theory and are as applicable to early motor development as they are to the advanced logical thought processes of the mature adult. Thus, Piaget cannot easily be dismissed as just another European "stage theorist."

The first two concepts of the stage-independent theory, schema and structure, appear to be almost interchangeable. A schema is a generalized or established behavior pattern of meaningful and repeatable action patterns, such as the sucking schema, the grasping schema, and later in adolescence, the "all-other-things-being-equal" schema of reasoning. As children continuously interact with their environment, the simple schemata become broadened and modified and combine with other schemata. Schemata, therefore, are not static, but are continuously growing and are even referred to as "mobile schemata." When referring to the thought processes of adolescents, Piaget uses such terms as "cognitive schema," "operational schema," "anticipatory schema," and "logical schema." It is in these latter instances that schema and structure become synonymous, except that schema is the behavioral equivalent and structure the internal thought patterns.

The structures are the organizational properties of thought that determine the nature of the child's actions, especially the more complex cognitive responses. Thus, the theory focuses on the qualitative changes of intellectual structure from birth to maturity. Each structure is built on earlier, simpler, less mature structures. The integration of older, lower-level structures into new, more advanced structures provides the continuity for cognitive development (Flavell, 1963b).

According to Piaget, when schemata and structures have developed to the extent that they can be used by interrelated systems of logic, they are called "operations." Piaget defines an operation as a reversible action or a reversible transformation of one structure into another. Consequently, operations are more complex and more differentiated than schemata and begin to approximate a logical model. It is possible to apply operations to a much wider spectrum of related problems. For example, memorized formulas that a student applies to a series of identical problems correspond to schemata. But when a student is able to solve a problem in a different context, or by using different symbols, or can understand the relationship of each specific piece of information to the whole problem, the student demonstrates operational thinking. In this situation the reliance on the memorized formula becomes unnecessary because the meaning of the problem is understood. To the extent that operations have become meaningful parts of the cognitive structure, they show resistance to forgetting. "Operations," to which Piaget devotes considerable emphasis in his theory, have two characteristics:

1. Operational thought is reversible. Logical operations in mathematics can be reversed by cancelling an operation. The operational child understands that subtraction can cancel the process of addition just as division can cancel multiplication. The addition $6 + 7 = 13$ can be cancelled by its reversal $13 - 7 = 6$. One can reverse an operation by reciprocity and return to the starting-point. A clay ball can be made into a clay sausage or a clay pancake and again be reversed into the original form of a clay ball.

2. Operational thought is associative. Thought is not limited to only one avenue, but has the flexibility and the freedom to pursue a problem by way of different routes, detours, and by way of a variety of methods and approaches. For example, the problem 25×25 can be solved in a number of ways: $(25 \times 20) + (25 \times 5)$; or $20^2 + (2 \times 20 \times 5) + 5^2$; or $25 \times 100 \div 4$; and so on.

The distinction between operational and preoperational thought constitutes the fundamental dividing line in Piaget's stage-dependent theory. Since such systems of logical operations, reversibility, and associativity of thought do not emerge until about the age of seven, Piaget speaks of the child prior to this age as the *preoperational child*, who relies predominantly on perception and intuition. After the age of seven the child enters the *operational stage of development*. Operations are seen as internalized actions that constitute a system of organized and related thoughts and correspond to the operations of mathematics and logic. Piaget speaks of logical operations, such as addition, multiplication, and reciprocity; and uses mathematics and logic as the models for his analysis of the thought of the operational child.

The three variables primarily responsible for development in general and cognitive development in particular are:

1. The maturation of the nervous system
2. Experiences gained through interaction with physical reality
3. The influence of the social environment

The maturation model of development constitutes only a general background for Piaget's equilibration-equilibrium model, which places major emphasis on the dynamic interaction between the developing child and his physical and social environment.

Cognitive adaptation to the environment takes place by way of assimilation and accommodation. The child's environmental experiences are first assimilated; that is, the new experience or event is structured or restructured to fit into the present intellectual organization. To intellectually assimilate "reality is to construct that reality, and to construct it in terms" of one's existing cognitive structure (Flavell, 1963a: 48). Accommodation refers to the process of internal change in the cognitive structure, a change brought about by utilizing and incorporating—that is, accommodating to the new experiences that were just assimilated. Piaget borrowed the terms assimilation-accommodation from biology, and biology provides an appropriate analogy: The organism assimilates food by chewing, swallowing, and breaking it down. In this process food is restructured to fit the biological needs of the organism. However, in the process the organism also changes. The organism accommodates food by incorporating (digesting) it into its own structure. As a result, the organism itself is restructured; it has more energy and it grows. Assimilation and accommodation are complementary processes. They bring about conceptual adaptation and cognitive growth through their continuous interaction. It is through this very process of assimilation and accommodation that the intellectual structure grows and expands. When a balance between assimilation and accommodation has been accomplished, a state of equilibrium exists.

Equilibrium is the harmony between sensory information and accumulated knowledge, or harmony between the individual and the environment. As new sensory information—in the form of questions, problems, and issues—disturbs existing, incomplete, or incorrect knowledge, the equilibrium is thrown into a new disequilibrium, and a new assimilation-accommodation process begins. As these new questions, problems, or issues are taken into the existing structure (assimilation) and the existing structure grows, changes, and expands in the process (accommodation), a new, higher-level equilibrium is attained. The accommodation of new experiences produces modifications in the structure and the schema, which means that the child has gained something that allows him to make more sophisticated observations, to solve more difficult problems, or to advance higher-level generalizations. Thus the theory allows for continuous progressive cognitive development. Assimilating and accommodating environmental experiences leads slowly but steadily to cognitive growth. In contrast to purely maturational theories, such as Gesell's (see Chapter 9), Piaget views children as active participants in their own development. This active conception of the nature of the child is well expressed in the often quoted statement by Piaget, "Every time we teach a child something, we keep him from reinventing it. On the other hand, every time a child discovers it for himself, it remains with him for the rest of his life" (from the film *Patron: Piaget in New Perspective*).

The concept of equilibrium is essential in Piaget's definition of intelligence as a "form of equilibration . . . toward which all functions lead" (Piaget, 1962: 120). Equilibration is defined as a compensation for an external disturbance. Intellectual development becomes a continuous progression moving from one structural disequilibrium to a new, higher, structural equilibrium. Intellectual operations never function in isolation but are regulated by organizing principles that relate to the total system. Consequently, Piaget frequently draws parallels from the basic cognitive structures of thinking to the child's level of moral judgment (1932), language development (1932a), reasoning, and conceptions of the world (1929), or physical causality (1930), or numbers (1952a), or space (1956). "It is possible to discern synchronized structures of operational development manifesting themselves in such diversified fields as logic, space, time, etc." (Inhelder, 1966: 304).

PIAGET'S STAGES OF COGNITIVE DEVELOPMENT

Piaget's theory originally focused on infancy and childhood but was later systematically expanded to include adolescence. The interrelationship of the various facets of Piaget's theory make it necessary to discuss briefly the essential characteristics of the earlier stages of development. The preadolescent and adolescent periods, which are characterized by operational thought, will be described in more detail and become the primary focus of this chapter. The following stage-dependent theory has to be understood in the light of the continuing disequilibrium-assimilation-accommodation-equilibrium process just discussed.

THE SENSORIMOTOR STAGE

The *sensorimotor stage of development* (from birth to two), described in great detail by Piaget, is subdivided into six developmental phases. The first phase (birth to one month), the *reflex* phase, consists primarily of exercising inborn reflexes such as the sucking reflex, which, as it becomes modified to meet the demands of different situations, becomes the sucking schema. During the second phase (one to four months), which Piaget calls the phase of *primary circular reactions*, the reflexes are slowly replaced by voluntary movements. The child may tirelessly practice an emerging schema, such as grasping, since he is motivated by "function pleasure"—a concept quite different from the behavioristic notion of "drive reduction" or "reinforcement." In the third phase (four to eight months), that of *secondary circular reactions*, infants begin to pursue objects and events unrelated to themselves—for example, following the slow movement of an attractive toy. Or, if an infant learns through trial and error to grasp a cord and make a bell jingle, he may repeat such behavior. That such an action sequence can be repeated is evidence of the beginning of intentionality and even an incipient form of goal-directed behavior. The fourth phase (eight to twelve months), that of *coordination of secondary schemata*, is characterized by the emergence of means-ends relationships. The child reaches for a box in order to obtain the toy that is inside the box. The child will begin to search or look for a toy hidden under a blanket, indicating that the concept of "object permanence" is beginning to emerge. During the fifth phase (twelve to eighteen months), that of *tertiary circular reactions*, the concept of "object permanence" becomes more stable. The child will search for and find the object even though in the process of hiding it, it may have been moved through a series of displacements. That is, the object may have been placed first under a blanket, then under a pillow, and finally under a box. The last of the six phases (twelve to twenty-four months) is that of *internalization of sensorimotor schemata*. The child begins to use foresight and symbolic representation in solving sensorimotor problems. For the first time, the child may investigate whether a hole is big enough before actually attempting to push an object through it, thus giving evidence that the strictly sensorimotor approach to problem solving is being replaced by thought.

THE PREOPERATIONAL STAGE

The second period of development (two to seven years), called the *preoperational stage*, is a transition period from the predominantly egocentric and motor stage of early childhood to the early forms of social behavior, sociocentric speech, and conceptual thought, all of which become more obvious as the child approaches the end of the preoperational stage. This stage is subdivided into two distinguishable phases. The first, that of *extracting concepts from experiences*, covers the years from two to four. Children learn new concepts on the basis of direct, first-hand sensory experiences—that is, they are still at the mercy of their own perceptions. Reality is what they perceive; no other alternatives are available to them. When a chocolate bar is broken up, they think there is more chocolate, because the pieces look more than the solid bar. During this phase, children's language develops at a phenomenal rate. From the rather rudimentary forms of language usage at the age of two, children normally develop language ability to such an extent that they are able to communicate their thoughts by the age of four. The words they hear and use become associated with objects, events, and relationships and thus contribute to conceptual growth.

The second, more advanced phase of the preoperational stage (four to seven years) is that of *intuitive thought*, or intuitive use of concepts. The differentiation from the previous stage is a fine one; the judgments are still intuitive and subjective, but they deal with more complex issues than in the previous stage. The child now can manipulate objects, tools, and toys much more effectively and the ability to communicate with others is enhanced by language development. Therefore, it becomes possible for children to make more systematic interrogations. Nevertheless, accurate judgment is limited by three factors:

1. Basically, children are still dependent on sensory experiences.
2. They cannot consider two or more dimensions at the same time; rather, they focus on one aspect and consequently neglect to consider the other.
3. They cannot rearrange or reorganize information in their minds.

Since these children are too dependent on sensory impressions, they do not yet comprehend the *principle of conservation*: that a given quantity remains the same, even though the way that quantity has been arranged has changed. The typical example is the clay ball being changed into a long clay sausage. The preoperational child thinks it is more "because it looks longer." Neither do they think in terms of a hierarchy of classes and supraclasses. A child may maintain, "We are not in Baltimore, we are in Maryland," not yet comprehending that one can be included in the other.

THE CONCRETE OPERATIONAL STAGE

At approximately age seven or eight, a major shift in the child's conceptual development takes place. He now begins to perform logical *concrete operations* in his mind. This period (from seven or eight to puberty) is referred to as the *operational stage in logical thinking*. Chronologically, this period of concrete operational thinking extends into the preadolescent period.

During the operational stage, the child learns to master the basic logical and mathematical operations, using material with concrete content. "Concrete" in this context does not mean that the child can only deal with tangible objects but that the problems have to be tied to reality. The major limitation still evident in the thinking at this level is the inability to think abstractly about a problem. Since concrete operations can now be performed mentally, overt trial and error becomes unnecessary. For the first time, the child begins to think in accordance with a model of logical reasoning. The important elements of concrete logical operations are:

1. *The logic of classes*, which is based on an understanding of whether or not an object belongs or does not belong in a given class. This enables children to work out problems of classification. They become concerned with the relationship between the parts and the whole. Understanding and classifying the parts that belong together helps them to gain a better understanding of the whole, the supraclass. Their ability to hold several pieces of information in mind and to reverse their thinking enables them to understand a hierarchy of classes and supraclasses. The operational child may actually become preoccupied with systems of classification.

2. *The logic of relations*, which makes it possible to order and organize several things in relationship to one another, according to specific criteria such as size. In a test situation, the child is asked to rank order a series of objects, such as dolls or sticks, according to their size. Such an "operation of serializing" is similar to the classification of a hierarchy, since it involves some understanding of the structure of the whole. "There is no class without classification; there is no systematic relation without serialization" (Piaget, 1962: 126). The

logic of relations gets elaborated when the child is asked to set two series of objects into correspondence with one another. An example would be to match a series of dolls with a corresponding set of hats or sticks. The operational child, possessing the "logic of relations," is able to order objects according to their size, height, or weight as long as objects are presented concretely. It is not until adolescence that such operations can be performed mentally on an abstract level.

The operational child now begins to develop an understanding of the *principle of conservation*, now realizing that changing a clay ball into a sausage or flattening it out into a pancake does not change its mass, weight, or volume. The concept of conservation of mass is established first, weight is of intermediate difficulty, and volume is the most difficult and may not emerge in the concrete operational stage (Elkind, 1961a; 1961b). Elkind (1961b) showed that the conservation of volume concept appeared later in American adolescents than suggested by Piaget; however, he did agree with Piaget that formal operations are necessary for the attainment of the conservation of volume concept.

An understanding of the principle of conservation leads to an awareness of the reversibility of thought processes. Reversibility is defined as "the permanent possibility of returning to the starting point of the operation in question" (Inhelder and Piaget, 1958: 272). The child can construct a chain of colored beads, copying the original pattern in reversed order. Awareness of the concept of reversibility is critical to operational thought. "An operation is an action capable of occurring internally and of which . . . the essential characteristic is its reversibility. Cognitive activity becomes operational when it acquires a mobility such that an action (or transformation) can be annulled in thought by an inverse action or can be compensated for by a reciprocal action" (Inhelder, 1966: 302). The ability to return to the starting point of an operation—which is implied in the concept "reversibility"—constitutes an important milestone in the intellectual development of the child. Operational children use addition and can reverse the findings by subtraction. They can judge the distance between point A and point B and conclude it to be the same as between B and A. Alice in Wonderland, after eating one side of the mushroom, demonstrates the idea of reversibility by nibbling on the other side in order to reverse her height. As a result of having reversible operations, the operational child can use various approaches to solutions of a problem without becoming committed to any one as the only one.

At the same time that the concrete operations emerge, the child's language, which has been predominantly egocentric until the age of seven, becomes primarily sociocentric. Sociocentric language implies a genuine effort to understand other people and to communicate thoughts objectively. "The child really exchanges his thoughts with others, either by telling his hearer something that will interest him and influence his actions, or by an actual interchange of ideas by argument or even by collaboration in pursuit of a common aim" (Piaget, 1932a: 9–10). Research does not substantiate the shift from egocentric to sociocentric speech as neatly as the shift from preoperational to operational thought as the theory does, but the research does support the more general idea that with increasing age the proportion of egocentric speech decreases as sociocentric speech increases.

The change from egocentric to sociocentric thought is not only reflected in the child's language, but permeates his thought processes as well. The sociocentric child can place himself in the situation of another person and take that person's point of view. When confronted with a model of three differently shaped mountains, he can identify correctly what they would look like from other positions (see Figure 11). He can rotate objects in his mind and might spontaneously ask, "What does the other side of the moon look like?"

Piaget identifies the properties of concrete operations and applies the term "elementary groupings," or "group-like structures," to the different ways in which the child's thought processes can manipulate classes and relations. Since Piaget postulates a direct relationship between logic and the child's cognitive processes, the concepts he introduces are conveyed in terms of the operations of logic and mathematics. An important set of four concrete operational groupings follows:

Combinativity. Two or more classes can be combined into one larger, more comprehensive class of the same grouping. For example, all men and all women equals all adults. Logical relationships such as A is larger than B and B is larger than C can be combined into a new statement that A is larger than C. The ability to combine subclasses into supraclasses is essential to the understanding of a hierarchy of classifications.

Reversibility. Every operation is reversible. Every mathematical operation has an opposite operation that reverses it. Supraclasses can be taken apart, so that the effect of combining subclasses is reversed. All adults except all women equals all men. The child's ability to reverse thought processes is an important indicator of cognitive development.

Associativity. The child whose operations have become associative can reach a goal in various ways, making detours in thought, but in such a fashion that the results obtained by these different routes remain the same. For example, $(3 + 6) + 4 = 13$, and $6 + (3 + 4) = 13$.

Identity or nullifiability. An operation that is combined with its opposite becomes nullified. Illustrations of nullifiability in mathematics are: give 3 and take 3 away results in null, or 5 times X divided by 5

Position 3

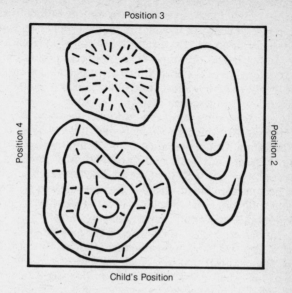

Position 4

Position 2

Child's Position

FIGURE 11. Schematic presentation of the three differently shaped mountains. The question is, when can a child accurately identify what the mountain range looks like from positions 2, 3, and 4?

equals X. All Americans except those who are American equals no one. If I drive one mile west and one mile east, I am where I started; my actions are nullified.

Primary groupings make combinativity, reversibility, and associativity in thought possible and thus aid the child in achieving an equilibrium that is considerably more mobile and flexible than the thought process of the preoperational child. Thus, the approach to problem solving is no longer intuitive or impulsive but rational and logical. However, reasoning is not yet integrated into a single total system of interrelated propositions.

THE FORMAL OPERATIONS STAGE

The final stage of cognitive development in Piaget's theory is the *stage of formal operations*, which is characterized by the use of propositional thinking, combinatorial analysis, and abstract reasoning. The concept ''formal'' implies that what matters is form rather than content. The major source of information about adolescent cognitive development is *The Growth of Logical Thinking* (Inhelder and Piaget, 1958). Piaget subdivides the stage of formal operations further into substages III-A, almost full formal function (eleven or twelve to fourteen or fifteen years) and III-B, full formal function (fourteen or fifteen years and up). This division of the adolescent period at the age of fourteen or fifteen implies another restructuring and a disequilibrium, which then leads to a higher level of equilibrium and intellectual structure during late adolescence. In this division III-A—the earlier substage, corresponding to early adolescence—appears to be a preparatory stage in which adolescents may make correct discoveries and handle certain formal operations, but the approach is still cumbersome, and they are not yet able to provide systematic and rigorous proof for their assertions. By the time adolescents reach substage III-B they have become capable of formulating more elegant generalizations and of advancing more inclusive laws. Most of all, they are now able to provide spontaneously more systematic proof for their assertions, since they understand the importance of the method of control. The difference in approach and reasoning of adolescents in substages III-A and III-B may be illustrated by actual responses.

In one of the experiments, "The Law of Floating Bodies . . .," the subject is presented with a great variety of objects. The problem is to distinguish those that float on water from those that do not float and to provide proof.

> Jim (12; 8) classifies floating or sinking objects according to whether they are *"lighter or heavier than water."* — "What do you mean?" — *"You would have to have much more water than metal to make up the same weight."* — "And this cover?" — *"When you put up the edges, there is air inside; when you put them down, it goes down because the water comes inside and thus makes more weight."* — "Why does the wood float?" — *"Because it is light."* — "And that little key?" — *"No, this piece of wood is heavier."* — "So?" — *"If you measure with a key* [= with the weight of a key], *you need much more wood than lead for the weight of the key."* — "What do you mean?" — *"If you take metal, you need much more wood to make the same weight than metal"* [Inhelder and Piaget, 1958: 38].

The subject who has reached substage III-B sees the problem more specifically in terms of units of measurements that are provided and uses the measures spontaneously. Furthermore, the subject more precisely appreciates that the weight of the object in relationship to the weight of the water that it replaces determines whether the object floats or sinks. There is a reduction in trial-and-error reasoning, and proof is provided with greater elegance and precision, as the following protocol illustrates.

Lamb (13; 3) correctly classifies the objects that sink: *"I sort of felt that they are all heavier than water. I compared for the same weight, not for the same volume of water."* — "Can you give proof?" — *"Yes, I take these two bottles, I weigh them . . . Oh!* [he notices the cubes] *I weigh this plastic cube with water inside and compare this volume of water to the wooden cube. You always have to compare a volume to the same volume of water."* — "And with this wooden ball?" — *"By calculation."* — "But otherwise?" — *"Oh, yes, you set the water level* [in the bucket]; *you put the ball in and let out enough water to maintain the original level."* — "Then what do you compare?" — *"The weight of the water let out and the weight of the ball"* [Inhelder and Piaget, 1958: 44].

It is obvious, as these illustrations show, that the reasoning from substage III-A to substage III-B becomes increasingly more abstract and shows a more sophisticated degree of mastery of the formal operations. Since Piaget postulates a direct correspondence between the structure of logic and the structure of the adolescent's cognitive operations, there is a developmental approximation of the operational thought process of the adolescent to the formal system of modern logic. The significance that Piaget attaches to the change from concrete operations to formal operations is even reflected in a change in the symbols of logic; for example, A + B used for concrete operations, changes to the symbols of logic "p o q" for the same operation. These changes in thought processes are seen as being directly related to maturational changes in the cortex that accompany puberty. While the child at the concrete operational stage was able to reason on the basis of objects, the adolescent begins to reason on the basis of verbal propositions. The principle difference between the operational and the formal operational stage is that the adolescent gains the ability "to reason in terms of verbally stated hypotheses and no longer in terms of concrete objects and their manipulation" (Piaget, 1980: 72). The adolescent can now make hypothetical deductions and entertain the idea of relativity. "Formal thought reaches its fruition during adolescence. An adolescent, unlike the child, is an individual who thinks beyond the present and forms theories about everything, delighting especially in consideration of that which is not" (Piaget, 1947b: 148).

Adolescents not only think beyond the present but analytically reflect about their own thinking. Piaget calls this kind of reasoning "second-degree thinking"; it involves operations that produce "thinking about thinking," "statements about statements," or more significantly, "operations on operations." The adolescent's theories may sometimes still seem to be oversimplifications of reality. Nevertheless, most adolescents in substage III-B have social and political theories and at least some also have religious, philosophical, and scientific theories. Formal operations give the adolescent the ability to understand and even form theories and "to participate in society and the ideologies of adults; this is often accompanied by a desire to change society and even, if necessary, destroy it (in his imagination) in order to elaborate a better one" (Piaget, 1980: 72). This preoccupation with theory can even be applied to the dreams girls have of their future husbands; these dreams are frequently quite "theoretical," as is their understanding of married life (Inhelder and Piaget, 1958).

In their thoughts adolescents can leave the real objective world behind and enter the world of ideas. They now control events in their minds through logical deductions of possibilities and consequences. Even the directions of thought processes change. Preadolescents begin by thinking about reality and attempt to extend thoughts toward possibility. Adolescents, who have mastered formal operations, begin by thinking of all logical possibilities and then consider them in a systematic fashion; reality has become secondary to possibility, reality now being reduced to a subset of possibility. To emphasize this important point further, one could say that in operational thinking reality is the foreground and possibility remains in the background. In formal operational thinking, this relationship is reversed—possibility has become the foreground and reality has become simply one of the many possibilities. "The most distincitve property of formal thought is this reversal of direction between *reality and possibility*; instead of deriving a rudimentary type of theory from the empirical data as is done in concrete inferences, formal thought begins with a theoretical synthesis implying that certain relations are necessary and thus proceeds in the opposite direction. . . . This type of thinking proceeds *from* what is possible *to* what is empirically real" (Inhelder and Piaget, 1958: 251). This reversal of the direction of thought between reality and possibility constitutes a turning point in the development of the structure of intelligence, since it leads to an equilibrium that is both stable and more flexible.

An illustration may serve to contrast preadolescent reasoning based on concrete operations with adolescent reasoning based on verbal propositions. The nine-year-old can arrange a series of dolls according to their height and can even supply each doll with a stick of a corresponding size from a series of different size sticks, even if the sticks are presented in reverse order. But not until the formal operations have developed can a similar, but verbally stated, abstract problem be solved: "If B is not as bad as C, and C is not as good as A, then who is worst?"

The attainment of formal operations is, of course, not an all-or-nothing proposition. Between the ages of eleven or twelve and fourteen or fifteen, considerable modification, systemization, and formaliza-

tion of thought processes can be observed. The complexity of the problems that the individual can handle increases substantially during these
years and reaches an equilibrium after substage III-B has been attained, at approximately fourteen or fifteen.

Piaget distinguishes between the concrete elementary, or primary,
groupings discussed earlier and formal, or second-degree, groupings
characteristic of the formal stage. He also refers to these more advanced groupings as operations to the second power, or the proposi-
tion-about-proposition attribute. Implied in the proposition-about-
proposition concept is the idea that adolescents think about their own
thoughts in a reflective way. (This idea will be developed in greater
detail in the chapter on adolescent egocentrism, Chapter 13). Turning
to a description of the formal operational schemata of adolescence,
one ought to remain aware that adolescents, even though they think
operationally, do not have a basic understanding of the kind of *formal
logic* by which Piaget analyzes and describes adolescent thought processes. The two important theoretical foundations of the formal logic of
adolescence are:

1. *The combinatorial system of operations*, defined as "the matrix
   of all possible combinations of all possible values of all possible
   variables inherent in the problem" (Dulit, 1972: 288).
2. *The INCR group of operations*, to be discussed later.

These two theoretical "building blocks" are comparable in significance to the "logic of classes" and the "logic of relations" in the
operational stage.

COMBINATORIAL SYSTEM OF OPERATIONS

Formal operations allow adolescents to combine propositions and
to isolate variables in order to confirm or disprove their hypotheses.
They no longer need to think in terms of objects or concrete events but
can carry out symbolic operations in their minds. This first grouping to
be presented constitutes a combinatorial system of operational schemata characterized by propositional operations. The formal-
operational thinker can make logical combinations in the following
ways.

1. *Combine by conjunction.* "Both A and B make a difference." The
subject was asked to determine why certain objects float and others do
not. In solving this problem the subject has to realize that "both weight
and volume make a difference" before being able to comprehend the
notion of density, which emerges once the relationship between weight
and volume is understood. As long as the subject attempts to explain

the phenomenon of floating or sinking on the basis of either weight or size—as the concrete operational child commonly does—he fails to make the correct generalization.

2. *Combine by disjunction.* "It's got to be this or that." In order to solve a given problem, variables have to be identified and tested individually so that a hypothesis can be confirmed or rejected. In one of the experiments, the subject is presented with a simple pendulum (see Figure 12). The variables that can be manipulated are the length of the string, the weight, the point at which the weight is released, and the force of the push. The problem is to discover what factors affect the frequency of the oscillation. Once the subject reasons, "It's got to be this or that" (length of string or weight), he begins to approach the solution hypothetically. By experimenting with each of these two variables independently, the subject discovers that weight is irrelevant and the length of the string is the important variable.

3. *Combine by implication.* "If it is this, then that happens." Once a relevant variable has been identified, a more specific explanation can be tested and stated. "If the string is short then the swing is fast; if the string is long then the swing is slow." That is in essence what one of Inhelder's and Piaget's (1958) sixteen-year-old subjects concluded, even though he initially believed that all four variables were involved. The hypothetical nature of the propositional thinking of adolescence finds a clear expression in the declining frequency of operational statements, such as: "This is true, therefore . . ." and an increase in hypothetical deductive statements, such as: "If this were true, then. . . ."

4. *Combine by incompatibility.* "When this happens, then that does not." In the pendulum experiment, increasing and decreasing the weight does not change the oscillation of the pendulum and thus serves to eliminate a hypothesis that is incompatible with the actual observation. A commonly made incorrect assumption in this experiment is that weight does make a difference. Consequently, the ability to combine by incompatibility appears in this instance relatively late in the operational stage.

Initially, in substage III-A adolescents cannot yet reason out the whole range of intrapropositional combinations, which means that they cannot produce systematic proof of their response by way of the schema, "all other things being equal." It is only at substage III-B that subjects can spontaneously use this method. They are now capable of holding all other variables constant and can systematically change one variable at a time to study the effects of each variable in isolation. As a result they not only advance hypotheses but subject them to empirical verification. As their thought processes simulate the controls of a scientific experiment, their proofs become more rigorous and their generalizations gain in precision.

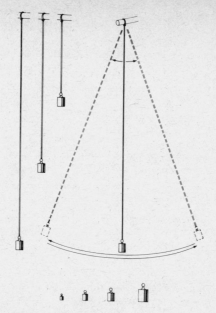

FIGURE 12. The pendulum problem utilizes a simple apparatus consisting of a string, which can be shortened or lengthened, and a set of varying weights. The other variables which at first might be considered relevant are the height of the release point and the force of the push given by the subject.

From *The Growth of Logical Thinking from Childhood to Adolescence*, by Bärbel Inhelder and Jean Piaget, © 1958 by Basic Books, Inc., Publishers, New York and Routledge & Kegan Paul, Ltd., London. Reproduced by permission.

Contrasting the responses of two adolescents in an experiment that involves five distinct variables may illustrate the difference in reasoning of a subject in substage III-A with a subject in substage III-B, only the latter apparently being able to use the important schema, "all other things being equal."

The apparatus consists of a vertical holder with clamps from which brass and nonbrass rods of different sizes and shapes can be horizontally suspended. The holder actually stands in a large basin of water. The subject is to determine the flexibility of the rods and to identify under what circumstances they would touch the water. The flexibility of the rods is dependent on the following variables:

1. The material (steel or brass)
2. The length of the rods (they can be shortened or lengthened)

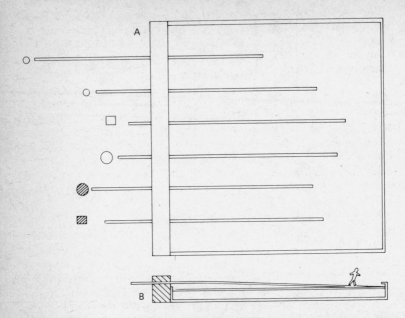

FIGURE 13. Diagram A illustrates the variables used in the flexibility experiment. The rods can be shortened or lengthened by varying the point at which they are clamped (see B for apparatus used). Cross-section forms are shown at the left of each rod; shaded forms represent brass rods, unshaded forms represent non-brass rods. Dolls are used for the weight variable (see B). These are placed at the end of the rod. Maximum flexibility is indicated when the end of the rod touches the water.

From *The Growth of Logical Thinking from Childhood to Adolescence*, by Bärbel Inhelder and Jean Piaget, © 1958 by Basic Books, Inc., Publishers, New York and Routledge & Kegan Paul, Ltd., London. Reproduced by permission.

3. The thickness of the rods (7mm², 10mm², 16mm²)
4. The cross section, or form (round, square, rectangular)
5. The weight attached to the suspended end of the rod (100g, 200g, 300g)

The problem is to determine under what circumstances the rod touches the water level and to provide proof for the assertions made.

Pey (12; 9) speculates that if the rod is to touch the water it must be "long and thin." After several trials he concludes: *"The larger and thicker it is, the more it resists."* — "What did you observe?" — *"This one* [brass, square, 50cm long, 16mm² cross section with 300 gram weight] *bends more than that one* [steel; otherwise the same conditions which he has selected to be equal]:

it's another metal. And this one [brass, round] *more than that one"* [brass, square; same conditions for weight and length, but 10 and 16mm² cross section]. — "If you wanted to buy a rod which bends the most possible?" — *"I would choose it round, thin, long, and made of soft metal"* [Inhelder and Piaget, 1958: 56-57].

The ability to combine the results of each pair of comparisons leads to an understanding of the "structured whole" and—in contrast to the one-by-one comparisons of earlier stages—demonstrates the operation of formal thought. Such an approach is "under construction" in substage III-A (as demonstrated above), not becoming fully operational until substage III-B, when it makes the process of verification much more convincing, as evidenced by the following protocol:

Dei (16; 10): "Tell me first [after experimental trials] what factors are at work here." — *"Weight, material, the length of the rod, perhaps the form."* — "Can you prove your hypotheses?" — [She compares the 200 gram and 300 gram weights on the same steel rod.] *"You see, the role of weight is demonstrated. For the material I don't know."* — "Take these steel ones and these copper ones." — *"I think I have to take two rods with the same form. Then to demonstrate the role of the metal I compare these two* [steel and brass, square, 50cm long and 16mm² cross section with 300 grams on each] *or these two here* [steel and brass, round, 50 and 22 cm by 16mm²]: *for length I shorten that one* [50 cm brought down to 22]. *To demonstrate the role of the form, I can compare these two"* [round brass and square brass, 50 cm and 16mm² for each]. — "Can the same thing be proven with these two?" [brass, round and square, 50 cm long and 16 and 7 mm² cross sectional]. — *"No, because that one* [7 mm²] *is much narrower."* — "And the width?" — *"I can compare these two"* [round, brass, 50cm long with 16 and 7mm² cross sectional] [Inhelder and Piaget, 1958: 60].

The elegance of reasoning demonstrated here is based on the systematic verification of one variable at a time with "all other things being equal." And if one were to give substage III-B a theoretical name, it ought to contain this "all other things being equal" quality.

INRC GROUP OF OPERATIONS

A second set of formal groupings that develop as part of the propositional logic of the adolescent is made up of four transformations, referred to as the INRC group. Each of these letters represents one of the logical transformations that can be performed on a proposition, changing it into a different operation. The acquisition of the INRC group is an important step in the development of logical thought in adolescence. An understanding of these four transformations is necessary in order to solve problems of proportionality and equilibrium.

1. *"I"—Identity or identity transformation.* The identity transformation refers to the starting operation that was initially given. This transformation is also referred to as the null transformation, since it results in no basic changes; the original proposition retains its identity. One of Piaget's experiments may provide an illustration. In a balance-type weighing scale, different size weights can be attached to several points on the crossbar (see Figure 14). The problem is to develop an understanding of the concept of equilibrium, which is based on an awareness of proportionality. In an "I" transformation, the subject may simultaneously increase the weight and the distance in such a way that the balance itself remains unaffected. Any change would be of such a nature that the basic relationship between the elements—the equilibrium of the scale— retains its identity.

2. *"N"—Negation or inversion.* A negative transformation simply means an undoing of the original operation. In an N transformation, everything in the initially given proposition is changed into the opposite of the original proposition. "All assertions become negations, and vice versa, and all conjunctions become disjunctions, and vice versa" (Flavell, 1963a: 216). The inverse to "all vertebrates" is "all nonvertebrates." Inversion or negation cancels out an operation and consequently constitutes one form of reversibility. Reversibility by inversion or negation means that the result of an operation is annulment. For example $+ 6 - 6 = 0$, or $+ n - n = 0$ (Piaget, 1980). In the crossbar scale experiment, an N transformation would be to "reduce the distance while increasing the weight or diminish the weight while increasing the distance or diminish both" (Inhelder and Piaget, 1958: 178).

3. *"R"—Reciprocal or reciprocity.* Reciprocity transformation means undoing the results of the original operation; however, in this transformation it is accomplished by changing some other variable in the system. The reciprocal of a proposition transforms the proposition without changing the conjunction or disjunction that joins the part of the proposition. "A is twice as large as B" in an R transformation becomes "B is twice as large as A." Reciprocity does not cancel a factor in the sense that negation does; rather, it neutralizes one factor, which makes it possible to vary the other. It allows for systematic testing of hypotheses and makes experimental manipulation of variables possible. In the crossbar scale experiment, "R compensates I by increasing both weight and distance on the other arm of the balance" (Inhelder and Piaget, 1958: 178). Reversibility by reciprocity involves operations of relationships. "For example, if A = B, then B = A, or if A is to the left of B, then B is to the right of A" (Piaget,

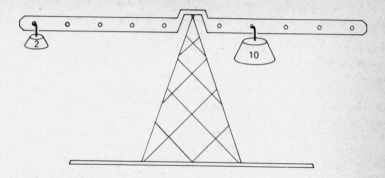

FIGURE 14. The balance scale used to assess children's concepts of proportionality. Different weights can be hung at different points on the crossbar.

1980: 71). A good illustration is Piaget's ring experiment, in which the subject is given a screen, a light source, a board with holes, and a series of different size rings with pegs. The task is to place two rings on the board, producing only one shadow on the screen. Ring size and distance from the screen bear a reciprocal relationship. One must compensate for the increase in the size of the ring by increasing the distance from the light source.

4. *"C"—Correlative.* Correlative transformation simply means the negation of a reciprocal. Piaget refers to the correlative as the "inversion of the reciprocal," or the "reciprocation of the inverse"; in other words, the relationship of C to R is the same as that of N to I. This transformation changes the conjunction or disjunction that joins the parts of the proposition but does not transform the remainder of the proposition. In the crossbar experiment, "C cancels R in the same way that N cancels I" (Inhelder and Piaget, 1958: 178).

The availability of propositional logic and the ability to make these transformations of propositions is one important aspect of formal thought. Another important dimension—closely interrelated with propositional operation—is the appearance of combinatorial operations. In an experiment conducted to illustrate the close relationship between propositional logical and combinatorial systems, the subject is exposed to five bottles:

1. Diluted sulfuric acid
2. Water
3. Oxygenated water
4. Thiosulfate

5. A bottle with a dropper, containing potassium iodine, referred to as "g"

The bottles are labeled 1, 2, 3, 4, and g. The subject does not know the chemical elements in each flask. While the subject is watching, the contents of three of these containers are mixed and produce a yellowish-brown liquid. Adding the contents of a fourth container returns the liquid to its original colorless state. The subject's problem is, first, to reproduce the yellow color using any combination of the bottles 1, 2, 3, 4, and g and then to return the liquid to its colorless state.

The approaches of concrete operational children are characterized by two forms of behavior: first, they systematically add "g" to all liquids since this is what they saw the experimenter do; second, they appear to think that color is attributed to only one of the elements, and this reveals the difference between a noncombinatorial and a combinatorial structure of intelligence.

> Gay (7; 6) also limits himself to $4 \times g$, $1 \times g$, $3 \times g$, and $2 \times g$, and discovers nothing else. "Could you try with two bottles together?" — [Silence.] — "Try." — [$4 \times 1 \times g$] *"It doesn't work."* — "Try something else." — [$3 \times 1 \times g$] — *"There it is!"* — "And that one [2], do you think that it will be as yellow?" — [No trial.] — "What do you think makes the color, the three together or only two?" *"Here"* [3]. — "And that one?" [1] — *"There isn't any color."* — "And that one?" [g]. — *"Yes, it's there inside."* — "Then what good are 1 and 3?" — *"There isn't any color"* [Inhelder and Piaget: 1958; 111].

Gay follows the pattern of the early operational child. He adds "g" to all combinations and ascribes the quality of color to one particular liquid, first to 3 and later to "g."

In substage III-A, systematic combinations become possible. In addition, even when III-As find the correct solution, $1 + 3 + g$, they are not satisfied and try other combinations. Their interest reaches beyond a solution of the problem to an understanding of the total structure and the total number of combinations.

> Sar (12; 3): "Make me some more yellow." — *"Do you take the liquid from the yellow glass with all four?"* — "I won't tell you." — [He tries first with $4 \times 2 \times g$, then $2 \times g \times 4 \times g$] *"Not yet.* [He tries to smell the odor of the liquids, then tries $4 \times 1 \times g$] *No yellow yet. Quite a big mystery!* [He tries the four, then each one independently with g; then he spontaneously proceeds to various two-by-two combinations but has the feeling that he forgot some of them.] *I'd better write it down to remind myself:* 1×4 *is done;* 4×3 *is done; and* 2×3. *Several more that I haven't done* [he finds

all six, then adds the drops and finds the yellow for $1 \times 3 \times g$]. *Ah! it's turning yellow. You need 1, 3, and the drops."* — "Where is the yellow?" — . . . — "In there?" [g] — *"No, they go together."* — "And 2?" — *"I don't think it has any effect, it's water."* — "And 4?" — *"It doesn't do anything either, it's water too. But I want to try again; you can't ever be too sure* [he tries $2 \times 4 \times g$]. *Give me a glass of water* [he takes it from the faucet and mixes $3 \times 1 \times$ water $\times g$—*i.e.*, the combination which gave him the color, plus water from the faucet, knowing that $1 \times 2 \times 3 \times 4 \times g$ produce nothing]. *No, it isn't water. Maybe it's a substance that keeps it from coloring* [he puts together $1 \times 3 \times 2 \times g$, then $1 \times 3 \times 4 \times g$]. *Ah! There it is! That one* [4] *keeps it from coloring."* — "And that?" [2]. — *"It's water"* [Inhelder and Piaget, 1958: 116–117].

Substage III-B, while not basically different from III-A, manipulates these materials more systematically, more quickly, and with an eye toward proof. Piaget describes this approach as a "generalization of substitution and addition."

Eng (14; 6) begins with $2 \times g$; $1 \times g$; $3 \times g$; and $4 \times g$: *"No, it doesn't turn yellow. So you have to mix them."* He goes on to the six two-by-two combinations and at last hits $1 \times 3 \times g$: *"This time I think it works."* — "Why?" — *"It's 1 and 3 and some water."* — "You think it's water?" — *"Yes, no difference in odor. I think that it's water."* — "Can you show me?" — [He replaces g with some water: $1 \times 3 \times$ water.] *"No, it's not water. It's a chemical product: it combines with 1 and 3 and then it turns into a yellow liquid* [he goes on to three-by-three combinations beginning with the replacement of g by 2 and by 4—*i.e.*, $1 \times 3 \times 2$ and $1 \times 3 \times 4$]. *No, these two products aren't the same as the drops: they can't produce color with 1 and 3* [then he tries $1 \times 3 \times g \times 2$]. *It stays the same with 2. I can try right away with 4* [$1 \times 3 \times g \times 4$]. *It turns white again: 4 is the opposite of g because 4 makes the color go away while g makes it appear."* — "Do you think that there is water in [any of the] bottles?" — *"I'll try* [he systematically replaces 1 and 3 by water, trying $1 \times g \times$ water and $3 \times g \times$ water, having already tried $1 \times 3 \times$ water]. *No, that means 3 isn't water and 1 isn't water."* He notices that the glass $1 \times 3 \times g \times 2$ has stayed clearer than $1 \times 3 \times g$. *"I think 2 must be water. Perhaps 4 also?* [He tries $1 \times 3 \times g \times 4$ again] *So it's not water: I had forgotten that it turned white; 4 is a product that makes the white return"* [Inhelder and Piaget, 1958: 120–121].

Another illustration of the same principle of combinatorial operations is suggested by Hunt (1961). His example is particularly relevant, since it clearly demarks the preadolescent thought processes from those found in the stage of formal operations. The task is to describe and identify *all possible combinations of animal life* on a newly discovered planet. The assumption is that animals on the planet can be classified into two basic classes:

1. Vertebrates (V) and their inverse, invertebrates (I)
2. Those animals that live on land, terrestrial (T), and those that live in water, aquatic (A)

The concrete operational child in all probability would answer with the following four classes of animal life:

1. (VT) vertebrates, terrestrial
2. (VA) vertebrates, aquatic
3. (IT) invertebrates, terrestrial
4. (IA) invertebrates, aquatic

The adolescent who possesses formal operations and can bring combinatorial analysis systematically to bear on the problem might be able to conceive of sixteen possible groups of animal life that are considered to be the inevitable outcome of combining two such propositions by modern logic.

1. No animals at all
2. Only (VT)
3. Only (VA)
4. Only (IT)
5. Only (IA)
6. (VT) and (VA), but not (IT) or (IA)
7. (VT) and (IT), but not (VA) or (IA)
8. (VT) and (IA), but not (VA) or (IT)
9. (VA) and (IT), but not (VT) or (IA)
10. (VA) and (IA), but not (VT) or (IT)
11. (IT) and (IA), but not (VA) or (VT)
12. (VT), (VA), and (IT), but not (IA)
13. (VT), (VA), and (IA), but not (IT)
14. (VT), (IT), and (IA), but not (VA)
15. (VA), (IT), and (IA), but not (VT)
16. All four classes (Hunt, 1961: 232)

The concrete grouping structure of the operational child does not possess the combinatorial system necessary to select the total number of possible combinations that produce the "structured whole." Concrete operations readily identify the four multiplicative classes VT, VA, IT, and IA; but to reason beyond these four concrete combinations requires an understanding of the structured whole and a combinatorial method that sees the relationship between the classes vertebrates and terrestrial as more than multiplicative. The fully operational adolescent can consider all possible combinations of all variables and work them out in a systematic fashion. Formal operations are necessary to see these four classes as the factors that, taken n-by-n, produce the sixteen possible combinations.

EVALUATION OF PIAGET'S FORMAL THINKING STAGE

An important question is being raised with increasing frequency: that is, what proportion of all adolescents do actually attain the full ability to perform the kind of logical operations that Piaget so skillfully described in *The Growth of Logical Thinking From Childhood to Adolescence*? Both Arlin (1975) and Kuhn (1979) cite the widely demonstrated estimate, according to which only approximately 50 percent of the adult population actually attain the full stage of formal thinking (III-B). Kuhn (1979) suggests, based on a review of the relevant literature, that the formal operations stage of adolescence, quite in contrast to the preceding childhood stages of Piaget's theory, may never be attained by a significant proportion of the general adolescent population. Piaget (1980) readily admits that the subjects of his study were "from the better schools in Geneva" and that his conclusions were based on a "privileged population." However, he ascribes differences between his own studies and those of others to "differences in speed of development without any modification in the order of succession of the stages." In spite of evidence critical of his assumptions, he maintains that "all normal individuals are capable of reaching the level of formal operation" (1980: 75) as long as the environment provides the necessary cognitive stimulation. However, he does admit to a differentiation in cognitive aptitude with increasing age, depending on interest, motivation, and environmental stimulation, so that some adolescents may show their operational skills in logic, mathematics, or physics, while others may show it in literature, linguistics, or artistic endeavor, and still others in practical skills such as are performed by the carpenter, the locksmith, or the mechanic. However, in spite of this concern, it is important to keep in mind that Piaget's theory has been studied, tested, and developed in the adolescent age range primarily with content material that came from science and mathematics. Piaget has shown little concern with the question of how formal operations might manifest themselves in artistic and literary endeavors. Gallagher (1978) has expanded the investigation of formal thought research to include analogy and metaphor. Gardner even suggests that formal operations might actually interfere with artistic development:

Formal operations may even at times serve to hinder artistic development, since the tendency to focus on underlying content, to abstract meaning, to be sensitive to the explicit demands of a task, to proceed in a systematic exhaustive manner, and, above all, to translate problems and questions into logical-propositional terms may all militate against the sensitivity to detail and nuance and the faithfulness to the particular properties of object and medium that are so vital for the artist (1973: 308).

Dulit (1972), utilizing Piaget's experiment, claims that among his group of average older adolescents only 20 to 35 percent actually functioned at the full formal level (III-B), and even in a selected group of scientifically gifted older adolescents that figure is only 75 percent. Actually, it is very difficult if not impossible to compare the various percentages reported in the literature for the presence or absence of formal operational reasoning ability. The problem is that Inhelder and Piaget never spelled out the methods they used in administering these tasks nor the exact criteria used for scoring. This lack of standardized procedures has plagued the formal operations research (Kuhn, 1979). Dulit, Kuhn, and others question the validity of the impression created by Piaget that the attainment of the formal-stage thinking is the norm in the same way that the attainment of the earlier Piagetian stages is apparently the rule for all younger children. Inhelder did report to Dulit that "not all cases were reported." The intent of the study was not to speak to the issue of "frequency" or "incidents"; rather, specific protocols were selected as illustrations of the theory. Dulit's own empirically derived frequency data throw serious doubts on the generalization that the full formal-stage thinking is the common or typical pattern in middle and late adolescence. He concludes that adolescence is indeed the characteristic age of the onset of formal operations, but such reasoning structure is not attained by all, or even by the majority, of adolescents. "Thus for adolescents the formal stage is more of a *characteristic of potential* only sometimes becoming an actuality" (Dulit, 1972: 298). The fully operational formal-stage reasoning ability must be viewed as an ideal kind of cognitive equilibrium. However, it is far from being normal or typical among adolescents. "It is more ideal than typical, more potential than actual."

Another related question is whether and to what extent changes in the subjects' problem-solving approach on the various cognitive problems (e.g., the pendulum, the floating bodies, colorless chemicals, the projection of shadows, the flexible rods, and others) develops synchronously—or to state it differently, whether the performances on these Piagetian tasks correlate with one another. If they do correlate or change synchronously, one could assume that such changes are the result of changes in the underlying cognitive structure. In general, the reported correlations for inter-tasks performances vary, but fall in the $r = .30$ to $.40$ range, not a very convincing piece of evidence for the existence of a coherent, underlying, and generalizable formal structure. Bart (1978) had hypothesized, in agreement with Piaget's theory, that the content of a test of formal reasoning should have little or no effect on formal reasoning performance. However, contrary to his hypothesis, he found that the correlations between three formal reasoning tests, quite different in content but structurally equivalent, were not between 1.0 and .9 as expected, but were actually only .46, .51, and .65. He concludes that formal reasoning, therefore, is not necessarily generalizable across content areas. Since the performance on Piaget's formal tasks has not been studied longitudinally, we do not know to what extent changes in reasoning are synchronized. Finally, there is the additional question whether and to what extent performance on Piaget's formal operations tasks correlates with more traditional measures of intelligence. If the correlations between various Piaget-type tasks were significantly larger than between such tasks and IQ, this again might add weight to the argument that solving Piaget-type problems has some uniqueness that might indeed relate to formal operations. Again the evidence is not very convincing.

IS THERE AN ADULT STAGE OF COGNITIVE DEVELOPMENT?

The question has been raised whether there exist cognitive structures that extend beyond and are different from those of the formal operational stage, moving the end of cognitive development into adulthood. Such a notion would place into question Piaget's statement that the formal operations of adolescence constitute the "final equilibrium" in cognitive development. Arlin (1975) contrasts, on the basis of theoretical considerations as well as some empirical evidence, the "problem-solving stage," which is identical to the formal operational stage, with the "problem-finding stage," which is assumed to constitute a new level of reasoning more advanced than the stage of formal operations. Such a problem-finding stage is described as a creative stage, and involves the ability to raise new questions and to discover. If such an assumption were proven, the stage of formal thinking would lose its special status as the "final equilibrium," since cognitive growth would continue in adulthood. However, the evidence for such a proposition is not entirely convincing and has been challenged on theoretical as well as empirical grounds.

EDUCATIONAL IMPLICATIONS

In his interaction with children in various experimental situations, Piaget observed that children often show resistance to learning from traditional instruction. Apparently, the subject's cognitive structure determines the degree of understanding that the individual can bring to the solution of a problem. Piaget was very skillful in challenging his subjects, by way of his clinical methods, to the limits of their understanding. Nevertheless, children seem incapable of being guided even through careful questioning and instruction beyond these limits. And even if correct answers with explicit explanations are provided, children appear to return to their own level of cognitive functioning as indicated by their earlier responses rather than to produce any generalized cognitive growth that would readily transcend the earlier established limits. Lovell (1961) investigated the influence of teaching on the child's ability to solve Piaget-type problems and the long-range benefits of such strategies. Apparently, the knowledge that a child might acquire before developing the corresponding cognitive structures either disappears very rapidly or, if it is retained, is retained as rote memorization without real understanding.

The interaction between a child and the experimenter, as reported by Piaget (1963: 294–295), may serve to illustrate the subject's resistance to change as a result of information that is still beyond his cognitive structure. The child is presented with the test material, an open box that contains twenty wooden beads; eighteen of these beads are brown and two are white. The child is asked: "Which are there more of, brown beads or wooden beads?" The preoperational child—who cannot yet classify and cannot consider two dimensions of a problem simultaneously—cannot distinguish brownness as a subclass to woodenness as a supraclass and consequently is most likely to answer: "There are more brown beads, because there are only two white ones."

Following such a typical preoperational response, Piaget might go to great length explaining the situation and the task to the child. Introducing an empty box he might ask: "If we were to put all the wooden beads in the box, how many would be left?" Whereupon the child might reply: "None, because they are all wooden." It thus becomes apparent that the child knows all beads are wooden. So Piaget continues: "Now, if we were to put all the brown beads in this box, how many would be left?" The child's reply would be: "These white ones," or "Two." Apparently the subject now clearly understands the situation that all beads are wooden, that most of the beads are brown, and that a few (two) are white. After these teaching efforts, the initial question is asked once more: "Which are there more of, wooden beads or brown beads?" The child may hesitate, indicating that he is more aware of the nature of the problem; nevertheless his response remains the same: "There are more brown beads, since there are only two white ones." Even though the elements necessary for solving the problem have been carefully explained, the child before age six to seven is still unable to consider both the color and the woodenness of the objects and is unable to free his thinking from the perceptual dominance of the many brown beads.

Development is seen as an increase in complexity, mobility, and systematization of schemata and logical structures, which result from equilibrium-equilibration processes, but which cannot be substantially accelerated by instruction. Obviously, in the assimilation-accommodation process, education plays a very significant role. However, the assimilation-accommodation process must move in very small logical steps in order to enhance learning. If the gaps in the presentation of educational material are too large or too advanced for the child, as they apparently are in the incident just cited, the individual cannot accommodate. The teacher has to be skillful in maintaining the proper level of tension between assimilation and accommodation, in starting at the child's level and in progressing in small steps in order to foster genuine conceptual and cognitive growth. On this particular issue Piaget appears to be very close to a maturational interpretation of development and reveals a somewhat conservative outlook on education. His objection to what he referred to as the American question, "How can we accelerate the child's progression through your developmental stages?" is that to do things faster or earlier is not necessarily a desirable thing and may be even worse than doing nothing.

Interestingly enough, it is on this issue that some of Piaget's close associates and followers seem to depart from his interpretation. Bruner, who apparently was greatly influenced by Piaget's theory, seems to take almost the opposite point of view when he says: "We begin with the hypothesis that any subject can be taught effectively in some intellectually honest form to any child at any stage of development" (Bruner, 1960: 33). On the other hand, Bruner quotes and appears to agree with Inhelder's statement that it may be worthwhile to devote two years of schooling "to a series of exercises in manipulating, classifying, and ordering objects in ways that highlight basic operations of logical addition, multiplication, inclusion, serial ordering, and the like" (Bruner, 1960: 46). Such an approach implies a rather direct structuring of the school curriculum in accordance with Piaget's theory.

Some research does provide evidence that Piagetian-type problems can be taught and that teaching such concepts does accelerate cognitive growth. Ojemann (1963) has shown that guided learning experiences, such as teaching preadolescents the reasons why objects sink or float, significantly affects the child's thought structure. Aebli (1963), a former associate of Piaget, has taken his teacher's theory of development and expanded it toward an educational theory. Aebli uses the sandbox in which the subject looks at three mountains of different shapes and is asked what the scenery would look like from different angles (see Figure 11). He was able to demonstrate that the method of presentation and the number and nature of significant cues were as important as the child's cognitive structures in facilitating solutions to the problems and learning. He varies the complexity of the problem by providing the subject with:

1. The contours of the mountains only
2. Contours and surface structure of the mountains
3. Contours, surface structure, and color of the mountains

Aebli and Bruner do not maintain that the child's logical structures can easily and substantially be accelerated through educational procedures. They are, however, somewhat more optimistic than Piaget in attributing a greater importance to the curriculum material, the curriculum planner, and the methods of teaching, since they feel that complex concepts can be simplified and presented so as to fit the logical structure of the child. The task of the teacher then becomes that of the "translator" who has to present the curriculum content on such a level and in such a way that it corresponds to the cognitive structure of the child; the goal is to correlate systematically the curriculum to the child's ability to assimilate and accommodate the material. Such a translation implies that, for any learning problem, the preoperational child should be presented with the problem in the form of direct sensory experiences, whereas the preadolescent would be able to work with concrete problems, and the adolescent could master abstract ideas, verbal propositions, and combinatorial analyses. More specifically, the formal operations found in the adolescent constitute the psychological prerequisite for teaching geometry, proportionality, propositions, and probabilistic reasoning. A Piagetian approach to teaching would make it mandatory for the educator to assess the operational structure of pupils. Piaget-type assessment and test materials (Burk, 1973; Furth, 1970; Patterson and Milakofsky, 1980; Pinard and Laurendeau, 1964; Uzgiris and Hunt, 1976) and curriculum material constructed with Piaget's developmental and educational theory in mind (Furth and Wachs, 1975; Lavatelli, 1970; Petrone, 1976; Sund, 1976; Weikart et al., 1971) have become available and have been used in schools and educational settings. Elkind (1978) reports that the rather dramatic upsurge of interest in Piaget-type curriculum and materials in the elementary schools peaked in the sixties when humanistic and child-centered values were cherished in education. This child development orientation has subsided as a result of the recent emphasis on basics, accountability, competence, and a more generally conservative attitude in American society. The effect of these trends, as well as some other factors, "such as ignoring the basic premises of Piaget's research and theory" has been the abandonment of Piaget-type elementary curriculum. However, on a more hopeful note, Elkind adds:

> Interestingly enough, where Piaget is now having a major impact is at the secondary level. Those concerned with physics and chemistry are, for example, examining the sequencing of materials, and the logical substructure (the requisite mental operations) of their tasks. Moreover, what is exciting about this work is that it is empirical rather than reflective. Various instructors are trying out different sequencing and ways of presenting materials and they are sharing their findings through meetings and journal articles. This to my mind is the way Piaget should be used in producing curriculum materials [1978: 2].

The ages that Piaget provides for the various developmental stages in some of his books are only approximations, or at best generalizations, and not statistical averages. Piaget is concerned with fundamental questions of genetic epistemology and the sequence and orderliness of cognitive changes and not with the variables that have always been of concern to the educational and developmental psychologist: individual differences, sex, socioeconomic class, IQ, reading level, and so forth. Piaget's theory has stimulated considerable research into these traditional developmental variables. For example, sex differences on Piagetian problems have been demonstrated (Keating and Schaefer, 1975; Dulit, 1972), especially on spatial processing tasks (Jamison and Signorella, 1980; Liben, 1974; 1975; 1978; Liben and Golbeck, 1980; Ray, Georgiou, and Ravizza, 1979; Thomas and Jamison, 1975; Thomas, Jamison, and Hummel, 1973). From childhood into early adulthood, males perform consistently better than females on Piagetian-type horizontal (judging the position of liquid in a tilted container) and vertical (judging the position of plumb lines in an oblique context) spatial tasks. Liben and Golbeck conclude that the persistence of such "sex differences suggests that there are actually competency differences in males and females" (1980: 596). Piaget himself devoted little attention to such variables. He never denied that they might exist; he simply focused on a different set of questions. "The order of succession of these stages has been shown to be extremely regular and comparable to the stages of an embryogenesis. The speed of development may vary from one individual to another and also from one social environment to another . . . but this does not change the order of succession of the stages through which they pass" (Piaget, 1980: 70–71). It is the order of succession in the acquisition of knowledge that was the focus of Piaget's research. However, knowledge of Piaget's theory gives the educator new insights into the limitations and abilities of children at various stages in their cognitive development. Piaget made it crystal clear that children think differently at various age levels and think quite differently from adults. Did it occur to anyone that children might think—assuming equality exists—that there is more milk in a thin, tall glass than in a wide, low glass before Piaget's experiments became widely known?

Finally, it is not only the content of Piaget's theory and the substance of his findings but also his methods that are relevant to the educator. He collects data by what is frequently referred to as the "clinical method," which means that the child actively searches for the solution to the problem. The examiner stimulates and challenges the child to reflect and elaborate on the answers and to use this discourse as a means to clarify thinking. Piaget (1947a) wholeheartedly believed in the autonomy of children and in their active participation in their own cognitive growth—an idea he shares with John Dewey. "There are two basic and correlated principles from which an educator inspired by psychology can never depart:

1. That the only real truths are those that one builds freely oneself and not those received from others
2. That moral good is essentially autonomous and cannot be prescribed" (Piaget, 1947a: 248).

Through this method, Piaget skillfully questioned children and provided for learning, pushing them to the limits of their operational structure without giving them ready-made answers.

Applying Piaget's findings about children's cognitive growth to teaching would have a revolutionary impact on the planning of the curriculum. The content itself would be influenced, or more important, the logical processes by which we think and by which we attempt to solve problems could become a major area of focus in any educational endeavor. Thus there would be a more systematic emphasis on systems of classification, on reversibility, on logical transformations, and on the process of logic in general.

11:
LAWRENCE KOHLBERG'S COGNITIVE-DEVELOPMENTAL APPROACH TO ADOLESCENT MORALITY*

PIAGET'S CONTRIBUTION TO AN UNDERSTANDING OF CHILDREN'S MORAL JUDGMENT

Piaget, in *The Moral Judgment of the Child* (1932b), postulated that the development of children's moral judgment follows the same basic patterns as those of cognitive development in general (discussed in the previous chapter), since moral schemata are based on the child's cognitive structures. Moral development is dependent on such cognitive skills as the perception of reality, the organization and evaluation of experiences, the making of fine discriminations and generalizations, and later, during adolescence, the ability to reason abstractly. Piaget's interest was primarily in moral judgment rather than in moral behavior. The distinction between moral judgment and moral behavior is an important one. Moral judgment refers to the evaluation of the "goodness" or "rightness" of a course of action in a hypothetical dilemma situation. Moral behavior refers to the individual's ability not to steal, to lie, to cheat, and so on, in an actual situation in which these temptations offer themselves. Piaget and Kohlberg have assumed that the structures underlying verbal moral judgment and nonverbal moral behavior are related but not identical. Various research studies have demonstrated that the relationship between moral judgment and moral behavior is not very high (Hartshorne and May, 1928–1930), although some positive relationships have been observed (Rubin and Schneider, 1973). The fact that a person knows the right behavior is no assurance that he will actually behave that way.

---

*Chapter 11 has been published as "Kohlberg's Cognitive-Developmental Approach to Adolescent Morality," *Adolescence*, 1974, *11*, 39–59.

Piaget found that a basic shift in the quality of children's moral judgment takes place when they progress from preoperational thought processes to operational thought processes at about the age of seven and again at twelve when concrete operational thought gives way to formal or abstract thought processes. The morality of the preoperational child is identified as "morality of constraint" or "moral realism" and is described as showing "blind obedience" to authority. Justice is seen as resting in the person who has authority. The child's moral concepts have developed from parental teaching of what is right and what is wrong; the child does not yet have the intellectual structure to consider other alternatives nor the emotional capacity to empathize with others. The preoperational child is not yet able to decenter—that is, to shift from one point of view to another or to take the view of another person into account. With an increase in the capability to decenter, the child becomes more altruistic in orientation and behavior (Rubin and Schneider, 1973). Preoperational children approach moral dilemmas from an "objective" viewpoint—that is, they are primarily concerned with the objective amount of physical damage caused by an act rather than the intent or motivation behind the behavior. As they begin to develop operational thought processes, their moral judgment is identified as "morality of cooperation" and begins to reflect a "subjective" morality—that is, their primary concern is no longer with the objective amount of damage caused but with the subjective intention or motivation of the act. The child begins to take the viewpoint of others into consideration and understands reciprocal relationships. In one of Piaget's stories, the question is who is naughtier: John, who opens a door and accidentally breaks fifteen cups that were behind the door and that he did not see, or Henry, who tries to snitch some cookies, climbs on a chair, and, in the process, breaks one cup. The preoperational child feels that John is naughtier since the primary concern is with the quantity of objective damage. The operational child judges Henry to be naughtier, since now subjective intention is given more weight than objective material damage.

The preoperational child's moral judgments have two essential characteristics: moral realism and immanent justice. Moral realism means that moral rules have an existence of their own and cannot be changed. Any suggested change in the rules strikes the child as a transgression (Piaget, 1932b: 18). Immanent justice refers to the child's belief that his misbehavior inevitably brings on pain or punishment as a natural consequence of the transgressions. For example, the child who steals and later, on the way home, falls and hurts himself becomes convinced that the fall was the punishment for his stealing. The shift from moral realism to "moral relativism" reflects that the child no longer blindly follows orders but considers the intent of the act rather than the letter of the law. And the law—or the rules that govern the child's behavior—can be changed. Most of Piaget's early work on the development of moral judgments was concerned with children rather than with adolescents.

The highest stage of moral development, characteristic of adolescence, is dependent on the attainment of formal reasoning or abstract operations and is referred to as moral autonomy. The development of this orientation begins at the age of eleven or twelve. In a game situation the adolescent is not only interested in the rules of the game but in anticipating all possible cases to which these rules apply. Now that abstract thought is possible, the adolescent develops a sense of ethical and moral responsibility that is based on abstract principles of what is right and what is wrong.

> The same is true of the concept of social justice and of rational, aesthetic, or social ideals. As a result of the acquisition of such values, decisions, whether in opposition to or in agreement with the adult, have an altogether different significance than they do in the small social groups of younger children. . . . The possibilities opened up by these new values are obvious in the adolescent, who differs from the child in that he is not only capable of forming theories but is also concerned with choosing a career that will permit him to satisfy his need for social reform and for new ideas [Piaget and Inhelder, 1969: 151].

LEVELS OF MORAL DEVELOPMENT

Kohlberg, inspired by Piaget's cognitive-developmental approach to moral development, expands the structural cognitive approach through more systematic longitudinal, cross-cultural, social class, and educational research (Blatt, 1959; Kohlberg, 1963; 1969; Kohlberg and Blatt, 1972; Kohlberg and Kramer, 1969; Turiel, 1966; 1969). Kohlberg distinguishes three basic levels of moral development: the preconventional, or premoral, level; the conventional level; and the postconventional, or autonomous, level. Morality begins as an idea of justice that is primitive, undifferentiated, and egocentric in young children, but that becomes more sophisticated and social as the adolescent moves through specific stages of moral thinking; it may reach, in some individuals, an awareness of universal values and ethical principles.

The preconventional level of moral thinking is prevalent during childhood and includes approximately the ages four to ten. Children are responsive to the definitions of what is good and bad provided by their social reference group, and they are often well behaved. However, the reasons for their moral judgments are different from those of adults, since their moral structure is still less differentiated. Moral decisions are primarily egocentric, based on self-interest and material considerations. They interpret acts as good and bad in terms of what Piaget calls "objective judgments."

The second level is the conventional, or moral, level, which is less egocentric and more sociocentric in basic orientation. Kohlberg describes it as conformity to social conventions, expressed by a strong desire to maintain, support, and justify the existing social structure. In general, most adolescents and even the majority of adults operate on the conventional level. As an individual progresses into adolescence, it becomes increasingly more difficult—in contrast to Freud's, Erikson's, and Gesell's theories, and even Piaget's cognitive stages of development—to associate any one chronological age, or even a developmental period such as adolescence, with any one level of thinking. Many adults continue to function at the conventional level, while some mature adolescents operate at the postconventional level.

The third level is the postconventional, or autonomous, level. The approach to moral issues is no longer based on egocentric needs, nor on conformity to the social order, but on autonomous, universal principles of justice that have validity even beyond existing laws, social conventions, or one's group of social peers. At the highest level of moral development, moral judgment and moral behavior are more closely related than at the earlier levels.

Kohlberg further subdivides each of his three levels into two stages and thus creates a more differentiated and elaborate theory of six stages of development, or, since it does refer to adults as well, a typology of moral orientation that has been applied to conservative, liberal, and radical political orientations (Hampden-Turner and Whitten, 1971). Each stage of moral development represents a distinct moral philosophy that has implications for social and political organization. The classification of individuals into these moral stages is based on their resolution of verbal moral dilemmas that Kohlberg presents to his subjects. The following story illustrates one of Kohlberg's philosophical dilemmas.

A woman is dying of cancer. A new drug that could save her life has been discovered by the local druggist. The druggist, who has not invested much in the drug, sells it for $2,000—about ten times what it cost him to make the drug. The sick woman's husband tries to borrow money from friends, but he can only raise $1,000. He approaches the druggist, asking him to sell the drug for half the price or let him, the husband, repay at a later time. The druggist refuses. The husband, in desperation, breaks into the store and steals the drug. Should he have done so? Why? The subject, if necessary, is questioned as to the rightness or wrongness of the husband's decision, the rights of the

druggist, the duties of the husband, the approp.
husband, and the obligations an individual ha.
nonrelatives. Classification of responses is not so
an adolescent decides to do in such a dilemma,
reasoning that leads to the proposed answer or the
behind the response. This means that all classificatio.   ...ed on
moral verbal judgment that may not be directly related   ...onverbal
moral behavior.

STAGES IN MORAL DEVELOPMENT

Stage One: Obedience and Punishment Orientation. The main motive given for obeying a rule at this stage is to avoid punishment and achieve gratification. The child's conscience is based on an irrational, egocentric fear of punishment. Children at this stage manifest an unquestioning submission to superior power and an effort to avoid trouble. They are still confused about human values and human life, and people are valued according to the benefits they can bring. The physical damage rather than the human intent of an act is considered in evaluating its goodness or badness. This confusion of the physical with the social-moral world is what Piaget calls "moral realism." In the previously described dilemma, the subject may fear that God will punish him if he lets his wife die.

Stage Two: Instrumental Relativist Orientation. Children can now distinguish between the physical and the social-moral world, but they confuse individual needs and what they think is right and wrong. At this stage, morally right behavior is based on what satisfies one's own needs, reflecting a basic hedonistic orientation. And the major motivation is to manipulate others in order to obtain rewards. The notion of reciprocity is beginning to emerge, and, consequently, under certain circumstances the needs of others are taken into consideration. However, interpersonal relationships are viewed as analogous to the economic marketplace. That is, reciprocity is based on an exchange of powers and favors rather than on considerations of loyalty and justice. A philosophy of "you scratch my back and I'll scratch yours" prevails. Fairness, reciprocity, and sharing do exist, but they are viewed in pragmatic, personal, utilitarian terms. Tom Sawyer's episode of the whitewashing of the fence is characteristic of this level of moral development. The criterion for making a moral judgment is based on selfish needs as in the case of the child who believed the man should steal the lifesaving drug for his ill wife because if she dies, nobody will look after his needs. Stage two subjects cannot yet decenter their thinking to take the position of another individual in an objective manner.

and two are typical of preadolescents and delinquents and ...ically premoral, since self-interest and material considerations ...termine moral decisions.

Stage Three: Interpersonal Concordance Orientation. Kohlberg refers to this first stage of the conventional level as the "good-boy"—"good-girl," approval-seeking orientation in moral development. Need and morality can be distinguished, but the confusion now is between social approval and right or wrong. Good behavior is now defined as behavior that pleases or helps others, and children will try to behave well in order to win the approval of others. Morality is now defined by the ties that individuals have to their social groups. Children seek to win the approval of their immediate social group through virtuous behavior and to live up to the expectations they think others have. There is conformity to what is believed to be majority opinion on "natural behavior." In an Ash-type experiment seventh-grade adolescents in stage three were more conforming than their age-mates who had attained higher or lower social judgment levels (Saltzstein, Diamond, and Belenky, 1972). Behavior is judged by intention, as in Piaget's subjective stage, frequently expressed in the child's concern with "he means well." Often this argument is overused, as with the cartoon character Charlie Brown in *Peanuts*. Stage three also describes the Mary Poppins type of moral philosophy. A stage three subject, as a husband, will do what any responsible husband is supposed to do—protect his wife.

Stage Four: Orientation Toward Authority, Law, and Duty. Morality at stage four is characterized by a strong belief in "law and order," which now becomes a primary value. Moral rules are separated from feelings of approval, but the rules are concrete, "thou shalt not . . . ," rather than abstract principles of justice. One obeys and respects the law in order to avoid the penalty that legitimate authority can impose. Breaking the law results in guilt feelings. Therefore, moral behavior is motivated by guilt and fear of legitimate censors. The basic orientation is a faith in existing authority, fixed rules, and the maintenance of social order at any price. The emphasis is on doing one's duty—exemplified, for instance, by Colonel Saito in the *Bridge over the River Kwai*, who rigidly maintained his lifelong orientation toward duty, authority, and a fixed social order. Moral behavior is obeying the law, doing one's duty, showing respect for authority, and maintaining the social order. "Life is conceived as sacred in terms of its place in categorical moral and religious order of rights and duties" (Kohlberg, 1970: 184). Since marriage is an institution essential to society and based on law, the stage four subject, as the husband in the earlier example, may consider it his lawful duty to steal the drug.

Stages three and four are conventional group- and law-oriented levels of moral development in which most adolescents and the majority of adults function. However, Kohlberg (1964) has argued that in late adolescence the continued endorsement of conventional morality reflects a deficiency in moral development.

Stage Five: Social Contract Orientation. Moral judgment at this postconventional level of moral development is defined in terms of general principles such as individual rights, human dignity, equality, contractual agreement, and mutual obligations. Consequently, this stage is referred to as the principled stage. Moral principles have been examined and are agreed on by the society as a whole. Moral behavior is motivated by a concern for the welfare of the larger community and a desire for community respect. The purpose of the law is to preserve human rights. Therefore, unfair or unjust laws must be changed. In contrast to the person in stage four, the individual in stage five is much more willing to view the law as flexible and works for changing the law, as long as these changes follow rational deliberations and considerations of social utility and are based on consensus. This is the official morality of the American Constitution and government. However, although the American democracy is philosophically based on the moral judgment represented by stage five, Kohlberg reports that only one out of three adult Americans has actually reached this level of moral development. The husband who is a stage five subject may decide to steal the drug in order to save his wife. The husband and wife promised to love each other regardless of the circumstances, and their moral commitment to each other is sanctioned by society.

Stage Six: Universal Ethical Principles Orientation. Morality at the highest principled stage of moral development is viewed as a decision of conscience that is based on self-chosen ethical principles that place the highest value on human life, equality, and dignity. The concept of justice goes beyond any particular existing social order that emerges. These ethical principles are characterized by consistency, logical comprehensiveness, and universality. They are abstract, such as the golden rule or Immanuel Kant's categorical imperative, rather than specific moral rules such as the Ten Commandments. One cannot be at the individual principled level without having been first at the social contract level and without having understood the basic contractual nature of the existing social order. The individual governed by universal ethical principles may practice civil disobedience, not out of disrespect for the law, but out of respect for a higher morality than the existing law. Unjust laws may be broken, because morality is grounded not in legality, but in ethical principles of justice and in respect for the rights of the individual. In practicing civil disobedience, the individual accepts the penalty in order to demonstrate the principles of justice, human rights, and the dignity of human beings to society at large. The stage six individual feels that no law, no contract, no moral obligation, and no fear of punishment can interfere with his desire to save those he loves. As the husband in the story, first, he will steal the drug to save the life of his wife; second, he will steal the drug and accept the penalty to demonstrate to society that the right to live is so fundamental that it must and should take precedence over the right to make a profit. The visionaries and moral leaders of society—Joan of Arc, Abraham Lincoln, Henry David Thoreau, Martin Luther King, Jr., and Claus Schenk von Stauffenberg, for example—seem to have been governed by universal ethical principles that challenged the existing morality of their society and times.

The thinking of a man oriented toward universal moral principles can best be expressed by a brief quote from Martin Luther King's "Letter from Birmingham Jail":

> I do not advocate evading or defying the law, as would the rabid segregationist. That would lead to anarchy. One who breaks an unjust law must do so openly, lovingly, and with a willingness to accept the penalty. An individual who breaks a law that conscience tells him is unjust, and who willingly accepts the penalty of imprisonment in order to arouse the conscience of the community over its injustice, is in reality expressing the highest respect for the law [King, 1964: 86].

THE INVARIANT DEVELOPMENTAL SEQUENCE IN MORAL THINKING

Kohlberg (1970) proposed that these six stages of moral development represent an invariant developmental sequence—they are universal and the thinking of any one stage is consistently applied to a variety of situations. Development moves from the lower to the higher stages in an invariant sequence, which means that the child moves step by step through each of the stages. The sequence of these stages is constant, and a child cannot skip a stage, but the age at which a person reaches a certain stage may differ from individual to individual and from culture to culture. An adolescent cannot function at stage five without having previously moved through stages three and four. Children may remain fixated at any one stage and not move on, but if they eventually do move on, it is in a stepwise progression. Children and adolescents do move through these stages with varying speeds so that the relationship between chronological age and stage of moral judgment becomes less precise as one grows older. To give approximations is no longer appropriate after the child has left stages one and two, which are generally associated with childhood. The moral thinking of stages three to six can be found in adolescents as well as adults, and some adults never reach stage five or six. Thinking at stages five and six is most commonly found in college-educated middle-class youth, and even they may regress to earlier stages of moral development after their college education has been completed. Only about 10 percent of American adults reach stage six, and many adults continue to function on the "law-and-order" level of moral development, giving this issue potency in election campaigns. Stages five and six, based on principled morality, do have as a prerequisite the attainment of abstract formal operations in cognitive development. Consequently, one cannot simply associate any one stage of moral development with adolescence. But since adolescence is a period of progression through several of these stages, all of Kohlberg's stages are relevant to a discussion of theories of adolescence. Much of Kohlberg's research deals with subjects in the age range from ten to sixteen and a follow-up in their twenties. Adolescents may be found at any one of Kohlberg's stages of moral development, though most have passed through stages one and two, excluding individuals whose concept of justice develops late or who are delinquent in their moral orientation. A few morally precocious adolescents may already have reached stage five, or in an exceptional case, stage six. However, adolescence is characterized by progression through at least some of these stages of moral thinking.

Kohlberg maintains that these stages are universal. He believes that the moral structure reflected in the decisions in his dilemma situations is not just a matter of learning cultural values, but that the sequential patterning of these stages occurs under varying cultural conditions and that the principles of justice reflected in stages five and six are free from culturally defined content.

Consistency does not imply "moral character" or moral trait. There is, however, a high degree of consistency from one moral stage to another, and within a moral stage. The thinking of about 50 percent of the individuals tested was within a single stage, even though the subjects responded to a variety of moral dilemma situations. Some, who apparently were progressing from one stage to another, were responding partly in stage three, partly in stage four, but rarely simultaneously in stages two and five.

CROSS-CULTURAL, SOCIOECONOMIC, AND POLITICAL DIFFERENCES IN MORAL THINKING

In support for the claim of cultural universality, Kohlberg (1964) has conducted research in the development of moral thinking of adolescents not only in the United States; he has also presented cross-cultural evidence from Great Britain, Canada, Taiwan, Mexico, and Turkey.

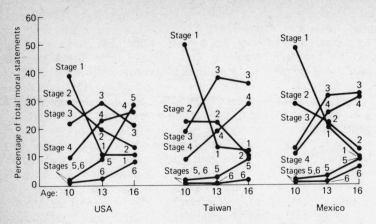

FIGURE 15. Middle-class urban boys in the U.S., Taiwan, and Mexico. At age 10, the stages are used according to difficulty. At age 13, stage 3 is most used by all three groups. At age 16, U.S. boys have reversed the order of age 10 stages (with the exception of 6). In Taiwan and Mexico, conventional (3-4) stages prevail at age 16, with stage 5 also little used.

From Lawrence Kohlberg, Moral Development and the Education of Adolescents. In R. F. Purnell, *Adolescents and the American High School.* © 1970 by Holt, Rinehart and Winston, Inc., New York. Reproduced by permission.

The data presented in Figures 15 and 16 support his claim of the universality of his developmental stages, although his sample includes few primitive societies. In all societies studied, he finds that stages one and two decline sharply as a function of age, especially between ages ten and thirteen. The thinking representative of stages three and four increases until middle adolescence, and in primitive societies until late adolescence, and then begins to decline or level off. Moral judgments representative of stages five and six show a very slow but steady increase during adolescence in all societies, although the total percentage of even late adolescents reaching these advanced stages remains very small—a fact that appears to be more pronounced in educationally and technologically underdeveloped societies (Kohlberg, 1970). These patterns of changes in moral thinking in adolescents apparently remain the same in all cultures studied. Kohlberg reports that anthropologists had warned him that he would have to throw away his culture-bound stories and stages. In a dilemma situation in which the wife is starving to death and the husband has no money to buy food and thus must choose between stealing or letting his wife die, Taiwanese adolescents typically gave stage-two responses: he should steal because if he lets her die,

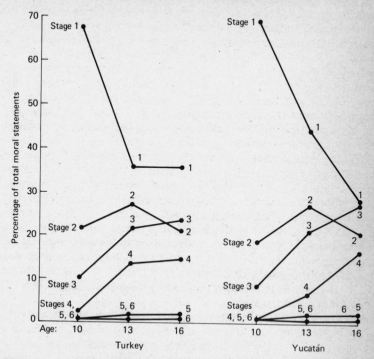

FIGURE 16. Two isolated villages, one in Turkey, the other in Yucatán, show similar patterns in moral thinking. There is no reversal of order, and preconventional (1-2) thought does not gain a clear ascendancy over conventional stages at age 16.

From Lawrence Kohlberg, Moral Development and the Education of Adolescents. In R. F. Purnell, *Adolescents and the American High School.* © 1970 by Holt, Rinehart and Winston, Inc., New York. Reproduced by permission.

he must pay for the funeral. In the Atayl village, where funerals are not so expensive, the typical stage-two response was that the husband should steal because he needed the wife to prepare his food. Thus, while the specific content of responses is influenced by prevalent cultural patterns of living, the underlying moral philosophy is basically the same in both responses.

Kohlberg did find that there are cultural differences in the specific stages when adolescents progress from one moral stage to a more advanced stage. In general, more advanced forms of moral judgment appear later in more primitive societies. For example, in Yucatán, more sixteen-year-old children were still in stage one and fewer in stages five and six than in the United States. Stages five and six are rarely attained in preliterate villages or tribal communities. The findings comparing socioeconomic classes in the United States are not too different from the results from cross-cultural comparisons. The basic pattern of moral development of middle- and lower-class youth is the same, but "middle-class children were found to be more advanced in moral judgment than matched lower-class children" (Kohlberg, 1970: 154). Kohlberg argues that basic moral values are not specifically related to social class, as frequently used terminology such as "middle-class values" implies, but that middle- and lower-class individuals subscribe to similar basic moral values.

Among young adults, those who are political conservatives and refer to law and order and the maintenance of the political system tend to make moral judgments characteristic of stage four. Adults in stage three emphasize "conformity to stereotyped roles" and think in terms of cultural stereotypes, such as Miss America, preppies, hard-hats, the drug addicts, our boys, red-blooded Americans, and so on. Liberals and moderates try to make stage five moral judgments, whereas radicals and revolutionaries are strangely divided between idealistic stage six and egoistic stage two responses (Hampden-Turner and Whitten, 1971). Individuals in stage six and less so in stage five provide for innovation, experimentation, and change in social values. Individuals in stages three and four represent the conventional and conservative elements in society.

RELATIONSHIP OF KOHLBERG'S STAGES OF MORAL JUDGMENT TO OTHER STAGE THEORIES

According to Kohlberg, there is a fairly specific relationship between his stages of moral judgment and Piaget's stages of cognitive development. Piaget's concrete operations correspond to the preconventional level of moral development. The earlier concern of the operational child with categorical classifications is related to the punishment-obedience orientation of stage one in moral thinking. The concrete reversibility of thought patterns, still part of Piaget's operational stage in logical thinking, has its analogue in Kohlberg's stage two of an instrumental relativistic moral orientation. The basic shift from childhood to adolescence is reflected in a dramatic shift from concrete to formal or abstract thought processes, just as the shift from preconventional to conventional morality constitutes the basic difference between child and adolescent moral structure. Piaget's earlier substage of formal operations concerned with relationships involving the inverse of reversibility corresponds to Kohlberg's interpersonal concordance orientation (stage three). Piaget's more advanced substage III-B of formal abstract operations encompasses Kohlberg's stage four orientation toward authority, law and order, and makes the more advanced postconventional principled stages five and six possible. Sixty percent of a group of sixteen-year-old adolescents had attained formal operational thinking, but only 10 percent had reached the postconventional levels of moral thinking. But all 10 percent who had reached the postconventional level of principled morality were able to think in terms of logical, abstract, formal operations. The relationship between Piaget's logical stages and Kohlberg's moral stages is such that the attainment of logical thought is a necessary precondition for the attainment of the corresponding level of moral thought. However, having attained a certain stage in logical thought, it does not follow that an individual has necessarily attained the same level in moral judgment. It may be, and frequently is, lower but never higher.

Kohlberg's stages of moral development have also been related to Erikson's stages of ego-identity. The research is based on Marcia's (1966) methodology and was conducted by Podd (1972). Podd classified college students into Marcia's four identity statuses: identity achievement, moratorium, foreclosure, and identity diffusion (see Chapter 4 for a definition of these statuses and discussion of Marcia's theory). Podd also independently classified the same individuals into four groups of moral development based on Kohlberg's moral stages: the preconventional level (stages one and two), the conventional level (stages three and four), the principled level (stages five and six), and a transitional group that he added. While the results do not provide simple, clear-cut relationships, interesting patterns between moral development and identity development emerge and, in general, support the theoretical links between identity status and moral thinking. Podd had hypothesized that the most mature level of reasoning would be found in the identity achieved subjects. About two-thirds of the morally principled subjects on Kohlberg's test were identified as having achieved a mature identity. None of the subjects who were transitional in their moral thinking had achieved a mature identity, but approximately two-thirds were identity diffused. Forty percent of the subjects subscribing to a conventional level of morality had also achieved a mature identity, and 30 percent of conventional subjects were foreclosures. Foreclosure subjects showed, as hypothesized, a strong tendency to use a conventional mode of moral thinking.

Those subjects who tended to be transitional in their moral orientation were also transitional in respect to their identity status. "People undergoing an identity crisis were found to be unstable and inconsistent in their moral reasoning" (Podd, 1972: 497). Before an individual can effectively question the conventional morality of his society, he must first have questioned his own identity—that is, he must first have completed his own moratorium issues.

Kohlberg's Moral Judgment Scale was administered to a large group of students at the University of California at Berkeley at the time when students had decided to take over the administration building in support of the Free Speech Movement (Haan, Smith, and Block, 1968). Of approximately 200 students arrested, the following patterns of moral thinking were observed. Stage six subjects verbally indicated that protest was a reflection of their principled morality and that they were more concerned with civil rights and civil liberties and the relationship between students as a group and the university as a community. Eighty percent of the stage six subjects had been arrested. For stage five subjects the issue was less clear-cut, and only 50 percent were arrested. For students in stages three and four subscribing to a conventional morality, the issue was again clear-cut against the protest, and only 10 percent participated in the sit-in leading to arrest. However, students at stage two were almost as likely to be arrested due to their participation in the protest as students at stage six. Sixty percent of stage two subjects were arrested; however, their protest was motivated by egoistic relativism and revenge, rather than by autonomous morality. They were more concerned with their own personal rights than with human rights. College students who still responded with stage two solutions to the moral dilemmas tended to use the protest movement to fight their own personal battle with society. The study illustrates that moral structure is not identical with moral behavior and that not all political civil disobedience is based on principled morality. College activists are comprised of individuals in the highest, as well as the lowest levels of moral development. While protesting may be a sign of mature and advanced morality, it can also be a sign of immature and selfish stage two morality. "Protest activities, like other acts, are neither virtuous nor vicious; it is only the knowledge of the good which lies behind them that gives them virtue" (Kohlberg, 1970: 159).

Kohlberg suggests that even though only a small majority of adolescents have actually reached a postconventional level of moral reasoning, some adolescents, particularly hippies and street people, live in what superficially appears to be a postconventional subculture, in that it challenges, questions, and criticizes the conventional morality of society on what may sometimes appear to be principles. Moreover, the moral philosophy of the individual hippie is largely based on "do your own thing" (stage two) morality and "be loving and nice" (stage three). The most frequent challenges to conventional morality are based on reasons that must be classified as stage three, as "laws being too harsh and mean," or on a more egoistic stage two rationale, as "why shouldn't I have fun?" rather than on more universal principles of morality. Hippies seem to have "adopted the style of the revolution without the awareness of the revolutionary" (Hampden-Turner and Whitten, 1971: 76). In other words, the morality of hippies, even though it may appear postconventional, is characterized by a high degree of relativism and fluidity, rather than by principles.

EDUCATIONAL IMPLICATIONS

The issue of teaching moral values and moral behavior in the public schools is a controversial one, and little time and effort is provided for "character education" in the curriculum of today. There is the fear among parents that arbitrary values may be imposed upon unsuspecting children. Consequently, the teaching of moral issues has been disguised in such "value-neutral" approaches as mental health, value clarification, life adjustment, and personality development. Parents, partly because of their own confusion as to what is right and partly because of their inability to teach effectively those moral virtues that they do believe in, increasingly demand that values and moral behavior be taught in school. However, there is little consensus as to what those values are and how they should be taught. Teachers and schools have been reluctant to teach moral values, partly because the teaching of middle-class values might offend and confuse the child who is exposed to lower-class values at home (and school critics such as Paul Goodman and Edgar Friedenberg feel that the teaching of middle-class values interferes with the learning process of lower-class children), and partly because of the wide endorsement of a relativistic moral philosophy, not only among adolescents, but even among theologians in the form of "situational ethics." A teacher might say: "I will expose them to my moral philosophy, but I will not impose it on them. Who am I to say that I am right and they are wrong?"

The relativistic philosophy of "doing your own thing" questions the schools' right and obligation to teach morality. Thus American schools have progressed from the formal teaching of Christian moral values in the strict Puritan tradition of the seventeenth century to the much more subtle and indirect approach of moral fables in which misbehavior inevitably results in painful consequences. This is the approach of the McGuffey readers and was quite prevalent in the public schools in the middle and latter part of the nineteenth century. During the earlier part of the twentieth century emphasis fell again on the teaching of virtues such as honesty, service, and self-control, an approach that Kohlberg identifies as the "bag of virtues" approach to teaching morality. More recently schools and teachers have denied that it is their role to teach virtues and values, especially when values were defined narrowly in terms of "white middle-class values." Consequently some teachers have abandoned the teaching of moral values in favor of teaching reading, writing, and arithmetic. Even among professionals the Supreme Court interpretation of the First Amendment concerning school prayer has been construed to eliminate any form of moral and ethical education from public schools, not only religious ones (Ball, 1967). Kohlberg (1967), in contrast, feels that the school can no more be committed to value neutrality than is the law, the Constitution, or the government. Two people obviously have the right to hold different values, but this does not mean that both sets of values are equally valid. It is a fallacy to believe that because a person has a sincere commitment to a set of values that these values are therefore necessarily valid, sound, mature, or beneficial. Public schools have a commitment to the development of the idea of justice in their pupils, and Kohlberg attempts to make this commitment explicit. Schools frequently do have what Kohlberg calls "a hidden moral curriculum"—be obedient, stay in your seat, make no noise—that becomes most obvious in the kind of behavior that teachers reward and punish. The underlying moral assumptions may actually be unconscious on the teacher's part and may be quite different from what a teacher would consciously define as a system of moral values.

The earlier version of moral education consisted of teaching a "bag of virtues." These included honesty, service, self-control, friendliness, and moral virtues. Aristotle already had proposed a similar bag of virtues including temperance, liberality, pride, good temper, truthfulness, and justice. The scout bag adds that a scout should be honest, reverent, clean, and brave.

Traditionally, children were encouraged to practice virtuous behavior—they were told about the advantages of good behavior and were warned of the harm that could befall them if they were not virtuous. Reward and punishment were used as well. To illustrate the point, teachers used didactic stories in which good little boys and girls were rewarded and bad boys and girls were punished. According to Kohlberg and Piaget, this amounts to training for an immature stage of moral development, since in mature moral development the abstract principle is more important than the material reward. The problem with the bag-of-virtues approach to moral education is that there are no such psychological traits; virtues such as honesty are evaluative labels that are not reflected in consistent behavior. The Hartshorne and May (1928–1930) studies pointed out that participation in the character-education program as provided in schools, Sunday schools, and Scouts did not contribute to improved moral behavior as measured by a test involving honesty, self-control, and service. Virtually all children cheated no matter what their moral education had been. Cheating was not a consistent trait but dependent upon the situation; some children cheated in one situation, but this did not predict their behavior in other situations. More recent follow-up studies have supported these findings, and moral knowledge and moral behavior often showed only low correlations. Children who did cheat were just as likely to say that cheating was wrong as those who did not cheat. Kohlberg, when asked "how can one teach morality?" answered as Socrates might have answered when asked the same question: "You must think I am very fortunate to know how virtue is acquired. The fact is that far from knowing whether it can be taught, I have no idea what virtue really is" (Kohlberg, 1970: 144).

Kohlberg is convinced that moral thinking can be enhanced through educational procedures that have been tried experimentally. The goal of his approach is to aid and encourage children in their natural developmental tendencies through educational intervention, to take the next step in a direction to greater moral maturity toward which the child is already predisposed. Kohlberg does have specific suggestions for the teacher wanting to teach moral values. His suggestions are radically different from teaching a bag of virtues by preaching, rewarding, punishing, cajoling, and demanding. Morality is not viewed by Kohlberg as a bag of virtues but as an understanding of justice; consequently, he wants schools to become concerned again with moral development, moral thinking, and an understanding of justice.

Progress from one stage to the next results—like development in Piaget's theory in general—from adaptation to a cognitive disequilibrium. Kohlberg assumes that the advance from one moral stage to the next higher one is not simply an addition of more or better understanding, but a reorganization and restructuring of earlier moral thinking modes. Cognitive disequilibrium can be brought about by challenges, interactions, and debate with one's peers. Consequently, social interaction with one's peers and with the moral ideas and ideals slightly ahead of one's own conceptual development are hypothesized to stimulate cognitive and moral development. Also moral development was described by Kohlberg (1969) as a function of role-taking ability through which people learn to restructure their own moral schemata and incorporate those of others. Consequently, role-taking opportunities and interaction with one's peers should facilitate moral development. Keasey (1971) investigated these hypotheses and found that the stages of moral development of early adolescents were positively related to the degree to which individuals were rated by themselves, their peers, and their teachers as high in social participation and social interaction. Adolescents with a significant amount of peer group involvement, role-taking opportunities, and social interaction advanced more rapidly through the moral stages than children who were socially withdrawn or lacking in social participation opportunities. Selman (1971a), too, found that "the ability to understand reciprocal social perspectives"—that is, role-taking skills—was positively related to higher levels of moral thought and was viewed as one precondition for progression in moral development (see Chapter 12).

Kohlberg's (1970) approach to teaching moral values involves several steps. First, it is essential to create in students a feeling of dissatisfaction about their concept of good and bad, right and wrong. This moral disequilibrium is brought about by exposing adolescents to choice situations involving a moral conflict for which they have no easy, readily available solution. The second step is to engage them in a discussion with their peers, a discussion in which different interpretations, disagreements, and conflicts are freely expressed, thereby inviting role taking. Ideally, the moral arguments should be those one stage beyond the subject's moral development, since arguments two or three stages ahead of a person are not as easily assimilated. Children and adolescents can understand the moral argument of all stages preceding their own, but they can rarely comprehend an argument that is more than one step ahead of their own (Turiel; 1966, 1969). By creating a cognitive dissonance and listening to the arguments of others, adolescents will see aspects of the moral dilemma that were inaccessible to them before. As they think about the problem, they incorporate into their thinking suggestions made by others. The advance from one moral stage to the next higher one is brought about by cognitive conflict, since resolution of conflict leads to a reorganization of structure—an idea not unlike Piaget's progression in cognitive development from equilibrium through disequilibrium to a higher level of equilibrium (Turiel, 1966; 1969).

Research (Blatt, 1959; Kohlberg and Blatt, 1972) in which this technique has been utilized has shown that 50 percent of the experimental subjects moved up one stage and an additional 10 percent moved up two stages. In a control group not exposed to the teaching of moral thinking, only 10 percent moved up one stage in the same period. Follow-up data suggest that the gain in moral structure was not temporary but permanent. In an experiment involving juvenile delinquents (Hickey, 1972)—who were originally in stages one or two and who espoused an "If I'm not getting nothing, I'm not giving nothing" philosophy—most had moved to a stage four law-and-order morality after exposure to Kohlberg's method of creating cognitive dissonance.

Kohlberg is concerned that schools themselves are not very highly developed institutions in terms of the moral philosophy that underlies their day-to-day operation. The school management seems to blend a fear of punishment (stage one) with an ever-present concern with law and order (stage four).

12: SOCIAL COGNITION. PART 1: ROBERT SELMAN'S THEORY OF ROLE TAKING*

SOCIAL COGNITION

The concept of social cognition, which has only recently emerged in the developmental literature, has rapidly gained popularity, recognition, and respectability, both as a popular research topic and as an important theoretical** construct. In contrast to most developmental theories, the theory of social cognition is not primarily associated with one particular person, or even one psychological school of thought; rather, it constitutes a new synthesis of several psychological positions. As a result, the concept of social cognition seems to suffer from diversification and a mushrooming of independent, interrelated minitheories and submodels. Because the important social cognition concepts come from different authors, different theories, and different research orientations, they do not have the unifying cohesiveness of theories developed by one person, such as those of Erikson or Piaget. Thus, social cognition theory constitutes the integration of several trends in the study of cognitive and social development.

Several major influences have contributed ideas to the theory of social cognition. On the one hand, there is the obvious influence of the vast literature concerned with the process by which children acquire their knowledge about the physical world, a process commonly referred to as cognitive development and heavily influenced by the writings of Jean Piaget, Heinz Werner, and Jerome Bruner. Even more relevant is Kohlberg's theory of moral development. However, his concepts of moral judgment and moral behavior are themselves frequently classified under the broader umbrella of social cognition; hence, Kohlberg's theory might be considered one aspect of social cognition.

---

*Chapter 12 is a revision of an article by the author "Social Cognition: Selman's Theory of Role Taking," *Adolescence* (in press).

**Many writers who have contributed to the development of the construct of social cognition prefer to speak about their "model" rather than their theory.

On the other hand, the vast literature on social development and social psychology also makes a significant contribution to the "social" side of social cognition theory. There is an extensive accumulation of information, much of it empirical in nature, about the developmental changes that take place in the social behavior of children and adolescents. The theoretical background for this approach is influenced by social learning theory and also by psychoanalytic theory.

Social cognition focuses on the processes by which children gain knowledge about their social world and their reasoning processes in social matters. Underlying all social cognition issues is the assumption that both children and adolescents apply cognitive abilities and cognitive skills to interpersonal situations and social problem-solving tasks (Youniss, 1975), such as anticipating or predicting how another person may feel or behave in a social dilemma. However, social cognition theory asks some important questions: How does the child learn to understand what children and adolescents think about one another's behavior? And how does the individual conceptualize the thinking of others? These will be explained further throughout the chapter.

The theoretical concept of "social role taking" as a significant construct in social and developmental psychology goes back to the writings of James Baldwin (1906) and George Herbert Mead (1934). Two specific concepts from Piaget's developmental theory are directly related to social cognition: egocentrism and decentering. Both will be treated in more detail in Chapter 13. Egocentrism and decentering are applicable to impersonal tasks such as Piaget's famous mountain range (see Figure 11, p. 187) where the child has to determine what the silhouette of the mountains looks like from a different position. However, egocentrism and decentering apply equally to interpersonal issues, such as putting one's self into another person's position. In Piaget's view, the emergence of role-taking ability must be viewed as a by-product of social and cognitive decentering.

An important question must be raised at this point: "Are social objects and physical objects known in the same or in different ways?" (Youniss, 1975: 173). Much information about social behavior, like much information about the physical world, will be acquired through observation, trial and error, exploration, direct first-hand experiences, and discovery. There also appears to be some parallel in the structural changes that accompany the development of impersonal and interpersonal cognition. Byrne (1974), for example, was able to demonstrate a close relationship between logical stages, moral stages, and role-taking stages. A certain level in logical thinking appears to be necessary before the equivalent stage in moral judgment is reached, and a certain level in role taking, in turn, is a prerequisite for the corresponding level of moral judgment. "Logical stages may be in evidence without the equivalent role taking or moral stage, but the role taking or moral stage rarely occurs without the corresponding stage of logical thinking" (Byrne, 1974: 5647B).

However, as Piaget (1932b) pointed out, there is one very important distinction between physical knowledge and social understanding: Scientific knowledge is objective and factual and can be proven or disproven through the scientific method. Social knowledge, in contrast, is quite arbitrary, and appropriate social behavior is determined to a very large extent by the specific social situation, as well as by social, cultural, and even subcultural definitions, requirements, and expectations.

> Because of the arbitrary nature of social rules and social protocol, the child will have to acquire some knowledge by direct instruction from adults or older children, by observing the behavior of mature people in the environment, and by experiencing approval and disapproval for appropriate and inappropriate behavior [Moore, 1979: 54].

Because social rules are less uniform, less specific, and more situation-dependent than physical phenomena, they are less predictable and more complicated to understand.

There is considerable debate in the literature about whether and to what extent physical knowledge and social cognition are correlated and about whether scientific problem-solving skills and social problem-solving skills are correlated or merely two relatively independent entities (Keating, 1978; Keating and Clark, 1980). At this point we are not justified in assuming that cognitive problem-solving skills can easily be transferred and applied to social problem-solving skills. Many writers have claimed that social problem-solving skills function independent of and are different from intellectual problem-solving skills and need to be taught in their own right. Shure and Spivack (1980) provide evidence that the cognitive abilities involved in interpersonal problem solving are not the same as those measured by the conventional IQ test. Furthermore, the improvement in social adjustment that resulted from their interpersonal skills training program was not a function of the child's level of intellectual functioning. Selman (1976b) reports that when a poorly adjusted clinical group of preadolescents was compared to a matched group of normally functioning peers no differences in level of cognitive functioning were found, but the poorly adjusted group was substantially below the normal group in the domain of interpersonal and moral reasoning. The individual with a deficient ego, according to Redl and Wineman, has greater difficulty in differentiating between physical and social reality. Such individuals are often surprisingly capable of figuring out problems posed on an impersonal, factual level, but they are unable to solve corresponding problems of social living or to see that their own aggressive behavior might have a negative impact on the group. Our present knowledge about the relationship between physical knowledge and social knowledge can best be summarized by a quote from Selman: "The development of social conceptions, reasoning, thought—social cognition—is distinct from, though not unrelated to, the development of nonsocial cognition" (1980: 14). Therefore, the investigation of social cognition development, independent of the development of reasoning ability, is justified and potentially a fruitful contribution to developmental psychology.

Although many writers on social cognition refer to the works of Piaget, Kohlberg, Bruner, and Heider, new and more specific social cognition theories of development have emerged, particularly in the writings of Flavell (1974; 1977), Shantz (1975), and Selman (1976a; 1976b; 1977; 1980).

Flavell's model of social cognition is not strictly developmental; rather, it is more of a "general information processing model." He identifies four components that are necessary for drawing inferences about the perspectives of other persons: the existence component, the need component, the inference component, and the application component (Flavell, 1977). The *existence component* simply implies a subject's recognizing the existence of psychological experiences or events in the other person and realizing that the other person's perspective of such experiences or events may differ from one's own. "There scarcely can be any thinking about social-cognitive phenomena if the very existence of such phenomena is not yet represented by the thinker" (Flavell, 1977: 20). The *need component* expands and includes the idea that the goal-directed behavior of another person is now understood as being motivated by a need. Other people are now being seen as having existence, feelings, and needs. The *inference component* leads to the construction of a representation of another person's subjective experiences. In other words, there is an attempt to figure out what the specific nature of the other person's needs or feelings may be. This kind of social thinking requires observing clues, integrating the clues, and probabilistic reasoning. The *application component* is the subject's adjusting his or her own behavior—as in game strategies or through verbal compliments—to apply the information obtained from the inference. A decision about an interpersonal issue or problem must go through all of these steps.

For example, assume an adolescent boy riding in a train is sitting next to a teen-age girl reading a book. He first becomes aware of her and finds her attractive. His interest increases until he is aware of little else. To assess her needs component he may begin to observe whether and how much she is absorbed in her reading, what she is reading, what she is wearing, whether she is wearing an engagement ring or other evidence of being attached; whether or not she looks at him, the openness and closedness of her body posture, and so on. He infers that she might be interested in talking to him.

The young man may never dare to make the necessary application and talk to her, in which case he will never know the correctness or incorrectness of his inferences. If he does complete the fourth step and makes the application by saying "Hi, I see you are interested in science fiction—so am I," he may find out whether his inferences about her were correct. She may look at him, smile, and respond. He also may be forced to reassess his initial inference if, for example, she abruptly turns the page or stares out of the window away from him without responding.

Shantz (1975) develops her theory around five related questions that address the fundamental issue of social cognition:

1. What is the other person seeing? This calls for the ability to make inferences about another person's visual perception of objects in space.
2. What is the other person feeling? The focus here is on understanding the emotional state of the other person; it involves empathy.
3. What is the other person thinking? At issue is the ability to make inferences about the thought processes of other people and to distinguish them from one's own.
4. What is the other person intending? This particular social cognition skill requires inferences about the motivation of the other person.
5. What is the other person like? This social cognition skill involves person-perception and can deal with overt (physical characteristics) and covert (personality traits) aspects of the other person.

The insights that can be ascertained from these social-cognitive developmental issues provide a theoretical model for understanding social behavior and social development (Selman, 1980). The discussion that follows will focus primarily on the contribution of Robert Selman, who has developed a social cognition theory that considers pre-adolescence and adolescence in more detail than anyone else. Taking the social perspective of someone else—which his theory emphasizes—appears to be at the very core of what social cognition is all about.

DEFINITION OF SOCIAL OR INTERPERSONAL COGNITION

Social cognition can be defined as "how people think about other people and about themselves," or how people come to know their social world. Social cognition is concerned with the processes by which children and adolescents conceptualize and learn to understand others: their thoughts, their intentions, their emotions, their social behavior, and their general point of view. Social cognition involves role taking, perspective taking, empathy, moral reasoning, interpersonal problem solving, and self-knowledge. Shantz has provided a formal definition of social cognition: "the child's intuitive or logical representation of others, that is, how he characterizes others and makes inferences about their covert inner psychological experiences" (Shantz, 1975: 1). Implied in the concept of social cognition is an ability to make inferences about other people's capabilities, attributes, expectations, feelings, and potential reactions. These inferential processes of social cognition are referred to as role taking or perspective taking. Selman differentiates between role taking and social-perspective taking. The former involves the question of what social or psychological information may look like from the position of the other person. Social-perspective taking more broadly involves an "understanding of how human points of view are related and coordinated with one another" (Selman, 1980: 22). Flavell makes a further distinction between perceptual and conceptual role taking. Perceptual role taking is limited to the process of assuming the visual perspective of another person, as in Piaget's famous mountain range experiment. Conceptual role taking implies taking another person's mental perspectives, including his motives, feelings, attitude, and knowledge.

In summary, our discussion of the defining characteristics of social cognition may be highlighted by a statement from Tagiuri, in which he captures the essense of that concept and focuses on the events and classes of objects toward which the efforts of social understanding and social problem solving are directed:

> The observations or inferences we make are principally about intentions, attitudes, emotions, ideas, abilities, purposes, traits, thoughts, perceptions, memories—events that are *inside* the person and strictly psychological. Similarly, we attend to certain psychological qualities of relationships *between* persons, such as friendship, love, power, and influence. We attribute to a person properties of *consciousness* and *self-determination*, and the capacity for *representation of his environment*, which in turn mediates his action [Tagiuri, 1969: 396].

Social Cognition Topics	Research References
Role taking	Byrne (1974); Chandler (1973); Flavell (1968); Selman (1971a; 1971b); Selman and Byrne (1974)
Perspective taking	Kurdek (1978); Selman (1971b)
Understanding the feelings of others	Feshbach (1973; 1975)
Understanding the motives of others	Berndt and Berndt (1974)
Interpersonal understanding	Selman (1980)
Interpersonal awareness	Selman, Jacquette, and Lavin (1977)
Social and interpersonal reasoning	Damon (1980); Keating and Clark (1980)
Social relations such as friendship and authority	Damon (1977)
Interpersonal acts such as kindness	Baldwin and Baldwin (1970); Youniss (1975)
Interpersonal problem solving skills	Spivack and Shure (1974); Spivack, Platt, and Shure (1976)
Social rules and conventions	Turiel (1975; 1978)
Moral judgment and behavior	Flavell (1977); Kohlberg (1969); Rest (1974)
Social institutions	Furth, Baur, and Smith (1976); Furth (1978)
Social competency	Elardo and Cooper (1977)
Communication skills	Gluecksberg, Krauss, and Higgens (1975)
Empathy	Eisenberg-Berg and Mussen (1978); Feshbach (1973); Hughes, Tingle, and Sawin (1981); Hoffman (1976)
Self-recognition	Flavell (1978); Hill and Tomlin (1981)
Attribution theory	Kelley (1973); Weiner (1974);
Egocentrism	Elkind (1967); Elkind and Bowen (1979); Looft (1971); Muuss (1981); Rubin (1973)
The self's own thought processes (Metacognition)	Flavell (1977; 1978)
Person perception	Livesley and Bromley (1973); Montemayor and Eisen (1977); Tagiuri (1969); Tagiuri and Petrullo (1958)

FIGURE 17. An Overview of Social Cognition: Topics, Models, and Research.

Social cognition or interpersonal cognition or social intelligence cannot be perceived as one uniform, consistent, theoretical construct. Under the umbrella "theory of social cognition," a variety of mini-theories, constructs, and models have emerged. The various social cognition constructs have stimulated considerable research to investigate these constructs, the interrelationship between the various social cognition concepts, and their relationship to the more general concepts of cognitive, moral, and social development. To provide the reader with a general overview of the multidimensional quality of social cognition theories and an understanding of some of the major conceptual constructs, as well as some references to the research literature, a summary of information is provided in Figure 17.

Most of the studies listed in Figure 17 used children as subjects and cannot be reviewed in detail here; however, the study by Montemayor and Eisen (1977) does focus on the developmental changes in self-conception from childhood through adolescence and hence deserves a more detailed review. The authors utilize Kuhn's (1954) "Who Am I" techniques, and the results are based on Gordon's (1968) thirty response classification categories. Responses at age levels ten, twelve, fourteen, sixteen, and eighteen show a significant increase in the following response categories: occupational role (e.g., I want to become a teacher); interpersonal style (I am lonely); psychic style (I am happy); a sense of unity (I am in harmony); a sense of self determination (I am a serious worker); ideological and belief references (I am a conservative); and existential and individuating responses (me, I, myself).

In the same group of adolescents a decrease in the following categories occurred as they grew older: territoriality (I am a New Yorker); possessions, resources (I own a motor scooter); physical self, body image (I am blond, slim, and tall).

The findings of the study suggest that with increasing age the self-conception of adolescents becomes more abstract and less concrete. Adolescents perceive themselves in terms of more abstract and subjective attributes; they emphasize personal beliefs and motivational and interpersonal qualities more than children do. Implied in the findings is the idea that the more abstractly thinking older individuals may be more effective in differentiating between overt appearance and deeper underlying dispositional qualities in themselves and others.

Returning to the previous listing (Figure 17) of social cognition concepts, it must be emphasized that the list of related social cognition concepts as well as the list of relevant research studies could be extended. The interested reader is referred to several of the more important summary reviews on social cognition: Chandler (1977), Hill and Palmquist (1978), Kurdek (1978), Shantz (1975), and Youniss (1975).

SELMAN'S STAGE THEORY OF SOCIAL COGNITION

Selman (1971b; 1976a; 1976b; 1977; 1980) and Selman and Byrne (1974) have advanced a stage theory of social cognition based on the concept of an ontogenetic, invariant sequence of predictable stages in social perspective taking. Selman was greatly influenced by Mead's theory of self, by Piaget's theory of cognitive development (logical thought), and by Kohlberg's theory of moral judgment (moral thought). "Conceptually, role taking can be described as a form of social cognition intermediate between logical and moral thought" (Selman, 1976a: 307). The developmental changes in logical structure seem to manifest themselves first in the thinking related to physical events, later in the thinking concerned with social events, and still later in the thinking concerned with the moral domain.

Selman's model focuses on the child's ability to draw interpersonal inferences about somebody else's perceptual or conceptual social awareness. It is based on an investigation of the developmental changes that take place in social perception or role-taking skills. The assumption, well supported by empirical evidence (Selman, 1971b; 1977; 1980; Selman and Byrne, 1974), is that social role-taking skills (that is, skill in differentiating between the perspective of self and others and accurate perception of the thinking of others) increase with age, at least into adolescence. Social role taking is viewed by Selman (1971b) as a proto-typical social cognitive skill. The basic theoretical issue rests on the assumption "that the unique aspect of social cognition and judgment that differentiates human from sub-human functioning is 'role-taking,' the ability to understand the self and the other as subjects, to react to others as like the self, and to react to the self's behavior from the other's point of view" (Selman and Byrne, 1974: 803).

The series of role-taking stages identified by Selman and Byrne are logically related and follow in a fixed developmental sequence. In that respect they meet the criteria for a structural developmental model. Selman makes an important distinction between the structure and the content of thought. What is being reasoned about is the content; in contrast, how the social reasoning is done is the structure. It is the structure of social reasoning that constitutes the theoretical basis for Selman's "Structural-Developmental Model of Social Cognition" (Selman, 1977). Selman hypothesizes that "each level of social perspective taking provides the structural basis for a stage in the development of conceptions of interpersonal role relations" (1976b: 160).

Originally, Selman identified only four developmental levels of social perspective taking skills between the ages of four and twelve. In his more recent work (Selman, 1976a; 1980; Selman, Jaquette, and Lavin, 1977), the model has been elaborated further and includes a fifth stage, corresponding to adolescence and reaching into adulthood. This theory has considerable empirical support, and since Selman places more emphasis on the developmental changes during adolescence than many of the previously mentioned social cognition models, his theory will be considered in greater detail.

Selman's model of interpersonal understanding is based on five distinct stages, although some further subdivision of these stages has been proposed. The names and the identifying characteristics of these stages are:

Stage 0. The egocentric undifferentiated stage (approximately age three to six)

Stage 1. The differentiated and subjective perspective-taking stage (age five to nine)

Stage 2. Self-reflective thinking or reciprocal perspective-taking stage (age seven to twelve)

Stage 3. The third-person or mutual perspective-taking stage (age ten to fifteen)

Stage 4. The in-depth and societal perspective-taking stage (age twelve to adulthood)

These five stage concepts constitute the developmental dimension in Selman's theory.

The progression through these five stages is assessed, analyzed, and described primarily in terms of four social domains that provide the specific content to understand the development in social cognition. The four social domains are:

1. The individual concepts domain
2. The friendship concepts domain
3. The peer-group concepts domain
4. The parent-child concepts domain

These content domains of social cognition provide the conceptual frame of reference within which the specific developmental changes are investigated. The specific responses revealing the child's social awareness are elicited in the individual interview through various social dilemma situations. An illustration of such a dilemma from the domain "Concepts of Individuals" (self-awareness) is:

> Eight-year-old Tom is trying to decide what to buy his friend Mike for his birthday party. By chance, he meets Mike on the street and learns that Mike is extremely upset because his dog Pepper has been lost for two weeks. In fact, Mike is so upset that he tells Tom, "I miss Pepper so much I never want to look at another dog again." Tom goes off, only to pass a store with a sale on puppies; only two are left and those will soon be gone [Selman, 1980: 94].

The dilemma that Tom faces is whether or not to buy the puppy and he wonders how Mike would receive such a gift. After posing a dilemma, the interviewer follows up with a number of standard questions, then with less structured questions to clarify the child's level of social reasoning. Sample questions from the interview are: "Mike said he never wanted to see another puppy again. Why did he say that?" Depending on the child's response level, the interviewer might pursue the issue through "stage-related" follow-up questions, such as these: "Can someone say something and not mean it?" "Is it possible that Mike does not know how he feels?" "Can you ever fool yourself into thinking you feel one way when you really feel another?" (Selman, 1980: 94).

This dilemma assesses the *issue* of self-awareness in the individual concepts domain. In each of the four social domains there are between four and seven issues (a total of twenty-two) that make up the practical concepts for assessing social cognition. Thus, for example, the six practical issues that are assessed in the friendship domain are:

1. The formation of friendships. How and why are friendships formed, and what might make an ideal friend?
2. The closeness of friendships. What are the different types of friendship? What constitutes the ideal kind of friendship? What is intimacy in friendship?
3. The role of trust in friendship. Under what circumstances does one do something for a friend and what is the role of reciprocity in friendship?
4. Jealousy in friendship. How does the person feel about the intrusion of others into an established friendship relationship?
5. Conflict resolution. How do friends resolve their conflicts when there is disagreement?
6. Termination of friendships. How and why are friendships terminated?

A similar group of issues are identified in the assessment of the other three social domains: individual, peer-group, and parent-child relations. In the following discussion of Selman's developmental stages of interpersonal understanding, at least one issue from each domain will serve as the focus of the presentation, in order to provide some specific illustrations. The issue of *self-awareness* will be the focus in the individual's concepts domain. *Conflict resolution* and *trust* will be used to illustrate the friendship concept domain. *Leadership* and *group loyalty* are the issues in the peer-group concepts domain, and *punishment* in the parent-child concepts domain. Having outlined the basic parameters of Selman's theory of social cognition, we will now turn to the five developmental stages of social perspective taking.

Individual	Friendship	Peer group	Parent-child relations
1. *Subjectivity:* covert properties of persons (thoughts), feelings, motives); conflicts between thoughts or feelings within the person	1. *Formation:* why (motives) and how (mechanisms) friendships are made; the ideal friend	1. *Formation:* why (motives) and how (mechanisms) groups are formed; the ideal member	1. *Formation:* motives for having children and why children need parents
2. *Self-awareness:* awareness of the self's ability to observe its own thoughts and actions	2. *Closeness:* types of friendship, ideal friendship, intimacy	2. *Cohesion–loyalty:* group unity	2. *Love and emotional ties:* between parents and children
3. *Personality:* stable or predictive character traits (a shy person, etc.)	3. *Trust:* doing things for friends; reciprocity	3. *Conformity:* range and rationale	3. *Obedience:* why children do as their parents tell them
4. *Personality change:* how and why people change (growing up, etc.)	4. *Jealousy:* feelings about intrusions into new or established friendships	4. *Rules–norms:* types of rules, and reasons for them	4. *Punishment:* the function of punishment from the parent's and the child's perspective
	5. *Conflict resolution:* how friends resolve problems	5. *Decision-making:* setting goals, resolving problems, working together	5. *Conflict resolution:* optimal ways for parents and children to resolve their differences
	6. *Termination:* how friendships break up	6. *Leadership:* qualities, and function to the group	
		7. *Termination:* why groups break up or members are excluded	

FIGURE 18. Issues of Interpersonal Understanding Related to Concepts of the Individual, Close Friendships, Peer-Group Organizations, and Parent-Child Relations (Selman, 1980). © 1980, Academic Press. Reproduced with permission.

STAGE 0. *EGOCENTRIC UNDIFFERENTIATED STAGE OF SOCIAL PERSPECTIVE TAKING* (age three to six)

At the egocentric undifferentiated stage of social perspective taking, children cannot make a clear distinction between their own interpretation of social situations and another's point of view. Nor can they understand that their own perception may not be the true or correct perspective. In social perspective-taking tasks, subject and object are not yet differentiated but are seen egocentrically from the subject's point of view. However, young children do seem to realize that the preferences and subjective experiences of others may be different from their own. Lacking still are the inferential skills to figure out what those subjective states of others could be. Children at this stage do not clearly distinguish between the physical and the psychological attributes of another individual. This confusion between subjective psychological and objective physical characteristics leads to difficulties in differentiating feeling from behavior, and it also interferes with the ability to distinguish intentional and unintentional behavior. While children understand that each person can have different feelings, they do not yet have the ability to determine how the thoughts and feelings of others might differ from their own (Forman and Siegl, 1979).

Characteristic of egocentric thinking is the cognitive inability to differentiate between different points of view. The differentiation between oneself and another is only accomplished in respect to physical qualities; the psychological characteristics remain undifferentiated.

FIGURE 19. The other person is seen egocentrically, or undifferentiated from the self's own point of view.

Since the subjective-psychological perception remains undifferentiated, children are not aware that another person may interpret a social event quite differently. Lacking is the awareness that another person possesses different perspectives; they cannot, so to speak, get "under the skin of another person," nor can they see the cause-effect relationship between thinking and behaving in other people. A girl may give her mother jelly beans for her birthday, not just because she herself likes jelly beans, or because she thinks her mother might like jelly beans, but because she views jelly beans as "things that are liked," without differentiating between her own point of view and those of others.

Self-Awareness in the Individual Concepts Domain. Stage 0 children are unable to differentiate an inner psychological experience from the more concrete nature of external experiences. They do possess an awareness of self; however, that self has quasi-physical attributes—for example, one part of the body tells another part what to do. When asked "When you think, where do you think?" the child may answer "In my mouth," or when asked "How do you think?" "My words tell me" (Selman, 1980: 95).

Conflict Resolution in the Friendship Concepts Domain. The young child at this level uses two methods to resolve conflict. The first may be characterized as noninteraction; the child may say "Go play with another toy," or just "Go away." The going away is not thought of as a cooling off period but as an "out of sight, out of mind" approach to conflict resolution. The second approach is physical attack—"Go and hit him." No reflective considerations are given to such psychological variables as motives, feelings, or attitudes. Conflict is often viewed not as a disagreement between two parties, but as a situation where one party does not get to do what he wants because of the behavior of the other party.

Leadership in the Peer-Group Concepts Domain. The young child views the leader as the one who has the physical power to tell group members what to do, and they must do it.

Punishment in the Parent-Child Concepts Domain. The Stage 0 child seems to be aware of the fact that punishment follows misbehavior but is unaware of the parents' motives for punishment. The child confuses punishment as a cause (I did something wrong because I was punished) and punishment as an effect (I was punished because I did something wrong).

The egocentric undifferentiated social perspective-taking stage seems to parallel closely the preoperational thinking structure in Piaget's theory of cognitive development and, in turn, seems to correspond to the premoral stage in Kohlberg's theory of the development of moral judgment.

STAGE 1. *THE DIFFERENTIAL OR SUBJECTIVE PERSPECTIVE-TAKING STAGE OR THE SOCIAL-INFORMATIONAL ROLE-TAKING STAGE* (age five to nine)

Children at this stage begin to realize that another person can have cognitive or social perspectives different from their own. One's subjective experiences are differentiated from the experiences of others; however, judgment of another person is still based on physical observations. The awareness dawns that others can interpret the same social situation differently. Children understand that another person may feel or think differently because that person is in a different social situation or has access to different information. However, children are still unable to determine accurately what the other person's perspective looks like (Oppenheimer, 1978). In other words, they cannot maintain their own perspective and simultaneously assume the perspective of another. The interpersonal perspective of the other person is conceived and conceptualized in one-way, unilateral terms. Even though children realize that different perspectives of an event do exist, they still assume that there is only one correct point of view, either their own or that of the "authority."

FIGURE 20. The other is seen as different from the self, but the other person's perception of the self is still undifferentiated.

There are three distinctive features of this level of social-perspective taking. First, children become aware that they themselves and their own inner thoughts can be the object of another person's thinking, but they cannot accurately judge their own behavior as seen from the perspective of another person. There is no reciprocity between perspectives of self and others; perspective taking is a one-way affair. Only physical experiences can be understood as a two-way reciprocity—for example, the child who was hit, hits back. People react to the actions of other people with the same action.

Second, the Stage 1 child, in contrast to the Stage 0 child, distinguishes between the physical and the psychological dimensions of another person and between intentionality and unintentionality in behavior and thus begins to consider personal reasons as causes of actions. The child now realizes that others have their own unique psychological life, understands the concept of personal reasons, and recognizes that personal reasons are the causes of choices.

Third, Stage 1 children are capable of inferring the other person's intentions, feelings, and thoughts with some degree of accuracy. They also realize that other people have their own reasons for their thoughts and actions; however, the reasons themselves are not apparent to the outside observer, and since these children base their judgment of the feelings of others on physical observations, they are not always correct.

Self-Awareness. Since Stage 1 children are not yet able to distinguish between overt physical behavior and inward-looking psychological experiences, they do not yet understand that people may hide their true inner feelings. They know how to lie and know that others lie; however, they are not yet cognizant "that one can purposefully misrepresent one's inner experiences" (Selman, 1980: 96). Even though these children are aware that intention and behavior are two different things, they assume that the internal feelings eventually must manifest themselves in overt behavior. This is well illustrated by the child's responses to questions about the previously cited dilemma:

HOW DOES MIKE FEEL INSIDE?
Sad.
HOW DO YOU KNOW?
Because of the way he looks.
COULD HE LOOK SAD AND BE HAPPY INSIDE?
He could but you would be able to tell if you watched him long enough; he'd show you he was happy [Selman, 1980: 97].

Finally, the distinction between awareness and unawareness is still quite vague and different from the more advanced levels that follow. "Fooling oneself" in the dilemma is seen more as changing one's feelings rather than as being unaware of them.

Conflict Resolution. The child begins to realize that the subjective or psychological effects in a conflict situation may be as important as the physical effects, the focus of attention of the Stage 0 child. However, awareness of the psychological effect is still a one-way proposition; that is, it can be applied to one of the two individuals involved in the situation. Thinking now expresses itself in two different approaches to the conflict situation:

1. to undo the actions that caused the conflict ("Give him back what you took from him.")
2. to perform a positive substitute action ("Give him something nice.")

The problem at this level is that the child assumes that a conflict is something started by one person, and reasons that the resolution of the conflict should come from that person; thus, conflict too is basically still a one-way proposition.

Friendship, Trust. Trust in a friendship relationship is also still a one-way proposition. The trust in a friendship is based, rather egotistically, on getting the other person to do what the child wants "his friend" to do. Selman quotes a child saying "You trust a friend if he does what you tell him" (Selman, Jaquette, and Lavin, 1977: 268).

Leadership. The child at Stage 1 of social perspective-taking sees the leader as someone who (1) has the best skills and knowledge, and (2) helps the other members of the group to acquire skills ("He teaches them tricks"). Group leadership is still based on unilateral authority. Cooperation and coordination of activities are not yet evident.

Peer-Group Loyalty. Loyalty to the peer group becomes important at this stage, but the child defines loyalty as the "unilateral obedience to the dictates of a leader or other group members." One of Selman's eight-year-olds defines loyalty as "always doing what you are told, 'cause they kick you if you don't" (Selman, Jaquette, and Lavin, 1977: 269).

Punishment. In contrast to the earlier stage, the child now does consider the parents' motives for punishment; however, this too is seen as a one-way proposition, since the child does not yet consider the recipient's reactions toward punishment. Punishment is identified as serving three functions: (1) parents use punishment to teach their children a lesson; (2) punishment may be seen as a method parents use to protect their children from danger; and (3) punishment is viewed as a way of restoring the equilibrium—that is, "setting things straight" or "paying someone back."

The beginning decentering in perspective taking characteristic of this stage of social cognition seems to find its counterpart in Piaget's transition from preoperational to operational thinking and is the developmental prerequisite for Kohlberg's stage one of moral judgment, "The Obedience and Punishment Orientation."

STAGE 2. *SELF-REFLECTIVE THINKING OR RECIPROCAL PERSPECTIVE TAKING* (age seven to twelve)

The preadolescent at Stage 2 realizes not only that other people have their own cognitive or social perspective because they think or feel differently, but the preadolescent also becomes aware that the other person thinks about his thinking and can take his, the subject's, role. Thus, the crucial developmental advance from Stage 1 to Stage 2 consists of the ability to leave oneself mentally and to take the perspective of another individual. The thought processes themselves can best be illustrated by the quote of a Stage 2 subject: "I know that she knows that I know she knows."

Individuals can now become capable of making inferences about the perspectives of other people; they can reflect about their own behavior and their own motivation as seen from the perspective of someone else. There is a self-reflecting anticipation of the other person's behavior toward the subject's own thought and purposes. However, such reflections about their own behavior and that of others are still limited since they do not occur simultaneously, but sequentially. Furthermore, they are aware that the other person can do the same thing.

This new ability to reciprocate social perspectives introduces an awareness of relativity, since each person might have quite different goals, values, ideals, feelings, and thoughts. No single individual's social perspective is necessarily correct or valid in an absolute sense. Another person's point of view may be as correct as one's own.

In contrast to the mutual role-taking ability of Stage 3, which follows, perspective taking at Stage 2 is still based only on a two-way reciprocity; it is sequential but not yet simultaneous or mutual. The preadolescent thinks only within a two-person frame of reference—"I think; you think"—and cannot yet take a more general third-person perspective or understand a more general social relationship system.

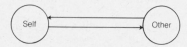

FIGURE 21.   The self can take the perspective of another person and becomes aware that the other person can also take the perspective of the self.

Other people are now seen as operating on multimotivational levels rather than being motivated by one factor. The preadolescent becomes cognizant of the fact that one can experience two opposing emotions (such as repulsion and attraction) toward the same person or the same object simultaneously. Furthermore, the preadolescent can differentiate thoughts and feelings, and thus can understand that one might do some things that one did not intend to do. Preadolescents establish a hierarchy of motives and perceive the possibility that altruistic and instrumental motives may conflict with one another, both in their own mind and in the minds of others. They can take into account the hierarchy of motives in a situation where a person wants to do one thing but actually does another. A person's behavior may be the expression of different layers; outward clowning, for example, may be a cover-up for true hidden feelings of insecurity or unhappiness.

Self-Awareness.   The Stage 2 preadolescent clearly distinguishes between outer (physical) and inner (psychological) reality and becomes aware that the two do not need to be congruent. Individuals may cover their true inner feelings to save face or avoid social embarrassment. Since preadolescents can take the perspective of another person, they can now monitor their own thoughts and actions from the perspective of another person. There emerges a new sense of priorities in that inner self-awareness matters more than outer appearances.

Conflict Resolution.   The preadolescent in Stage 2 becomes aware that quite commonly both parties contribute to a conflict. Therefore, it becomes obvious that both parties must cooperate in seeking an effective solution. This is often done by appealing to the individual's sensitivity and good judgment. Lacking still is the notion of conflict resolution by mutual consensus. As in Stage 0, he may suggest a resolution of the conflict by getting away from each other; however, the idea that emerges in this suggestion is the establishment of a psychological space, or a cooling-off period.

Leadership. The preadolescent sees the issue of leadership as a reciprocal relationship. Leadership is based on bilateral equality and a reciprocity of interest. The role of the leader is that of a mediator, organizer, and coordinator of group efforts. The leader encourages the efforts of group members through friendliness, recognition, support, and reward.

Friendship, Trust. Trust at Stage 2 is based much more on reciprocity between two friends than it was in Stage 1. However, self-interest still dominates the quality of trustworthiness in a friendship relationship, finding its clearest expression in the simple statement, "If you do something for me, I will do something for you."

Peer-Group Loyalty. Peer-group loyalty, like trust, is based on an even exchange of favors or mutual expression of affection, such as "I like you, if you like me," or "If he is loyal, the guys will be nice to one another."

Punishment. Punishment by parents may now be seen as an expression of the parent's concern for the child's well-being. He can conceptualize that parents use punishment to communicate with their children; thus, one purpose of punishment may be to make the child think about certain behavior. "Punishment is a message from one self-reflecting being to another" (Selman, 1980: 125). In addition, punishment is also seen as serving as a deterrent—it is likely to instill fear, which will become an internal agent of control in a similar situation.

The self-reflective perspective taking of Stage 2 finds its developmental parallel in Piaget's stage of operational thinking and sets the stage for the movement to stage two, "Instrumental Relativist Orientation," in Kohlberg's theory.

STAGE 3. *THE THIRD PERSON OR MUTUAL PERSPECTIVE-TAKING STAGE*
(age ten to fifteen)

The perspective-taking skills of early adolescence lead to a capacity for a more complex type of social cognition. The adolescent moves beyond simply taking the other person's perspective (in a back-and-forth kind of approach) and is able to see all parties from a more generalized third-person perspective. The third-person perspective "allows the adolescent to abstractly step outside an interpersonal interaction and simultaneously and mutually coordinate and consider the perspectives (and their interaction) of self and other(s)" (Selman, 1980: 39). In other words, the emerging concept of mutual role taking implies that adolescents can step outside of their own perspective and outside the partner's perspective and assume the perspective of a neutral third person. They thus can consider the mutual relationship involved, even as one of the participants. As third-person observers they see themselves as both actor and object. Adolescents know that both they and their thoughts can also be the object of the other person's thought and vice versa (Oppenheimer, 1978).

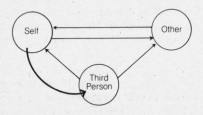

FIGURE 22. The self can view the self–other interaction from the perspective of a neutral third person.

Furthermore, there emerges the ability to distinguish between one's own point of view and a more generalized perspective that might be taken by an "average" member of the group. Adolescents can assume the role of such a disinterested average spectator and view the social interaction between themselves and somebody else from that spectator's position; they can see each party's perspective simultaneously and mutually. Furthermore, they reflect on their own self interacting with the self, an idea that Selman characterizes as "the observing ego."

Self-Awareness. The degree of self-awareness increases and the mind is seen as the observer of the self-aware self. Thus, the mind becomes the active psychological manipulator controlling the inner life. In other words, the mind is now viewed not as a storehouse of information but as an active participant deciding which ideas go where and which are kept out. Thus it becomes possible to fool the mind through an act of will. Thoughts and feelings may emerge even when opposed by will and mind. There is now a much more basic comprehension of the relationship between the self-as-subject and the self-as-object (Selman, 1980: 103).

Conflict Resolution. Friendship is now viewed not as a process of reciprocal back scratching but as a series of interactions over an extended period of time. They validate mutuality and involve emotional support and sharing of common feelings. Conflicts are seen as a natural, almost inevitable, part of a friendship relationship rather than as a problem of one individual. To resolve conflict in a friendship both sides must feel satisfied and both must be able to place themselves in the other person's shoes and be satisfied. Conflicts are seen as possibly emerging from different personality characteristics. Implied is the idea that a permanent conflict resolution might require some personality changes. In addition, there emerges the interesting notion that conflict resolution may actually contribute to strengthening a friendship—especially if there is a mutually satisfying way to work it out and find a harmonious compromise. Effectively working through a mutual problem seems to strengthen the commitment to the relationship. The adolescent can distinguish between the immediate or superficial reaction and the value of the long-term affectionate relationship. The bond that constitutes the friendship between the individuals becomes a factor contributing to conflict resolution. Mutual perspective taking, characteristic of early adolescence, implies an "active interpersonal communication and sharing" and relies on "verbal or mental rather than physical-action resolutions" (Selman, 1980: 112).

Trust. Friendship and trust during this stage is no longer defined as a fair exchange of favors. Friendship is built on a more basic and lasting mutual support system. More personal concerns and intimacies are shared; the relationship has more lasting consistency and one friend will stand up for the other "through thick and thin" even if there is no immediate benefit. "One thirteen-year-old said that trust in a friendship is when they get it off their chest if they talk to you; things that are going on in your life and in the other person's life" (Selman, Jaquette, and Lavin, 1977: 269).

Leadership. The group is viewed as a social system, and the role of the leader is to coordinate the efforts of the group, to hold the group together, to express the feelings of the group, and to encourage group solidarity. The leader encourages a sense of community and is seen as a catalyst in that process.

Loyalty. Loyalty to the group now requires a willingness to contribute to the welfare of the peer community, a kind of all-for-one loyalty. The underlying philosophy can be expressed by paraphrasing Kennedy's famous statement: "Ask not what the group can do for you, but what you can do for the group."

Punishment. Adolescents in this stage clearly distinguish between punishment as a general childrearing procedure and punishment that might be applied to themselves. They often feel that punishment is less applicable to them than to younger children. At this stage punishment is mutually perceived as serving a need for parents and a purpose for the child. Both parent and child have needs, characteristics, interests, and personalities that must be considered and, ideally, carefully weighed in a punishment decision. Adolescents now recognize that there may be methods other than punishment to achieve control or obedience and to ensure safety.

The mutual role-taking advances of adolescence seem to indicate the emergence (transition) of formal operations in.the impersonal thinking domain and make possible the development of an "Interpersonal Concordance Orientation" in Kohlberg's moral judgment theory.

STAGE 4. *IN-DEPTH AND SOCIETAL PERSPECTIVE TAKING* (adolescence to adulthood)

During adolescence the individual may move to a still higher and more abstract level of interpersonal perspective taking, which now involves the "coordination of all possible third person perspectives—a societal perspective." The adolescent can conceptualize that the subjective perspectives of persons toward other persons not only operates on a level of common expectations and awareness but exists "simultaneously at multidimensional or deeper levels of communication" (Selman, 1980: 40). Thus, role taking is raised from the level of didactic relationships between people to the level of a general social system. "At this level the subject can compare and qualitatively contrast different sets and levels of perspectives" (Selman, 1976b: 160). Adolescents become aware of the relativity of perspectives held by themselves and by the social group. In other words, social facts are now understood as being interpreted by each individual according to that individual's own system of analysis.

Stage 4 subjects understand that each person can consider the shared point of view of the "Generalized Other"—that is, the social system—

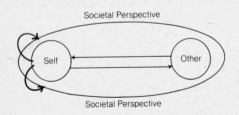

FIGURE 23.   The self can take a generalized societal perspective of the self–other interaction.

which, in turn, makes possible accurate communication with and understanding of other people. Furthermore, the notion of law and morality as a social system depends on the idea of consensual group perspective, implied in Stage 4 role-taking ability. "At this level, the adolescent or young adult can abstract multiple mutual (generalized other) perspectives to a societal, legal or moral perspective in which all individuals can share" (Selman, 1980: 40).

There are two distinguishing features of the adolescents' conception of other people. First, they become aware that motives, actions, thoughts, and feelings are shaped by psychological factors. This notion of psychological determinants now includes the idea of the unconscious processes, although adolescents may not express this awareness in psychological terminology. Second, they begin to appreciate the fact that a personality is a system of traits, beliefs, values, and attitudes with its own developmental history.

Self-Awareness. Since adolescents are now discovering the idea of the unconscious mind, they become cognizant that there may be influences on thoughts, feelings, and motivations that they are not aware of and that, therefore, are not available for self-analysis. This means that beneath the inner reality of feelings and fantasies exists an even deeper reality that the individual is not aware of but that influences actions and behavior.

Friendship. The Stage 3 conception of friendship was characterized by an awareness that friendships are based on close-knit mutuality. The adolescent in Stage 4 seems to reject that idea of mutuality partially, at least as long as it interferes with the autonomous growth and development of the individual. There is striving for independence, which may result in a rejection of overdependence and overbonding characteristic of Stage 3. However, friendship is based on an understanding that total independence is not the goal either, just as mutuality based on overdependence is not ideal. There is a striving for a balance between independence and dependence with a focus on the mutual relationships in the sense of "keeping the lines of communication open." The adolescent becomes aware that conflicts within one person may cause conflict between that person and his friend.

Trust. Adolescent and adult trust in friendship relationships becomes an ongoing process. "Trust means openness to change and growth, as well as stability in a relationship" (Selman, Jaquette, and Lavin, 1977: 269). The idea is well expressed by a college student who said, "Trust means that you've got to grow to let your friend grow. The more you hold on, the less you have. You have to have confidence in yourself as a good friend, then you'll have trust in your relationship" (Selman, Jaquette, and Lavin, 1977: 269).

Leadership. The leadership position is seen as being created by the

	Piaget's Stages of Cognitive Development	Selman's Stages of Social Perspective Taking	Kohlberg's Stages of Moral Judgment
Stage 0	Sensorimotor and preoperational stages	The egocentric undifferentiated stage of social perspective taking	The premoral stage
Stage 1	Beginning of concrete operations	The differential or subjective perspective-taking stage or the social-informational role-taking stage	The obedience and punishment orientation
Stage 2	Well-developed concrete operations	Self-reflective thinking or mental perspective-taking stage	The instrumental relativist orientation
Stage 3	Beginning formal operations (Piaget's stage III-A)	The third-person or mutual perspective-taking stage	The interpersonal concordance orientation
Stage 4	Well-developed formal operations (Piaget's stage III-B)	The in-depth and societal perspective-taking stage	The orientation toward authority, law, and duty
Stage 5			The social contract orientation
Stage 6			The universal ethical principles orientation

FIGURE 24. The parallels between Piaget's stages of cognitive development, Selman's stages of social-perspective taking, and Kohlberg's stages of moral judgment. According to Byrne (1974) at each stage, cognitive development appears to be a prerequisite for the corresponding stage of social-perspective taking which in turn precedes the emergence of the corresponding stage of moral judgment.

Adapted from Selman (1976a) and Papalia and Olds (1979).

group, and the leader's role, to enhance the collective good of the group. The leader is thus viewed as the embodiment of the group, and the function of the person is clearly separated from the leadership function. Leadership serves a fundamental social purpose that is abstracted from the members of the group. Furthermore, there now is a clearer understanding and differentiation of several different kinds of leadership.

Loyalty. Loyalty to the group takes on the quality of a contractual agreement. Loyalty presupposes that an individual member of the group is willing to relinquish personal goals for the benefit of the collective goals of the group. "Loyalty is the unity of the group; that means that each member is willing to make a sacrifice for the good of the group—a sacrifice of himself" (Selman, Jaquette, and Lavin, 1977: 269).

Punishment. The one new idea that seems to emerge in the adolescent's conception of punishment is that punishment now may be seen as an unconscious effort to maintain psychological control over others.

The social perspective-taking ability identified as Stage 4, which constitutes the final and mature stage in social cognitive development, will not be reached by all adults. It corresponds to Piaget's ability to perform formal operations in logical reasoning and is the prerequisite for an orientation to the maintenance of social morality and social order as well as Kohlberg's postconventional level of moral judgment.

Byrne (1974) investigated the relationship of these stages to Piaget's stages of logical development and Kohlberg's stages of moral judgment. He found that a relationship exists between Piaget's logical thinking stages and Selman's role-taking stages. However, the adolescent may reach a certain level of logical thinking without having reached the equivalent role-taking stage or moral judgment stage. On the other hand, rarely can an individual reach a given role-taking or moral judgment stage without having first attained the corresponding level of logical thinking. Furthermore, an individual may reach a certain social role-taking stage without evidence of an equivalent attainment in moral judgment, but it is unlikely that a specific moral judgment stage can be reached without the necessary role-taking stage. It thus appears that role taking is an intermediate step in social cognitive development that falls between the development of logical operations and the development of moral judgment during the years from ten to adulthood.

EDUCATIONAL IMPLICATIONS

Selman's theory supports an educational philosophy that emphasizes affective education, altruism, sympathy, social problem solving, and an increased social awareness. It implies a movement away from a limited concern with only the cognitive side of learning, toward an inclusion of interpersonal, social-cognitive awareness.

The application of social cognition theory to education in general and curriculum in specific rests in the assumption that training in social reasoning will lead to more adequate forms of social functioning and produce an increase in the complexity and the effectiveness of social reasoning (Enright, 1976). Marsh, Serafica, and Barenboim (1980) were able to demonstrate that early adolescents could actually be trained in perspective-taking skills and that such training did indeed have a positive effect on the ability to solve interpersonal problems. Social problem solving was assessed by asking each subject to assume that one of his three close friends must be excluded from a rock concert and to develop an appropriate excuse. There were several interpersonal problems of this nature, and subjects had to decide: What is the problem? What factors must be considered? What are alternative ways of solving the problems? What are the consequences for each solution?

In another study it was shown that children who had developed better perspective-taking skills are more likely friendly, helpful, and show social problem-solving behavior when confronted with a child in need of assistance than are children with less social perspective-taking skill (Hudson, Peyton, and Brian-Maisels, 1976). Other researchers (Rosen, 1974; Spivack and Shure, 1974; 1978; Elardo, 1974) have reported similar positive effects of perspective-taking training on younger children. However, in these studies the perspective-taking part of the program was embedded in a more general social problem-solving context. The Shure and Spivack (1978) interpersonal problem-solving script is not designed only to help children in solving specific problems "now"; it is also intended to teach them to cope with new social problems, which inevitably will arise in the future. The two most important interpersonal problem-solving skills are *alternative-solution thinking* (the social skill to produce many different solutions to a problem), and *consequential thinking* (the social skill to predict what is most likely to happen with each alternative solution).

The movement from lower to higher levels of social cognition is a matter of interaction between nature and nurture. Social cognition growth comes in part as a result of maturation, hence its strong association with age. However, social reasoning develops also as a result of experiences, stimulation, and education. The educational method that appears to be particularly valuable in stimulating interpersonal growth is not a lecture or expository mode of teaching, but an exploratory mode of teaching, such as discussion and debate (Selman, 1976a).

A quite different educational issue suggests that methods of childrearing and the disciplinary methods of control used at home and in school may have an influence on social interpersonal development, and that certain kinds of childrearing practices help develop interpersonal skills, social cognition, and moral judgment.

Martin reviewed the literature investigating the influence of childrearing methods on moral development, and he reports that the following conditions foster moral development: "the parents of children with more mature conceptions of right and wrong favored high 'cognitive structuring,' including making clear statements of parental expectations, involving general moral principles to guide behavior, and emphasizing the consequences to others of the child's misbehavior" (Moore, 1979: 57). Other factors that were identified as making similar contributions to social cognitive development were a high degree of warmth toward children and low frequency in threat of punishment.

Spivack and Shure provide an entire training program or curriculum for teaching social problem-solving skills, and Elardo has developed a similar program to foster children's social awareness (Spivack and Shure, 1974; Elardo, 1974).

Recognizing the social cognitive stages of each child may help the teacher in several ways:

1. The teacher can better understand the behavior of the class by understanding how children view social relationships, rights, and obligations.
2. The teacher can better determine his/her own expectations for student's developmental goals, and
3. The teacher learns not to overestimate the affective, as well as the cognitive capacity of children [Selman, 1976a: 310].

Selman's work gives emphasis to an important, often neglected, educational goal: the development of understanding, sensitivity, and skills in social awareness, interpersonal relationships, and social problem-solving skills.

13: SOCIAL COGNITION. PART 2: DAVID ELKIND'S THEORY OF ADOLESCENT EGOCENTRISM*

THE CONCEPT OF EGOCENTRISM

"Egocentrism" refers to the inability to clearly differentiate the nature of the subject-object interaction, or the subject-object relationship. Egocentric children cannot yet differentiate themselves from the rest of the world. The separation of the self from others and from objects is incomplete or difficult. Egocentric children consider their own *subjective point of view* as representing objective reality and even as the only possible point of view. They assume that others automatically share their pains and pleasures. The essential meaning of egocentrism has been defined as "an embeddedness in one's own point of view" (Looft, 1971: 485), and in that sense egocentrism is the opposite of role taking or perspective taking. Egocentric children thus are unable to put themselves phenomenologically into the situation or the position of someone else because they are not aware that other people have a different point of view. They think that everybody else thinks as they do. In its more primitive form, children believe that objects or landscapes do not look different from other perspectives, but that their own perspective is the "real," the only, perspective. In the early phases of development, egocentrism is so pervasive that it permeates virtually all spheres of functioning: cognition, perception, speech, emotions, and attitudes.

In the history of mankind, egocentrism is analogous to the earlier belief that the whole universe revolved around the earth. Copernicus, by discovering that the sun rather than the earth is the center of the universe, replaced the egocentric view of the world with a scientific

---

*Chapter 13 is a revision, extension, and modification of two earlier publications by the author: "Die Entwicklung der Egozentrizitat in der Kindheit und der Adoleszenz." *Der Kinderarzt*, 1981, 12, 189-193, 339-343, 519-531, and "Social Cognition: Elkind's Theory of Adolescent Egocentrism," *Adolescence* (in press).

view, contributing to the decentering process in man's view of himself in the larger scheme. Egocentric children still view themselves as the center of the universe.

The concept "egocentrism" stems originally from Piaget's theory of cognitive development and is defined as the lack of differentiation between one's own point of view and those of others. Piaget is concerned with fundamental laws of cognitive development. Samples of such laws relevant to a discussion of the developmental decline in egocentrism are:

1. All mental growth moves in a specific direction; that is, it moves from an egocentric orientation toward a sociocentric orientation toward reality.

2. Mental growth is characterized by an increasing differentiation between subject and object, between thought and reality (Elkind, 1968: 143).

3. The child's language patterns change with increasing age from egocentric to sociocentric speech patterns.

4. Increasing cognitive maturation is characterized by the ability to decenter one's own thought processes. Abundant research evidence shows that egocentric thought processes decrease with age and the ability to decenter increases with age.

5. The entire process of cognitive development is an orientation process. Step by step, children realize that they are not the center of the world and that other persons and objects have their own independent existence. Children also slowly realize that the perceptions of other people are quite independent of their own.

6. The process of decentration of thinking is the essence of intellectual development. As intellectual maturity is developed, one's own limited egocentric point of view is replaced by the recognition of many possible different viewpoints.

According to Elkind (1967), as cognitive development progresses through the familiar stages identified by Piaget (sensorimotor, preoperational, operational, and formal), the nature, quality, and characteristics of egocentrism change correspondingly, and each developmental stage has its own unique egocentric characteristics. The transition from one stage to another proceeds in a dialectic fashion: The emerging new and more sophisticated cognitive structures, which free the child from the entanglement in a lower-level egocentrism, lead to a higher-level egocentrism. In this sense egocentrism can be said to be a negative but necessary by-product of cognitive development, for it creates at each stage "a new set of unrealistic, non-object representations of the world" (Looft, 1971: 486), and thus the concept egocentrism enriches our understanding of the social and emotional domains that accompany the cognitive development of the child.

The major mechanism that contributes to the decline of egocentrism and to movement from lower to higher levels of egocentrism is the developmental process of decentering. The decentering process makes it possible to shift the focus of awareness from one limited aspect of reality or the self to several features and eventually to a whole array of different dimensions. Each of these steps produces a reorganization and expansion of earlier perceptions. The child decenters by becoming aware that he is not the center of the world and realizing that an object or another person has an existence of its own, quite independent of how it is perceived or who perceives it. Being able to assume the point of view of another person indicates a social decentration, that is, an increase in role-taking ability. The concepts of decentration and role-taking have been used in the literature as synonyms rather than as two different processes (Shantz, 1975). One can distinguish between social, emotional, and cognitive perspective-taking skills. Essentially, the development of decentration is facilitated by social interaction, because one-sided and one-dimensional perceptions are challenged and must be reexamined in view of the ideas expressed by others. In reconciling the dissonance beteen one's own one-sided perspective and the point of view of others, the individual progresses to see several aspects or dimensions of an issue and learns to take another person's point of view.

STAGES OF EGOCENTRISM

For each major stage of egocentrism, Elkind (1967) has identified a special problem of cognition that, although not the only problem, gives the egocentric thought at that stage its unique qualities and characteristics.

SENSORIMOTOR EGOCENTRISM (birth to age two)

The first stage can best be characterized as radical egocentrism, since infants lack the ability to differentiate between themselves and the larger world. The major cognitive task of the sensorimotor child is the conquest of the object.

Sensorimotor egocentrism implies a lack of ability to differentiate between the actual object and the sensory impressions that the object produces. Egocentrism, at this stage, is the belief that one's sensory impressions are essential for the existence of the object. "At the sensorimotor level, the infant does not at first know how to separate the effects of his own actions from the qualities of external objects or persons" (Inhelder and Piaget, 1958: 342). Egocentrism begins to decline when the infant realizes that the existence of an object is independent of his subjective perception of it; that is, as the concept of *object permanence* develops, sensorimotor egocentrism begins to decline.

PREOPERATIONAL EGOCENTRISM (age two to six)

The major cognitive task during the preschool period is the *conquest of the symbol*, and the most important symbolic system to be acquired is speech. Other areas where symbol confusion is common are self-created play symbols representing unavailable objects (e.g. the chair is made into a train) and symbols that appear in dreams.

In general, the preoperational egocentrism consists of the inability to differentiate between the symbol and its referent. The egocentric child does not yet understand the relationship between the signifier and what is signified (Elkind, 1968: 144). Initially, the symbols are viewed as *identical to their referents*. Furthermore, children believe that their personal perspective of the world is shared by others. The child has a particular understanding of the world and believes that everybody shares this particular view (and takes for granted that others think the same way). Egocentrism at the preoperational level takes the form of a "relative lack of differentiation both between ego's and alter's point of view, between subjective and objective, but this time the lack of differentiation is representational rather than sensori-motor" (Inhelder and Piaget, 1958: 343).

CONCRETE OPERATIONAL EGOCENTRISM (age seven to eleven)

The major cognitive task of the operational child is the mastery of classes, relations, and quantities. Thinking has progressed to the point where elementary deductive and concrete logical thinking have become possible. In the concrete operational stage the process of decentering has gone so far that the child is "able to structure relationships between classes, relations and numbers objectively. . . . He acquires skills in interindividual relations in a cooperative framework" (Inhelder and Piaget, 1958: 343).

The school age child can nest classes, seriate relations, and conserve quantities; furthermore, he can now perform elementary syllogistic reasoning and advance hypotheses as long as they concern concrete objects (Elkind, 1967). These newly acquired operational skills of logical thinking lift children out of the egocentrism of the preoperational stage; however, at the same time they lower them into a new kind of egocentrism.

Children can advance concrete hypotheses about reality, but they do not realize that their hypotheses are their own mental constructs and must be tested against reality to be verified. Egocentric children too readily accept their own hypotheses as something factually given and believe that the facts must adapt to fit their hypotheses. Concrete operational egocentrism consists of the inability to differentiate with some degree of accuracy between the products of one's own mental reasoning and what is perceptually given. To say it differently, it is the inability to differentiate between what one thinks and what one perceives. The inability to differentiate clearly between an assumption and a fact is what constitutes concrete operational egocentrism (Looft, 1971).

The failure to differentiate between hypothesis and fact means that the child may treat hypotheses as if they were facts and treat facts as if they were hypotheses. When these children produce a mental construct, they believe that the products of their thinking are real rather than the result of mental reasoning. When challenged, they do not change their mental constructions but reinterpret the data to fit the initial assumption. For example, when a child makes up an excuse or a story, he begins believing his own fabrications and defends them as if they were the truth. His own mental constructions "are experienced as imbued with a [logical] necessity" (Elkind, 1967: 1028).

The concept of concrete egocentrism can best be illustrated by the findings of a research study by Weir (1964) entitled "Developmental Changes in Problem Solving Strategies." The subjects, age four to seventeen, were exposed to a probability learning task involving a candy delivery machine with three knobs; one paid 66 percent of the time, one 33 percent, and one never. The child's task is to find a maximum pay-off strategy. Preoperational children maximized surprisingly early. They solved the problem without trying to figure it out cognitively. Their strategy was based primarily on trial and error. Adolescents developed various hypotheses, tested and rejected them, and eventually settled down to pressing the 66 percent knob all the time. They came to the right solution by reasoning it out. Operational children had considerably more difficulties; they persisted rather stubbornly with wrong hypotheses, even though they had not found a strategy that paid off continuously. They tended to blame the machine ("It's rigged!") rather than attacking their own rigid adherence to incorrect hypotheses.

ADOLESCENT EGOCENTRISM (age eleven to adulthood)

The major cognitive task of adolescence is the *mastery of thought processes* that are logical and abstract. During adolescence, in the stage of formal operations, "the adolescent not only tries to adapt his ego to the social environment but, just as empathetically, tries to adjust the environment to his ego. . . . The result is a relative failure to distinguish between his own point of view . . . and the point of view of the group" (Inhelder and Piaget, 1958: 343). The adolescent learns to use formal operations in logic, to use combinatorial analysis, to construct contrary-to-fact propositions, and to form theories. This new mode of formal operational thinking is characterized by two abilities:

a) the ability to think about one's own thinking, and
b) the ability to recognize possibility as well as actualities [Looft, 1971: 487].

These abilities eliminate the egocentrism of the concrete operational stage, but at the same time contribute to the emergence of adolescent egocentrism.

Since adolescents in the formal operational stage acquire the ability to conceptualize their own thought processes, they now become able to submit their own thinking to introspection and to reflect on their own mental processes and personality traits (Elkind, 1967/68: 429). They also begin to conceptualize in their own minds the thought processes of others, especially their peers, and they are able to differentiate between their own thoughts and those of other people, but not between the objects that the thoughts of others are directed toward and objects that are the focus of their own concern. "It is this capacity to take account of other people's thought, however, which is the crux of adolescent egocentrism" (Elkind, 1967: 1029). Adolescents surmise that they become the object of the thoughts of others as if all others were personally concerned with them. "This egocentrism is one of the most enduring features of adolescence; it persists until the new and later decentering which makes possible the true beginnings of adult work" (Inhelder and Piaget, 1958: 343).

Actually, as has been repeatedly demonstrated, the thoughts of early adolescents are very much concerned with their own behavior, body changes, and physical appearance. There is a great deal of self-absorption, and psychoanalysts even speak of a resurgence of narcissism in adolescence (Blos, 1962). "It is this belief that others are preoccupied with his appearance and behavior that constitutes the egocentrism of the adolescent" (Elkind, 1967: 1030). The young child was unable to take another person's point of view; the adolescent, however, "takes the other person's point of view to an extreme degree. He is so concerned with the point of view of others and how they regard him that he often loses sight of his own point of view" (Elkind, 1968: 153). The concept of egocentrism thus can explain the power of the peer group over the individual during early and middle adolescence.

Egocentrism in thinking leads to a preoccupation with physical characteristics, so that each individual adolescent attaches much greater significance to his or her own physical attributes, especially shortcomings, than the peer group does. The egocentric dimension of the problem is that the adolescent does not yet recognize this. As soon as they realize that others are much less critical than they themselves are their egocentrism begins to disperse.

This kind of egocentrism is often exaggerated when individuals have an actual physical defect or abnormality. They feel that the eyes of everyone are focused on them and that their defect is the topic of conversation when they are absent, or behind their back. Surprisingly, this is even more true with minor defects or developmental deviations that are not immediately noticeable than with serious defects, the obvious reality of which cannot be denied by children and adults. For this reason those with physical deformities or developmental deviations, though relatively happy and well adjusted as children, often experience their first real depression as they enter adolescence and begin to reflect on what others may think (Godenne, 1978).

Another illustration of egocentric thinking is the not uncommon occurrence of an adolescent girl wearing a new dress or a new hair style and who cannot understand why others do not notice these new and carefully selected attributes. She egocentrically thinks that everybody is as concerned with her appearance as she is—and gets sulky if she does not receive the expected comments and compliments. Most people indulge in this kind of egocentric thinking once in a while.

The idea of adolescent egocentrism can even be applied as an explanatory principle to several common characteristics of youth in contemporary society:

> attention getting behavior may well express this egocentric need to be noticed, evaluated, visible, and "on stage." . . . shortlived romantic affairs, conformity to the influence of the peer group, and even friendships may serve an egocentric need for self-definition and self-respect [Elkind, 1968: 153, 154].

The egocentrically thinking adolescent feels that others (especially peers) are as critical and as concerned and as admiring as he himself is. Consequently, he constructs and reacts and plays to what Elkind (1967) has effectively characterized as an *imaginary audience*. The adolescent imagines that he is the center of attention of this audience of peers—a product of his own thinking rather than a real audience. This construct of the imaginary audience may help to account for the adolescent's common feeling of self-consciousness. Furthermore, since the audience is actually the product of the adolescent's own mental construction, each boy or girl knows precisely what this imaginary audience is looking for (or at) in terms of clothes, hair style, breast development, physical skills, improprieties, blemishes, being too fat or too thin, overall body configuration, and so on. In other words, the individual's own critical self-evaluations and preoccupations are superimposed or projected on this self-made audience. The adolescent boy believes that they are aware of the hardly noticeable spot on his trousers, or that he has been biting his fingernails again, or even that he has masturbated. The imaginary audience is assumed to be just as repulsed by these atrocities as he is. Adolescents will wear outlandish clothes to please this audience, sass the teacher to gain applause, or participate in other wild and risk taking behavior that may earn the audience's respect and admiration. Thus the adolescent is constantly on stage, and sees himself as the principal actor, and all peers are the audience. The adolescent's great need for privacy and reluctance toward self-disclosure in other situations may well be a reaction against the egocentric feeling of being constantly evaluated, watched, and compared by peers.

Actually, most of the adolescent's peers are preoccupied with themselves and their own imaginary audience. Hence, in actuality they pay much less attention to each other than each assumes they do. For example, before a formal date the boy may spend a long time in front of the mirror making himself attractive, imagining his girl friend's reactions. The girl similarly changes her clothes repeatedly, rearranges her hair, and experiments with make-up in front of the mirror for hours, imagining the boy's reactions. When the two actually meet, they are much more concerned with being observed than with being the observer (Elkind, 1967).

A corollary concept that defines the nature of the adolescent's egocentrism is each individual's belief in his own *uniqueness*. Elkind uses the term "the personal fable" to identify this notion of uniqueness. The personal fable is seen in many adolescents' convictions that their beliefs, their feelings, their ideals are very special, even unique, and that others do not have and cannot even understand such feelings. The conviction that emerges is: I am a unique individual, nobody else has my experiences or my feelings. This idea of the uniqueness of feelings, thoughts, and experiences is a very common theme of many adolescent diaries. And puberty is the time when this kind of egocentric thinking is at its peak. The diaries of adolescents frequently illustrate a mixture of both acute egocentricity and an emotional and selfless devotion to humanity (Piaget, 1967). The diary becomes the only "confidante" to whom one can speak and who understands. At the same time parents are admonished by their offspring, "But, you don't know how it feels. . . ." Blos (1962) speaks of the vicarious relationship between outer reality and internal processes and experiences during adolescence proper. However, in a more general sense—and here Blos writes about the same idea of *egocentric uniqueness* that Elkind developed from a cognitive point of view—"the fact remains that the adolescent does experience the outer world with a unique sensory quality which he thinks is not shared by others: 'Nobody ever felt the way I do.' 'Nobody sees the world the way I do.' Mother Nature becomes a personal respondent to the adolescent; the beauty of nature is discovered and exalted emotional states are experienced" (Blos, 1962: 93).

Another part of the personal fable is the belief in one's own *indestructibility*, which impairs judgment in critical situations since it provides a false sense of power, often with catastrophic consequences (Blos, 1962: 100). This attitude may find expression in the following convictions:

Death will never happen to me.
Pregnancy will never happen to me (adolescent sexual behavior is notorious for the lack of use of contraceptives).
Accidents will never happen to me (adolescent drivers are notorious for taking risks).
Drug addiction will never happen to me.
Alcohol addiction will never happen to me.
Marriage problems will never happen to us.

Egocentrism in the cognitive structure of the adolescent makes it difficult to differentiate between his own highly idealistic thought processes (how things ought to be) and the real world (how things are). "Adolescent egocentricity is manifested by belief in omnipotence of reflection, as though the world should submit itself to idealistic schemes rather than to systems of reality. It is the metaphysical age *par excellence*; the self is strong enough to reconstruct the universe and big enough to incorporate it" (Piaget, 1967: 64). Adolescents cannot and will not understand why the rest of the world does not accept their idealistic solutions to social, economic, or ecological problems, and they may get angry and express unwillingness to accept reality. The adolescent tries to adjust his ego to the real world. "In effect, the adolescent not only constructs ideal families, religions and societies, he also constructs ideal persons. The short-lived adolescent crush is a case in point" (Elkind, 1967/68: 432).

The results of this untested idealism is that adolescents dream "of a glorious future" which they hope to attain by transforming the world through ideas. They are idealistically critical of the way things are and unwilling to compromise between contending parties or ideas. Indeed, adolescents are often exceedingly effective in changing the real world.

RESEARCH SUPPORT FOR AN ADOLESCENT EGOCENTRISM THEORY

The concept of egocentrism has been investigated extensively during the last decade. However, most studies have used younger children as subjects, and much of the methodology is based on Piaget's classical study of the child's perspective-taking skills, using a model landscape of the three different-sized mountains or some adaptation of that approach to perspective taking.

Research using adolescent subjects and focusing on adolescent egocentrism, in contrast, is sparce. However, those few research studies that do investigate the imaginary audience, the personal fable, adolescent self-consciousness, and adolescent role-taking skills contribute significantly to an understanding of adolescent social and emotional development and will be reviewed here.

Several generalizations emerge from egocentrism research with children, some of which cut across several developmental periods, and hence are relevant to our overall considerations:

1. Most widely supported is the theoretical assumption that egocentrism decreases with age and is replaced by a sociocentric point of view as the individual matures. With increasing age, the ability to decenter expands (Rubin, 1973; Stuart, 1967; Sullivan and Hunt, 1967). This fundamental theoretical assertion seems to hold true for several dimensions of egocentrism:

   spatial or cognitive egocentrism—visual perspective taking
   social egocentrism, or role-taking egocentrism
   communicative egocentrism
   egocentric speech
   affective or emotional egocentrism

2. Rubin (1973) has shown that a significant interrelationship exists among such social cognition concepts as spatial egocentrism, role-taking egocentrism, communicative egocentrism, and Piaget's concept of conservation. Rubin defines the commonality of these concepts as the "centration factor."

3. Piaget suggested in *Language and Thought of the Child* (1932a), that as the child moves from the preoperational stage to the operational stage of thinking, egocentric speech patterns decline and socio-

centric speech patterns increase. Furthermore, he assumed as a correlate that the more egocentric children would be less popular (since they cannot take their peers' point of view) than children who are less egocentric. There is at least some evidence for this assertion, especially with younger children (Deutsch, 1974).

4. A negative relationship was found between egocentric speech patterns and the quality of peer interaction. Rubin calls this "communicative egocentrism" (Rubin, 1972; 1976).

5. More egocentric children have less adequate social schemata to understand such concepts as conformity and independence (Weinheimer, 1972) and are more likely to conform than less egocentric children (Tierney and Rubin, 1975).

6. The ability to decenter has been shown to be positively correlated with the ability to make mature moral and causal judgments (Stuart, 1967; Rubin and Schneider, 1973).

7. Institutionalized emotionally disturbed children are significantly more egocentric than noninstitutionalized children (Neale, 1966).

8. The idea of egocentric thought versus nonegocentric thought is not the same as Piaget's fundamental distinction between concrete and abstract thinking. Concrete evaluations can be egocentric or nonegocentric. Abstract evaluations, on the other hand, are most likely nonegocentric. In general, research has demonstrated that the basic developmental progression from concrete to abstract evaluation is paralleled by a corresponding transition from egocentric to nonegocentric thinking (Wegner, 1977).

More recently, Elkind and Bowen (1979) have begun to examine the concept of adolescent egocentrism empirically, the focus of their investigation being the *imaginary audience* (defined as the belief that others are as concerned with our thoughts and behavior as we are). In their investigation they distinguished between (1) the *abiding self*, or long-lived permanent personality traits, such as mental ability, and (2) the *transient component of the self*, which is the momentary issue and transient behavior, such as the reaction of the adolescent to a bad haircut or a spot on an outfit or an unguarded inappropriate comment.

In agreement with the theoretical assumption of an imaginary audience created by the early adolescent, eighth-graders were significantly more self-conscious than both younger children and older adolescents. This finding was true for both subscales of the test, the abiding self and the transient self of the Imaginary Audience Scale. Elkind and Bowen also reported that females were more concerned about the imaginary audience at all age levels than males. This sex difference is consistent with previous research that has shown girls to be more self-conscious, more conforming, and more concerned about an imaginary audience than boys (Simmons, Rosenberg, and Rosenberg,

1973). Early adolescents are more self-conscious about imperfections and less willing to reveal their abiding self or transient self. Even if they were to go to a party with a grease spot on their clothes, they would be much more likely than either younger children or older adolescents to modify their behavior so that the spot would not be revealed to others. They say, for example, "I would stand in a dark corner," "I would hold my hand over the spot," or "I would spill something on the spot during the party."

Young adolescents, more than either the younger or the older age groups, think that they are able to conceal facts of the transient self (such as the spot) from peers. The desire to conceal imperfections in attire, appearance, and manners is interpreted as evidence of the awareness and the influence of the imaginary audience.

Enright and his colleagues (Enright, Lapsley, and Shukla, 1979; Enright and Sutterfield, 1980), in two methodologically similar studies using different population samples, investigated the relationship between adolescent egocentrism, sociocentrism, self-consciousness, and age, and thus contributed further to an understanding of egocentrism theory. These investigations focused on three components of egocentrism: the personal fable, the imaginary audience, and general self-focus. In addition, they included two additional subscales, identified as sociocentrism and nonsocial concerns, the assumption being that with increasing maturity, adolescents become more concerned with general social and political issues rather than with just their own world and their immediate social group.

The findings, even though based on a different methodology, are quite consistent both with Elkind's (1976) theoretical construct of adolescent egocentrism and with the Elkind and Bowen (1979) findings reported above. Specifically, Enright et al. found support in their data for the following generalizations:

1. As adolescents move from early adolescence to late adolescence, there is a decline in the personal fable (that is, the belief that one is special and unique). Females are more inclined to believe the personal fable than are males.

2. Similarly, as a function of adolescent development, there is a decline in the importance of the imaginary audience (believing that others pay more attention to the individual than they actually do). Females, again, are more aware of an imaginary audience than are males.

3. Nonsocial concerns (such as watching TV) lose their importance as a function of adolescent development.

4. Political awareness or sociocentric focus (keeping up with the news) increases in importance with increasing age.

5. Self-consciousness is moderately correlated with adolescent egocentrism.
6. Egocentrism and sociocentrism are negatively correlated during adolescence, suggesting that as a function of development the former declines while the later increases in importance.
7. Self-focus is high in early adolescence and declines during the high school years, but a surprising heightening of self-focus takes place in college. Females are reported as more self-focused than males.

However, while egocentrism theory receives substantial support from these studies, the authors do suggest that egocentrism is not a unidimensional factor, but that different dimensions may unfold at different times during the adolescent period.

Michael Chandler (1973) explored the role that a persistent social egocentrism might play in the development and maintenance of chronic antisocial behavior. Egocentrism was defined as the "relative inability to recognize or take into account the privileged character of one's own private thoughts and feelings." Social egocentrism, when it becomes a developmental deficit, interferes with the ability to assess the needs of others and to perform adequately in situations requiring empathy and social cooperation. As was shown in the studies cited above, in normal development, social egocentrism declines with age and makes space for a more sociocentric orientation that includes an understanding of other people's needs and the ability to take their perspective into account, to cooperate, and to empathize. Chandler hypothesized that a prolonged adherence to social egocentrism or a developmental delay of social perspective-taking skills during adolescence may be a crucial variable in the maintenance of antisocial behavior. Developmental delay in sociocentric thought has been shown to be related to a misunderstanding of social expectations, a misjudgment in the actions and intentions of others, and a disrespect for the rights and feelings of others. Social deviancy is therefore assumed to be associated with persistent egocentric thought if the latter is age-inappropriate. In accordance with these theoretical propositions, Chandler observed that a group of chronic delinquent adolescents did indeed have much greater difficulties in assuming the roles or perspectives of others than a nondelinquent control group. The assessment of social egocentrism was based on a series of ten cartoon sequences in which the behavior of a major character was shaped by a series of events. In the middle of such a sequence of events, a second character was introduced who did not know what had happened earlier. The question was, to what extent could subjects distinguish between their own complete, but partly privileged information and the more limited information of the late-arriving bystander.

Example: A boy had brought his father to the airport and was deeply saddened by his father's departure. Later he received a package with a toy airplane, which made the boy cry again as he remembered his father's departure. The mailman who witnessed the boy's distress on opening the package had, of course, no knowledge of the antecedent events [Chandler, 1973].

The subject who had all the information of the story was to assume the role of the mailman. The purpose was to determine whether the subject could set aside the privileged information known only to him and take the perspective of the late-arriving mailman, or whether he would intermingle the two perspectives, assigning to the mailman information that he could not have.

Chandler did find, as hypothesized, that the group of chronic delinquent adolescents had much greater difficulty in correctly assuming the role or perspective of the late-arriving bystander. A nondelinquent control group had little difficulty in separating their own privileged information of the full story from the partial information of the late arriver.

The second contribution to egocentrism theory in Chandler's study dealt with the value of intervention, examining two issues: (1) Can social perspective-taking skills be taught? and (2) Does a reduction in social egocentrism have an effect on delinquent behavior? The training in social perspective-taking skills involved acting out dramas and making video films in which the subject takes the perspective, or the role, of a particular character.

When chronic delinquent adolescents were given systematic training in social perspective-taking skills, their level of egocentrism declined significantly. Since only half of the chronic delinquents received such training, Chandler was able to show, in a long-range follow-up study, that those chronic delinquents who had received special training in role-taking skills had a much lower recidivism rate than the delinquent control group. Apparently, social deviance is associated with egocentric thinking, and reducing social egocentrism through training in social perspective-taking skills tends to reduce the rate of delinquent behavior. Although one study may be insufficient evidence to start large-scale social action programs in an attempt to fight juvenile delinquency, nevertheless adolescent egocentrism theory does hold promise of having far-reaching implications.

EDUCATIONAL IMPLICATIONS

Assuming that the intriguing findings by Chandler (1973) are generalizable and replicable, it would appear most appropriate to provide children and adolescents with systematic learning opportunities that would require them to project themselves into the psychological situation of another human being. Some possibilities would be role playing, theatre productions, movie making, and verbal exercises similar to the one discussed on page 267 and used as a method to assess egocentrism. Shantz, after an extensive review of the social cognition literature, concludes that role-taking skills "seem to be fostered by the opportunity to enact various roles" (1975: 310). Some role-taking activities are, of course, offered in schools, but usually only on the initiative of an especially interested teacher or for children and adolescents who are attracted to such activities and volunteer for such courses and/or programs. However, role playing and related "acting" activities are not generally and systematically offered as tools for aiding the social and personal development in a way that reaches all children.

Steinberg and his associates (1981) have suggested that early work experiences—including part-time and summer work—may enhance the development of social understanding during adolescence and thus serve as a partial antidote to adolescent egocentrism. Working experiences are assumed to have a potentially positive impact on the worker by advancing social as well as cognitive development. In the work setting, the adolescent must learn to shift between very diverse roles quickly and effectively. In a certain situation he must act authoritatively (e.g., in relationship to customers or to a junior worker), at other times he must behave deferentially (e.g., toward a supervisor or boss), at still other times he is expected to react to people on an egalitarian basis (e.g., toward coworkers). Furthermore, many jobs require frequent interaction with strangers who may be quite different in age, background, and attitude.

Social interaction patterns among the typical high school students frequently are limited to peers, teachers, and family members, and relationships with the latter two are often based on stereotyped attitudes and/or long established response patterns. In the economic marketplace egocentrism, pseudostupidity, and social insensitivity (afflictions from which adolescents supposedly suffer and about which teachers frequently complain) are not rewarded, but are quickly extinguished. Steinberg and his associates observed that egocentricity, pseudostupidity, and social insensitivity decline dramatically when the adolescent is paid in accordance with his willingness to behave in a nonegocentric fashion. It has been claimed that the kind of role-taking skills that the work setting requires will enhance the acquisition of skills that are not usually taught in school, and thus will contribute "to the development of responsibility and a sense of competency, lessen feelings of alienation and purposelessness and help to break down intergenerational barriers" (Steinberg et al., 1981: 142) and, more importantly, will show how to interact with various other people.

Teaching adolescents formally about the concept of egocentrism might better help them understand and deal with the problems that emerge from egocentric thoughts. Problems related to peer group conformity, preoccupation with physical development and physical appearance, excessive concern with what others think, and the egocentric need for risk-taking behavior with its social and health implications are fairly common during adolescence. And even if such understanding does not necessarily solve these problems, the individual would at least have a frame of reference within which to evaluate his own thinking. Furthermore, the idiosyncratic behavior of their peers would begin to be seen in a new light.

For the educator the most important insight to be gained from these considerations is the fact that adolescent egocentrism exists as a common, normal developmental phenomenon. Adolescents, even though they may have reached the operational stage of thinking—and partly because they are beginning to think operationally—still think in ways that are qualitatively different from those of the mature adult whose thought processes have become sociocentric. These differences need to be more fully recognized and appreciated in the daily interaction with adolescents in the classroom. Their comments and their behavior, which may appear silly or immature by adult standards, become meaningful when viewed as a manifestation of egocentric thought.

In order to avoid unnecessary repetition, the reader is referred to the Educational Implications section at the end of Chapter 12, Social Cognition, Part I: Robert Selman's Theory of Role Taking. The implications of the two social cognition chapters are to a large extent compatible and supplementary.

14:
THE IMPLICATIONS OF SOCIAL LEARNING THEORY FOR AN UNDERSTANDING OF ADOLESCENT DEVELOPMENT*

SOCIAL LEARNING THEORY

Social learning theory, especially with its unique implications for child and adolescent development, has emerged fairly recently. Baldwin (1967) described it as "a theory in the making," partly because its formalizations are not as rigidly stated as those of behavioristic learning theories or psychoanalytic theory and partly because, from its inception, social learning theorists have been firmly committed to verification of hypothetical relationships by way of empirical research. Since social learning theorists have objected to the use of theoretical constructs without empirical support, they have been thoroughly committed to a position in which theory and empirical research findings are viewed as closely interrelated and interdependent. However, since research findings in relatively complex forms of social behavior frequently do not systematically and unequivocally support theoretical hypotheses, continuous revisions of and additions to theoretical postulates have been an essential characteristic of social learning theory.

Social learning theory is eclectic in that it draws on concepts, hypotheses, and methodology from a variety of different psychological sources. Some research hypotheses are influenced by psychoanalytic constructs such as identification, frustration, aggression, regression, repression, rejection, dependency, ego strength, and transference, but they are investigated within the methodological approach of the experimentalist rather than the clinician. While social learning theory develops its own theoretical constructs, of which modeling and imitation are the most important for our discussion, it freely draws on constructs of behavioristic learning theory, especially reinforcement. But

---

*Chapter 14 has been published as "The Implications of Social Learning Theory for an Understanding of Adolescent Development," *Adolescence*, 1974, 11, 61–85.

even Skinner's concept of direct reinforcement is expanded to include social dimensions: vicarious reinforcement and self-reinforcement. Consequently, the nature of problems and concerns of social learning theorists go far beyond those of the narrow connection between a stimulus and a response and include the contribution of the mother-child relationship to personality development, the importance of models, and the imitation of models (that is, modeling) in the learning process. In addition, social learning theory has drawn freely on the findings of cultural anthropology. In short, the realm of investigation for the social learning theorist is the whole spectrum of the socialization process by which children learn, often through indirect teaching, to conform to the cultural expectations of acceptable behavior. The significance of the socializing agents as "a source of patterns of behavior" has been neglected in other theories, even though observational and empirical evidence indicates that this social aspect of the learning process is fundamental to socialization and personality development. Because of its eclectic orientation, social learning theory has contributed as much to an understanding of learning as to development and personality theory.

The advent of social learning theory cannot easily be credited to a single individual, since it constitutes a merger of thought that came not only from Clark Hull's drive reduction theory and from Skinner's reinforcement theory, but also from Freud's psychoanalytic theory. Social learning theory has been described as the translation of psychoanalytic constructs into behavioristic terminology. Men such as Miller and Dollard, as well as Mowrer, who for a long time have been concerned with the relationship between psychoanalytic theory and behavioristic theory and who have attempted to bridge the gap between these diverse points of view, seemed to give an early impetus to an approach to basic human, social, and developmental problems that developed into social learning theory. The concern with social aspects of learning is not new, but the systematic development of a theory of social learning begins with the publication of Miller and Dollard's *Social Learning and Imitation* (1941) and has been continued in the works of Mowrer and Sears. Miller and Dollard systematically integrated the concept of imitation—which will be discussed later—into behavior theory. They referred to subjects imitating the behavior of their leader as "matched dependent behavior," because the subjects depended on their leader for cues in order to produce matching responses; but imitation was still viewed as only a special case of instrumental conditioning.

However, within social learning theory, especially the more recent developments, there is diversity rather than unanimity in point of view, in emphasis, and in some rather basic conceptualizations. Some theorists tend to be closer to S-R (stimulus-response) explanations, whereas others are more oriented toward psychoanalytic constructs, and it is this cross-fertilization and open-mindedness that give social learning theory its vitality. Common to all appears to be the application of behavioristic constructs to basic social and developmental problems and a belief that environmental, situational, and social, rather than biological and maturational factors are primarily responsible for learning and development. They believe that the rewarding of imitative responses is the psychological explanation of the socialization process. Rotter and Crandall have placed particular emphasis on the efforts expended in obtaining goal satisfaction, the value of the goal, and the expectancy of obtaining it. For them the individual's subjective expectation is the central construct of social learning theory. Sears selected the parent-child relationship and especially the mother-child relationship as the focus of his research and theory. He suggested the study of dyadic units, rather than the monadic units of the stimulus-response type learning of an individual without social interaction, as in a Skinnerian program. The study of dyadic units illustrates his social emphasis and includes the combined actions and interactions of two or more people.

"Individual and group behavior are so inextricably intertwined both as to cause and effect, that an adequate behavior theory must combine both in a single internally congruent system" (Sears, 1951: 476). Sears has concentrated his efforts on the study of both the antecedents and the consequences of early child development, and while initially the parents' behavior is seen as the antecedent and the child's behavior as the consequent, both behaviors later become a matter of interaction. Antecedent-consequent statements are characteristic of social learning theory, since it is the relationship between social and environmental antecedents and their behavioral consequences that is the focus of investigations and theorizing. A well-known statement in this regard is Miller's (1941) hypothesis that frustration is the inevitable antecedent of aggressive behavior.

While Sears has contributed a considerable amount of information about patterns of childrearing (1957), the focus of his work has been on childhood rather than adolescence. It is primarily through the work of Bandura (1925–   ) and Walters (1918–1967) that a number of studies emerge that express an explicit concern with the application of social learning theory, or, as they refer to it, a sociobehavioristic approach to adolescence. Bandura, a student of Sears, has remained closer to Sears, while Walters was closer to Skinner. Their major works relevant to theories of adolescence are *Adolescent Aggression* (Bandura and Walters, 1959) and, concentrating more specifically on child behavior, *Social Learning and Personality Development* (Bandura and Walters, 1963), as well as innumerable research studies. Since Bandura and

Walters are more concerned than other social learning theorists with the period of adolescence, the major emphasis in this chapter will be on the work of these two men and their collaborators. However, it would be incorrect to identify Bandura and Walters' contribution as a "theory of adolescence," since they do not view adolescence as a separate stage, qualitatively different from either childhood or young adulthood, but are convinced of the continuity of human development from infancy to adulthood. Indeed, the contribution of social learning theory to an understanding of adolescence consists of seriously questioning the widely held assumption that adolescence is a distinct stage in human development that has its own unique characteristics and requires its own set of theoretical explanations. A sociobehavioristic approach to adolescence implies that the principles of learning that help explain child development (Sears, 1951; 1957) are equally applicable to adolescent development, since no fundamental qualitative differences exist among childhood, adolescence, and adulthood. What may differ at different age levels are sociocultural expectations, and adolescents frequently select models different from those of children. On many important social learning theory concepts, such as imitation, the frustration aggression hypothesis, and the nature of adolescence,* Bandura and Walters are almost as critical of Miller and Dollard's earlier writing as they are of Freudian and Skinnerian theory.

MODELING, IMITATION, AND IDENTIFICATION

Bandura and his collaborators have shown that children watching the behavior of a model are quick in imitating the specific responses as well as the generalized response patterns of the model. This phenomenon of modeling has been observed repeatedly in a variety of experimental situations. Furthermore, personal observation of children and adolescents imitating mannerisms, language idiosyncrasies, and habits of their parents and teachers, often to the embarrassment of the model, are commonplace. Bandura, Ross, and Ross (1963b) demonstrated that watching unusual aggressive behavior heightened children's aggressive responses significantly when compared to controls who had observed a nonaggressive model. The first experimental group watched a real-life aggressive model; the second group saw the same model portraying aggressive behavior on film; the third group observed an aggressive cartoon character depicting the same behavior. Many of the

---

*Early learning theory in sharp contrast to Bandura and Walters maintained "Adolescence is known in our society as a period of increased aggressiveness and irritability . . ." (Dollard et al., 1939: 72).

children's responses in the test situation were rather accurate imitations of the unusual aggressive acts of the model, especially of the real-life and the film model. The overall increase in aggressive behavior was highly significant and about the same for all three experimental situations, but the cartoon aggressive model elicited less precise imitation. Walters and his associates have shown that the increase in aggressive behavior as a result of watching an aggressive model is not limited to children; they produced similar findings with high school students, young women, and male hospital attendants. These social learning theory studies on imitation of aggressive behavior have been influential in awakening social concern about the potential danger of children and adolescents repeatedly watching aggressive behavior on the television screen, since "exposure to filmed aggression heightens aggressive reactions in children" (Bandura, Ross, and Ross, 1963b: 9).

The potency of watching and imitating a model in altering response patterns has been demonstrated in such divergent areas as moral judgment (Bandura and McDonald, 1963); self-imposed delay of reward pattern exhibited by the model (Bandura and Mischel, 1965); and self-reinforcement patterns closely following those of the model (Bandura and Kupers, 1964). And in contrast to popular belief, Bandura and Walters' (1959) findings suggest that adolescent boys may be more likely to engage in sexual intercourse when double and multiple dating, thereby imitating the sexual advances of each other. When behavior patterns are inhibited in the subject, observing a model perform that behavior seems to remove personal inhibitions. The factor that predicts drug use in an adolescent most accurately is whether or not friends use drugs. Apparently, an "if he can do it, I can do it" viewpoint prevails. According to Bandura, a great variety of social learning phenomena are acquired because a learner observes a model's behavior and imitates the behavior observed.

As children grow older they tend to imitate different models from their social environment. The young child usually identifies with parents and attempts to imitate their behavior, including language, gestures, and mannerisms as well as more basic attitudes and values. Identification with a teacher is not uncommon for the child entering school or for the preadolescent. The child does imitate speech patterns and mannerisms observed in the teacher. Ideas about social or community issues that the child expresses in dinner conversations and that are new to the family are often those of the teacher. With the onset of adolescence, parents and teachers frequently decline as important models, at least in regard to issues and choices that are of immediate consequence. During adolescence it is the peer group and selected entertainment heroes who become increasingly important as models, especially if communication between parents and adolescent breaks down. The adolescent peer group is particularly influential as a model in the use of verbal expressions, hair style, clothing, food, music, and entertainment preferences, as well as in regard to decisions related to rapidly changing social values (Brittain, 1963). Some of the problems that arise during adolescence may be the result of an individual modeling the behavior of peers who may be no more knowledgeable, intelligent, mature, and wise than the individual himself is.

Related to modeling and important in Bandura's social learning theory are the concepts of identification and imitation. In his earlier writing Bandura uses the concept of identification frequently, but later he rejects it as lacking specific content. Different definitions have been advanced for the concepts "identification" and "imitation." Although there is no complete agreement about the specific meaning of these concepts, identification is viewed as a more general way of modeling the behavior of another person even without the person's presence. Identification includes the incorporation of the model's values, beliefs, roles, and attitudes. Imitation, on the other hand, refers to the rather specific reproduction or matching of behavior sequences almost in the nature of mimicking behavior while the person whose behavior is imitated is or was personally present. Experimental psychologists speak of "imitation" whereas personality theorists speak of "identification." Bandura and Walters (1963) discuss the difference in existing definitions but prefer to use "imitation," which they define as referring to "the occurrence of matching responses."

The role of imitation has been recognized since antiquity as an important method of learning, and it is indeed surprising that behavioristic learning theory has shown so little concern for imitating and modeling. Imitation is particularly relevant for learning complex social behavior, such as language, self-control, altruism, aggression, sexual behavior, and so on. Imitation also plays an essential role in the learning of basic perceptual-motor skills such as handwriting, and much of the learning in the gymnasium and on the sports field is the result of observing and imitating a model who shows how to play correctly. In many languages the term "to teach" is synonymous with "to show" or, as in Hebrew, has the same root, revealing that modeling, or showing, is the basic method of teaching when the emphasis is on skills that can be acquired through observational learning (Bandura and Walters, 1963). The adolescent who wants to learn to drive a car does so first of all by observation and imitation. A youth totally naïve in the use of cars would endanger his own life and those of others if he were to attempt driving solely on the basis of trial and error or reinforcement. Bandura (1962) reports that natives in a Guatemalan subculture learn to operate a cotton textile machine by observing the correct operation of the machine for a number of days. During this training period the youthful trainee asks no questions and is given neither verbal instruction nor reinforcement. Yet, when she feels confident that she can master the process herself, she takes over the operation of the machine and usually succeeds on the very first trial in operating the machine without any difficulties and without further instruction. This kind of learning is based only on the apprentice observing an appropriate social model and imitating the behavior of the model.

SOCIAL LEARNING THEORY CONTRASTED WITH STAGE AND TRAIT THEORIES

Stage theorists of development, such as Gesell, Freud, Erikson, and even Piaget, have postulated fairly specific age-related behavior dispositions that follow an invariant developmental sequence, possess cross-situational consistency, and are more or less universal and predetermined. Social learning theory, in contrast, assumes that behavior is primarily determined within a social situational context. Consequently, social learning theory focuses on the interrelationship between environmental and social changes as antecedents and the behavioral changes that occur in a given individual as consequences rather than as a function of age. Descriptions and statements about adolescence are not of such a general, all-encompassing nature, as is Erikson's theory, for example, which predicts that an adolescent will inevitably experience an identity crisis, or Piaget's prediction that adolescent thought processes will begin to follow formal logic and become increasingly more abstract. Rather, social learning theory statements are predictions of relationships between external factors and behavior. The strong emphasis in the sociobehavioristic approach on the influence of social conditions and cultural expectations, even on adolescent sexual behavior, becomes obvious in a statement such as: "In North American society, the marked increase in heterosexual behavior in middle and late adolescence is certainly due less to hormonal changes than to cultural expectations" (Bandura and Walters, 1963: 150). It appears as if they overstated their case, for hormonal changes during adolescence have been found to be related to sexual drive (Beach, 1974). Even Margaret Mead—who is certainly not an advocate of biological determination in adolescent development—recognizes that "the development of heterosexual interest and activity at puberty does serve to distinguish this period from the period preceding it and from maturity" (Mead, 1952: 537). The word "puberty" carries distinct connotations of physiological and hormonal changes. While Bandura admits that such changes in behavior do occur, he explains the phenomenon differently. In general, pronounced changes in behavior may occur during adolescence, not because of internal maturational forces but because of sudden changes in the social training situation, family structure, peer group expectation, or other environmental factors; and, according to Bandura, such changes are less common than much of the literature on the so-called rebirth or storm and stress of adolescence leads one to believe.

Bandura, in an article, "The Stormy Decade: Fact or Fiction," has seriously questioned the stage theory assumption that adolescence is a turbulent decade inevitably characterized by "storm and stress, tension, rebellion, dependency conflicts, peer-group conformity, black leather jackets and the like" (Bandura, 1964: 224). While he does not deny that some of these kinds of behavior occur in some individuals, such behaviors are viewed as being due to cultural conditioning and social expectation rather than as inevitable developmental phenomena characteristic of the period of adolescence per se. Aggressive behavior in adolescence—when it does occur—is viewed as the consequence of specific antecedent conditions in the childrearing pattern and the parent-child relationship such as dependency training, socialization pressure, imitation, and modeling, rather than as the result of adolescent adjustment problems. Whenever such behaviors occur, they are viewed as being lawfully related to existing situations or to the preadolescent social situation—that is, the antecedent environmental conditions. The prototypical adolescent with turmoils and anxieties,* sexual tensions, compulsive conformity, and acute identity crisis so commonly described in the literature, according to Bandura (1964), fits only the actual behavior of perhaps "the deviant ten percent of the adolescent population." The "myth" that such behavior is believed to be a normal aspect of adolescent development is due more to cultural expectations and the representation of teen-agers in movies, literature, and the mass media than based on actual facts. Bandura (1964) does find, as does Offer in *The Psychological World of the Teenager* (1969), that responsible, happy, well-adjusted, parent-respecting youth are more common than had been assumed. Such positive findings are also interpreted not as characteristics of adolescence per se but in the light of antecedent home conditions such as having experienced a warm, supportive preadolescence in which firmness and socialization pressure in childhood slowly gave way to increasingly more freedom during adolescence. As a general law of social and personal development, social learning theory assumes that there is continuity in human growth

---

*Cattell and Scheier (1961) do find—in contrast to Bandura's claim—that during adolescence a noticeable increase in anxiety distinguishes that period from childhood and adulthood. "In the normal person, free anxiety is very high in adolescence, drops sharply as adulthood is reached. . . ."

patterns and in the learning process and that no basic changes or clear-cut new stages in the mode of thinking appear at any one age level. Bandura and McDonald (1963) tested Piaget's (1932) theory that objective moral judgment, which considers the material damage in an act, gives way at about the age of seven to subjective moral judgment, which considers the intent of the wrongdoers rather than the amount of damage. They did not find a distinct or abrupt change in the moral responses of their subjects, but there was a pronounced increase in subjective moral judgment and a decrease in objective moral judgment as a function of age. Bandura and McDonald consider changes in moral judgment to be primarily the result of changes in reinforcement contingencies in combination with the effects of modeling, rather than a function of maturation or a change from the preoperational to the operational stage in logical thinking. Bandura and McDonald (1963) demonstrated further that age-specific social responses such as moral judgment can be modified through the utilization of appropriate models and the application of social learning principles. Since the age-specific behavior postulated by Piaget's theory of two distinct stages of moral judgment can be modified through modeling and social reinforcement, some doubt is cast on the validity of the stage concept. It appears as if external social experiences have greater impact on behavior changes than the internal maturational forces postulated by stage theorists. Bandura and Mischel (1965) also show that delay of reward behavior can be modified through modeling techniques.

In contrast to stage theories, social learning theory is concerned with *interindividual* rather than with *intraindividual* differences. Some of the environmental variables in behavior are intelligence, sex, age, race, socioeconomic status, culture, home atmosphere, exposure to models, and different reinforcement schedules. "To the extent that children representing such diverse backgrounds experience differential contingencies and schedules of reinforcement, as well as exposure to social models who differ widely in the behavior they exhibit, considerable interindividual behavior variability would be expected" (Bandura and McDonald, 1963: 274).

Trait theorists, such as Raymond Cattell (1961), have measured the basic components or traits of personality and postulated cross-situational consistency and developmental stability of behavior patterns, since they assumed that it was not so much the external situation but the internal trait or disposition that determined behavior. Since the primary cause of behavior is located within the person, trait theorists have searched for consistency in people's behavior across situational changes and ascribe consistency in behavior to such traits as ego strength, reality orientation, self-control, self-concept, maturity, and energy-binding ideation. Social learning theorists, in contrast, see situational changes in a lawful way related to behavior changes and, consequently, investigate the observable external causes of behavior. An adolescent may be rebellious, disobedient, insensitive, nonconforming, and tough, and yet the same person may also be obedient, sensitive, conforming, and considerate. Social learning theory would not look at some of these traits as real and at the other group as defenses or compensations; nor would it view these diverse traits as inconsistent, arbitrary, or capricious. Social learning theory would consider all of these behaviors as lawfully related to specific social situations and antecedent factors. In other words, the issues then become when, how, where, and in interaction with whom did what behavior occur? Or what happened to the individual prior to the occurrence of a particular behavior?

Any consistency in behavior that can be observed is the result of similarity in the antecedent external social conditions rather than an internal trait. If antecedent conditions differ markedly or are expected to differ, behavior will differ and may appear quite inconsistent. A widely held assumption, especially among stage theorists, is that a consistent characteristic of middle adolescence is an antagonism toward adult authority. However, to illustrate the importance of antecedent social conditions, one might consider the common observation of an adolescent who has pronounced feelings of antagonism toward his father while, at the same time, expressing a great deal of admiration and respect for other adult authority figures such as his football coach, adult Boy Scout leader, or minister.

SOCIAL LEARNING THEORY CONTRASTED WITH BEHAVIORISTIC LEARNING THEORY

Social learning theory also recognizes the very limited applicability of reinforcement theory to a wide variety of especially complex forms of social behavior such as language learning. Bandura (1962) considers the use of operant or instrumental conditioning as "tedious and ineffective" for most human learning. Skinner and others have assumed, without sufficient empirical verification, that reinforcement principles based on the findings of studies in highly structured laboratory situations apply equally to complex social situations. However, for a novel response to be reinforced, at least an approximation of that response must occur. Many complex forms of social learning would not easily emerge if they had to rely on reinforcement or drive reduction alone. A response that has never been made and observed has a zero probability of occurring and can hardly be acquired if there is no reliable eliciting stimulus. Reinforcement theory assumes that learning takes place only after a response has been made and is reinforced. However, reinforcement is not a precondition for the acquisition of a new response; it can only change the probability that an existing response will occur in the future. Bandura (1962) feels that people would not be socialized and many vocational and recreational skills would never be learned if they depended solely on reinforcement. A new behavior repertoire can only be learned from observing a model exhibiting that behavior and matching or imitating the behavior modeled. Operant conditioning effectively explains how the learned behavior is maintained and strengthened but not how it is initially acquired. The initial acquisition of a response pattern is more effectively explained by imitation, and this kind of observational learning can take place without direct reinforcement. Similarly, trial-and-error learning can be eliminated, or the number of trials reduced, by providing an opportunity to observe the necessary behavior performed by an appropriate model. This process of observing and imitating is referred to as modeling and constitutes the cornerstone of Bandura's sociobehavioristic approach. "What you know and how you behave depends on what you see and hear and not just on what you get" (Mischel, 1971: 71).

Social learning theory makes a clear and important distinction between the acquisition of potential response patterns and actual performance or responding. The acquisition of potential response patterns is a function of observing the behavior of others and depends on social variables, sensory input, and cognitive operations. Acquisition learning does take place before the subject responds, and many response patterns are acquired but not performed. Acquisition learning is particularly obvious in language learning. However, whether the acquired behavior will actually occur and the probability that it will occur are dependent on reinforcement (Mischel, 1971). In social learning theory, reinforcement takes the place of a secondary, supportive role in the learning process. Most complex learning is viewed primarily as social—namely, the imitation of social models, especially in the learning of novel response patterns. The difference between acquisition and performance may be illustrated by the fact that most adolescent boys may know how to use lipstick and cosmetics—the response patterns having been acquired through observation. However, because these responses have never been reinforced, their probability of occurring is very low and may actually be zero. Many response patterns are acquired through observing a model but are not expressed as long as the learned behavior is not functional. However, if the social situations change so that the acquired response patterns become functional, the previously acquired behavior may be performed without further observations, without trial and error, and without reinforcement. When social situations change, for example, children may surprise parents with language patterns or language skills that were acquired earlier but that had never before been used.

Some social behaviors may seem to be much more dependent on the behavior of the model that is observed and imitated rather than upon the reinforcement or punishment. One fairly persistent research finding is that parental punitiveness toward aggressive behavior appears to be associated with more rather than less aggressive behavior in the child.

> Indeed, parental modeling behavior may often counteract the effects of their direct training. When a parent punishes his child physically for having aggressed toward peers, for example, the intended outcome of this training is that the child should refrain from hitting others. The child, however, is also learning from parental demonstration how to aggress physically and this imitative learning may provide the direction for the child's behavior when he is similarly frustrated in subsequent social interactions [Bandura, 1967: 43].

"Do as I say, not as I do" is exactly the reverse of what social learning theory predicts will happen. The imitation of the model, the "as I do" part, apparently is more potent than the reinforcement or the punishment provided by the "as I say" part. And many adolescents complain about their parents' "hypocrisies," since their "model" behavior belies their verbal recommendations and admonitions. Many manuals on discipline emphasize that the modeling of desirable behavior is actually a much more potent influence than any verbalization or reward-punishment system. And the most valid general rule in regard to the training of children and adolescents is: "There is no sure way to guarantee that your child will grow up to be the kind of person you would like him to be. The most likely way is for you to be the kind of person you would like him to be."

In addition to its establishment, the maintenance of response patterns or learning in the behavioristic sense does not depend only on direct external reinforcement as in Skinner's theory. Bandura expands the traditional concept of reinforcement to include *vicarious reinforcement* and also *self-reinforcement*. Vicarious reinforcement depends on the positive or negative consequences that the subject observes in others—that is, in the model. Observing social models that are rewarded for aggressive behavior increases the likelihood of this behavior occurring in the observer; just as aggressive behavior punished in the model inhibits the same behavior in the subject.

Bandura, Ross, and Ross (1963c) showed two films of Rocky the Villain exhibiting almost identical aggressive behavior, except that in one instance his aggressive behavior was rewarded and in another it was punished. Children who watched the movie and saw that the aggressive behavior of Rocky was rewarded were quick in imitating both the physical violence and the verbal abuse that they had observed. Actually, they showed about two times as much aggressive behavior as a control group. However, in the situation in which the children observed that the villain was punished after his aggressive act they showed little imitation of the behavior they had watched. However, even though punishing the villain inhibited the overt learning effects that resulted from observing the "bad" model, it did not suppress the latent tendencies. Children did acquire these response patterns and could describe them with considerable accuracy, but they did not perform them unless such response patterns became functional under either the impact of provocation or the prospect of reward.

Self-reinforcement means that learners actually reward themselves for work that they consider of good quality. Verbal self-evaluations, which people administer frequently, are part of the self-reinforcing event. Bandura claims that "most human behavior is altered and maintained in the absence of immediate reinforcement" (Bandura, 1971: 248). In a variety of experiments children give themselves candy or tokens for attaining self-selected levels of performance on a miniature bowling game. The standards for their self-reinforcement are adopted from the comparison model (Bandura and Kupers, 1964; Bandura and Whalen, 1966); if the standards of the model are stringent, self-reinforcement is infrequent, but if the standards of the model are lenient, self-reinforcement is generous. Bandura and Perloff (1967) demonstrated that self-reinforcement and external reinforcement are equally effective, and both are significantly more effective than noncontingent reward or a nonreward condition. Once the performance of a desirable response pattern has acquired a positive value, such as an adolescent shooting baskets, the person can administer self-reinforcement by producing the desired basket and feeling good about the improving skills. Common observation illustrates that this kind of self-reinforcement can keep such behavior as basket shooting going for several hours on a Saturday afternoon. Adolescents are learning to set their own level of performance, and reaching that level makes them feel good, proud, or satisfied and, therefore, carries its own reward. In other words, as we grow more mature, self-reinforcement patterns stabilize and become less and less dependent on parents, teachers, and bosses giving us our rewards. We increasingly judge the appropriateness and the quality of our own responses and reward them accordingly. Successful socialization requires that our own judgment for a piece of work become a more important reinforcer than some outsider administering praise, candy, money, or other reinforcers. Mature adolescents may be able to make themselves feel good about work well done—that is, provide self-reinforcement—even though a critical teacher or an impatient father expresses dissatisfaction. In contrast to Skinner's emphasis on direct reinforcement often contingent on fairly specific piecemeal types of responses, social learning theorists maintain that the more important reinforcers in terms of mature complex social behavior are self-administered.

THE ANTECEDENTS OF ADOLESCENT AGGRESSION

Bandura (1973b) rejects all hydraulic motivational theories of aggression—such as Freud's aggressive instinct theory, Lorenz's aggressive urge theory, and even Miller and Dollard's reactive drive theory—since they view aggression as the natural response to frustration. Aristotle believed that emotional expression purges the emotions. Similarly, hydraulic models hold that as long as the cause of aggression is within the individual, the aggressive energy must find an outlet. Aggression is assumed to be reduced by aggressive behavior, and therapy provides safe and approved outlets for aggression.

Plato, in contrast, held that the overt expression of emotion arouses rather than reduces emotions. Bandura feels that Plato is the better psychologist. Social learning theory postulates that the causes of aggression are external, social, and environmental and can be found in the dependency training in childhood, imitation of aggressive models, and lack of internalization of social values. Numerous studies (Bandura, Ross, and Ross, 1963b; 1963c) have shown that exposure to aggressive models increases aggressive behavior in the observer. As an alternative to the frustration-aggression hypothesis, Bandura assumes that, rather than frustration leading to aggression, frustration produces

> emotional arousal that can elicit a variety of behaviors depending on the types of reactions people have learned for coping with stressful conditions. When distressed, some people seek help and support; others display achievement behavior; others show withdrawal and resignation; some aggress; others exhibit heightened somatic activity; others anesthetize themselves with drugs or alcohol; and most intensify constructive efforts to overcome their problems [Bandura, 1973b: 204].

Bandura and Walters' interest in the period of adolescence finds its most explicit expression in an extensive study, *Adolescent Aggression* (1959). The study is—as the subtitle, "A Study of the Influence of Child Training Practices and Family Interrelationships," suggests—concerned with the antecedent variables in the parent-child relationship that contribute to the development of antisocial aggressive behavior in adolescents. The specific antecedent home conditions investigated were derived from social learning theory hypotheses and involve such variables as dependency training, sex attitudes and behavior, the handling of discipline in the home, identification processes, and the socialization process in general. The socialization process is viewed as "the development of habitual response patterns that are acceptable in the society in which the individual lives. The learning of such habits, or cue-response associations, requires the presence of some kind of drive or motivating process and the occurrence of a reward or reinforcement" (Bandura and Walters, 1959: 23).

The conditions that contribute to effective socialization include the development of a dependency motive, so that the child desires approval and affection from others. In addition, since dependency alone is not sufficient, socialization pressure needs to be exerted by way of demands, restrictions, and limitations—in short, through discipline—so that the child learns to conform to the patterns of society. This socialization process is facilitated by the amount and quality of personal contact parents give their child and by withholding of secondary rewards such as approval and attention, while at the same time keeping the child in a dependent relationship. The socialization process is delayed or disrupted if dependency behavior is punished or discouraged, if parental discipline methods are inconsistent within the home, and if the parents' values are in conflict with the prevalent values of the community and society. One basic assumption of Bandura and Walters' study is that antisocial aggression develops from a disruption in the adolescent's earlier dependency training in relationship to parents. Dependency needs could be frustrated by lack of affectional nurturance, by parental rejection, or by lack of close dependency ties with one or both parents. An impairment in the development of healthy dependency relationships may directly contribute to feelings of hostility and to aggressive behavior. In addition, children without dependency motives experience less guilt and lack the capacity to control aggressive feelings sufficiently when aroused.

Bandura and Walters obtained their data from two groups of carefully selected boys aged fourteen to seventeen. Twenty-six pairs of boys were matched on a one-to-one basis in regard to age, intelligence, father's occupational status, and area of residence. They differed in that the aggressive boys had a history of repetitive antisocial, aggressive patterns of behavior, and many of them were on probation. The nonaggressive control boys were neither markedly aggressive nor withdrawn. Both groups came from intact families, had average or above-average intelligence, did not live in a high-delinquency neighborhood, and were free from withdrawal tendencies, known organic involvement, or other psychiatric problems. Data were collected through extensive personal interviews of both groups of adolescents as well as their parents. In theoretical orientation, in content, and in methodology the study may be considered an extension of Sears, Maccoby, and Levin's *Patterns of Child Rearing* (1957).

Sociological approaches relate incidence of delinquency to population density, poverty, broken homes, deteriorated houses and neighborhood, lack of recreational facilities, and social and personal discontent. The investigators, in contrast, looked at the nature of the parent-child relationship and related it to the absence or presence of aggressive behavior in the adolescent subjects, controlling most of the sociological factors by matching procedures. In contrast to the psychodynamic disease model of deviant behavior, Bandura and Walters assume that both deviant and prosocial behavior are governed by the same learning principles, rather than by hidden, subconscious, internal dynamics or traits. It is the external stimulus condition that controls normal as well as deviant behavior, rather than underlying dispositions.

Furthermore, since social learning theorists believe in the continuity of human development, antisocial aggressive behavior in adolescent boys is seen not as a problem that emerges with puberty or as related to hormonal changes, but as a failure in the socialization process that begins very early in childhood and continues during development.

The first group of hypotheses developed from social learning theory compared the dependency behavior, dependency anxiety, feelings of rejection, and aggressive behavior in the aggressive adolescents with those of the nonaggressive adolescents. In general, there was no significant difference in mothers' warmth and affection with both groups of boys. However, the aggressive boys were, as social learning theory predicted, less dependent on their fathers, felt more rejected by their fathers, and spent less time with their fathers than the control boys.

The fathers of the two groups of boys did not report any difference in the amount of overt aggression directed toward them. Only a few of the mothers of aggressive boys reported physical aggression directed toward them, but they also admitted that they were more tolerant of aggressive behavior. The control mothers had firmer limits in the amount of aggression they would tolerate. In general, the differences in expression of aggression against parents and parents' tolerance of aggressive behavior between these two groups were not very pronounced. However, it became quite obvious that both the fathers and the mothers of the aggressive adolescents actively encouraged their sons to show aggression outside the home, to use their fists, to stand up for their rights; and the fathers seemed to get some vicarious enjoyment from the aggressive acts of their sons. This difference, especially between the fathers of aggressive sons and the control fathers, was most pronounced. In a follow-up study of aggressive and inhibited preadolescent boys, Bandura (1960) found that the parents of the inhibited boys were nonpermissive and nonpunitive toward aggressive behavior, which means that they neither reinforced nor did they model aggressive behavior. The parents of aggressive boys, in contrast, were nonpermissive and punitive when the aggressive behavior was directed toward themselves, but they encouraged aggression toward other children and permitted sibling aggression.

Aggressive boys had more dependency anxiety—that is, they were less willing to express their dependency, seek help, talk about their problems, and show affection, even though they did have dependency needs. The dependency anxiety generalized from parents to peers and school. The control boys sought and appreciated help from their fathers more, and they also showed more help-seeking and approval-seeking behavior in relationship to their peers, while the feeling of being rejected in relationship to school and peers was more pronounced among the aggressive boys.

In relationship to sexual behavior, no difference was found in the handling of sexual behavior in both groups of parents, except that the fathers of the aggressive boys were more permissive concerning sexual behavior. However, it was found that the aggressive boys had had significantly more heterosexual experiences and expressed less anxiety about sex. Apparently, the permissive attitude in the fathers contributed to the greater sexual experience of the aggressive boys.

Several significant relationships were found in respect to the handling of rules, limitations, and the disciplining of these two groups of boys. The control parents used more reasoning as a disciplinary method and had higher achievement expectations for their sons. The control mothers were more consistent in enforcing rules and were more restrictive—that is, they used more socialization pressure, at least in the home. The methods used significantly more in disciplining the aggressive boys were physical and verbal punishment by their fathers, isolation, and more deprivation of privileges, although the latter method was common in both groups. The relationship between punitive parents and aggressive behavior in their children has been reported repeatedly in the literature. Apparently, the more children are punished at home for aggressive behavior, the more aggressively they act toward their peers (Eron, Walder, Toigo, and Lefkowitz, 1963; Sears, Maccoby, and Levin, 1957). The mothers of the aggressive boys reported that their sons resisted their demands, and the aggressive boys themselves admitted that they ignored parental requests and refused to do what they were told to do. The parent-child relationship of the aggressive adolescents may best be described as lacking in warmth and affection.

The final and crucial question from a social learning theory point of view relates to the identification of these two groups of boys with their parents and the internalization of controls. While there was no difference in terms of identification with the mother, control boys identified more strongly with their fathers. The control fathers, in turn, were more demanding of masculine behavior in their boys. The aggressive boys experienced more disruption in affectional relationships between their fathers and their mothers and also more of a disruption in the emotional relationship between themselves and their parents, especially their fathers. In terms of internalization of controls, the nonaggressive group experienced more guilt when they transgressed, whereas the aggressive boys did not. The conscience development of the aggressive boys differed from that of the control boys. The behavior of the control boys was governed by guilt, an internal avoidance, when confronted with temptation. The aggressive boys, in a situation involving transgression of rules, were not governed by guilt but, if they were inhibited at all, by fear of punishment. Since identification is not encouraged and rewarded in the aggressive boys, the internalization of values seems to suffer.

In summary, more important than the shortcomings in the dependency training of the aggressive boys—which were theoretically predicted, but actually only weakly supported—was the imitation process. Aggressive boys seem to imitate their aggressive parents, who tend to use more physical punishment as a method of discipline and who encourage and reward the aggressive behavior of their sons, at least outside the home. By reinforcing aggressive behavior outside the home, by inhibiting aggressive behavior inside the home directed toward the parents, and by modeling aggressive behavior through physically punishing the boys, these parents "fostered displacement of aggression toward òbjects and situations eliciting much weaker inhibitory response" (Bandura, Ross, and Ross, 1961). These findings resulting from the study of aggressive behavior of adolescent boys in their natural environment are quite consistent with the results of laboratory studies of aggressive behavior of young children (Bandura, Ross, and Ross, 1961; 1963b; 1963c), discussed earlier.

Antisocial aggressive behavior in adolescent boys is the consequence of identifiable socialization variables in the parent-child relationship.

EDUCATIONAL IMPLICATIONS

Social learning theory's basic assumption is that children and adolescents learn most complex skills more effectively by imitating the behavior of their parents, teachers, and peers rather than by reinforcement, trial and error, and, in certain situations, even better than by verbal instruction. Verbal instructions and verbal cues, if they represent the modeling behavior symbolically, can facilitate the learning process, at least for behavior already in the subject's response repertoire. An often neglected aspect of the role of the teacher is the effective model role, demonstrating correct response patterns to be imitated. Only secondarily is the teacher a good reinforcer who uses reinforcement to shape and maintain already learned response repertoires. A teacher serves the model function, and some pupils will imitate this behavior regardless of whether or not the teacher consciously chooses for them to do so. A teacher cannot limit her influence on students to academic competencies only but must be aware that some pupils will be influenced by her altruism or selfishness, cleanliness or slovenliness, organization or disorganization, and whether or not she is observed participating in political activities, religious activities, and so on.

Evidence indicates that there are at least three types of effects that observing the model's behavior has on the learner (Bandura, 1965; Bandura and Walters, 1963). First, there is the already discussed *modeling effect*. By imitating the model's behavior, children acquire response patterns that they did not have before, and the modeling responses closely match those of the model. Bandura provides strong evidence that modeling as a teaching-learning technique is more economical than the techniques of operant conditioning, at least in learning novel responses. Second, there is the *inhibitory or disinhibitory effect*, which is based on the consequence the model experiences. If the consequences of the model's behavior are pain or punishment, watching the model's reaction to pain or punishment has an inhibitory effect on the observer. On the other hand, if the model is rewarded for a certain behavior, this has a disinhibitory effect on the observer, and the probability that the observer will imitate that behavior is increased. Vicarious reinforcement contributes to the disinhibitory influence of modeling. Third, there is the *eliciting effect*, meaning that the model's behavior provides specific cues, or serves as an eliciting stimulus that facilitates the release of similar responses in the observer, thus aiding the learning process. In the case of the eliciting effect of the model the behavior that is imitated is not new, nor was it previously inhibited, but at least similar responses are already in the subject's response repertoire. For example, a study by White (1967) was concerned with the effects of instruction and modeling on the altruistic behavior of preadolescent children. It was shown that in eliciting altruistic responses in students, what the teacher *did* was more important than what the teacher *said*. Apparently, altruistic behavior can be elicited more effectively by modeling than by verbal instruction. Bandura and McDonald (1963) demonstrated that modeling procedures, especially when both the model and the observer are reinforced, are very powerful in changing preadolescents' moral judgments. Live and symbolic models have been found to have a significant influence on the learning of self-control (Bandura and Mischel, 1965).

LaFleur and Johnson (1972) were concerned with the application of social learning theory principles in influencing the behavior of adolescents in a counseling situation. The treatment condition consisted of having the subjects watch cartoon stick-figure models, who were similar to themselves in important characteristics, request information about educational and vocational goals. The cartoon characters in the modeling treatment group remained without reward. However, for the second experimental group, the cartoon characters not only served as models, but they were also reinforced for information-seeking behavior, thus providing modeling and vicarious reinforcement for subjects. A control group of adolescents received information about educational and vocational planning, but they were given no model to observe and imitate. Modeling in the first experimental group was as effective as modeling with vicarious reinforcement in the second experimental group; but both experimental groups were significantly more effective than the control situation, in which merely information was provided. The first two experimental groups imitated the modeled behavior; these adolescents became more interested in seeking information about planning their future, and they actually acquired more knowledge.

Teachers have an indirect but potent influence on children and adolescents in shaping the latter's values and attitudes by what they, the teachers themselves, are and what they do. This is in addition to the influence they exert through the cognitive, instructional curriculum that relates to their subject matter and teaching methods. Teachers can indirectly encourage altruism, moral values, social conscience, and human decency by exhibiting these virtues themselves. Even though adolescents as a group may reject teachers in general as identification models, it is not at all uncommon that an individual student may experience occasional infatuation, crushes, and adoration of an individual teacher. Furthermore, an adolescent may imitate the behavior of a teacher, even though a more general identification with the teacher as a person is lacking. Consequently, it is important to consider the conditions contributing to the imitation-identification process. First, the behavior to be imitated must be within the subject's perceptual and motor capacity. Furthermore, studies have shown that the identification process is facilitated if the model is warm, friendly, and supportive rather than cold and rejecting. However, each of the factors that generally contributes to imitation and learning must be evaluated in relationship to other factors and the overall context. For example, an overindulgent teacher or parent providing too much warmth and giving the child too much nurturance may inhibit rather than facilitate the learning or behavior that demands effort and self-denial.

Learning is more likely to occur if imitative or matching responses are directly rewarded, so that modeling and reinforcement jointly contribute to the acquisition of response patterns. Imitation, or matching of responses, can be further enhanced by vicarious reinforcement —that is, if the model who is being observed is also being rewarded for the behavior.

Social power and the control of rewards make up another variable that influences imitation, and these factors are of importance in the school situation in which teachers do control the rewards and have social power. In an experiment, Bandura, Ross, and Ross (1963a) utilized an adult model who controlled the distribution of highly attractive toys. A second adult model received some of these toys as did the children who served as subjects. Consequently, the children might have viewed the second model as a rival. Bandura observed that the children were much more likely to imitate the behavior of the first model who had the control (social power) over the toys rather than the behavior of the second model. Related to the findings of this study is the common observation that the higher-status model is much more likely to be imitated than the lower-status model. President Kennedy contributed to the popularity of rocking chairs and President Reagan to that of jellybeans.

In addition, it has been demonstrated (Bandura, 1962) that the effectiveness of the model in producing matching responses in the observer depends on a variety of factors, such as the model's attractiveness, prestige, competence, and willingness to dispense rewards and praise. If the model has some characteristics in common with the observing subject, the observer is more inclined to imitate the model's behavior. For children, adults often serve as more powerful models than peers, since they have status, prestige, competence, power, and are the dispensers of rewards. However, with adolescents, peer group members do serve as models and may actually have greater influence on imitative behavior than parents and teachers, partly because they share common characteristics, partly because the peer group has control over the rewards that matter to adolescents.

The model's influence on imitative behavior of the subject also depends on the motivation and other characteristics of the subject. The person who has strong dependency needs, who is lacking in self-esteem or competence, and who, in the past, has been reinforced for producing matching responses, is more likely to imitate the model.

It appears crucial that adolescents have teachers with whom they can and want to identify. Since much learning occurs inadvertently due to the fact that the teacher serves as a socializing agent, it becomes more important that teachers be selected in the light of their qualities as models for youths and their potential for identification. The demand of radical groups that black students be taught by black teachers—since black children tend to identify better with black teachers with whom they share a number of common characteristics—seems to receive some implicit support from social learning theory. Bandura (1962) has also pointed out that the sex of the model and the sex of the subject do influence the imitation of behavior. The power of imitating a model is so great that children will imitate the sex-inappropriate play behavior of a same sex model. Boys watching a male model play with a toy stove increase their stove-playing behavior when the model is gone, just as girls increase their truck-playing behavior after having observed a female model play with the truck (Wolf, 1973).

Social learning theory could also provide a potential explanation as to why school integration does work and does produce results—although often only modest results—that are more effective than other compensatory reforms. As lower-class children move into academic settings in which peer models value learning, take school seriously, and aspire for academic success, their own attitudes and behavior will change to the extent that they accept and imitate the academic striving of their new peers.

REFERENCES

Abraham, K. The influence of oral eroticism on character formation. In *Selected papers on psychoanalysis*. London: Hogarth, 1948. (Originally published 1921.)

Aebli, H. *Über die geistige Entwicklung des Kindes*. Stuttgart: Klett, 1963.

Andrews, J. The relationship of values to identity achievement status. *Journal of Youth and Adolescence*, 1973, *2*, 133–138.

Aristotle. Magna moralia. In W. D. Ross, ed., *The works of Aristotle* (G. Stock, trans.), Vol. 9. Oxford: Clarendon Press, 1925.

———. Ethica Nicomachea. In R. McKeon, ed., *The basic works of Aristotle* (W. D. Ross, trans.). New York: Random House, 1941(a).

———. Historia animalium. In R. McKeon, ed., *The basic works of Aristotle* (D. W. Thompson, trans.). New York: Random House, 1941(b).

———. Politica. In R. McKeon, ed., *The basic works of Aristotle* (B. Jowett, trans.). New York: Random House, 1941(c).

———. Rhetorica. In R. McKeon, ed., *The basic works of Aristotle* (W. R. Roberts, trans.). New York: Random House, 1941(d).

Arlin, P. K. Cognitive development in adulthood: A fifth stage? *Developmental Psychology*, 1975, *11*, 602–606.

Ausubel, D. P. *Theory and problems of adolescent development*. New York: Grune & Stratton, 1954.

———. *Theory and problems of child development*. New York: Grune & Stratton, 1958.

Baldwin, A. L. *Theories of child development*. New York: John Wiley & Sons, 1967.

Baldwin, C. P., and Baldwin, A. L. Children's judgments of kindness. *Child Development*, 1970, *41*, 29–47.

Baldwin, J. M. *Social and ethical interpretations in mental development*. New York: Macmillan, 1906.

Ball, W. B. Religion and public education: The Post-Schempp years. In T. R. Sizer, ed., *Religion and public education*. Boston: Houghton Mifflin, 1967.

Bandura, A. Relationship of family patterns to child behavior disorders.

Progress Report, U.S.P.H. Research Grant M-1734. Stanford, Calif.: Stanford University, 1960.

_____. Social learning theory through imitation. In M. R. Jones, ed., *Nebraska Symposium on Motivation*, Vol. 10. Lincoln: University of Nebraska Press, 1962.

_____. The stormy decade: Fact or fiction? *Psychology in the Schools*, 1964, *1*, 224-231.

_____. Behavioral modifications through modeling procedures. In L. Krasner and L. P. Ullmann, eds., *Research in behavior modification*. New York: Holt, Rinehart & Winston, 1965.

_____. The role of modeling processes in personality development. In W. W. Hartup and N. L. Smothergill, eds., *The young child: Reviews of research*. Washington, D.C.: National Association for the Education of Young Children, 1967.

_____. *Principles of behavior modification*. New York: Holt, Rinehart & Winston, 1969.

_____. Vicarious and self-reinforcement processes. In R. Glaser, ed., *The nature of reinforcement*. New York: Academic Press, 1971.

_____. *Aggression: A social learning analysis*. Englewood Cliffs, N.J.: Prentice-Hall, 1973(a).

_____. Social learning theory of aggression. In J. F. Knutson, ed., *The control of aggression: Implications from basic research*. Chicago: Aldine Publishing Company, 1973(b).

Bandura, A., and Kupers, C. J. Transmission of patterns of self-reinforcement through modeling. *Journal of Abnormal and Social Psychology*, 1964, *69*, 1-9.

Bandura, A., and McDonald, F. J. Influence of social reinforcement and the behavior of models in shaping children's moral judgments. *Journal of Abnormal and Social Psychology*, 1963, *67*, 274-281.

Bandura, A., and Mischel, W. Modification of self-imposed delay of reward through exposure to live and symbolic models. *Journal of Personality and Social Psychology*, 1965, *2*, 698-705.

Bandura, A., and Perloff, B. Relative efficacy of self-monitored and externally imposed reinforcement systems. *Journal of Personality and Social Psychology*, 1967, *7*, 111-116.

Bandura, A., Ross, D., and Ross, S. A. Transmission of aggression through imitation of aggressive models. *Journal of Abnormal and Social Psychology*, 1961, *63*, 575-582.

_____. A comparative test of the status envy, social power, and secondary reinforcement theories of identificatory learning. *Journal of Abnormal and Social Psychology*, 1963, *67*, 527-534(a).

_____. Imitation of film-mediated aggressive models. *Journal of Abnormal and Social Psychology*, 1963, *66*, 3-11(b).

_____. Vicarious reinforcement and imitative learning. *Journal of Abnormal and Social Psychology*, 1963, *67*, 601–607(c).

Bandura, A., and Walters, R. H. *Adolescent aggression.* New York: Ronald Press, 1959.

_____. *Social learning and personality development.* New York: Holt, Rinehart & Winston, 1963.

Bandura, A., and Whalen, C. K. The influence of antecedent reinforcement and divergent modeling cues on patterns of self-reward. *Journal of Personality and Social Psychology*, 1966, *3*, 373–383.

Barker, R. G., Wright, B. A., Meyerson, L., and Gonick, M. R. *Adjustment to physical handicap and illness: A survey of the social psychology of physique and disability.* Bulletin 55 (rev.). New York: Social Science Research Council, 1953.

Bart, W. M. Issues in measuring formal operational reasoning. *The Genetic Epistemologist*, 1978, *7*, 3–4.

Beach, F. A. Levels of plasma testosterone in human males at different ages. In W. Montagna and W. A. Sadler, eds., *Reproductive behavior.* New York: Plenum Publishing Corporation, 1974.

Bell, N. D. The relationship of occupational choice to ego identity and self-concept. Unpublished doctoral dissertation, Utah University, 1969.

Benedict, R. *Patterns of culture.* New York: New American Library, 1950.

_____. Continuities and discontinuities in cultural conditioning. In R. E. Muuss, ed., *Adolescent behavior and society: A book of readings*, 3rd ed. New York: Random House, 1980.

Berndt, T. J., and Berndt, E. G. Children's use of motives and intentionality in person perception and moral judgment. *Child Development,* 1975, *46*, 904–912.

Blatt, M. Experimental studies in moral education using a developmental approach. Unpublished doctoral dissertation, University of Chicago, 1959.

Block, J. Ego identity, role variability, and adjustment. *Journal of Consulting Psychology*, 1961, *25*, 392–397.

Blos, P. *The adolescent personality: A study of individual behavior.* New York: D. Appleton-Century, 1941.

_____. *On adolescence: A psychoanalytic interpretation.* New York: Free Press, 1962.

_____. The initial stage of male adolescence. *The psychoanalytic study of the child.* New York: International Universities Press, 1965, Vol. 20, 145–164.

_____. The second individuation process of adolescence. *The psychoanalytic study of the child.* New York: International Universities Press, 1967, Vol. 22, 162–186.

_____. *The young adolescent: Clinical studies.* New York: Free Press, 1970.

_____. The child analyst looks at the young adolescent. *Daedalus*, 1971, *100*, 961–978.

_____. *The adolescent passage: Developmental issues*. New York: International Universities Press, 1979.

_____. Modifications in the traditional psychoanalytic theory of female adolescent development. In S. C. Feinstein, P. L. Giovacchini, J. G. Looney, A. Z. Schwartzberg, and A. D. Sorosky, *Adolescent Psychiatry*, Vol. 8. Chicago: University of Chicago Press, 1981.

Bob, S. An investigation of the relationship between identity status, cognitive style, and stress. Unpublished doctoral dissertation, State University of New York at Buffalo, 1968.

Bourne, E. The state of research on ego identity: A review and appraisal. Part I. *Journal of Youth and Adolescence*, 1978, *7*, 223–251.

Boyd, W. *The history of Western education*. New York: Barnes & Noble Books, 1965.

Breuer, H. Ego identity status in late-adolescent college males, as measured by a group-administered incomplete sentence blank and related to inferred stance toward authority. Unpublished doctoral dissertation, New York University, 1973.

Brittain, C. V. Adolescent choices and parent-peer cross-pressures. *American Sociological Review*, 1963, *28*, 385–391.

_____. Age and sex of siblings and conformity toward parents versus peers in adolescence. *Child Development*, 1966, *37*, 709–714.

Bronson, G. W. Identity diffusion in late adolescents. *Journal of Abnormal and Social Psychology*, 1959, *59*, 414–417.

_____. Fear of visual novelty: Developmental patterns in males and females. In L. J. Stone, H. T. Smith, and L. B. Murphs, eds., *The competent infant*. New York: Basic Books, 1973.

Brownstone, J. E., and Willis, R. H. Conformity in early and late adolescence. *Developmental Psychology*, 1971, *4*, 334–337.

Bruner, J. S. *The process of education*. New York: Vintage Books, 1960.

Bunt, M. E. Ego identity: Its relationship to the discrepancy between how an adolescent views himself and how he perceives that others view him. *Psychology*, 1968, *5*, 14–25.

Burk, D. *Piagetian attainment kit*. Monterey, Calif.: Publishers Test Service, 1973.

Byrne, D. F. The development of role taking in adolescence. *Dissertation Abstract*, 1974, *34*, No. 11, 5647B.

Calhoun, J. F. *Abnormal psychology: Current perspectives*, 2nd ed. New York: CRM/Random House, 1977.

Cattell, R. B., and Scheier, I. H. *The meaning and measurement of neuroticism and anxiety*. New York: Ronald Press, 1961.

Cauble, M. A. Formal operations, ego identity, and principled morality: Are they related? *Developmental Psychology*, 1976, *12*, 363–364.

Chandler, M. J. Egocentrism and antisocial behavior: The assessment and training of social perspective-taking skills. *Developmental Psychology*, 1973, *9*, 326–332.

_____. Social cognition: A selective review of current research. In W. F. Overton and J. McCarthy Gallagher, eds., *Knowledge and development: Advances in research and theory*, Vol. 1. New York: Plenum Publishing Corporation, 1977.

Comenius, J. A. *The great didactic* (M. W. Keatinge, ed. and trans.). London: A. & C. Black, 1923.

Committee on adolescence, group for the advancement of psychiatry. *Normal adolescence*. New York: Charles Scribner's Sons, 1968.

Conger, J. J. *Adolescence and youth: Psychological development in a changing world*, 2nd ed. New York: Harper & Row, 1977.

Constantinople, A. An Eriksonian measure of personality development in college students. *Developmental Psychology*, 1969, *1*, 357–372.

Corsini, R. J. *Current personality theories*. Itasca, Ill.: F. E. Peacock, 1977.

Costanzo, P. R. Conformity and development as a function of self-blame. *Journal of Personality and Social Psychology*, 1970, *14*, 366–374.

Costanzo, P. R., and Shaw, M. E. Conformity as a function of age level. *Child Development*, 1966, *37*, 967–975.

Cross, H. J., and Allen, J. G. Paternal antecedents of identity status in college males. Paper presented at The Eastern Psychological Association Annual Meeting, Philadelphia, 1969.

_____. Ego identity status, adjustment, and academic achievement. *Journal of Consulting and Clinical Psychology*, 1970, *34*, 288.

_____. Antecedents of identity status: Differences between males and females. Paper presented at the Eastern Psychological Association Meeting, New York, 1971.

Damon, W. *The social world of the child*. San Francisco: Jossey-Bass, 1977.

_____. Patterns of change in children's social reasoning: A two-year longitudinal study. *Child Development*, 1980, *51*, 1010–1017.

Darwin, C. R. *The origin of species by means of natural selection*. London: J. Murray, 1859.

Davis, A. Socialization and adolescent personality. In *Adolescence, Yearbook of the National Society for the Study of Education*, 1944, *43*, Part 1.

Deutsch, F. Observational and sociometric measures of peer popularity and their relationship to egocentric communication in female preschoolers. *Developmental Psychology*, 1974, *10*, 745–747.

Dollard, J., Miller, N. E., Doob, L. W., Mowrer, O. H., and Sears, R. R. *Frustration and aggression*. New Haven, Conn.: Yale University Press, 1939.

Donovan, J. M. A study of ego identity formation. *Dissertation Abstract*, 1971, *B31*, 4986–4987.

_____. Identity status and interpersonal style. *Journal of Youth and Adolescence*, 1975, *4*, 37–55.

Douvan, E., and Adelson, J. *The adolescent experience.* New York: John Wiley & Sons, 1968.

Dufresne, J., and Cross, J. H. Personality variables in student drug use. Unpublished master's thesis, University of Connecticut, 1972.

Dulit, E. Adolescent thinking à la Piaget: The formal stage. *Journal of Youth and Adolescence,* 1972, *1,* 281–301.

Dye, P., Marquiss, J., and LaVoie, J. C. Ego identity in normal and socially maladjusted adolescent females. Unpublished manuscript, University of Nebraska at Omaha, 1975.

Eisenberg-Berg, N., and Mussen, P. Empathy and moral development in adolescence. *Developmental Psychology,* 1978, *14,* 185–186.

Elardo, P. Project AWARE: A school program to facilitate social development of children. Paper presented at the Fourth Annual H. Blumberg Symposium, Chapel Hill, N.C., 1974.

Elardo, P., and Cooper, M. *AWARE: Activities for social development.* Menlo Park, Calif.: Addison-Wesley, 1977.

Elkind, D. Children's discovery of the conservation of mass, weight, and volume: Piaget replication study II. *Journal of Genetic Psychology,* 1961, *98,* 219–227(a).

_____. Quantity conceptions in junior and senior high school students. *Child Development,* 1961, *32,* 551–560(b).

_____. Egocentrism in adolescence. *Child Development,* 1967, *38,* 1025–1034.

_____. Cognitive structure and adolescent experience. *Adolescence,* 1967/68, *2,* 427–434.

_____. Cognitive development in adolescence. In J. F. Adams, ed., *Understanding adolescence.* Boston: Allyn & Bacon, 1968.

_____. Is Piaget passé in elementary education? *Genetic Epistemologist,* 1978, *7,* 1–2.

Elkind, D., and Bowen, R. Imaginary audience behavior in children and adolescents. *Developmental Psychology,* 1979, *15,* 38–44.

Engelmann, W. Reifungsentwicklung und Reifungsveränderung im gefühls betonten Wertungsbereich unserer Jugend. *Psychologische Rundschau,* 1962, *12,* 131–140.

Enright, R. D. Social cognition in children: A model for intervention. *Counseling Psychologist,* 1976, *6,* 65–70.

Enright, R. D., Lapsley, D. K., and Shukla, D. G. Adolescent egocentrism in early and late adolescence. *Adolescence,* 1979, *14,* 687–695.

Enright, R. D., Shukla, D. G., and Lapsley, D. K. Adolescent egocentrism-sociocentrism and self-consciousness. *Journal of Youth and Adolescence,* 1980, *9,* 101–116.

Enright, R. D., and Sutterfield, S. J. An ecological validation of social cognition development. *Child Development,* 1980, *51,* 156–161.

Erikson, E. H. *Childhood and society.* New York: W. W. Norton & Co., 1950.

———. *Young man Luther.* New York: W. W. Norton & Co., 1958.

———. Identity and the life cycle: Selected papers. *Psychological Issues Monographic Series I.,* No. 1. New York: International Universities Press, 1959.

———, ed. *The challenge of youth.* Garden City, N.Y.: Doubleday/Anchor Books, 1965.

———. *Identity, youth and crisis.* New York: W. W. Norton & Co., 1968.

———. *Gandhi's truth.* New York: W. W. Norton & Co., 1969.

———. Autobiographic notes on the identity crisis. *Daedalus,* 1970, *99,* 730–759.

Eron, L. D., Walder, L. O., Toigo, R., and Lefkowitz, M. M. Social class, parental punishment for aggression, and child aggression. *Child Development,* 1963, *34,* 849–867.

Feshbach, N. D. Empathy: An interpersonal process. Paper presented at the meeting of the American Psychological Association, Montreal, 1973.

———. Empathy in children: Some theoretical and empirical considerations. *Counseling Psychologist,* 1975, *5,* 25–30.

Fisher, S., and Greenberg, R. P. *The scientific credibility of Freud's theories and therapy.* New York: Basic Books, 1977.

Flanagan, J. C. Findings from project TALENT. *Educational Forum,* 1979, *43,* 489–490.

Flavell, J. H. *The developmental psychology of Jean Piaget.* New York: D. Van Nostrand, 1963(a).

———. Piaget's contributions to the study of cognitive development. *Merrill-Palmer Quarterly,* 1963, *9,* 245–252(b).

———. *The development of role-taking and communications skills in children.* New York: John Wiley & Sons, 1968.

———. The development of inferences about others. In T. Mischel, ed., *Understanding other persons.* Oxford: Blackwell, Basil, Mott, 1974.

———. *Cognitive development.* Englewood Cliffs, N.J.: Prentice Hall, 1977.

———. Metacognition. In E. Langer (Chair), *Current perspectives on awareness and cognitive processes.* Symposium presented at the meeting of the American Psychological Association, Toronto, 1978.

Flynn, W. R. The pursuit of purity: A defensive use of drug abuse in adolescence. *Adolescence,* 1970, *5,* 141–150.

Forman, G. E., and Sigel, I. E. *Cognitive development: A life-span view.* Monterey, Calif.: Brooks/Cole Publishing Co., 1979.

Freud, A. *Introduction to psychoanalysis for teachers.* London: George Allen & Unwin, Ltd., 1931.

———. *The ego and the mechanisms of defense* (C. Baines, trans.). New York: International Universities Press, 1948.

Freud, S. *Further remarks on the neuro-psychoses of defense*. Standard edition, Vol. 3. London: Hogarth, 1962. (Originally published 1896.)

_____. *The interpretation of dreams*. Standard edition, Vols. 4 & 5. London: Hogarth, 1953. (Originally published 1900.)

_____. *Notes upon a case of obsessional neurosis*. Standard edition, Vol. 10. London: Hogarth, 1955. (Originally published 1909.)

_____. *The unconscious*. Standard edition, Vol. 14. London: Hogarth, 1957. (Originally published 1915.)

_____. *The ego and the id*. Standard edition, Vol. 19. London: Hogarth, 1961. (Originally published 1923a).

_____. *The infantile genital organization of the libido*. Collected Papers, Vol. 2. London: Hogarth, 1949. (Originally published 1923b).

_____. Three contributions to the sexual theory. *Nervous and Mental Disease Monograph Series*, No. 7. New York: Nervous and Mental Disease Publishing Co., 1925.

_____. *New introductory lectures on psycho-analysis*. Standard Edition, Vol. 22. London: Hogarth, 1964. (Originally published 1933.)

_____. *Analysis, terminable and interminable*. Collected Papers, Vol. 5. London: Hogarth, 1950. (Originally published 1937.)

_____. *A general introduction to psychoanalysis* (J. Riviere, trans.). New York: Permabooks, 1953.

Furth, H. G. *An inventory of Piaget's developmental tasks*. Washington, D.C.: Catholic University Center for Research in Thinking and Language, 1970.

_____. Children's societal understanding and the process of equilibration. In W. Damon, ed., *New directions for child development*, Vol. 1. San Francisco: Jossey-Bass, 1978.

Furth, H. G., and Wachs, H. *Thinking goes to school: Piaget's theory in practice*. New York: Oxford University Press, 1975.

Furth, H. G., Baur, M., and Smith, J. W. Children's conceptions of social institutions: A Piagetian framework. *Human Development*, 1976, *19*, 351–374.

Gallagher, J. M. The future of formal thought research: The study of analogy and metaphor. In B. Z. Presseisen, D. Goldstein, and M. Appel, eds., *Topics in cognitive development: Language and operational thought*, Vol. 2. New York: Plenum Publishing Corporation, 1978.

Gardner, H. *The arts and human development*. New York: John Wiley, 1973.

Gesell, A. Maturation and the patterning of behavior. In C. Murchison, ed., *A handbook of child psychology*, 2nd ed. Worcester, Mass.: Clark University Press, 1933.

_____. Reciprocal interweaving in neuromotor development: A principle of development evidenced in the patterning of infant behavior. *Journal of Comparative Neurology*, 1939, *70*, 161–180.

_____. Twins T and C from infancy to adolescence: A biogenetic study of individual differences by the method of co-twin control. *Genetic Psychology Monographs*, 1939, *24*, 3–121.

———. The ontogenesis of infant behavior. In L. Carmichael, ed., *Manual of child psychology*. New York: John Wiley & Sons, 1946.

———. *Studies in child development*. New York: Harper and Brothers, 1948.

———. *The first five years of life*. New York: Harper and Brothers, 1940.

Gesell, A., and Ilg, F. L. *Infant and child in the culture of today*. New York: Harper and Brothers, 1943.

———. *The child from five to ten*. New York: Harper and Brothers, 1946.

Gesell, A., Ilg, F. L., and Ames, L. B. *Youth: The years from ten to sixteen*. New York: Harper and Brothers, 1956.

Gesell, A., and Thompson, H. Learning and growth in identical infant twins. *Genetic Psychology Monographs*, 1929, *6*, 1–124.

Glucksberg, S., Krauss, R. M., and Higgens, T. The development of referential communication skills in children. In F. D. Horowitz, ed., *Review in child development research*, Vol. 4. Chicago: University of Chicago Press, 1975.

Godenne, G. Counseling handicapped adolescents. In R. E. Muuss, ed., *Adolescent behavior and society: A book of readings*, 3rd. ed. New York: Random House, 1980, Chap. 31.

Gordon, C. Self-conceptions: Configurations of content. In C. Gordon and K. J. Gergen, eds., *The self in social interaction*, Vol. 1. New York: John Wiley & Sons, 1968.

Green, R. Human sexuality: Research and treatment frontier. In S. Arieti, ed., *American handbook of psychiatry*, 2nd ed., Vol. 6. New York: Basic Books, 1976.

Greulich, W. W. Physical changes in adolescence. In *Adolescence, Yearbook of the National Society for the Study of Education*, 1944, *43*, Part I.

Gruen, W. Rejection of false information about oneself as an indication of ego identity. *Journal of Consulting Psychology*, 1960, *24*, 231–233.

Haan, N., Smith, M. B., and Block, J. Moral reasoning of young adults: Political-social behavior, family background, and personality correlates. *Journal of Personality and Social Psychology*, 1968, *10*, 183–201.

Hall, C. S. *A primer of Freudian psychology*. New York: World Publishing, 1954.

Hall, G. S. *Adolescence*. 2 vols. New York: Appleton, 1916.

Hamburg, D. A., and Lunde, D. T. Sex hormones in the development of sex differences in human behavior. In E. E. Maccoby, ed., *The development of sex differences*. Stanford, Calif.: Stanford University Press, 1966, pp. 1–24.

Hampden-Turner, C., and Whitten, P. Morals left and right. *Psychology Today*, 1971, *4*, No. 11, 39–43.

Harris, D. B. The climate of achievement. *Child Study*, 1958, *34*, 8–14.

Hartshorne, H., and May, M. A. *Studies in the nature of character*. 3 vols. New York: Macmillan, 1928–1930.

Hartsoeker, N. *Essai de Dioptrique*. Sect. 88, Paris, 1964.

Havighurst, R. J. The development of the ideal self in childhood and adolescence. *Journal of Educational Research*, 1946, *40*, 241–257.

_____. *Developmental tasks and education*. New York: Longmans, Green, 1951.

Havighurst, R. J., and MacDonald, D. V. Development of the ideal self in New Zealand and American children. *Journal of Educational Research*, 1955, *49*, 263–273.

Hayes, J. M. Ego identity and moral character development in male college students. Unpublished doctoral dissertation, The Catholic University of America, 1977.

Healy, W., Bronner, A. F., and Bowers, A. M. *The structure and meaning of psychoanalysis*. New York: Alfred A. Knopf, 1930.

Hickey, J. E. The effects of guided moral discussion upon youthful offenders' level of moral judgment. *Dissertation Abstracts International*, 1972, *33* (4–A), 1551.

Hill, J. P., and Palmquist, W. J. Social cognition and social relations in early adolescence. *International Journal of Behavioral Development*, 1978, *1*, 1–36.

Hill, S. D., and Tomlin, C. Self-recognition in retarded children. *Child Development*, 1981, *52*, 145–150.

Hobbes, T. *Leviathan*. London: 1651.

Hoffman, M. L. Empathy, role-taking, guilt, and the development of altruistic motives. In T. Lickona, ed., *Moral development and behavior: Theory, research and social issues*. New York: Holt, Rinehart & Winston, 1976.

Howard, M. R. Ego identity status in women, fear of success, and performance in a competitive situation. Unpublished doctoral dissertation, State University of New York at Buffalo, 1975.

Hudson, L. M., Peyton, E. F., and Brion-Maisels, S. Social reasoning and relating: An analysis of videotaped social interactions. In H. Furth (Chair), *Integrations of development in social cognition and social behavior*. Symposium presented at the meeting of the American Psychological Association, Washington, D.C., 1976.

Hughes, R. Jr., Tingle, B. A., and Sawin, D. B. Development of empathic understanding in children. *Child Development*, 1981, *52*, 122–128.

Hunt, J. McV. *Intelligence and experience*. New York: Ronald Press, 1961.

Inhelder, B. Cognitive development and its contribution to the diagnosis of some phenomena of mental deficiency. *Merrill-Palmer Quarterly*, 1966, *12*, 299–319.

Inhelder, B., and Piaget, J. *The growth of logical thinking* (A. Parsons and S. Milgram, trans.). New York: Basic Books, 1958.

Iscoe, I., Williams, M., and Harvey, J. Modification of children's judgments by a simulated group technique: A normative developmental study. *Child Development*, 1963, *34*, 963–978.

Jamison, W., and Signorella, M. L. Sex-typing and spatial ability: The association between masculinity and success on Piaget's water-level task. *Sex Roles*, 1980, *6*, 345–353.

Jessor, S. L., and Jessor, R. Transition from virginity to nonvirginity among youth: A social-psychological study over time. *Developmental Psychology*, 1975, *11*, 473–484.

Jones, R. M. *An application of psychoanalysis to education.* Springfield, Ill.: Charles C Thomas, 1960.

Jordan, D. Parental antecedents of ego identity formation. Unpublished master's thesis, State University of New York at Buffalo, 1970.

———. Parental antecedents and personality characteristics of ego identity statuses. Unpublished doctoral dissertation, State University of New York at Buffalo, 1971.

Josselson, R. L. Psychodynamic aspects of identity formation in college women. *Journal of Youth and Adolescence*, 1973, *2*, 3–52.

Josselson, R., Greenberger, E., and McConochie, D. Phenomenological aspects of psychosocial maturity in adolescence. *Journal of Youth and Adolescence*, 1977, *6*, 25–55, 145–167.

Kaplan, L., and Baron, D. *Mental hygiene and life.* New York: Harper & Brothers, 1952.

Keasey, C. B. Social participation as a factor in the moral development of preadolescents. *Developmental Psychology*, 1971, *5*, 216–220.

Keating, D. P. A search for social intelligence. *Journal of Educational Psychology*, 1978, *70*, 218–223.

Keating, D. P., and Clark, L. V. Development of physical and social reasoning in adolescence. *Developmental Psychology*, 1980, *16*, 23–30.

Keating, D. P., and Schaefer, R. Ability and sex differences in the acquisition of formal operations. *Developmental Psychology*, 1975, *11*, 531–532.

Kelley, H. H. The processes of causal attribution. *American Psychologist*, 1973, *28*, 107–128.

Keniston, K. Social change and youth in America. In E. H. Erikson, ed., *The challenge of youth.* Garden City, N.Y.: Doubleday/Anchor, 1965.

———. Youth: A "new" stage of life. *The American Scholar*, 1970, *39*, 631–654.

———. The tasks of adolescence. In *Developmental psychology today.* Del Mar, Calif.: CRM Books, 1971, Chap. 20.

King, M. L. *Why we can't wait.* New York: Harper & Row, 1964.

Kohlberg, L. The development of children's orientations toward a moral order. *Vita Humana*, 1963, *6*, 11–33.

———. Development of moral character and moral ideology. In M. L.

Hoffman and L. W. Hoffman, eds., *Review of child development research,* Vol. 1. New York: Russell Sage Foundation, 1964.

_____. Moral and religious education and the public schools: A developmental view. In T. R. Sizer, ed., *Religion and public education.* Boston: Houghton Mifflin, 1967.

_____. Stage and sequence: The cognitive-developmental approach to socialization. In D. A. Goslin, ed., *Handbook of socialization theory and research.* Chicago: Rand McNally & Company, 1969.

_____. Moral development and the education of adolescents. In R. F. Purnell, ed., *Adolescents and the American high school.* New York: Holt, Rinehart & Winston, 1970.

Kohlberg, L., and Blatt, M. The effects of classroom discussion on level of moral development. In L. Kohlberg and E. Turiel, eds., *Recent research in moral development.* New York: Holt, Rinehart & Winston, 1972.

Kohlberg, L., and Gilligan, C. The adolescent as a philosopher. In J. Kagan and R. Coles, eds., *Twelve to sixteen: Early adolescence.* New York: W. W. Norton & Co., 1972.

Kohlberg, L., and Kramer, R. Continuities and discontinuities in childhood and adult moral development. *Human Development*, 1969, *12*, 93–120.

Kubie, L. S. *Neurotic distortion of the creative process.* Lawrence Kans.: University of Kansas Press, 1958.

_____. Introduction. In R. M. Jones, *An application of psychoanalysis to education.* Springfield, Ill.: Charles C Thomas, 1960.

Kuhn, D. The significance of Piaget's formal operations stage in education. *Journal of Education*, 1979, *161*, 34–50.

Kuhn, M. H., and McPartland, T. S. An empirical investigation of self-attitudes. *American Sociological Review*, 1954, *19*, 68–76.

Kurdek, L. A. Perspective taking as a cognitive basis of children's moral development: A review of the literature. *Merrill-Palmer Quarterly*, 1978, *24*, 3–28.

LaFleur, N. K., and Johnson, R. G. Separate effects of social modeling and reinforcement in counseling adolescents. *Journal of Counseling Psychology*, 1972, *19*, 292–295.

Lambert, G. B., Rothschild, B. F., Atland, R., and Green, L. B. *Adolescence: Transition from childhood to maturity*, 2nd ed. Monterey, Calif.: Brooks/Cole Publishing Co., 1978.

Lavatelli, C. *Early childhood curriculum: A Piaget program.* Boston: American Science and Engineering, 1970.

LaVoie, J. C. Ego identity formation in middle adolescence. *Journal of Youth and Adolescence*, 1976, *5*, 371–385.

Lewin, K. Environmental forces in child behavior and development. In C. Murchison, ed., *Handbook of child psychology.* Worchester, Mass.: Clark University Press, 1931.

———. *A dynamic theory of personality*. New York: McGraw-Hill Book Company, 1935.

———. *Principles of topological psychology*. New York: McGraw-Hill Book Company, 1936.

———. The conceptual representation and the measurement of psychological forces. Duke University Series, *Contributions to Psychological Theory*, 1938, *1* (4).

———. Field theory and experiment in social psychology: Concepts and methods. *American Journal of Sociology*, 1939, *44*, 868–896.

———. Studies in topological and vector psychology: I. Formalization and progress in psychology. *University of Iowa Studies in Child Welfare*, 1940, *16*, 9–42.

———. Field theory and learning. In *The Psychology of Learning, the Yearbook of the National Society for the Study of Education*, 1942, *41*, Part II.

———. Behavior and development as a function of the total situation. In L. Carmichael, ed., *Manual of child psychology*. New York: John Wiley & Sons, 1946.

———. *Resolving social conflicts*. New York: Harper and Brothers, 1948.

———. *Field theory and social science*. New York: Harper & Row, 1951.

Liben, L. S. Operative understanding of horizontality and its relation to long-term memory. *Child Development*, 1974, *45*, 416–424.

———. Long-term memory for pictures related to seriation, horizontality, and verticality concepts. *Developmental Psychology*, 1975, *11*, 795–806.

———. Performance on Piagetian spatial tasks as a function of sex, field dependence, and training. *Merrill-Palmer Quarterly*, 1978, *24*, 97–110.

Liben, L. S., and Golbeck, S. L. Sex differences in performance on Piagetian spatial tasks: Differences in competence or performance? *Child Development*, 1980, *51*, 594–597.

Livesley, W. J., and Bromley, D. B. *Person perception in childhood and adolescence*. New York: John Wiley & Sons, 1973.

Locke, J. *An essay concerning human understanding*. London: 1753.

———. Treatise on civil government. In *The work of John Locke*. London: 1768.

Loevinger, J. The meaning and measurement of ego development. *American Psychologist*, 1966, *21*, 195–206.

———. *Ego development*. San Francisco: Jossey-Bass, 1976.

Looft, W. R. Egocentrism and social interaction in adolescence. *Adolescence*, 1971, *6*, 485–494.

Lovell, K. A follow-up study of Inhelder and Piaget's *The growth of logical thinking*. *British Journal of Psychology*, 1961, *52*, 143–154.

McCandless, B. R. *Adolescents behavior and development*. Hinsdale, Ill.: Dryden Press, 1970.

Mahler, C. The assessment and the evaluation of the coping styles of two ego identity status groups: Moratorium and foreclosure, to identity conflict arousing stimuli. Unpublished master's thesis, State University of New York at Buffalo, 1969.

Mahler, M. S. Thoughts about development and individuation. *The Psychoanalytic Study of the Child*, 1963, *18*, 307–324.

Marcia, J. E. Development and validation of ego-identity status. *Journal of Personality and Social Psychology*, 1966, *3*, 551–558.

———. Ego identity status: Relationship to change in self-esteem, "general maladjustment," and authoritarianism. *Journal of Personality*, 1967, *35*, 118–133.

———. The case history of a construct: Ego identity status. In E. Vinacke, ed., *Readings in general psychology*. New York: Van Nostrand Reinhold, 1968.

———. Identity six years after: A follow-up study. *Journal of Youth and Adolescence*, 1976, *5*, 145–160(a).

———. Studies in ego identity. Unpublished research monograph, Simon Fraser University, 1976(b).

———. Identity in adolescence. In J. Adelson, ed., *Handbook of adolescent psychology*. New York: John Wiley & Sons, 1980.

Marcia, J. E., and Friedman, M. L. Ego identity status in college women. *Journal of Personality*, 1970, *38*, 249–263.

Marsh, D. T., Serafica, F. C., and Barenboim, C. Effect of perspective-taking training on interpersonal problem solving. *Child Development*, 1980, *51*, 140–145.

Martin, B. Parent-child relations. In F. D. Horowitz, ed., *Review of child development research*, Vol. 4. Chicago: University of Chicago Press, 1975.

Matteson, D. R. Alienation vs. exploration and commitment: Personality and family correlaries of adolescent identity statuses. *Report from the Project for Youth Research*. Copenhagen: Royal Danish School of Educational Studies, 1974.

Mead, G. H. *Mind, self and society*. Chicago: University of Chicago Press, 1934.

Mead, M. The primitive child. In C. Murchison, ed., *A handbook of child psychology*, 2nd ed. Worcester, Mass.: Clark University Press, 1933.

———. Educative effects of social environment as disclosed by studies of primitive societies. *Environment and Education: A Symposium, Human Development Series*, 1942, *1* (54).

———. What is happening to the American family? *Journal of Social Casework*, 1947, *28*, 323–330.

———. *Male and female*. New York: William Morrow & Co., 1949.

———. *Coming of age in Samoa*. New York: New American Library, 1950.

———. Adolescence in primitive and in modern society. In G. E. Swanson,

T. M. Newcomb, E. L. Hartley, eds., *Readings in social psychology*, rev. ed. New York: Henry Holt, 1952.

―――. *Growing up in New Guinea*. New York: New American Library, 1953.

―――. Age patterning in personality development. In W. E. Martin and C. B. Stendler, eds., *Readings in child development*. New York: Harcourt, Brace, 1954.

―――. The young adult. In E. Ginzberg, ed., *Values and ideals of American youth*. New York: Columbia University Press, 1961.

Mead, M., and Macgregor, F. C. *Growth and culture*. New York: G. P. Putnam's Sons, 1951.

Meilman, P. W. Cross-sectional age changes in ego identity status during adolescence. *Developmental Psychology*, 1979, *15*, 230–231.

Miller, N. E. The frustration-aggression hypothesis. *Psychological Review*, 1941, *48*, 337–342.

Miller, N. E., and Dollard, J. *Social learning and imitation*. New Haven, Conn.: Yale University Press, 1941.

Mischel, W. *Introduction to personality*. New York: Holt, Rinehart & Winston, 1971.

Montemayor, R., and Eisen, M. The development of self-conceptions from childhood to adolescence. *Developmental Psychology*, 1977, *13*, 314–319.

Moore, S. G. Social cognition: Knowing about others. *Young Children*, 1979, *34*, 54–61.

Mowrer, O. H. A stimulus-response analysis of anxiety and its role as a reinforcing agent. *Psychological Review*, 1939, *46*, 553–565.

Muuss, R. E. *First-aid for classroom discipline problems*. New York: Holt, Rinehart & Winston, 1962.

―――. Adolescent development and the secular trend. *Adolescence*, 1970, *5*, 267–284(a).

―――. Puberty rites in primitive and modern societies. *Adolescence*, 1970, *5*, 109–128(b).

―――. Eine Taxonomie der Psychologie der Adoleszenz. *Der Kinderarzt*, 1979, Vol. 10, #10, 1471–1475; #11, 1637–1642; #12, 1801–1809.

―――. Die Entwicklung der Egozentrizität in der Kindheit und der Adoleszenz. *Der Kinderarzt*, 1981, Vol. 12, #2, 189–193; #3, 339–343; #4, 519–531.

―――. Psychosoziale Probleme der Sexualität in der Adoleszenz. In T. Hellbrügge, ed., *Entwicklung der kindlichen Sexualität*. Berlin: Urban & Schwarzberg (in press).

Neale, J. M. Egocentrism in institutionalized and noninstitutionalized children. *Child Development*, 1966, *37*, 97–101.

Neuber, K. A., and Genthner, R. W. The relationship between ego identity, personal responsibility, and facilitative communication. *Journal of Psychology*, 1977, *95*, 45–49.

Offer, D. *The psychological world of the teenager*. New York: Basic Books, 1969.

Ojemann, R. H., and Pritchett, K. Piaget and the role of guided experiences in development. *Perceptual and Motor Skills*, 1963, *17*, 927–940.

Oppenheimer, L. The development of the processing of social perspectives: A cognitive model. *International Journal of Behavioral Development*, 1978, *1*, 149–171.

Orlofsky, J. L. Identity formation, nAchievement, and fear of success in college men and women. *Journal of Youth and Adolescence*, 1978, *7*, 49–62.

Orlofsky, J. L., Marcia, J. E., and Lesser, I. M. Ego identity status and the intimacy versus isolation crisis of young adulthood. *Journal of Personality and Social Psychology*, 1973, *27*, 211–219.

Oshman, H., and Manosevitz, M. The impact of the identity crisis on the adjustment of late adolescent males. *Journal of Youth and Adolescence*, 1974, *3*, 207–216.

Papalia, D. E., and Olds, S. W. *A child's world*, 2nd ed. New York: McGraw-Hill, 1979.

Patel, A. S., and Gordon, J. E. Some personal and situational determinants of yielding to influence. *Journal of Abnormal and Social Psychology*, 1960, *61*, 411–418.

Patterson, H. O., and Milakofsky, L. A paper-and-pencil inventory for the assessment of Piaget's tasks. *Applied Psychological Measurement*, 1980, *4*, 341–353.

Petrone, F. R. *The developmental kindergarten: A Piagetian basic skills program*. Bryn Mawr, Pa.: Educational Consultation Services, 1976.

Piaget, J. *The child's conception of the world*. New York: Harcourt, Brace, 1929.

_____. *The child's conception of physical causality*. London: Kegan Paul, 1930.

_____. *The language and thought of the child*, 2nd ed. New York: Harcourt, Brace, 1932(a).

_____. *The moral judgment of the child*. London: Kegan Paul, 1932(b).

_____. The moral development of the adolescent in two types of society, primitive and "modern." Lecture given to the United Nations Educational, Scientific and Cultural Organization, Paris, 1947(a).

_____. *The psychology of intelligence* (M. Piercy and D. E. Berlyne, trans.). New York: Harcourt, Brace, 1947(b).

_____. *The child's conception of number*. New York: Humanities Press, 1952(a).

_____. *The origins of intelligence in children* (M. Cook, trans.). New York: W. W. Norton & Co., 1952(b).

_____. *The construction of reality in the child*. New York: Basic Books, 1954.

_____. Three lectures. *Bulletin of the Menninger Clinic*, 1962, *26*, 120–145.

_____. The attainment of invariants and reversible operations in the development of thinking. *Social Research*, 1963, *30*, 283–299.

_____. *Six psychological studies*. New York: Random House, 1967.

_____. Intellectual evolution from adolescence to adulthood. In R. E. Muuss, ed., *Adolescent behavior and society: A book of readings*, 3rd ed. New York: Random House, 1980.

Piaget, J., and Inhelder, B. *The psychology of the child* (H. Weaver, trans.). New York: Basic Books, 1969.

_____. *The child's conception of space*. London: Routledge & Kegan Paul, 1967.

Pinard, A., and Laurendeau, M. A scale of mental development based on the theory of Piaget: Description of a project. *Journal of Research in Science Teaching*, 1964, *2*, 253–260.

Plato. *The republic* (B. Jowett, trans.). Oxford: Clarendon Press, 1921.

_____. Phaedo. In *The dialogues of Plato* (B. Jowett, trans.), Vol. 1, 3rd ed. New York: Random House, 1937.

_____. Laws. In *The dialogues of Plato* (B. Jowett, trans.), Vol. 4, 4th ed. Oxford: Clarendon Press, 1953.

Podd, M. H. Ego identity status and morality: The relationship between two developmental constructs. *Developmental Psychology*, 1972, *6*, 497–507.

Podd, M. H., Marcia, J. E., and Rubin, B. M. The effects of ego identity and partner perception on a prisoner's dilemma game. *Journal of Social Psychology*, 1970, *82*, 117–126.

Poppen, P. J. The development of sex differences in moral judgment for college males and females. Unpublished doctoral dissertation, Cornell University, 1974.

Rank, O. *Will therapy and truth and reality*. New York: Alfred A. Knopf, 1945.

Rasmussen, J. E. Relationship of ego identity to psychosocial effectiveness. *Psychological Reports*, 1964, *15*, 815–825.

Ray, W. J., Georgiou, S., and Ravizza, R. Spatial abilities, sex differences, and lateral eye movements. *Developmental Psychology*, 1979, *15*, 455–457.

Rest, J. R. The cognitive developmental approach to morality: The state of the art. *Counseling and Values*, 1974, *18*, 64–78.

Rosen, C. E. The effects of sociodramatic play on problem-solving behavior among culturally disadvantaged preschool children. *Child Development*, 1974, *45*, 920–927.

Rosen, G. M., and Ross, A. O. Relationship of body image to self-concept. *Journal of Consulting and Clinical Psychology*, 1968, *32*, 100.

Rousseau, J. J. *Émile* (W. H. Payne, trans.). New York: Appleton, 1911.

Rowe, I., & Marcia, J. E. Ego identity status, formal operations, and moral development. *Journal of Youth and Adolescence*, 1980, *9*, 87–99.

Rubin, K. H. Relationship between egocentric communication and popularity among peers. *Developmental Psychology*, 1972, *7*, 364.

_____. Egocentrism in childhood: A unitary construct? *Child Development*, 1973, *44*, 102–110.

_____. Social interaction and communicative egocentrism in preschoolers. *Journal of Genetic Psychology*, 1976, *129*, 121–124.

Rubin, K. H., and Schneider, F. W. The relationship between moral judgment, egocentrism, and altruistic behavior. *Child Development*, 1973, *44*, 661–665.

Saltzstein, H. D., Diamond, R. M., and Belenky, M. Moral judgment level and conformity behavior. *Developmental Psychology*, 1972, *7*, 327–336.

Schenkel, S. Relationship among ego identity status, field-independence, and traditional femininity. *Journal of Youth and Adolescence*, 1975, *4*, 73–82.

Schenkel, S., and Marcia, J. E. Attitudes toward premarital intercourse in determining ego identity status in college women. *Journal of Personality*, 1972, *40*, 472–482.

Schmuck, R. Sex of sibling, birth order position, and female dispositions to conform in two-child families. *Child Development*, 1963, *34*, 913–918.

Schoeppe, A., and Havighurst, R. J. A validation of development and adjustment hypotheses of adolescence. *Journal of Educational Psychology*, 1952, *43*, 339–353.

Sears, R. R. *Survey of objective studies of psychoanalytic concepts*. New York: Social Science Research Council, 1943.

_____. A theoretical framework for personality and social behavior. *American Psychologist*, 1951, *6*, 476–483.

Sears, R. R., Maccoby, E. E., and Levin, H. *Patterns of child rearing*. Evanston, Ill.: Row, Peterson, 1957.

Selman, R. L. The relation of role taking to the development of moral judgment in children. *Child Development*, 1971, *42*, 79–91(a).

_____. Taking another's perspective: Role-taking development in early childhood. *Child Development*, 1971, *42*, 1721–1734(b).

_____. Social-cognition understanding: A guide to educational and clinical practice. In T. Lickona, ed., *Moral development and behavior: Theory, research and social issues*. New York: Holt, Rinehart & Winston, 1976(a).

_____. Toward a structural analysis of developing interpersonal relations concepts: Research with normal and disturbed preadolescent boys. In A. D. Pick, ed., *Minnesota symposia on child psychology*, Vol. 10. Minneapolis: University of Minnesota Press, 1976(b).

_____. A structural-developmental model of social cognition: Implications for intervention research. *Counseling Psychologist*, 1977, *6*, 3–6.

_____. *The growth of interpersonal understanding: Developmental and clinical analyses*. New York: Academic Press, 1980.

Selman, R. L., and Byrne, D. F. A structural-developmental analysis of levels of role taking in middle childhood. *Child Development*, 1974, *45*, 803–806.

Selman, R. L., Jaquette, D., and Lavin, D. Interpersonal awareness in children: Toward an integration of developmental and clinical child psychology. *American Journal of Orthopsychiatry*, 1977, *47*, 264–274.

Shantz, C. U. The development of social cognition. In M. F. Hetherington, ed., *Review of child development research*, Vol. 5. Chicago: University of Chicago Press, 1975.

Sherif, M., and Cantril, H. *The psychology of ego-involvements*. New York: John Wiley & Sons, 1947.

Shock, N. W. Physiological changes in adolescence. In *Adolescence, Yearbook of the National Society for the Study of Education*, 1944, *43*, Part I.

Shure, M. B., and Spivack, G. *Problem-solving techniques in childrearing*. San Francisco: Jossey-Bass, 1978.

_____. Interpersonal problem solving as a mediator of behavioral adjustment in preschool and kindergarten children. *Journal of Applied Developmental Psychology*, 1980, *1*, 29–44.

Simmons, R. G., Rosenberg, F., and Rosenberg, M. Disturbance in the self-image at adolescence. *American Sociological Review*, 1973, *38*, 553–568.

Spiegel, L. A. A review of contributions to a psychoanalytic theory of adolescence: Individual aspects. In R. S. Eissler, A. Freud, H. Hartman, and E. Kris, eds., *The Psychoanalytic Study of the Child*, Vol. 6. New York: International Universities Press, 1951.

Spivack, G., and Shure, M. B. *Social adjustment of young children*. San Francisco: Jossey-Bass, 1974.

Spivack, G., Platt, J. J., and Shure, M. B. *The problem-solving approach to adjustment*. San Francisco: Jossey-Bass, 1976.

Steinberg, L. D., Greenberger, E., Jacobi, M., and Garduque, L. Early work experience: A partial antidote for adolescent egocentrism. *Journal of Youth and Adolescence*, 1981, *10*, 141–157.

Stuart, R. B. Decentration in the development of children's concepts of moral and causal judgment. *Journal of Genetic Psychology*, 1967, *111*, 59–68.

Sullivan, E. V., and Hunt, D. E. Interpersonal and objective decentering as a function of age and social class. *Journal of Genetic Psychology*, 1967, *110*, 199–210.

Sund, R. B. *Piaget for educators: A multimedia program*. Columbus, Ohio: Charles E. Merrill, 1976.

Tagiuri, R. Person perception. In G. Lindzey and E. Aronson, eds., *The handbook of social-psychology*, Vol. 3, 2nd ed. Reading, Mass.: Addison-Wesley, 1969.

Tagiuri, R., and Petrullo, L., eds., *Person perception and interpersonal behavior*. Stanford, Calif.: Stanford University Press, 1958.

Tanner, J. M. *Growth at adolescence*, 2nd ed. Oxford: Blackwell, 1962.

_____. Earlier maturation in man. *Scientific American*, 1968, *218*, 21–27.

Thomas, H., and Jamison, W. On the acquisition of understanding that still water is horizontal. *Merrill-Palmer Quarterly*, 1975, *21*, 31–44.

Thomas, H., Jamison, W., and Hummel, D. Observation is insufficient for discovering that the surface of still water is invariantly horizontal. *Science*, 1973, *181*, 173–174.

Tierney, M. C., and Rubin, K. H. Egocentrism and conformity in early childhood. *Journal of Genetic Psychology*, 1975, *126*, 209–215.

Toder, N. L., and Marcia, J. E. Ego identity status and response to conformity pressure in college women. *Journal of Personality and Social Psychology*, 1973, *26*, 287–294.

Turiel, E. An experimental test of the sequentiality of developmental stages in the child's moral judgments. *Journal of Personality and Social Psychology*, 1966, *3*, 611–618.

_____. Developmental processes in the child's moral thinking. In P. Mussen, J. Langer, and M. Covington, eds., *Trends and issues in developmental psychology*. New York: Holt, Rinehart & Winston, 1969.

_____. The development of social concepts: Mores, customs, and conventions. In D. J. DePalma and J. M. Foley, eds., *Moral development: Current theory and research*. Hillsdale, N.J.: Erlbaum, 1975.

_____. Social regulations and domains of social concepts. In W. Damon, ed., *New directions for child development*, Vol. 1. San Francisco: Jossey-Bass, 1978.

Urberg, K. A. Sex role conceptualizations in adolescents and adults. *Developmental Psychology*, 1979, *15*, 90–92.

Uzgiris, I. C., and Hunt, J. McV. *Assessment in infancy: Ordinal scale of psychological development*. Urbana: University of Illinois Press, 1976.

Wachtel, P. L. *Psychoanalysis and behavior therapy*. New York: Basic Books, 1977.

Wagner, J. A study of the relationship between formal operations and ego identity in adolescence. Unpublished doctoral dissertation, State University of New York at Buffalo, 1976.

Waterman, A. S., and Goldman, J. A. A longitudinal study of ego identity development at a liberal arts college. *Journal of Youth and Adolescence*, 1976, *5*, 361–369.

Waterman, A. S., and Waterman, C. K. The relationship between ego identity status and satisfaction with college. *Journal of Educational Research*, 1970, *64*, 165–168.

_____. Relationship between freshman ego identity status and subsequent academic behavior: A test of the predictive validity of Marcia's categorization system for identity status. *Developmental Psychology*, 1972, *6*, 179.

Waterman, C. K., Beubel, M. E., and Waterman, A. S. Relationship between resolution of the identity crisis and outcomes of previous psychosocial crises. *Proceedings 78th Annual Convention American Psychological Association*, 1970, 467–468.

Waterman, C. K., and Nevid, J. S. Sex differences in the resolution of the identity crisis. *Journal of Youth and Adolescence*, 1977, *6*, 337–342.

Waterman, C. K., and Waterman, A. S. Ego identity status and decision styles. *Journal of Youth and Adolescence*, 1974, *3*, 1–6.

Wegner, D. M., and Vallacher, R. R. *Implicit psychology: An introduction to social cognition*. New York: Oxford University Press, 1977.

Weikart, D. P., Roger, L., and Adcock, C. *The cognitively oriented curriculum*. Washington, D.C.: National Association for the Education of Young Children, 1971.

Weiner, B., ed., *Achievement motivation and attribution theory*. Morristown, N.J.: General Learning Press, 1974.

Weinheimer, S. Egocentrism and social influence in children. *Child Development*, 1972, *43*, 567–578.

Weir, M. W. Developmental changes in problem-solving strategies. *Psychological Review*, 1964, *71*, 473–490.

White, G. M. The elicitation and durability of altruistic behavior in children. *Research Bulletin* No. 67–27. Princeton N.J.: Educational Testing Service, 1967.

White, R. W. Competence and the psychosexual stages of development. *Nebraska Symposium on Motivation*, Vol. 8. Lincoln: University of Nebraska Press, 1960.

Williams, F. E. *Adolescence: Studies in mental hygiene*. New York: Farrar and Rinehart, 1930.

Wolf, T. M. Effects of live modeled sex-inappropriate play behavior in a naturalistic setting. *Developmental Psychology*, 1973, *9*, 120–123.

Wylie, R. C., and Hutchins, E. B. Schoolwork-ability estimates and aspirations as a function of socioeconomic level, race, and sex. *Psychological Reports*, 1967, *21*, 781–808. Monograph Supplement 3–V21.

Youniss, J. Another perspective on social cognition. In A. D. Pick, ed., *Minnesota symposia on child psychology*, Vol. 9. Minneapolis: University of Minnesota Press, 1975.

INDEX

Abraham, K., 41, 293
abstract thinking, 190–193, 264
accommodations, 178–182, 205–206
acculturation, 168, 173
adaptation, 178, 180–181
Adelson, J., 91, 298
adolescence:
  age norms in, 2–7, 116–118, 148–150, 166–170
  aggression and, 114–115, 273–274, 277, 281–287
  biology of, 3–5, 109, 111, 113, 152–153
  concept of, 2–3, 6–7, 26, 28–29, 98, 167
  early, 4, 7, 77, 98–99, 102, 107, 114–116, 124, 164, 260
  egocentrism, 228, 233, 259–263
  late, 2, 7, 77, 98, 100, 105, 117–120, 202, 215, 265, 276
  as marginal man, 2, 95, 149–152, 155–156
  middle, 7, 87–88, 98, 115–117, 171, 202, 218, 260, 276
  personality development in, 45–48, 98–100, 133–135
  psychosexual conflicts of, 45–47
  sexuality in, 13, 56–58, 117, 120, 122–123, 131–132, 137
adolescent behavior, 142, 145–146, 152–159, 160–161, 170–174
adolescent development:
  Aristotle on, 12–14
  Barker on, 153–157
  Blos on, 96–99, 107–120
  cultural anthropology, 131–136, 152–154, 167, 169, 273, 276–278
  egocentrism in, 233, 254–263

  Erikson on, 61–64, 68–72
  Freud on, 39–48
  Gesell on, 166–173
  Hall on, 27–28
  Havighurst on, 162–164
  individual variability and, 98, 100–104, 124–125, 152–154, 167, 169
  Lewin on, 145–152
  libidinal drive and, 47, 110, 114–118
  Marcia on, 74–76, 81–82
  maturation in, 124, 165–175
  moral, per Kohlberg, 211–217
  personality structure vs., 99–100, 134–135, 278
  physical vs. emotional changes in, 157–158
  physiological changes in, 3–5, 109, 111, 113, 152–153
  Piaget on, 86, 178–191, 209–211
  Plato on, 9–12
  retardation of, 86–87, 122, 137
  Rousseau on, 23–25
  social reinforcement vs., 273, 276–279
Aebli, H., 205, 206, 293
aggressive behavior:
  in adolescence, 14, 102–103, 118, 273–274, 277, 283–287
  dependency and, 284, 286, 287
  in early adolescence, 114–115
  frustration and, 272, 283
  imitation in, 273–274, 281–282
Ames, L. B., 2, 165–173, 301
anal stage, 32–33, 40–46, 55, 98, 112
Andrews, J., 90, 293
anxiety, 36, 38, 48, 286
  in adolescent development, 86–87, 100, 102–104, 137, 160–162
  choice making and, 139–140

identity status and, 86–87
socialized vs. neurotic, 161
application component of social cognition, 230–231
Aristotle, 8, 12–14, 16, 18, 23, 26, 27, 165*n,* 224, 283, 293
Arlin, P. K., 201, 203, 293
asceticism, 33, 47, 52–53, 117
assimilation, 178, 180–182, 205–206
Ausubel, D. P., 2–5, 8, 16, 131, 293
authoritarianism, 78, 86–87
autoerotic phases, 41–42
autonomy, 62, 65–66, 74, 90, 96, 100, 103, 107, 109–111, 211

Baldwin, A. L., 44, 233, 270, 293
Baldwin, C. P., 233, 293
Baldwin, J. M., 228, 293
Ball, W. B., 224, 293
Bandura, A., 272–291, 294
Barker, R., 14, 145, 152–157, 295
Bart, W. M., 203, 295
Beach, F. A., 3–4, 276, 295
behavioristic learning theory, 270, 279–283
Bell, N. D., 91, 295
Benedict, R., 126–133, 140, 295
Berndt, T. G., 233, 295
biological evolution, 25–26
biological factors:
    in adolescence, 109, 111, 113, 123–124, 305
    in cognitive approach, 177–178
    per cultural anthropologists, 126, 131–132, 134–135
    in developmental tasks, 162–163
    Gesell on, 166–169, 173–174
bisexual tendencies, 109, 115–116
Blatt, M., 211, 226, 295, 304
Block, J., 78, 222, 295, 301
Blos, P., 60, 96–124, 164, 259, 262, 295–296
Bob, S., 84–85, 296
body image, 70, 148, 158
Bourne, E., 84, 296
Bowen, R., 233, 264–265, 298
Boyd, W., 17, 296
boys:
    aggressive behavior in, 285–286
    body changes in pubescent, 4–5
    identity development in, 78
    oedipal conflict in, 42–43, 47–48, 104
    phallic stage in, 42–43

relations with fathers/mothers, 38, 42–43, 47–48, 89, 105–106, 113
sexual maturation retard in, 86–87, 122, 137
Breuer, H., 86, 87, 296
Brittain, C. V., 101, 275, 296
Bronson, G. W., 74, 78–79, 98, 120, 296
Brownstone, J. E., 101, 296
Bruner, J. S., 205–206, 227, 230, 296
Bunt, M. E., 296
Burk, D., 206, 296
Byrne, D. F., 228–229, 233–235, 250–251, 296, 310

Calhoun, J. F., 50, 296
Calvin, J., 14–15
castration anxiety, 38, 43, 47–48, 96–97, 104–106, 111, 113–114
cathexis, 52
Cattell, R. B., 102, 136*n,* 277*n,* 278, 296
Cauble, M. A., 86, 296
Chandler, M. J., 233–234, 266–267, 296
childhood, 12, 18, 24
    Aristotle on, 12–13
    development in, 180–187
    Erikson on, 65–68
    Hall on, 28
    life space in, 144, 147
    Locke on, 21–22
    maturation in, 2, 24, 166–168
    minority group status of, 154–155
    Plato on, 10–11
    Rousseau on, 22–25
childrearing:
    aggressive behavior and, 277
    in family disorganization, 122–123
    Gesell on, 167–168, 173
    permissiveness in, 24, 27, 56–57, 130
    in primitive societies, 127–136
choice making, 13, 135, 138–139
clinical method, 176, 208
cognitive development, 176–208, 212, 217, 220–221, 225–227, 234–235, 240, 255–256
combinatorial system of operations, 191–195, 200, 259
Comenius, J. A., 17–19, 25, 28, 297
concrete operational stage, 178, 184–187, 250, 257–258
conflict formation, 98, 107–109
conflict resolution, 43, 73, 98, 107–110, 237–247
conformity, 14, 69, 72, 81, 85–86, 101,

119, 136, 138, 155–156, 212, 214, 220, 238, 264, 269, 277
Conger, J. J., 36, 49, 102, 297
conscience, 24, 38, 47, 118, 215–216, 287, 289
conscious, 32, 33–35, 37, 39–40, 52
consciousness, 20, 24, 34, 46, 50, 53, 62
Constantinople, A., 73, 76, 297
continuity in development, 24, 27, 126–130, 133–135, 152–159, 166–168, 172–173, 273, 276–278
conventional moral level, 211–212, 214–215, 219, 220–222
Corsini, R. J., 56, 297
Costanzo, P. R., 101, 297
crisis, adolescent, 74–75, 146
Cross, H. J., 74, 84–85, 88, 90, 297–298
cultural anthropology, 3, 27, 125–139, 169, 271
cultural behavior, 160
cultural conditioning, 126–130, 139
  in adolescent heterosexuality, 276
  in adolescent social learning, 160–162, 170–172
  discontinuities of, 126–128, 139, 153–154
  in primitive societies, 135–136
cultural relativism, 21, 126, 131–132, 135

Damon, W., 233, 297
Darwin, C., 8, 12, 25–27, 30, 32, 52, 297
Davis, A., 160–162, 297
decentered thinking, 177, 189–190, 210, 213, 243, 245–246, 255–256
defense mechanisms, 33, 35, 37, 47, 49–56, 111, 114
delinquent behavior, 36, 59, 72, 110, 171, 285
democratic values, 20–22, 81, 173
denial, 33, 47, 50, 54–55, 111
dependency anxiety, 284, 286–287
despair, 62, 74
Deutsch, F., 264, 297
developmental tasks, 59, 61, 74, 97, 105, 116, 118, 120, 162–164
differential perspective stage, 236, 240–243, 250
discipline, 16, 57, 122, 129, 131, 173
displacement, 33, 51, 55, 111
Dollard, J., 271, 273*n*, 283, 297, 307
Donovan, J. M., 74, 85, 87, 89, 297
Douvan, E., 91, 298

drive organization, 98–99, 101, 107–108, 115, 117–120
drug use, 77, 90, 262, 274
Dufresne, J., 90, 298
Dulit, E., 191, 202, 207, 298
Dye, P., 87, 298

early adolescence, 4, 7, 77, 98–99, 102, 107–108, 113–116, 124, 164, 260
education:
  Blos on, 120–124
  in child development, 18–19
  in field theory, 157–159
  Gesell on, 173–175
  identity development and, 92–95
  Mead on, 135–139
  moral values in, 223–226
  Piaget on, 203–208
  psychoanalytical approach in, 56–59
  Rousseau on, 22–25, 57
  social cognition and, 251–253, 267–269
  in social learning, 287–291
ego, 32–40, 47, 70–71, 97, 111, 114, 117, 120, 229
ego, defense of, 33, 49–56
ego development, 36–40, 63, 70, 107–110, 114, 117–119, 122
ego function, 86, 98, 101
ego ideal, 38, 108, 118–120
ego identity, 61, 63, 66, 70, 72, 81, 137, 164, 221
ego organization, 98–99, 118, 120
ego reorganisation, 107–108
ego strength, 83, 270, 278
ego, tripartite model, 35–40, 118
egocentric undifferentiated stage, 236, 239–240, 250
egocentric uniqueness, 261–262
egocentrism, 228, 233, 254–269
  Piaget on, 177–178, 228
Eisenberg-Berg, N., 233, 298
ejaculation, 4, 5
Elardo, P., 233, 252–253, 296
Elkind, D., 185, 206–207, 233, 254–269, 296
empiricism, 19–21
Engelman, W., 114, 298
Enright, R. D., 252, 265, 298
epigenetic principle of development, 61–62, 107
epistemology, 177, 207
equilibrium, cognitive, 178, 181, 187, 202–203, 226

Erasmus, Desiderius, 17
Erikson, E. H., 33, 60–97, 99, 103, 118, 125, 128, 137, 145, 164, 212, 221, 227, 276, 299
Eron, L. D., 286, 299
existence component, 230

father:
  in homosexual male orientations, 48, 106
  in oedipal conflict situations, 38, 42, 43, 105
  son relations with, 88–89, 113
fear of success, 85
femininity, 98, 106, 117
Feshbach, N. D., 233, 299
field independence, 85–86
field theory, 140–159
Fisher, S., 32, 35, 38, 42, 43, 48, 99, 299
fixation, 40, 41
Flanagan, J. C., 119, 154, 299
Flavell, J. H., 178–180, 196, 230, 232–233, 299
Flynn, W. R., 90, 299
foreclosure subjects, 75–76, 79–81, 85–86, 89, 221
Foreman, G. E., 239, 299
formal operations, 86, 185–191, 200–203, 217, 220–221, 255–262
free movement, in life space, 142–145
Freud, A., 33, 52–53, 57, 59–60, 117, 299
Freud, S., 9, 30–60, 67, 94, 97–99, 106, 125, 140, 145, 164, 212, 271, 276, 300
Friedenberg, E., 13, 82, 92, 223
friendship, 14, 29, 45, 73, 111, 114, 171, 233, 238–242, 245–247
friendship concepts domain, 236–237, 240, 250
frustration, 40, 49, 54, 56, 57, 94, 141, 154, 270, 283
frustration-aggression hypothesis, 272, 283
Furth, H. G., 176, 206, 233, 300

Gallagher, J. M., 201, 300
Gardner, H., 201–202, 300
generativity, 62, 73
genital stage, 33, 40, 45–48, 98
Gesell, A., 2, 9, 13, 27, 145, 165–175, 181, 212, 300–301
Gestalt psychology, 140, 159, 177

girls:
  adolescent stage, per Gesell, 170
  body changes in pubescent, 4–5
  heterosexual aggressiveness in, 114, 125
  identity status, 74–91
  puberty rites for, 149
  pubescent spurt in, 112, 121
  in Samoa, 3–4, 127–132
Gluecksberg, S., 233, 301
Godenne, G., 260, 301
Gordon, C., 234, 301
Green, R., 98, 301
Greenberg, R. P., 32, 35, 38, 42–43, 48, 99, 299
Greulich, W. W., 4–5, 301
growth gradients, 165–172
Gruen, W., 78, 88, 120, 301
guilt, 38, 47–48, 62, 66–67, 100, 117, 214

Haan, N., 222, 301
Hall, C. S., 39, 101
Hall, G. Stanley, 6, 8, 23, 25–29 passim, 125, 165, 169, 301
Hamburg, D. A., 98, 301
Hampden-Turner, C., 212, 220, 223, 301
Harris, D. B., 143, 301
Hartshorne, H., 209, 224, 301
Hartsoecker, N., 17, 302
Havighurst, R. J., 19, 114, 151–164, 302, 310
Hayes, J. M., 89, 302
Healy, W., 46, 302
Helvetius, C. A., 20
heredity, in development, 165–168
heterosexual development:
  in adolescence, 45–48, 114–119
  cultural factors in, 276
  premature, 121, 136
Hickey, J. E., 226, 302
Hill, J. P., 234, 302
Hill, S. D., 233, 302
Hobbes, T., 20, 302
Hoffman, M. L., 233, 302
homosexual development/personality, 32, 45, 47–48, 105, 112–115, 127
homunculus theory, 9, 15–17, 19, 23
Howard, M. R., 85, 88, 302
Hudson, L. M., 252, 302
Hughes, R., 233, 302
Hull, C., 271
human nature, 125, 132
  empiricist view of, 19–21

Greek philosophers on, 9–14
medieval view of, 14–18, 21
psychoanalytic view of, 32
Rousseau on, 22
Hunt, J. McV., 199–200, 206, 302, 312

id, 9, 32–33, 35–40, 47, 110, 118
identification, 80, 114
as defense mechanism, 33, 51–52, 54
in social learning, 270, 273–276, 284, 287, 289–290
identity, 60, 67–72, 137
in cognitive operations, 188, 196
search for, 188
identity crisis, 61–72, 75, 76, 96, 277
identity/development/status, 52, 62, 68–72, 74–92, 94, 221
achievement, 69, 75–79, 83–92, 221
confusion, 62–65, 68–75
crises, 61, 63–75, 83, 90, 93, 96, 221
diffusion, 63, 65–69, 75–79, 86–92, 221
foreclosure, 75–76, 79–93, 221
moral reasoning, 89, 221
moratorium, 75–76, 81–93, 137, 221–222
research, 84–92
Ilg, F. L., 2, 165–174, 301
imaginary audience, 260–261, 264–265
imitation, 51, 270–271, 273–276, 280, 287–290
independence, 116–118, 126, 159
indestructibility, belief in, 262
individual concepts domain, 236–237, 239, 240
individual differences, 6, 11, 16, 123–124, 151–153, 166–168, 278
individuation processes, 97, 99–104, 107
industry, 62, 67–68, 96
infancy:
autistic isolation in, 65
ego development in, 37
egocentrism in, 256–257
Freud on, 36–37, 41–42
Gesell on, 167–168, 173
life space in, per Lewin, 142–143
maturation in, 167–168
phases of, per Piaget, 182–183
self-regulation in, 172
inference component, 230–231
inferiority, 62, 67–68
Inhelder, B., 176–181, 185, 188–199, 202, 211, 257, 259, 302, 309

initiative, 62, 66–67, 96
innate ideas, 11–12, 15, 19–21
integrity, 62, 73–74
intellectualization, 33, 47, 52–53, 117
intelligence, 10
cognition and, 176–180, 190, 198, 203
identity status and, 84–86
structure of, 190, 198
intelligence tests, 176–177, 202–203
interindividual differences, 278
internalization, 54, 182
interpersonal cognition, 228–229, 232–235
interpersonal concordance orientation, 214, 220–221, 250
intimacy, 53, 62, 70–73, 83, 91, 137, 238
introjection, 33, 54
Iscoe, I., 101, 302
isolation:
as defense mechanism, 52
identity achievement vs., 62, 68–69, 72–73

Jacquette, D., 233, 235, 242–243, 247, 249, 251, 310–311
Jamison, W., 207, 303, 311–312
Jessor, R., 115, 122, 303
Jones, R. M., 57–58, 303
Jordan, D., 88–89, 303
Josselson, R. L., 90, 92, 303

Kaplan, L., 40, 303
Keasey, C. B., 225, 303
Keating, D. P., 207, 229, 233, 303
Kelley, H. H., 233, 303
Keniston, K., 2, 69, 80, 84, 303
King, M. L., Jr., 216, 303
Kinsey report, 45, 59, 119
Kohlberg, L., 89, 209–227, 230, 233, 235, 240, 243, 245, 248, 250–251, 303–304
Kubie, L. S., 34, 58, 80, 304
Kuhn, D., 201–202, 304
Kuhn, M. H., 77, 79, 82, 234, 304
Kurdek, L. A., 233–234, 304

LaFleur, N. K., 289, 304
Lambert, G. B., 50, 304
language, 18, 59, 66, 70, 83–85, 137, 183, 186, 255, 257, 275, 279–281
Lapsley, D. K., 265, 298
late adolescence, 2, 7, 77, 98, 100, 105, 117–120, 202, 215, 265, 276

latency, 33, 40, 43–48, 58, 67, 98, 102, 104–107, 109
Laurendeau, E., 176, 206, 309
Lavatelli, C., 206, 304
Lavin, D., 233, 235, 242–243, 247, 249, 310–311
LaVoie, J. C., 84, 86–89, 298, 304
law and order, 214, 217, 226
leadership, 237, 240–247, 249–251
learned behavior, 127
learning:
  cultural, 161
  empirical approach to, 20
  Erikson on, 68, 92–95
  imitation and, 275
  in field theory, 158–159
  maturation and, 174–175
  Plato on, 11–12
  Renaissance change in, 17–18
  resistance to, 203–204
  social learning, 270–291
Lesser, I. M., 72, 83, 90, 308
Lewin, K., 14, 126, 140–157, 164, 169, 170, 304–305
Liben, L. S., 207, 305
libido, 39–44, 47, 53, 55, 104–106, 110, 114–118
life space, 100, 140–147, 164
Livesley, W., 233, 305
Locke, J., 8–9, 15, 19–21, 305
Loevinger, J., 118–119, 122, 305
logical inversion, 196
logical thinking, 176–180, 183–191
  combinatorial systems in, 191–200
  egocentrism and, 257–258
  moral judgment and, 220–221, 228–229
  social cognition and, 229–230
  utilization of, 201–208
Looft, W. R., 233, 254–255, 258–259, 305
Lovell, K., 204, 305
loyalty, 213, 237, 243, 245, 247, 251

Maccoby, E. E., 285–286, 310
Mahler, C., 87, 305–306
Mahler, M. S., 99, 306
Marcia, J. E., 72, 74–93, 221, 306, 308–309, 310, 312
marginal man concept, 2, 95, 149–152, 155–156
Marsh, D. T., 252, 306
Martin, B., 253, 306
masculinity, 106, 117, 121, 124

masturbation, 3–4, 40–42, 45, 51, 111, 114–115, 129
Matteson, D. R., 86, 306
maturation, 123–124, 165–175
  genetic factors in, 167–168
  Hall on, 27
  Piaget on, 180
  Rousseau on, 24
  stresses of, 126–140
mature identity, 74, 221–222
maturity profiles, of Gesell, 169–172
McCandless, B. R., 102, 305
McConochie, D., 92, 303
McDonald, F. J., 274, 278, 288, 294
Mead, G. H., 228, 235, 306
Mead, M., 4, 13, 81–82, 122, 125–126, 129–149, 276, 306–307
mechanisms of defense, 33, 35, 37, 47, 49–56, 111, 114
Meilman, P. W., 76, 77, 307
menstruation, 5, 127, 132–133
middle adolescence, 7, 87–88, 98, 115–117, 171, 202, 218, 260, 276, 279
Miller, N. E., 271–273, 283, 297, 307
Mischel, W., 274, 278, 280, 289, 294, 307
mistrust, 53, 61–65, 77
modeling, 270, 273–276, 280–281, 288–290
Montemayor, R., 233–234, 307
Moore, S. G., 229, 253
moral behavior, 209–211, 215, 222–227
moral development, 209–227, 234
moral judgment:
  age and, 212, 215, 277–278
  cognition, 220–221, 227, 235, 251, 253, 264
  cultural differences in, 217–220
  in identity development, 89
  Piaget on, 177–178, 209–211
moral reasoning, 89, 213, 216–221, 229, 232, 278
moratorium subject/status, 75–76, 81–83, 86–88, 90–93, 137, 221–222
mother, in oedipal conflict, 38, 42–43, 47–48, 51, 104–107, 114
Mowrer, O. H., 160, 271, 297, 307
mutual perspective taking stage, 236, 245–248, 250
Mussen, P., 233, 298
Muuss, R. E., 57, 95, 120, 122, 136, 233, 307

narcissism, 41, 46, 58, 102–103, 259
Neale, J. M., 264, 307

need component, 230, 231
negative oedipal conflict, 104, 106, 112–113
Neill, A. S., 57
Neuber, K. A., 90, 307

obedience, 16, 94, 210, 213, 220, 224, 238, 240, 250
object choice, 36, 42, 44, 46–47, 108
object permanence, 182–183, 257
oedipal conflict, Oedipus complex, 32–33, 38, 42–43, 46–48, 51, 67–68, 98–100, 103–107, 110, 113–114, 116–117
Offer, D., 277, 308
Ojemann, R. H., 205, 308
Olds, S. W., 250, 308
operational egocentrism, 257–258
operational stages, 178–180, 183–186, 191, 210, 220, 255, 257–258, 278
Oppenheimer, L., 241, 246, 308
oral stage, 32–33, 40–42, 46, 98, 111
Orlofsky, J. L., 72, 74, 83, 85, 90, 308
Oshman, H., 87, 89, 308

Papalia, D. E., 250, 308
parent-child concepts domain, 236, 238, 240
parents, 38, 42–43, 80, 103, 122
   adolescent ambivalence toward, 116–117
   in adolescent development, 47–48, 79, 100–101, 122–123
   in aggressive behavior formation, 285–287
   behavior modeling by, 100, 281
   peer groups vs., 101–102, 138, 274
   in socialization, 122, 284
   social learning role of, 272, 281
Patel, A. S., 101, 308
Patterson, H. O., 176, 206, 308
peer group concepts domain, 236–238, 240, 243, 245
peer groups, 109, 119, 136, 149–151, 153–158, 269, 277
   in adolescent individuation, 100–101
   in identity development, 69–72, 80
   parents vs., as models, 101–102, 138, 274
penis envy, 43, 96, 111
perceptual role taking, 232
personal fable, 261, 265
personality, 10
   ego development and, 35–36, 63
   Gesell on, 165

personality confusion, 72
personality consolidation, 118
personality development:
   in adolescence, 45–48, 98–100, 133–135
   anal stage in, 32–33, 42
   in late adolescence, 118
   life space and, 143
   oral type, 32–33, 41–42
personality traits, 278
Petrone, F. R., 206, 308
phallic stage, 40, 42–44, 46–47, 98, 103, 106, 111
phenomenological viewpoint, 159, 254
Piaget, J., 10, 18, 19, 86, 110, 145, 176–212, 220–221, 227, 229–230, 232, 235, 240, 243, 245, 250–251, 255, 257, 259, 261–264, 276, 278, 308–309
Pinard, M., 176, 206, 309
Plato, 9–12, 16, 19, 283, 309
pleasure principle, 36, 39–40, 105
Podd, M. H., 86–89, 221, 309
Poppen, P. J., 89, 309
postadolescence, 98–99, 107, 119–120
postconventional moral development, 211–212, 215, 221–223
preadolescent stage, 48, 107–108, 110–113, 231, 243–244, 274, 277, 288
   age norms for, 7
   aggressive drive in, 110–112
   cognitive development in, 190–191
   development in, 24, 98, 110–113
   of girls, 106, 111–113
   regresssion and delinquency in, 110–111
preconscious, 32–34, 39–40, 108
preconventional moral level, 211–212, 219–221
preformationist childhood, 8–9, 16–17
preoperational egocentrism, 257
preoperational stage, 178–184, 186, 210, 250, 255, 278
prepuberty, 45, 98, 109–110
primary sex characteristics, 2–5, 108, 123, 148, 169
primitive societies, 2–4, 6, 125–139, 149, 218
projection, 33, 49, 54, 111
promiscuity, 33, 36, 53, 73, 117, 127
psychoanalytical theory, 30–59, 270
   Blos on, 96–124
   child training, 56–58
   cultural anthropology and, 125, 135

Erikson on, 60–95
Freud on, 30–59
in education, 56–59, 92–95, 120–124
psychosexual development, 33, 38–48,
62, 98–99
puberty/pubescence:
adolescence vs., 2–3, 98–100, 136–137
Ausubel on, 2–5
biological onset of, 4–5, 7
genital stage as, 45–48
homosexual component in, 48, 105
as new birth, 23, 28
oedipal conflict revival in, 47–48, 103
superego development and, 38–39
puberty rites, 3, 95, 150
punishment, 16, 38, 56, 67, 160, 210,
213, 216, 220, 237–238, 240–243, 245,
247–251, 281, 286–288

radicalism, 222–223
Rank, O., 33, 53, 117, 164, 309
rationalization, 33, 47, 49–50, 54, 90,
120
Ray, W. J., 207, 309
reaction formation, 33, 46, 53–54, 111
reality:
in adolescent development, 147–148,
158–160
in cognitive development, 183, 190,
191
Gesell on, 165*n*
in operational thinking, 100, 191
principle, 36–38, 104
social vs. logical, 229–230
reality-irreality level, 145–147, 158
recapitulation theory, 9, 25, 27–29, 100,
104, 165
reciprocal operations, 196–197
reciprocal social perspectives, 236,
243–245, 250
Redl, F., 229
regression, 40–41, 47, 74, 96–97, 102–
106, 111, 168, 270
reinforcement:
behavioral, 271–272, 274
in learning, 290–291
in social learning, 270, 275, 278–284,
288, 290
relations, logic of, 184–185
repression, 33, 35, 39, 46–47, 50–51, 58–
59, 111, 129, 270
Rest, J. R., 233, 309

reversibility, 179–180, 185–187, 196, 208,
220
role change:
ego identity and, 63, 67, 68
role diffusion, 68–69, 71–72, 75
role taking, 225–226, 232–235, 254, 256,
263, 268
romantic naturalism, 22–25
Rosen, C. E., 252, 309
Rosen, G. M., 148, 309
Rosenberg, F., 264–265, 311
Ross, A. D., 148, 281, 309
Rousseau, J. J., 8, 17, 22–25, 57, 138,
173, 309
Rowe, I., 86, 89, 309
Rubin, K. H., 86, 88, 209, 210, 233,
263–264, 309, 310, 312

Saltzstein, H. D., 214, 310
Samoan society, 3–4, 127–132, 149
savage stage, 24
Scheier, I. H., 277*n*, 296
schema, 178–179, 182, 191, 209, 225, 264
Schenkel, S., 74, 84–86, 91–92, 310
Schmuck, R., 101, 310
Schoeppe, A., 163, 310
Sears, R., 271, 273, 285–286, 297, 310
second individuation process, 97–103
secondary sex characteristics, 2–5, 69,
108, 123, 148, 169
self-awareness, 66, 109, 171, 228, 234,
237–238, 240–241, 244, 246, 249
self-consciousness, 24, 66, 102, 108,
110–111, 263–265
self-doubt, 62, 65, 66, 72
self-esteem, 25, 78, 87–88, 91, 118–120,
290
self-reinforcement, 271, 274, 281–282
Selman, R. L., 68, 226–253, 269, 310–
311
sensorimotor egocentrism, 256–257
sensorimotor stage, 178, 182–183, 250,
255–256
serialization, 184–185
sex differences:
Blos on, 97–98, 112
in egocentrism, 263–264
Freud on, 32
in identity development, 86–87, 90–92
in maturation, 121, 136
in oedipal conflict resolution, 97, 104–
106
in Piagetian tasks, 207

sex roles, 78, 92–93, 117, 127, 129, 148, 163, 164
sexual identity, 67, 70, 93, 100, 118–119
sexual latency, 44–45, 67, 98, 104, 109–110, 133
sexual maturation, 2, 97–98, 120–121, 136, 158
sexual regression, 40–41
sexuality, 31, 33, 42, 53–54, 56–58
  adolescent, 13–14, 56–58, 115–117, 120
  aggressive boys and, 286
  in ego identity, 67, 70, 72, 75–76
  frustration avoidance in, 56–57
  peer group, 101, 274
  premature development of, 121–122
  projection of, 54
  in Samoan society, 130–131
  sublimation of, 58–59
shame, 62, 65–66
Shantz, C. U., 230–232, 234, 256, 268, 311
Sherif, M., 3, 131, 311
Shock, N. W., 5, 311
Shure, M. B., 229, 233, 252–253, 311
Simmons, R. G., 264–265, 311
Skinner, B. F., 271–273, 279, 281, 283
social cognition, 68, 178, 227–269
social egocentrism, 266–269
socialization, 69, 134, 143, 160–167, 271–272, 277, 282–287
socialized anxiety, 160–162
social learning, theory of, 3, 9, 21, 143, 228, 270–291
social perspective taking, 226, 232, 236–239, 241, 250–253, 266–267
social problem solving, 228–229, 232, 252–253
social role taking, 228, 235, 251
societal perspective taking stage, 236, 248–251
sociobehavioristic approach, 272–273, 276–283
sociocentric development, 212, 263–266
sociocentric language, 183, 185–186, 225, 255, 263–264
somatic maturation, 98, 107, 110, 116–118, 123, 153–154
somatopsychology, 152–157
speech patterns, 155, 183, 186, 263–264, 274–275
Spiegel, L. A., 48, 311
Spivack, G., 229, 233, 252–253, 311
stagnation, 62, 73, 77

Steinberg, L. D., 268, 311
storm and stress *(Sturm und Drang),* 28–29, 129, 169, 277
Stuart, R. B., 263–264, 311
sublimation, 46, 55–56, 58–59
Sullivan, E. V., 263, 311
Sund, R. B., 206, 311
superego, 32–33, 35, 38–40, 43–44, 47, 51–52, 58–89, 105, 110–111, 114, 118–120
suppression, 50

tabula rasa, 8–9, 20–21, 133
Tagiuri, R., 232–233, 311
Tanner, J. M., 108, 120–121, 153, 311
teachable moment, 19, 162
Tertullian, Q. S. F., 14
Thomas, H., 207, 311–312
Tierney, M. C., 264, 312
time confusion/perspective, 62–64, 145–147, 154, 157–158, 174
Toder, N. L., 86–87, 312
toilet training, 31, 37, 41–42, 65, 160
trust, 14, 61–65, 77, 96, 237, 242, 245, 247, 249–250
Turiel, E., 211, 226, 233, 312

unconscious, 30–36, 39–40, 47, 50–51, 53, 55, 57–58, 108, 249, 251
undoing, 33, 49, 51, 56
uniformism, 101
Urberg, K. A., 117, 312
Uzgiris, I. C., 206, 312

valence, 70, 141–142, 154–155, 157
vicarious reinforcement, 271, 281, 288–289
virginity, 4, 116, 129
Vives, Juan Luis, 17
vocational expectations, 71, 91, 120, 154, 158

Wachtel, P. L., 99, 312
Wagner, J., 86, 312
Walters, R. H., 272–276, 283–284
Waterman, A. S., 74, 86, 88, 92, 312–313
Waterman, C. K., 74–75, 86, 88, 92, 312–313
Wegner, D. M., 264, 313
Weikart, D. P., 206, 313
Weiner, B., 233, 313
Weinheimer, S., 264, 313

Weir, M. W., 258, 313
White, G. M., 288, 313
White, R. W., 44, 313
will, 10–11, 19, 22, 25
Williams, F. E., 163, 313
Wolf, T. M., 291, 313

Wylie, R., 154, 313

Youniss, J., 228, 233–234, 313
youth, 2, 3, 28, 77, 80–81, 94, 165–166, 169